LANDMARK CASES IN DEFAM,

Landmark Cases in Defamation Law is a diverse an_ _ _ _ _ _ _ _ tion that brings together eminent scholars from the United Kingdom, the United States, Australia, Canada and New Zealand to analyse cases of enduring significance to defamation law. The cases selected have all had a significant impact on defamation law, not only in the jurisdiction in which they were decided but internationally. Given the formative influence of English defamation law in the United States, Australia, Canada and New Zealand, the focus is predominantly on English cases, although significant United States and Australian decisions are also included in the collection. The authors all share a common interest in defamation law but bring different expertise and emphasis to their respective chapters. Among the authors are specialists in tort law, legal history and internet law. The cases selected cover all aspects of defamation law, including defamatory capacity and meaning; practice and procedure; defences; and remedies.

Landmark Cases in Defamation Law

Edited by
David Rolph

·HART·

OXFORD · LONDON · NEW YORK · NEW DELHI · SYDNEY

HART PUBLISHING

Bloomsbury Publishing Plc

Kemp House, Chawley Park, Cumnor Hill, Oxford, OX2 9PH, UK

1385 Broadway, New York, NY 10018, USA

29 Earlsfort Terrace, Dublin 2, Ireland

HART PUBLISHING, the Hart/Stag logo, BLOOMSBURY and the Diana logo
are trademarks of Bloomsbury Publishing Plc

First published in Great Britain 2019
First published in hardback, 2019
Paperback edition, 2021

A catalogue record for this book is available from the British Library.

Library of Congress Cataloging-in-Publication data

Names: Rolph, David, editor.
Title: Landmark cases in defamation law / edited by David Rolph.
Description: Oxford, UK; Chicago, Illinois: Hart Publishing, 2019. |
Series: Landmark cases | Includes bibliographical references and index.
Identifiers: LCCN 2019007695 (print) | LCCN 2019009136 (ebook) |
ISBN 9781509916740 (EPub) | ISBN 9781509916702 (hardback}
Subjects: LCSH: Libel and slander–English-speaking countries–Cases. |
BISAC: LAW / Media & the Law.
Classification: LCC K930 (ebook) | LCC K930.L36 2019 (print) |
DDC 346.03/40264–dc23
LC record available at https://lccn.loc.gov/2019007695

ISBN: HB: 978-1-50991-670-2
PB: 978-1-50994-668-6
ePDF: 978-1-50991-671-9
ePub: 978-1-50991-674-0

Typeset by Compuscript Ltd, Shannon

To find out more about our authors and books visit www.hartpublishing.co.uk.
Here you will find extracts, author information, details of forthcoming events
and the option to sign up for our newsletters.

Preface

THE HISTORY OF any private law cause of action is important for an understanding of the present state of the law. This is acutely so for defamation. The history of defamation law as a cause of action in English law spans over eight centuries. Defamation law derives from multiple sources: the ecclesiastical courts; the Star Chamber; the statutory offence of *scandalum magnatum*; and the royal courts. Arguably, it has not completely reckoned with its long past, or successfully reconciled or rationalised its disparate origins. In many ways, modern defamation law bears the hallmarks of historical accident. It is not the rational product of a balancing between the protection of reputation and freedom of speech.

In the long and varied history of defamation law, there are many cases which can properly lay claim to being a landmark case. It is not possible to cover them all. Indeed, there is room to argue as to what constitutes a landmark case in defamation law. The cases included in this collection cover the three major aspects of defamation law: liability; defences; and remedies. In relation to liability, the issues of defamatory capacity and meaning are explored in the chapters on *Lewis v Daily Telegraph Ltd* and *Charleston v NGN* (chapters five and eight), whilst the increasingly vexed issue of publication is explored in the chapters on *Byrne v Deane* and *Dow Jones & Co Inc v Gutnick* (chapters three and ten). In relation to defences, the important but technical defence of fair comment is examined in the chapters on *Campbell v Spottiswoode* and *Kemsley v Foot* (chapters one and four), and the recent common law revision of qualified privilege is analysed in the chapter on *Reynolds v Times Newspapers Ltd* (chapter nine). In relation to remedies, the principal one has been, and continues to be (notwithstanding the periodic attempts of law reformers in some jurisdictions), an award of damages. The purposes for which defamation damages are awarded and the difficult issue of exemplary damages for defamation are explored in the chapter on *Uren v John Fairfax & Sons Ltd* (chapter seven). Less commonly, an interim or interlocutory injunction may be sought and, more likely than not, refused. The reasons for this are analysed in the chapter on *Bonnard v Perryman* (chapter two).

The impact of English defamation law has not only come about due to the length of its history but also due to its wide, geographical influence, as a consequence of British imperialism. In various ways, the common law of defamation has been modified, adapted, rejected or replaced, by courts and legislatures in the jurisdictions that received English law several centuries ago. The common law of defamation has not been static and has become less common. Whilst the common heritage remains, each jurisdiction has developed its own distinctive defamation law. Many of the chapters document the complex relationship between English defamation law and the national, state or provincial laws derived from them. Chapter seven is an illustration of this point: *Uren v John Fairfax & Sons Ltd* is a landmark in defamation law concerning awards of damages for defamation but it is also a landmark in the development of an independent Australian private law jurisprudence, representing a significant occasion on which the High Court of Australia no longer regarded itself bound to follow the House of Lords, a position which was upheld by the then apex court in the Australian judicature, the Privy Council.

Not all of the cases included in this collection were decided by English courts. This is because some landmarks in defamation law were first reached by courts outside the United Kingdom. For instance, the High Court of Australia was the first court of appeal to hear and determine the issue of jurisdiction over internet defamation. Given the profound changes in communication technologies, it is unlikely to be the last time that this issue arises for determination. Also included is what is indisputably *the* landmark United States defamation case, *New York Times v Sullivan*. The constitutionalisation of United States defamation law and the primacy given to freedom of speech at the expense of the protection of reputation combined to make *New York Times v Sullivan* a radical departure in defamation law in the Anglophone world and a benchmark or counterpoint, depending upon one's perspective, by which all subsequent speech-protective developments may be assessed.

A remarkable feature of the common law of defamation is its continuity in the face of change. Defamation law has proven to be highly adaptable to the changes in the ways in which people communicate. In the earliest stages of the history of defamation law, most complaints of defamation law concerned slander. Cases involving libel were rare, reflecting the control exercised by the State over the printed work at that time. Defamation law has adapted to accommodate 'new media' over time: newspapers; radio; television. It is in the process of adapting again to accommodate the latest 'new media': online publications in all their forms and platforms. The extent of defamation law's surprising adaptability, its capacity to use established principles to address novel problems, is starting to be recognised through the revitalisation of publication by omission derived from *Byrne v Deane*: a case which was a curiosity in the twentieth century, applied only twice in reported cases, given new life in the twenty-first century, deployed to deal with the problems presented by whether internet intermediaries, such as internet service providers and search engines, are publishers for the purposes of defamation law. Perhaps now more than ever, an understanding of landmark cases of defamation law can help resolve the problems of the present and the future.

Professor David Rolph
December 2018
Sydney

Table of Contents

List of Contributors

Eric Barendt is an Emeritus Professor at University College London.

Jason Bosland is an Associate Professor at the Melbourne Law School, as well as the Deputy Director of the Centre for Media and Communications Law at the University of Melbourne.

Ursula Cheer is the Dean of Law at the University of Canterbury, Christchurch.

Mark Lunney is a Professor of Law at the University of New England Law School in Armidale, New South Wales; Visiting Professor at the Dickson Poon School of Law, King's College, London; Visiting Professor at the Faculty of Laws, University College, London; and a Fellow of the Australian Academy of Law.

Barbara McDonald is a Professor of Law at the University of Sydney Law School, University of Sydney and a Fellow of the Australian Academy of Law.

Kylie Papparlardo is a Lecturer at the Queensland University of Technology Faculty of Law.

David Partlett is the Asa Griggs Candler Professor of Law at Emory Law School in Atlanta, Georgia.

David Rolph is a Professor of Law at the University of Sydney Law School, University of Sydney, and a Fellow of the Australian Academy of Law.

Nicolas Suzor is an Associate Professor at the Queensland University of Technology Faculty of Law.

Paul Wragg is an Associate Professor at the University of Leeds Law School.

Hilary Young is an Associate Professor at the University of New Brunswick Faculty of Law.

Table of Cases

Australia

Brunei

Canada

France

Hong Kong

India

Malaysia

New Zealand

Northern Ireland

Singapore

South Africa

United Kingdom

United States

Court of Justice of the European Union

European Court of Human Rights

Table of Legislation

Ireland

New Zealand

United Kingdom

United States

International

1

Campbell v Spottiswoode *(1863)*

PAUL WRAGG

'And the *Saturday* would have had a column of sneering jocosity
on the irrepressibly sanguine temperament of authors'[1]

I. INTRODUCTION

THE FACTS OF *Campbell v Spottiswoode* ('*Campbell*') are well-known:
Spottiswoode, the publisher of the *Saturday Review* (known colloqui-
ally as 'the *Saturday*'), had printed an article called 'The Heathen's Best
Friend' ('the Heathen article'), about Campbell, a proselytiser, which alleged
he was defrauding his followers. Its significance, though, is more debatable.
On Tuesday, 30 June 1863 (several months after it was decided), the *Sydney
Morning Herald* presciently declared '[it] will stand among the landmarks of
law, and will be often appealed to in similar questions ... '[2] This was certainly
Lord Phillips's view of it in 2010, when he said it is 'perhaps the most important foundation stone of the modern law of fair comment'.[3] What, though, did
it decide? Commentators at the time were uncertain, as Mitchell notes: they
agreed that *Campbell* disentangled fair comment from qualified privilege, but
could not agree on what this meant: was fair comment now the companion to
justification? Was it something else? Was it even a defence?[4] Partially, the problem is explained by the concepts of fair comment, qualified privilege, and justification lacking the neat distinctions of today.[5] But it was also not helped by
the ambiguity of the phrase 'privilege' which is used prominently in *Campbell*
(and prior cases) to describe qualified privilege (as we know it) as well as fair

---

[1] George Gissing, *New Grub Street* (Oxford, Oxford World's Classics, 2016) 388.
[2] *The Sydney Morning Herald*, 30 June 1863.
[3] *Joseph v Spiller* [2010] UKSC 53, [2011] 1 AC 852, [34].
[4] Paul Mitchell, *The Making of the Modern Law of Defamation* (Oxford, Hart Publishing, 2005)
183–86.
[5] *Sutherland v Stopes* [1925] AC 47 is the start of this process.

comment and justification. Indeed, even in 1906, the Court of Appeal noted the problem this 'etymological inexactitude'[6] caused in elucidating the concept of fair comment. Allied to this, judicial fickleness toward *Campbell*, in which the case has fallen into and out of favour, has introduced the danger of seeing the case through modern perspectives. Consequently, a sort of Chinese whispers has seen the case assume a significance and meaning now that, arguably, it never had.

Instead, it will be argued, the court's view, in *Campbell*, of the distinction between fair comment and qualified privilege (and justification) was less radical. For them, the case facts raised no new points of law. The novelty of the case lay with counsel's argument that the imputation of dishonesty was the same as the imputation of folly or wrongheadedness: all were capable of being matters of fair comment where the underlying facts supported the opinion. In the court's view, this argument could not succeed (though there was some disagreement about why). In retrospect, then, although courts and commentators have used *Campbell* to tease out important distinctions between fair comment and qualified privilege, this was not the court's intention. Indeed, qualified privilege (as we know it) was never pleaded (nor was justification). This more prosaic account arises from the contemporary newspaper reports of the trial, and a greater understanding of the characters involved in the trial, especially, the redoubtable Rev Dr John Campbell, whose claim it was.

II. THE FACTS

A. Dr Campbell is 'not altogether unknown'

The Reverend Dr John Campbell was a colourful character. Born in Scotland, in 1795, he moved to London in 1829, and died there in 1867 (some four years after his successful libel suit).[7] He was a zealot, a fierce antagonist and a wily businessman. He wrote prodigiously, including books, pamphlets, letters and newspaper articles. He also part-owned *British Standard* and *Ensign* – the newspapers at the centre of the *Campbell* litigation. Such endeavours prompted a commentator to dub him 'the most bustling man in … the Dissenting world of London'.[8]

His nature seems well-captured in an anecdote from the mid-1830s. When Campbell moved to London, he was co-pastor at two chapels (George Whitfield's chapel on the Tottenham Court Road and the Tabernacle in Finsbury). In 1834,

---

[6] *Thomas v Bradbury Agnew* [1906] 2 KB 627, 638.

[7] Frederick Douglas, *The Frederick Douglas Papers: Series 3, Correspondence, 1842–1852, Vol 1*, John R McKivigan, ed (New Haven, Conn, Yale University Press, 2009) 136.

[8] J. Ewing Ritchie, *Christopher Crayon's Recollections: The Life and Times of the Late James Ewing Ritchie as Told by Himself* (1898) ch XI.

Campbell had 'a serious difference with the Trustees of Tottenham Court Road about the exclusion of a member of the congregation'.[9] This resulted in his dismissal. Whilst the specifics are unknown, it is known that Campbell did not go quietly. Or at all. For we are told, in the *Metropolitan Ecclesiastical Directory* ('*Directory*') of 1835, that Campbell's successor – Rev Ragsdell – was prevented from taking up his ministration of the chapel: every time he tried to hold a service, Campbell would 'attend and demand the pulpit'[10] and, once rebuffed by Ragsdell, would leave and take the congregation with him.

But Campbell prevailed. By, at least, 1850, he had returned to both chapels as minister. Yet – and here is a hint of how Campbell's pecuniary interests courted controversy – he preached at neither.

> He still held the pastorate, resided in the parsonage, and drew the salary; but he supplied his pulpit by employing, for a few weeks at a time, the most popular ministers that could be employed, to preach to his people ... [whilst he] gave his time to the editing of [his] papers.[11]

It should come as no surprise that Campbell was not universally liked. As one former colleague put it:

> I found Dr Campbell to be an earnest, but a very belligerent, man. He was always given to controversy. To use an American expression, he was given to 'pitching into' everybody and everything that did not correspond with his views. In this way he did a great deal of good; and occasionally, I fear, some harm.[12]

Campbell's 'zeal' saw him lose a libel case.[13] On another occasion, he lost his popular support by 'unwisely' entering the fray over a controversial hymn book[14] (controversial because Dissenters like Campbell thought it lacking in Evangelical truth).[15] It was this that caused Campbell to commence the *British Standard*.

It is unsurprising, then, that, in the Heathen article, the *Saturday* should refer to Campbell as 'not altogether unknown'. Indeed, he was well-known to George Spottiswoode, the publisher of the *Saturday*, whom Campbell sued. In November 1840, his father, Andrew, felt Campbell's wraith over a dispute about the monopoly then existing for the right to print the Bible. As King's Printer, Andrew had defended his right, in a letter to *The Times*, in which he expressed fear that 'well-intentioned people' might be 'deceived' by Campbell: 'I cannot but look upon the barefaced assertions ... as a deliberate misrepresentation to

---

[9] ibid.

[10] *The Metropolitan Ecclesiastical Directory*, (London, T Hurst, 1835) 165.

[11] Charles Grandison Finney, *Memoirs of Rev Charles G Finney*, (Bedford, Mass, Applewood Books, 1876) 401.

[12] ibid 402–03.

[13] Ritchie, *Christopher Crayon's Recollections* (1989).

[14] ibid.

[15] See Rev Brewin Grant, *What's It All About? Or Both Sides of the 'Rivulet' Controversy* (London, Collingridge, 1856).

catch the unaware, to assist in forming an opposition Bible Society, and *to raise a subscription*. His own statements, in fact, prove it to be so' (emphasis added). To this, Campbell published a long and theatrical response, in which the phrase '*I charge Mr Spottiswoode with misrepresentation!*' (emphasis in original) is a constant refrain. Note, though, the allegation of financial dishonesty made by Spottiswoode.

The *Saturday*'s reference to Campbell's notoriety, though, alludes to a previous article about him written in August 1861, entitled 'The Rev Dr Campbell, The Last Defender of the Faith' ('the Defender article'). (We can assume this is the first – possibly only other – article written about Campbell since it states, 'we never heard of Dr Campbell hitherto'.) This ridiculed Campbell for his part in a hoax (which the *Saturday* may have implemented). Campbell had written letters to Prince Albert accusing him of being a Jesuit.[16] He published these in the *Ensign* and *British Standard* (and, later, a handy volume) and encouraged his followers to buy multiple copies for distribution amongst the ignorant. Later, he published encouragement received from 'Rev Henry Wilkins', who praised his efforts – and was mocked by the *Saturday* for doing so: 'Alas! For human credulity. It might have occurred to anybody of less boundless vanity and matchless impudence than the editor of the *British Standard* to look at the *Clergy List* ... [since the correspondent] only existed in the ingenious imagination [of a hoaxer]'.

Two features of this article relate to the Heathen. First, the allegation that Campbell's chief motivation was profit appears here: 'Among other dodges for circulating his newspaper, [Campbell] started the scheme of getting contributions to "assist in distributing 100,000 copies of the *Ensign*." This is the euphemism of Dr Campbell for pocketing exactly 100,000*d*.' Secondly, the *Saturday* mocks the reference to the 'Honourable Charlotte Margaretta Thompson', who, Campbell claims, is pivotal to the success of scheme by subscribing generously. These two features tell us much about the *Saturday*'s grounds for the claims they would later make in the Heathen article; it is why they thought Campbell was a swindler (as Andrew Spottiswoode had too).

That later scheme, as with this one, involved Campbell writing more letters, this time to Queen Victoria herself, imploring the Queen to evangelise the Chinese 'heathen'. As before, he implored his followers to buy multiple copies of his letters (published in the *British Standard* and *Ensign*) to fund missionary work in China. 'He addressed his readers as his friends of truth as it is in Jesus, and after speaking of the salvation of man and the glory of God called upon them to increase the circulation by five times what it was on the publication of the Prince Consort letters'.[17] Also, as before, Campbell praised the 'noble example' of Mrs Thompson, who had pledged 5,000 copies, and also, the Earl

---

[16] See Lytton Strachey, *Eminent Victorians* (Oxford, Oxford World's Classics, 2009).
[17] *The Morning Post*, 20 April 1863.

of Gainsborough, the Earl of Shaftesbury, and various anonymous individuals, including those described as 'R.G', 'a London Minister' and 'an Old Soldier'.

B. The *Saturday Review*: 'One thing I always like to have – ... hatred of the *Saturday* ... and the love of God'[18]

The *Saturday*, a weekly newspaper, was an important source of 'leading critical opinion' in mid-Victorian times.[19] It boasted an impressive array of writers (albeit articles were published anonymously, as was the custom). Although non-partisan, its outlook was non-radical: it believed, for example, that England should be ruled 'by governing classes made up of a well-born, intelligent, educated, and propertied minority' and that total enfranchisement was 'likely to destroy the whole fabric of civilised society'.[20] It 'ridiculed socialism', was 'bitterly hostile' to trade unions, and 'detested' the dictatorial leadership in France and Italy.[21]

On religion, although it sought to 'avoid ... controversy' by advocating 'moderation and tolerance ... decorum and decency,' it became 'the unsparing critic of the bigotry, vulgarity, sensationalism, obscurantism, and puritanism of the extremists of the dominant middle class'.[22] The *Saturday* attacked Nonconformism (of which Campbell was an adherent) at every opportunity. Evangelical 'intolerance of other people's pleasures was a frequent subject for laughter and indignation'.[23] Such was the shared distrust of 'emotionalism and enthusiasm' of this puritanism that articles written about the chief culprits of this movement (Rev Charles Spurgeon and Dr John Cumming) were almost equal to those about Disraeli and Gladstone.[24] It is unsurprising, then, that the *Saturday* would write about Campbell.

The *Saturday* was published by Spottiswoode & Co of New-Street Square (between Fetter Lane and Shoe Lane in central London), a printing business whose lineage extended back to about 1739.[25] By 1863, Andrew had retired from the business and had passed control to his sons, William and George. While William became Queen's Printer, George ran Spottiswoode & Co. The firm had only recently begun printing the *Saturday* (perhaps as early as 1860), as it branched out from solely bookwork to periodicals.[26]

---

[18] Reverend Charles Spurgeon, quoted in Merle Mowbray Bevington, *The Saturday Review 1855–1868* (New York, Columbia University Press, 1941) 89.

[19] Bevington (ibid) vii.

[20] ibid 58–59.

[21] ibid 60–65.

[22] ibid 77.

[23] ibid 86.

[24] ibid 88.

[25] Richard Arthur Austin-Leigh, *The Story of a Printing House*, 2nd edn (London, Spottiswoode & Co Ltd, 1912) 51.

[26] ibid 44.

C. 'The Heathen's Best Friend': 'There was a great deal of banter about it'[27]

It is unknown who wrote the Heathen (or Defender) article. Although Bevington, in his thorough history of the *Saturday* under John Douglas Cook's editorship from 1855 to 1868, provides an extensive list attributing authorship to various articles, there is no mention of the article. Although Cook kept a list of who wrote what, even in 1941, those records had 'long since disappeared'.[28] Bevington reports that (at least) some 113 commentators contributed pieces to the *Saturday* between 1855 and 1868, including Walter Bagehot, Joseph Blakesley (friend of Alfred Tennyson), Lord Robert Gascoyne-Cecil (Prime Minister 1885–92 and 1895–1902), George Eliot, and Charles Kingsley.

There are several candidates who may have written the article, but it was probably Rev William Scott (1813–72), a vicar and long-time contributor. As a 'High Church' adherent, Campbell's views would have been anathema. If not him, then possibly Edward Freeman, John Morley or George Venables. Freeman, an historian, was also a 'regular' and known for his 'savagery in reviewing'[29] (though he tended to write only on general literature).[30] John Morley (later Viscount Morley of Blackburn), a barrister, journalist and, later, politician, was a staunch liberal. His strong conviction against paternalism (he opposed state intervention in many forms, including, foreign affairs) rings true with the mockery of Campbell's naïve belief that the 'heathen' could be evangelised through missionary work.[31] George Stovin Venables, a close friend of Carlyle, Tennyson and Thackeray, was, like Freeman, a prolific writer, and, according to Bevington,[32] 'more than anyone else set the political tone' of the *Saturday*. His father, Richard Venables, was Archdeacon of Carmarthen. Although it was the sort of thing James Fitzjames Stephen would write, he left the *Saturday* in 1861 (following a dispute with Cook) and did not return until 1863.

The Heathen article was published on 14 June 1862. It remains an engaging, humorous piece of work, rich in sarcasm from the beginning:

> A GREAT discovery has been made, and, strange to say, only a select few have heard anything whatever about it. It is not often that genius retreats into a corner and hides its light under a bushel; and when a scheme is devised for the regeneration of about four hundred millions of our race, it is but proper that the whole world should be acquainted with it ... To [Campbell's] misfortune, rather than to his modesty, must be ascribed the ignorance of his plan that so lamentably prevails in society.

---

[27] Bovill's description, *Morning Post* (n 17).
[28] Bevington, *Saturday Review* (1941) 331–32.
[29] ibid 30, fn 61.
[30] ibid 342–46.
[31] ibid 361.
[32] ibid 383.

It proceeds to mock Campbell's scheme for evangelising the Chinese:

> It has hitherto been thought a difficult and sometimes dangerous task to attempt to change the religion of any race, and men have spent years in preparing a way for the work, only to be disappointed at last. The reason is that they worked in the dark. They lived before Dr Campbell's time, or they neglected to avail themselves of his light.

And the evangelism of the *British Ensign*:

> It has, according to Dr Campbell (than whom no man should be better qualified to judge), half rooted out infidelity from the land. It has struck a deadly blow at the Papacy. It has extirpated sundry heresies and schisms of long standing. It has awakened the churches, stirred up the backsliders, reproved vice in high places ... and all at the exceedingly low charge of one penny. It seems an excess of generosity to set so low a price on so invaluable an instrument.

Campbell urged Queen Victoria to lead the evangelism; since (in Campbell's words) England and China were 'neighbours', it was her 'duty' to convert the Chinese because 'the ties resulting from neighbourhood, next to those of blood, are the strongest known to earth' (to which the *Saturday* retorts: 'People who have lived for years without even knowing their next door neighbours may be rather staggered at this statement'.)

Reference is then made to Mr Thompson in a passage that the plaintiff would complain of at trial: 'The doctor refers frequently to Mr Thompson as his authority – so frequently that we must own to having had a transitory suspicion that Mr T was nothing more than another Mrs Harris' (this refers to Sairey Gamp, the incompetent nurse in *Martin Chuzzlewit*, whose oft-mentioned friend, Mrs Harris, is generally acknowledged to be a 'phantom of Mrs Gamp's brain').[33] But, the passage should be seen in context. In full, it says:

> Among Dr Campbell's many gifts, a good memory does not appear to be included, and it is a pity that the fact should be so, for he makes a great variety of statements and challenges a good deal of attention to his own achievements. Fortunately, when he is in a dilemma, a Mr Thompson, of Bath, is ever at hand to help him out.

This clearly refers to the Defender article, where 'the Honourable Mrs Thompson' had rescued Campbell by 'finishing [his] pyramid'. *Quelle surprise*, then, that Mr[s] T should be the chief subscriber here.

Read today, the article is primarily a criticism of Campbell's gullible audience, as seen in its conclusion:

> For whatever may be the private views of the editor of the *Ensign*, there can be no question that his followers are sincere enough in the confidence they repose in his plan ... The past cannot be very sad, nor the future very dreadful, to him who has the capacity for hoping all things and believing all things without hesitation.

---

[33] Charles Dickens, *Martin Chuzzlewit*, (Oxford, Oxford World's Classics, 1998) 348.

Considering the *Saturday*'s position on religion and politics, this criticism is typical – and also unremarkable. Sadly, neither Campbell, nor, eventually, the courts, read it this way.

D. Dr Campbell's Response

Two weeks after publication, Campbell's solicitor requested a published, 'ample apology ... with a declaration ... that the charges made against him were utterly unfounded'.[34] Campbell offered his ledgers to prove the subscribers were genuine.[35] Such an apology would have provided a complete defence under s 2 of the Libel Act 1843, so long as payment into court, by way of amends, followed.[36]

Spottiswoode's advisors, though, denied there was a libel and invited the plaintiff to specify which words were libellous (a request that the plaintiff dismissed: 'there [can] be no difficulty in discovering what those passages were'). They maintained:

> [I]t appears to us, from the context, that the words complained of are used merely as part of a criticism on a newspaper article, and are not intended to attack Dr Campbell's character. If you will point out any statements of matter of fact which you consider erroneous, it shall be corrected in the 'Review'.

The only reply they received was a writ, which prompted them to express regret that they had not been 'afforded [the opportunity] of correcting any erroneous statement of ... fact'.[37]

Why did the defendant's advisors adopt this cavalier position? Possibly, they may have dismissed Campbell's complaints as mere posturing. Said a commentator at the time,

> The parties who wince under hostile strictures seldom find it worth while to put themselves on their trial by appealing to a jury. Such an action as that of 'Campbell v Spottiswoode' is now very rare ... the publishers of journals are so seldom brought to account for slanderous articles.[38]

They offer two grounds for this conclusion: first, the 'reluctance ... to seek redress ... by legal means is the probability that further exposure will [lead to] increased currency [being] given to stories which the aggrieved party has good reason for wishing to suppress'. Secondly, that rather than engage in lengthy

---

[34] *Campbell v Spottiswoode* (1863) 176 ER 188, 3 F&F 421 (the 'Trial decision') 190.

[35] Reported in the *Sydney Morning Herald* (n 2).

[36] See, eg, AV Dicey, *Introduction to the Study of the Law of the Constitution*, 9th edn, ECS Wade, ed, (London, MacMillan & Co, 1952) 588.

[37] This chain of events is described in the Trial decision (n 34) 190–91.

[38] 'The Action for Libel against the "Saturday Review"', taken from *the Times*, republished in *North and South Shields Gazette*, 5 March 1863.

litigation, 'the wrong done may be remedied by a retraction'. The *Saturday* seemed willing to consider this, but Campbell wanted his day in court.

III. THE DECISION

A. The Trial: 'Your verdict should be for the plaintiff'[39]

The trial took place, around the end of February 1863, at Guildhall, which is in the northern part of the City of London, east of St Paul's Cathedral. (Serious libels were held in the Old Bailey.) Of course, in 1863, libel could still be tried as a criminal offence, though in this case Campbell was after financial recompense, which he valued at £1,000 (around £47,500 today). The case was heard by Lord Chief Justice Cockburn and a jury. It was said of Cockburn CJ, a notorious character himself,[40] that 'his knowledge of law was not profound' and that, as judge, he 'acquired his knowledge by sitting on the bench with Mr Justice Blackburn'[41] – which he did in the *Campbell v Spottiswoode* appeal.

Spottiswoode's legal team was impressive: it was led by (later Sir) William Bovill QC, accompanied by Mr (Sir) John Coleridge (the great-nephew of poet Samuel Taylor Coleridge, whose writings had done so much to alleviate John Stuart Mill's nervous breakdown) and Mr (Sir) William Vernon Harcourt. Bovill was a very experienced barrister. He was called to the bar in 1841 and took silk in 1855. At the time of the trial, he was 48 years old. He would later become Chief Justice of the Common Pleas and, in 1871, would preside over the infamous Tichborne case,[42] in which Thomas Castro from Wagga Wagga in Australia sought to persuade the court that he was the long-lost, rightful heir to the Tichborne estate. Before Bovill then, and acting on behalf of the Tichborne family, was John Coleridge. He was 42 years old at the time of Campbell's trial and had been called to the bar in 1846. He would later become Lord Coleridge and, prior to succeeding Cockburn (on his death in 1880) as Lord Chief Justice, became Chief Justice of the Common Pleas, in 1873, when Bovill died suddenly at the age of 59.

Intriguingly, Sir William Vernon Harcourt, who became, in the 1880s, Home Secretary then Chancellor of the Exchequer under Gladstone, before becoming leader of the opposition (1896–98), had been a writer for the *Saturday* from 1855

---

[39] The Trial decision (n 34) 194, per Cockburn CJ.

[40] 'There is a story told of Chief Justice Cockburn, that he was in the habit of going down on Sundays to Richmond or elsewhere with a woman, and generally a different one, and the landlady of the inn he went to remembered that Sir A. Cockburn always brought Lady Cockburn with him, but that she never saw any woman who looked so different on different days.' Edward Manson, *Builders of our law during the reign of Queen Victoria*, 2nd edn (London, Neville Cox, 1904) 138.

[41] *Dictionary of National Biography*, vol 11, Leslie Stephen and Sidney Lee, eds (London, Smith, Elder & Co, 1887) 177–81. Manson claims that this was said 'jestingly', ibid 161.

[42] See, eg, Robyn Annear, *The Man Who Lost Himself* (London, Robinson, 2002).

to early 1859, but left when his legal career flourished.[43] He was 35 years old at the time of the trial.

Campbell argued that it was libel to say (1) that the listed subscribers were non-existent and a mere 'decoy' to lure unsuspecting acolytes to subscribe generously; and, more importantly, (2) that the scheme was a fraud; Campbell simply wanted to generate profit.[44] He called Mr Thomas Thompson[45] (Charlotte's husband) as a witness. His wife, Charlotte,[46] was the sister of the Earl of Gainsborough – which explains how he became a subscriber of Campbell's paper. Thompson himself was a successful business man involved with the Worshipful Company of Merchant Taylors (one of the 12 great livery companies of the City of London) and the London Stock Exchange. (He died almost two years later, on December 1865 at Prior Park, his home in Bath. Charlotte survived him by only four years.)

Thompson would have been a formidable character witness for Campbell. As Odgers later recalled:

> [T]he insinuation about Mr. Thompson is quite unfounded. I had the honour of knowing that worthy gentleman when I was a boy at Bath, and he was just the sort of person who would subscribe for a thousand copies of any paper of an evangelical type, if he thought that any good would result to the Chinese or any one else.[47]

Such was Thompson's influence on the trial that Cockburn CJ instructed the jury to find for the plaintiff.[48] As he would later say, in the appeal, 'the charges made against the plaintiff were unquestionably without foundation'.[49]

Bovill argued that the *Saturday* was entitled to criticise Campbell for treating increased subscriptions as 'a religious act, or as likely to promote the welfare of the heathen',[50] and that those comments were fair, honest and 'within the privilege of comments by one public writer upon the published proposals' (the meaning of 'privilege' here is discussed below). Certainly, this is the view of the commentator who wrote the case report:

> It had been well settled that a public writer might freely comment on any public matter, put forth by the plaintiff, even so as to convey moral imputations undoubtedly defamatory, provided they arose out of the matter so put forth and were thus 'fair comment'.[51]

---

[43] Bevington (n 18) 27.

[44] See Trial decision (n 34) 193.

[45] Much of my knowledge about Thomas Thompson is taken from an account of his genealogy: www.mikesclark.com/genealogy/thompson.html.

[46] Charlotte Margaret Thompson: she was born in 1792 and married her first husband, Thomas Welman, in 1813.

[47] W Blake Odgers, *An Outline of the Law of Libel* (London, MacMillan & Co, 1897) 41.

[48] ibid 194.

[49] *Campbell v Spottiswoode* (1863) 122 ER 288, 3 B&S 769 (the 'Appeal decision') 291.

[50] Trial decision (n 34) 194.

[51] ibid. The commentator may have been Bovill, but probably not since Foster and Finlason tended to write their own (see Mitchell, *Modern Law of Defamation* (2005) 171).

It would not be libel 'to ridicule a literary composition, or the author of it, in as far as he has embodied himself with his work',[52] unless the comment went 'beyond the limit of the matter thus raised' and used 'terms of general abuse'.[53]

According to Cockburn CJ, though, the comment *had* exceeded the spirit of criticism: although the plaintiff's scheme was 'a subject not only of public interest but of sacred and universal interest',[54] which was open to 'discussion and criticism of severe and hostile character', no writer was entitled to attribute 'base and sordid motives' to the plaintiff's evangelism: 'it cannot be said that because a man is a public man a public writer is entitled not only to pass a judgment upon his conduct, but to ascribe to him corrupt and dishonest motives'.[55]

Although Cockburn CJ was clear that liability should be decided in the plaintiff's favour, he did direct the jury, on damages, to consider whether the *Saturday* had attributed these base and sordid motives 'under an honest and genuine belief that the plaintiff was fairly open to these charges' since such would lessen the award. He also noted, at Bovill's request, that if this honest belief was established, he would allow the defendant to appeal its decision to the Queen's Bench.[56] The jury awarded Campbell £50 (around £2,500 today) and stated that 'the writer ... believed his imputations to be well founded'.

B. The Appeal: 'If he had stopped there no one could have blamed him'

i. Introduction

The appeal was heard before Crompton J, Blackburn J and Mellor J – and Cockburn CJ (which, to modern eyes, looks decidedly suspect). The decision was handed down on Saturday, 18 April 1863. Cockburn CJ delivered the main judgment, with which his brethren agreed (albeit there are subtle, but important, distinctions between what each says).

Making sense of the judgments is not an easy task; contemporary commentators could not agree amongst themselves (as noted above). More recently, Loveland has said 'the defence rested primarily on fair comment, but it was also claimed that any factual assertions made in the story should attract qualified privilege on the basis that they were directed towards an issue of considerable public concern' and also that the court 'rejected the suggestion that ... qualified

---

[52] The commentator refers to *Macleod v Wakeley* (1828) 172 ER 435, 3 C & P 311; *Carr v Hood* (1808) 170 ER 983, 1 Camp 355; *Tabart v Tipper* (1808) 170 ER 981, 1 Camp 350; and *Soane v Knight* (1827) 173 ER 1086, Mood & M 74 in support.
[53] *Dunne v Anderson* (1825) 130 ER 447, 3 Bing 88.
[54] Trial decision (n 34) 193.
[55] ibid 194.
[56] ibid 195.

privilege should arise on these facts'.[57] Mitchell says similarly that the decision is significant for deciding 'that fair comment was not part of qualified privilege' (and that the 'person pleading fair comment raised the question "libel or no libel"').[58] Certainly, the commentator on the trial case note thought qualified privilege (or something like it) was at stake, for where Cockburn CJ found dishonourable motives could not be ascribed as a matter of fair comment, he wrote 'that, it is submitted, was not the question; but whether inferences of fact might not be drawn, honestly, though erroneously, from the admitted effect of the proposals'.[59]

Yet, the appeal can be understood differently. Rather than a comment on the relationship between fair comment and qualified privilege (as we know it), the decision is more prosaic. By examining a contemporary report of the appeal, alongside the decision itself, it will be argued that: (1) the reference to 'libel or no libel' is short-hand for the proposition that fair comment could not be relied upon; and, (2) Bovill's appeal was, solely, that the direction to the jury on damages ought to have been the direction on liability; he did not claim qualified privilege. In this way, the trial report commentator means 'opinions about facts' when they say 'inferences of fact' might be drawn honestly but erroneously. (It is odd that they should mean qualified privilege when there is no other mention of the concept in the report itself or the commentary.)[60]

ii. The Tone of Proceedings

A *Morning Post* report of the decision provides some fascinating insights into the proceedings, from which the following is drawn.[61] It suggests proceedings were dialectic, convivial and dominated by Bovill. Indeed, not only does it seem he was without Coleridge and Vernon Harcourt but also that the plaintiff's legal team were absent (or else, silent). Also, there is much mirth at Campbell's expense, suggesting he was not there either. For example, when discussing the Prince Albert letters, Bovill recalls the danger that Campbell apprehended of:

> [The Prince] becoming an infidel from his going to Oxford University. (Laughter.)
>
> The Lord Chief Justice – And also from his visiting Rome. (Laughter.)
>
> Mr. Bovill – Yes ... Having been so successful with the Prince Consort's letters he entered on a new subject in the autumn of 1861, that of the salvation of the

---

[57] Ian Loveland, *Political Libels: a Comparative Study* (Oxford, Hart Publishing, 2000) 34.

[58] Mitchell (n 4) 183.

[59] Trial decision (n 34) 194.

[60] See, ibid 195, *(b)* where the commentator says of the jury's finding about the defendant's honest belief: 'the jury must have meant, that the plaintiff's publications were such as would naturally, although ... erroneously, lead to such a belief ... [otherwise] a public writer, commenting on the plaintiff's own publications, must always be liable for criminatory inferences, however natural and reasonable, if they were untrue'.

[61] Above, n 17.

Chinese – (laughter) – by the publication of a series of letters in the Ensign and Standard, and he called on the public in the most solemn manner to participate in attaining that end by subscribing towards the gratuitous circulation of the two papers.

Mr Justice Mellor – Were they for circulation amongst the Chinese? (Laughter).

iii. Libel or No Libel

'The first question,' said Crompton J, in his judgment (which appears second), 'is, whether the article on which this action is brought is a libel or no libel, – not whether it is privileged or not.'[62] His brethren agreed. 'It is important to bear in mind that the question is, not whether the publication is privileged, but whether it is a libel,' said Blackburn J. 'And I agree,' said Mellor J, 'that the question in this case is, libel or no libel'. Strangely, Cockburn CJ, who gave the leading judgment, did not use this phrase, or anything of the sort. This is understandable, if the others were of a different opinion – but all three say that they agree with him. Crompton J is most explicit: 'I am of the same opinion: for the reasons given by the Lord Chief Justice'. Blackburn J said, 'I also think that the law governing this case is so clearly settled that we ought not to grant a rule'. Finally, Mellor J said, 'I am of the same opinion'.

This apparent inconsistency raises two questions: (1) if *Campbell* is a case that recasts fair comment, then why do the judges not acknowledge this radical departure? Why, instead, do they suggest that they are simply applying, in Blackburn J's words, 'settled' law? (2) Why did Crompton J, Blackburn J and Mellor J say the appeal was about 'libel or no libel' when Cockburn CJ said it was about the 'line ... drawn between criticism upon public conduct and the imputation of [wicked] motives'? If they are saying something different to Cockburn CJ, why are they not explicit?

Mitchell argues that the question 'libel or no libel' speaks to the court's conclusion that fair comment was different from qualified privilege (and he sets out some tangential problems with their conclusion).[63] But, alternatively, it may be more straightforward: that the 'privilege' of fair comment could not arise on the facts because the imputation of bad motives destroyed the right. The court used the term 'privilege' ambiguously throughout the decision, as both a collective noun (to refer to the bundle of defendant's rights to defeat the defamation claim) and when referring not only to qualified privilege (as we know it) but also fair comment and justification.

Seen in this light, (1) and (2) are resolved by understanding the decision as confirmation that Cockburn CJ had not erred because neither fair comment nor the other plausible defences (justification or qualified privilege) arose; thus, the only question for the appeal panel to determine was whether Cockburn had

---

[62] Appeal decision (n 49) 291.
[63] Mitchell (n 4) 183–85.

instructed the jury correctly on how to distinguish libellous words from non-libellous words. In other words, the question for the jury could not be: is this article privileged or not, because there were no privileges (no rights) at stake that the writer could fall back upon. He was not exercising his liberty to attack public men on issues of public importance in the true spirit of criticism, nor were the allegations demonstrably true, nor was he (the writer) under a duty to comment which would otherwise have allowed for false statements of fact where honestly believed.

The reason why fair comment could not arise is slightly hazy: either the court believed the accusation itself was a statement of fact, not opinion, or that it was opinion, but not one flowing from facts with a substantial basis in truth. The former interpretation seems to be Crompton J's and the latter Cockburn CJ's. But, even so, the decision does leave open the question of where fair comment sits, is it a defence, properly called, or does it prevent the defamation claim being actionable? As Mitchell notes, this is a question that the courts did not agree on;[64] indeed, the question was not settled until the twentieth century (see below).

To demonstrate this interpretation, the issues are split into two: to show (1) how Bovill's plea, for a ruling that fair comment had been at stake, played out; and (2) how the alternative 'privilege as right' interpretation arises.

iv. The Fair Comment Misdirection

Cockburn CJ had directed the jury to find for the plaintiff because the attribution of 'base and sordid motives' went beyond the limits of fair comment – unless they thought 'the *only* effect of the article was *fairly* to discuss the proposal of the plaintiff'.[65] Bovill argued that this was a misdirection. His position is reflected in the trial report commentary, which notes that the direction given to the jury on damages ought to have been the direction on liability.[66] There, Cockburn CJ had acknowledged that the plaintiff's scheme was regrettably of 'a somewhat doubtful character' so that the insinuation of deceitful motivation, which the jury might think groundless, was neverthe-less understandable: 'if it might naturally suggest itself to the mind, you must make some allowance for the position of the writer' since 'the matter' arose out of 'a public controversy, and not as one in which there was any intention to wound and injure the plaintiff'.[67]

Since the jury agreed with Cockburn CJ on this point, Bovill argued that it showed the jury was for the defendant. His appeal, therefore, was that Cockburn CJ had been wrong to say the imputation of 'sordid and base motives'

---

[64] Mitchell (n 4) 186–88.
[65] Trial decision (n 34) 195.
[66] Trial decision (n 34) 194, *(d)*.
[67] ibid 194–95.

went beyond the limits of fair criticism, given that it was an understandable conclusion arising from the facts. The fair comment doctrine rescued the defendant from liability, he said, since, as was also recognised by the jury, the comment was not made maliciously. The appeal panel, though, clearly thought that this argument represented a novel point of law, which they were not prepared to grant. This can be seen in the dialogue between Bovill and the bench (taken from the *Morning Post* – part of which I paraphrase):

> Bovill: '[T]his was a matter that had been brought before the public by the plaintiff, and was open to public criticism.'
>
> Cockburn CJ: '[M]ost certainly, if fair and proper.'
>
> Bovill: '[I]t was fair and proper because there was no evidence of express malice.'
>
> Crompton J: '[N]o, the law does not allow one 'to make charges of dishonesty.'
>
> Bovill: '[T]his was not a statement of fact, but opinion, as shown by its humorous nature: "there was a great deal of banter about it".'
>
> Cockburn CJ: 'I do not know that an imputation is the less painful or effective when put in the shape of a banter. It was a laughing way of putting it to say, "So many copies for the 'Old Soldier'. We know who the old soldier is;" but it was none the less libellous.'

The *Morning Post* reports that, later, 'Mr Bovill contended that the moment it was shown that an article was privileged, it became necessary to show express malice'. This (for reasons that are not clear) was interpreted by the court (certainly, by Crompton J and Blackburn J) as a special plea for the press to receive differential treatment. Crompton J's responds:

> It is a mistake to speak of a newspaper being privileged. The editor of a newspaper had no different privilege from any other of her Majesty's subjects. He certainly was not privileged to make charges of dishonestly. The jury had very properly found the article libellous.[68]

It is possible that Bovill was alluding to the decision in *Dibdin v Swan*[69] and his understanding that this case decided that 'the editor of a public newspaper may fairly comment on a place of public entertainment kept by the plaintiff, so as to reflect upon him, unless it can be proved that the comment is unjust, is malevolent, and exceeding the bounds of fair opinion'.[70] This quote is taken from the case commentary (which Bovill might have written).[71] The most telling case, though, from that commentary is *Gathercole v Miall*,[72] on which the commentator notes: '[it] held … that a public writer, on a public matter, has a right to make comments *or draw inferences in a fair spirit*; even though untrue

---

[68] Above, n 17.
[69] (1793) 170 ER 269, 1 Esp 28.
[70] Trial decision (n 34) 191, *(b)*.
[71] See n 51 about the authorship of the case note.
[72] (1846) 153 ER 872, 15 M&W 319.

and defamatory; provided that they appear to be *bona fide*, in the absence of actual malice' (emphasis added).

This sheds a different light on Bovill's claim. It also explains the bench's response because, in their view, the accusation of fraud was an attack on the man, not his work – and thus outside the 'fair spirit' of criticism. This can be seen from the following exchange, recorded in the *Morning Post*:

> Bovill: '[I]f a man honestly believed it he had a right to publish it, and let the great man stand upon his character. There was no question of truth or falsehood in a case of privilege. The observation that Dr Campbell's intention was to put money into his own pocket was a fair comment.'

> Crompton J: 'I have no wish to see the liberty of the press diminished in the slightest degree. Persons might expression their opinions upon the charges of judges, bishops, or decisions of magistrates, and they might say they were foolish and ridiculous, but they must not say that they acted from corrupt motives or had received a bribe.'

Bovill's argument here expounds fair comment in terms familiar to modern readers: opinion is not subject to proof. Indeed, Bovill's position here foreshadows the statement Lord Phillips of Worth Matravers PSC would make, in 2010, when exploring the possible developments that could have occurred in the nineteenth-century common law:

> The damage that such a comment can do is relatively limited. Actions speak louder than words. Most people judge their fellow men by the way that they behave, not … general opinions expressed by others. The common law might have held that bare comments were not actionable at all. Or it might have held that a defence of fair comment would lie in respect of a bare comment provided that the defendant could identify the factual basis for his comment by giving evidence of what it was that he had had in mind.[73]

Crompton J's response seems to be, not that the comment was a statement of fact, but that the opinion attacked the private not public character of the man. Indeed, this is explicit in Cockburn CJ's follow-up:

> Cockburn CJ: '[A] public man's public character might be criticised, and the accuracy of his judgment questioned, but his private reputation must not be attacked, or base motives attributed to his acts.'

> 'Mr Bovill said he should contend that it might, so long as it was connected with the subject matter under discussion. Was not this such a case as would render it necessary for the public interest that the matter should be brought forward to prevent the public from being mulcted of their money?'

> 'The learned counsel proceeded to argue that this case stood in the same position as giving a character to a servant, and a person stating that the servant was dishonest was not actionable if he made the statement in the honest bona fide belief that it was true.'

---

[73] *Spiller v Joseph* (n 3) [88].

Crompton J: '[A] man giving an answer to a question was a very different thing from publishing the charge in an advertisement.'

'Mr Bovill said he could not perceive a more important object than that of informing persons that the money was wanted for one purpose when it was wanted for another.'

Cockburn CJ: 'Why did you not justify, and ask the jury to come to your opinion?'

Thus, Bovill makes two points here: that a man's private character can be attacked when it is embodied in his work and, as with qualified privilege, only malice extinguishes the right. Crompton J disagrees though: where private character is at stake, fair comment and qualified privilege are different. Cockburn CJ meanwhile asks Bovill: if the defendant was so convinced of Campbell's base motives, why did he not plead justification? (the *Morning Post* does not record an answer).

In conclusion, the judgments focus on the availability of a defence in these circumstances. Most clearly, they are adamant that fair comment cannot extend to an *ad hominem* attack unless there is a substantial basis in fact, as is evident in Cockburn CJ's summation (reported in the *Morning Post*):

[I]t seems to me the line must be drawn between hostile criticism, between a man's public conduct and the motives by which he was actuated; and you have no right to impute base, sordid, dishonest, and wicked motives. It turns out that this imputation was most undoubtedly without foundation. It may have been that Dr Campbell, in addition to the religious enthusiasm and zeal that actuated him, may not have been altogether insensible to the collateral object of promoting the circulation of his weekly publication, but there is no foundation for saying that it assumed on his part the character of imposture, or that he had resorted to a fraudulent and false device to induce the public to contribute towards it … The doctrine cannot be pushed further than a full right to comment in the true spirit of criticism.

Similarly, Mellor J says:

And, as far as I am aware, this is the first time it has been contended that a libel which imputes the obtaining of money under false pretences, and is not excused by being true, nor made on an occasion in which the exigencies of society required it, is excused by the fact that the person making it believed it to be true.[74]

Thus, the decision stands for the proposition that to call a man a fool is fair comment; to call him a cheat is not. Only the most charitable can say the distinction is not arbitrary; it calls to mind a passage from John Stuart Mill's 1825 article on libel law: 'All censure is invective. To censure is to ascribe misconduct … It is impossible, therefore, to prohibit invective, without prohibiting all discussion, or leaving it to the rules to decide what sort of discussion shall be punished, and what left free'.[75]

---

[74] Appeal decision (n 49) 293.
[75] JS Mill, 'Law of Libel and Liberty of the Press', *The Westminster Review*, April 1825, 301.

v. Qualified Privilege in Campbell

Like Mitchell, *Gatley* hails *Campbell* for its contribution to fair comment doctrine: it notes that it introduced the principle that only qualified privilege (not fair comment) could apply to misstatements of fact.[76] Yet *Campbell*'s treatment of qualified privilege is not straightforward, not least because of the ambiguous use of 'privilege' throughout. Careful unpicking of this usage suggests that *Campbell* is not as profound on the nature of qualified privilege (or fair comment) as it appears. At that time, the term 'privileged' meant 'right' or 'liberty'. So, for example, in an 1854 copyright dispute, the Privy Council notes that: 'the purchaser of a copyright from an English author would not, I conceive, be deprived of the **privileges** conferred by the Copyright Acts',[77] and, in a case under the Legitimacy Declaration Act 1858, the court says: 'his object in that proceeding was to rescue from a state of bastardy, and introduce into the world with all the **privileges** appertaining to those who are born under the influence of the law'.[78]

Thus, at trial, Cockburn CJ had said, dismissing the defendant's claim: 'that, in my view, is not the law, and the privilege of comment does not go to that extent'.[79] This colloquial usage is recognised (and used) in the *Campbell* appeal. Both Crompton J and Blackburn J note (using the same phrase): 'the word 'privilege' is used loosely'.[80] Crompton J's statement in full is:

> Though the word 'privilege' is used loosely in some of the cases as applied to the right which every person has to comment on public matters, I think that in all the cases cited the real question was whether the alleged libel was a fair comment such as every person might make upon a public matter, and if not there was no privilege.

In other words, if the comment was not such as one might make on a public matter, it fell outside the right (to fair comment). Blackburn J and Mellor J, though, do discuss qualified privilege (as we know it). But only to confirm that that privilege (ie, right) could not be pleaded – and neither could justification (another privilege). Thus, when Blackburn J refers to it, I think he means to expand upon what Crompton J had just said, which was:

> In the present case it is clear, as found by the jury, that the article is beyond the range of fair comment, and, this not being a case within the rule as to privilege, the only other available mode of defence was by proving the truth of the article ... I think the case is so clear that we ought not to throw any doubt upon the subject by granting a rule ...[81]

---

[76] See Alastair Mullis and Richard Parkes, *Gatley on Libel and Slander*, 12th edn (London, Sweet & Maxwell, 2013) [12.6].

[77] *Jefferys v Boosey* (1854) 155 ER 675, IV House of Lords Cases (Clark's) 815, 865.

[78] *Shedden and Shedden v Attorney-General & Others* (1858) 164 ER 958, 2 S & T 170, 200.

[79] Trial decision (n 34) 194.

[80] Appeal decision (n 49) 292.

[81] ibid 292.

For Blackburn J begins 'I also think that the law governing this case is so clearly settled that we ought not to grant a rule ... ' His (eventual) key point (which adds to what has already been said) is 'if it could be shewn that the editor or publisher of a newspaper stands in a privileged position, it would be necessary to prove actual malice' otherwise 'I take it to be certain that he has only the general right which belongs to the public to comment upon public matters ... in such cases every one has a right to make fair and proper comment; and so long as it is within that limit, it is no libel'. He concludes 'Bona fide belief in the truth of what is written is no defence to an action; it may mitigate the amount, but it cannot disentitle the plaintiff to damages'.

Thus, it seems to me, Blackburn J means to say that Bovill's claim (that fair criticism is anything other than words spoken maliciously) is not a description of fair comment, but of qualified privilege (as we know it). This can be seen from his initial explanation where he sets out what he means by privilege:

> [I]t is important to bear in mind that the question is, not whether the publication is privileged, but whether it is a libel. The word "privilege" is often used loosely, and in a popular sense, when applied to matter which are not, properly speaking, privileged. But for the present purpose, the meaning of the word is that a person stands in such a relation to the facts of the case that he is justified in saying or writing what would be slanderous or libellous in any one else. For instance, a master giving a character of a servant stands in a privileged relation ...[82]

In other words, Blackburn J is saying: when I say the publication is not privileged, I mean it in a specific sense: I mean, that the *Saturday* was not in the same position as someone under a duty to 'say what she believed to be true';[83] I mean that the limits of fair criticism are *narrower* than a right to say anything honestly believed to be true.

Mellor J's judgment is also capable of the same interpretation, though I think he is more explicit than the others, for he says 'if comment is beyond the limits of fair criticism it becomes a libel ... If the words were used upon a justifiable occasion, no action could be maintained' (by which I assume he means, since the doctrine of fair comment could not apply, the only means by which the *Saturday* could have avoided liability was to show the accusation was truthful, or if qualified privilege applied). This interpretation gains support from a subsequent decision involving Mellor J, where he said '*Campbell v Spottiswoode* ... shews that it is the excess of comment only that makes the publication of such a matter libellous'.[84]

So, it may be said *Campbell* says nothing profound about qualified privilege and its relationship with fair comment. Prosaically, it decides that fair comment, qualified privilege and justification do not arise on the facts. It further notes that

---

[82] Appeal decision (n 49), 292.
[83] ibid.
[84] *Kelly v Tinling* (1865–1866) LR 1 QB 699, 701.

allegations of fraud cannot constitute fair comment unless it has substantial factual support.

IV. THE INFLUENCE OF *CAMPBELL v SPOTTISWOODE*

A. Contemporary Reception

News of the trial verdict in Campbell's favour was not well received by the popular press. Commentators thought it too radical and not warranted by precedent. *The Examiner*, of 7 March 1863 noted:

> If forty-nine pounds nineteen and elevenpence three farthings will evangelize China, we hope that the Rev Dr Campbell will settle the spiritual affairs of that Empire with the conscience-money that must be burning in his pocket as excess of damages obtained [in his trial] … It is hardly fair to fine a journal of high standing and undoubted honesty for giving its attention to pretentious insignificance.

The Times had hoped the appeal would see the defendant victorious. Writing shortly after the Trial, it accepted that the line between public criticism and private character attack was 'not easy to draw' but that:

> [T]he reports of former cases of libel [had not] prepared us for so strong a statement as that the imputation of sordid motives cannot be excused by proof that it was made bona fide, but only by proof of its truth – a proof of which the subject-matter may not admit. We are glad to observe that this point was so reserved by the form of the verdict that it can be raised again and argued before the full Court.[85]

The Times concluded:

> We have no sympathy with a claim of impunity for those who malign others out of spite or revenge, but if a journalist may not honestly warn the public against an attempted fraud, without being able to demonstrate its criminality, a most useful function of the press will be seriously impeded.

The Examiner, of 23 April 1863, was similarly incredulous after the appeal:

> The judges, one after another, harped on the distinction between allowable fair comment and the opposite, but the real question was whether the construction put by the *Saturday* Reviewer was not rational and fair, taking into consideration the suspicious aspect of Dr Campbell's scheme and its boasted supporters. If quackish expedients wear the appearance of something worse, we repeat that the quack has only himself to blame, and is not entitled to any remedy for the misjudgment he has provoked.

In their view, the High Court had been wrong to take the question of fair comment away from the jury:

> We fully admit that bad motives are not to be lightly imputed, and we claim no privilege of comment for the press, which is not the right of every individual, but we

[85] Above, n 38.

maintain that the whole circumstances of every case of alleged libel should be left to the consideration of the jury. This is the principle of the improved law of libel, and this is what was not done in the trial ...

Indeed, the writer for *The Examiner* fretted that in 30 years of journalism, they too had committed libel, if the *Campbell* standard was followed:

'[W]e look back with some uneasy feeling, like that of one who has passed a precipice unconsciously, at the escapes we must have had, if indeed it be law that motives are not to be inferred from conduct, and never to be ascribed unless susceptible of positive, palpable, impossible proof.

As *The Examiner* put it, if the subject of the libel engages in a scheme whereby one possible explanation is malevolent, why should the press not call attention to it?

B. The Legacy

i. *The Foundation of Fair Comment?*

The claim that *Campbell* had a major role on the development of fair comment stems from later judicial comment on the case, starting in 1908, when Fletcher Moulton LJ, in the Court of Appeal, described it as 'a case of the highest authority'[86] and, in the same year, Vaughan Williams LJ, also in the Court of Appeal, called it 'the foundation of the modern doctrine'.[87] Although this attachment to the decision has remained, the modern judge is slightly more tentative: '[it] is perhaps the most important foundation stone of the modern law of fair comment'.[88]

How, though, has this attachment arisen? Arguably, not from poor advocacy or from the judges involved in the case: the lawyers seemed clear that *Campbell* stood for no more than that fair comment required 'the comments were no stronger than the occasion fairly justified'.[89] Likewise, Mellor J,[90] the only judge from that case to refer to it, held the same view.[91] Otherwise, the decision itself was ignored. The late Victorian judges, it seemed, saw little significance in it.

That is, until *Merivale v Carson*.[92] Had it not been for this case, the decision might have passed into obscurity. This case involved newspaper criticism of a stage play, written by Mr and Mrs Herman Merivale, which, the plaintiffs

---

[86] *Hunt v Star Newspaper Co Ltd* [1908] 2 KB 309, 320.
[87] *Walker v Hodgson* [1909] 1 KB 239, 250.
[88] *Joseph v Spiller* (n 3) [34].
[89] *Wason v Walter* (1868–69) LR 4 QB 73, per Karslake QC, Coleridge (now a QC) and Wood.
[90] *Kelly v Tinling* (n 84); *Jenner v A'Beckett* (1871–72) LR 7 QB 11, 12.
[91] *Wason v Walter* (n 89); *Ridsdale v Clifton (No 1)* (1876) 1 PD 316, 335; *Purcell v Sowler* (1876) 1 CPD 781, 784 per Edwards QC.
[92] *Merivale v Carson* (1887) 20 QBD 275, CA.

argued, went beyond fair criticism by implying the play was immoral. Odgers, for the defendant, argued:

> [T]his being a criticism upon a matter of public interest, the occasion was privileged, and the plaintiffs were bound to prove express malice and this they did not do ... *Campbell v Spottiswoode* may appear opposed to this view, but the judgments in that case must be read with reference to the facts of the case, and there the criticism was not confined to the work itself, but contained an attack on the character of the author.[93]

Lord Esher MR disagreed. After saying that the jury must first decide what the words complained of mean, he said:

> What is the next question to be put to the jury? Are they to be told that the criticism of a play is a privileged occasion, within the well-settled meaning of the word 'privilege,' and that their verdict must go for the defendant, unless the plaintiff can prove malice in fact, that is, that the writer of the article was actuated by an indirect or malicious motive? I think it is clear that that is not the law, and that it was so decided in *Campbell v Spottiswoode*, which has never been overruled. All the judges, both before and ever since that case, have acted upon the view there expressed, that a criticism upon a written published work is not a privileged occasion.[94]

Lord Esher continues: 'Blackburn J ... shews why it is not a privileged occasion. A privileged occasion is one on which the privileged person is entitled to do something which no one who is not within the privilege is entitled to do on that occasion'.[95] Is that what Blackburn J had said? Or had he said, as observed above, that the press was not entitled to special fair comment right in which an accusation of fraud counted as opinion?

From this point, *Merivale v Carson*, not *Campbell*, became the leading authority on fair comment, with the latter becoming a footnote to it. Also, Cockburn CJ's judgment (which holds the key to understanding its significance) became unfashionable. Instead, Lord Esher's view that Blackburn J's judgment was instructive took hold. The only notable dissension was that Crompton J's judgment was also significant. This treatment of *Merivale v Carson* emerges from the important 1903 Court of Appeal decision, *McQuire v Western Morning News Co Ltd*.[96] Here, we see Collins MR, in a thoughtful, considered judgment explaining the meaning of fair criticism, concentrate on *Merivale v Carson* (*Campbell* is cited but not discussed). Also, he says some interesting things about qualified privilege and fair comment whilst discussing *Henwood v Harrison* (above):

> The decision, so far as I know, has never been questioned, though exception has been taken to the use of the word 'privilege' to describe the public right of fair comment,

---

[93] ibid 277.
[94] ibid 279.
[95] ibid 280. Bowen LJ agreed with him; see 283.
[96] *McQuire v Western Morning News Co Ltd* [1903] 2 KB 100.

and some eminent judges have preferred not to use a word which, according to its technical etymology, denotes the special right of an individual, as extending to cover the common rights of the whole community at large.[97]

He later expanded upon this view in 1906 in another Court of Appeal decision (again referring to *Merivale v Carson* as the key decision on fair comment):

> The dicta no doubt assert the etymological inexactitude of the word 'privilege' as connoting a right common to the public at large, and the limits of the right itself are pointed out which, whether it be called privilege or by any other name, does not extend to cover misstatements of fact however bona fide; but they in no degree affect the standard by which the fairness of the comment is to be judged or relieve the commentator from liability, if the comment be malicious, if, indeed, it can then be described as comment at all. The right, though shared by the public, is the right of every individual who asserts it, and is, qua him, an individual right whatever name it be called by, and comment by him which is coloured by malice cannot from his standpoint be deemed fair.[98]

Apart from the odd mention, usually by counsel,[99] *Campbell* was not discussed again, significantly, until 1951–52 in the bizarre libel suit brought by Lord Kemsley against Michael Foot (a complaint about the headline: 'Lower than Kemsley'). Here we find the second source (after *Merivale*) of sentimental attachment to *Campbell*, for Diplock KC, in his submissions to the court about the development of fair comment, marked *Campbell* as a turning point (one of three) in the history of fair comment.[100] Even here, though, *Campbell* is dealt with only briefly by the court – Lord Porter acknowledges it as one of several cases that decide that the underlying facts must be established for fair comment to apply.[101]

Intriguingly, by 1969, *Campbell* had been largely forgotten again. In the Court of Appeal decision in *London Artists Ltd v Littler*,[102] the judges did not refer to it when discussing the meaning of fair comment; even when discussing imputations of dishonourable motives.[103] Similarly, there is no mention of it in the 1989 Privy Council decision in *Jeyaretnam v Goh Chok Tong*[104] (albeit counsel mentions it) – instead, the court refers to a passage from *Gatley on Libel and Slander* (on the difference between fact and comment when imputing bad motives).[105] Similarly, in the House of Lords decision in *Telnikoff v Matusevitch*,[106] counsel referred to it (and many other cases) but their Lordships did not. Indeed, it is

---

[97] ibid 111.
[98] *Thomas v Bradbury Agnew* (n 6) 638.
[99] See, eg, *Sutherland v Stopes* (n 5).
[100] *Kemsley v Foot* [1952] AC 345, 349. For further discussion of this landmark case, see ch 4.
[101] *Kemsley v Foot* (n 99) 358.
[102] *London Artists Ltd v Littler* [1969] 2 WLR 409.
[103] Instead (ibid 420), the court refers to *Walker v Hodgson* (n 87).
[104] *Jeyaretnam v Goh Chok Tong* [1989] 1 WLR 1109.
[105] ibid 1113.
[106] *Telnikoff v Matusevich* [1992] 2 AC 343.

not until 1999 that the UK judiciary saw significance in *Campbell*. In *Reynolds v Times Newspapers Ltd*, the House of Lords notes Crompton J's comment that fair comment is 'the right of all the Queen's subjects'.[107]

Interestingly, the Court of Appeal mentioned *Campbell* in the section marked 'English authorities on qualified privilege' – noting Cockburn CJ's concluding remarks that it is not in the interests of society for the private character of public men to be attacked without foundation.[108] This adds weight to the popular view that *Campbell* is also a qualified privilege case – although it does not add specifics. Eady J, in 2006, added a little more when he said *Campbell* was decided at a time when 'the distinction between fair comment and privilege as separate defences had not fully emerged'[109] – although he uses it only as a source of principles for fair comment.[110]

ii. Imputation of Bad Motives

The minor role that *Campbell* plays in fair comment doctrine is that the imputation of bad motives falls outside the right unless there is a substantial factual foundation.[111] Even this may be an exaggeration of *Campbell*'s influence, for there is an earlier case, *Robertson v M'Dougall*,[112] where it was said the law did not protect 'imput[ations of] base motives' unless true (albeit this *was* a qualified privilege case).[113]

Even if *Campbell* was novel on this point, its influence has now waned considerably. The Faulks Committee, in its report on defamation law had said in 1975 that there should be no special rule preventing imputations of 'base motives' from being fair comment.[114] In 2002, Eady J doubted the point could be reconciled with the European Court of Human Rights jurisprudence on Article 10, freedom of expression.[115] For example, in *Nilsen and Johnsen v Norway*,[116] the Court held that the imputation of bad motives was a matter of opinion rather than fact (though the decision may be confined to its facts). In 2010, Andrew Caldecott QC invited the Supreme Court, in *Joseph v Spiller*, to rule that 'there should not be a more stringent test for opinions imputing dishonourable motives'.[117] The Court, though, confined the principle to bare

---

[107] *Reynolds v Times Newspapers Ltd* [2001] 2 AC 127, 193.
[108] Appeal decision (n 49) 291.
[109] *Lowe v Associated Newspapers Ltd* [2006] EWHC 320 (QB), [2007] QB 580, [51].
[110] ibid [51] and [53].
[111] See, eg, Cameron Doley and Alastair Mullis, *Carter-Ruck on Libel & Privacy*, 6th edn (London, Lexis Nexis, 2010) 10.42–10.44.
[112] *Robertson v M'Dougall* (1828) 4 Bingham New Cases 670.
[113] ibid 679.
[114] Faulks Committee, *Report of the Committee on Defamation* (1975, Cmnd 5909) [161].
[115] *Branson v Bower* [2002] QB 737, [21].
[116] *Nilsen v Johnsen v Norway* (2000) 30 EHRR 878, [50].
[117] *Joseph v Spiller* (n 3), [82].

comments (the 'courts have always held that the only defence to a bare comment which infers the existence of discreditable conduct but does not identify it is justification').[118] *Campbell*, though, is not a bare comment case (the Heathen article explained the source of its suspicion in some detail).

Campbell's minor role, assuming it has contemporary significance for honest opinion under s 3,[119] Defamation Act 2013, seems to be this: that (1) the court must decide whether the imputation of bad motives is a claim of fact or opinion. This depends entirely on context: (2) if it is fact, then the only defence available is justification or qualified privilege;[120] (3) if it is opinion, then there is no special rule that the underlying facts need to be established beyond the usual level in fair comment.

V. CONCLUSION

It is tempting to treat *Campbell* as a case of its times, in which trustworthiness was a most valuable commodity. That would explain why dishonesty ranked differently to folly. But that would ignore the incredulity with which popular commentators greeted the decision. For them, Bovill's powerful defence ought to have succeeded. Thus, even then, *Campbell* was a contentious decision.

Do we read too much into *Campbell*? Despite being contemporaneously contentious, the decision itself is prosaic, if understood as confined to fair comment. As all four judges admit, or seem to, the law in this area was so clearly settled that the answer, to them at least, was straightforward. So, we might treat *Campbell* as wrongly decided – that the special rule it contains (but does not create) regarding imputations of dishonesty ought not to have been applied because the underlying facts had a substantial basis (across not one but two articles), and the inference arising from them was one that could be *honestly* held. But we would not think it a landmark for this reason. It may be that, just as Cockburn CJ and his brethren did for Campbell, we too attribute a nobler significance to *Campbell* than we ought to.

---

[118] ibid [89].

[119] *Gatley* (n 76) [12.4].

[120] See, ibid [105] where Lord Walker of Gestingthorpe endorses Lord Nicholls of Birkenhead's summary on this point in *Tse Wai Chun v Cheng* [2001] EMLR 777, [17] where he cites, with approval, the New South Wales case of *Myerson v Smith's Weekly Publishing Co Ltd* (1923) 24 SR (NSW) 20, 26, 'To say that a man's conduct was dishonourable is not comment, it is a statement of fact. To say that he did certain specific things and that his conduct was dishonourable is a statement of fact couple with a comment'.

2

Bonnard v Perryman *(1891)*

DAVID ROLPH

I. INTRODUCTION

A NY CASE AFTER which a rule is named has a fair claim to be regarded as a landmark case. The rule in *Bonnard v Perryman*[1] has been applied and reaffirmed for over 125 years, not only by English courts but also by Australian, New Zealand, Canadian, Hong Kong and Singaporean courts.[2] Its effect is that a claimant will ordinarily be unable to obtain an interim or interlocutory injunction to restrain an apprehended, allegedly defamatory publication. It is an aspect of defamation doctrine and practice in which freedom of speech is decisively preferred over the protection of reputation. This is significant because defamation law, in most common law countries, may be characterised as claimant-friendly.[3]

---

[1] *Bonnard v Perryman* [1891] 2 Ch 269 ('*Bonnard v Perryman*').

[2] As to the position in Australia, see *Royal Automobile Club of Victoria v Paterson* [1968] VR 508, 510 (McInerney J); *Healy v Askin* [1974] 1 NSWLR 436, 441–42 (Lee J). However, see now *Australian Broadcasting Corporation v O'Neill* [2006] HCA 46, (2006) 227 CLR 57. As to the position in New Zealand, see, for example, *McSweeney v Berryman* [1980] 2 NZLR 168, 175 (Barker J); *New Zealand Mortgage Guarantee Co Ltd v Wellington Newspapers Ltd* [1989] 1 NZLR 4, 6 (Cooke P); *Ron West Motors Ltd v Broadcasting Corporation of New Zealand (No 2)* [1989] 3 NZLR 520, 527–28 (Smellie J); *TV3 Network Services Ltd v Fahey* [1999] 2 NZLR 129, 132 (Richardson P). As to the position in Canada, see, for example, *Canada Metal Co v Canadian Broadcasting Corporation* (1974) 44 DLR (3d) 329, 344 (Holland J); *Church of Scientology of British Columbia v Radio NW Ltd* (1974) 46 DLR (3d) 459, 462–64 (Branca JA). As to the position in Hong Kong, see *Target Newspapers Ltd v Narain* [1989] HKCA 242, [1989] 2 HKC 16, 23; *Ki Ming Po v Yeung Wai Hong* [1993] HKCFI 117, [3] (Godfrey J), [1993] 1 HKC 595; *Poon Ying Hon v CCT Telecom Holdings Ltd* [2001] HKCFI 735, [28] (Leong J). As to the position in Singapore, see, for example, *Kwek Juan Bok Lawrence v Lim Han Yong* [1989] 1 SLR(R) 675, [1989] SGHC 55.

[3] This is certainly the case in comparison to the United States following its constitutionalisation of its defamation law in its landmark defamation case, *New York Times v Sullivan* 376 US 254 (1964), as to which, see ch 6. Recent reforms to defamation law in England and Wales may also have had the effect of making the bringing of defamation claims more difficult for claimants. See generally A Mullis and A Scott, 'The swing of the pendulum: reputation, expression and the re-centering of English libel law' (2012) 63 *NILQ* 27. See further D Rolph, *Defamation Law*, 1st ed (Sydney, Thomson Reuters, 2016) [2.20].

Bonnard v Perryman was the culmination of a line of cases in which English courts attempted to work out, following the passage of the *Judicature Acts*, the powers of a court exercising both common law and equitable jurisdiction to grant the equitable remedy of an injunction for a common law cause of action, the tort of defamation, as well as the circumstances in which such a remedy would be granted. It was not the first Court of Appeal decision to consider the issue. As Lord Coleridge CJ's judgment in *Bonnard v Perryman* itself through its lengthy, direct quotation, coupled with express endorsement, Lord Esher MR in the earlier Court of Appeal decision in *William Coulson and Sons v James Coulson and Co*[4] had dealt directly with the very same issue of the proper approach to the grant of an interlocutory injunction in a defamation case. Yet it is the rule in *Bonnard v Perryman* that defamation practitioners and judges invoke. That *Bonnard v Perryman* was a decision of the full Court of Appeal and that there is an authorised report of the judgment gave this case a prominence and an imprimatur over the earlier decision. A landmark case need not always be the first case on point.

Bonnard v Perryman has not been without its critics. The judgment itself was not unanimous. It is frequently overlooked that there was a dissent from Kay LJ.[5] There was some initial doubt about, even resistance to, its application.[6] It has been the subject of extensive judicial debate in Australia.[7] However, for a long period of time, in most Commonwealth jurisdictions, the rule in *Bonnard v Perryman* has been consistently and uncontroversially applied to ensure a restrictive approach to the grant of injunctive relief in defamation claims.

Given that applications for interim injunctions will ordinarily need to be determined on an urgent basis, the clarity provided by the rule in *Bonnard v Perryman* is important. One consequence of the way in which such applications arise is that appeals are rare, certainly to intermediate appellate courts, even more so to courts of final appeal.[8] The High Court of Australia's decision in *Australian Broadcasting Corporation v O'Neill* is a rare example of the issue of the proper approach to the grant of an interlocutory injunction in a defamation case being determined by an ultimate appellate court.[9]

Bonnard v Perryman has proven to be remarkably resilient. It has been tested by the Court of Appeal since the introduction of the Human Rights Act 1998 and survived.[10] Given the significant developments in the tort of misuse of private information and the growing recognition of reputation as an aspect of

---

[4] *William Coulson and Sons v James Coulson and Co* (1887) 3 TLR 846. For a recognition of *William Coulson and Sons v James Coulson and Co* (1887) 3 TLR 846 as 'the starting point of the jurisprudence', see *Holley v Smyth* [1998] QB 726, 738 (Auld LJ).

[5] *Bonnard v Perryman* (n 1) 285–89.

[6] See, for example, Lord Halsbury's judgment in *Monson v Tussauds Ltd* [1894] 1 QB 671.

[7] As to which, see section V B below.

[8] *Chappell v TCN Channel Nine Pty Ltd* (1988) 14 NSWLR 153, 163 (Hunt J).

[9] *Australian Broadcasting Corporation v O'Neill* [2006] HCA 46, (2006) 227 CLR 57.

[10] *Greene v Associated Newspapers Ltd* [2004] EWCA Civ 1462, [2005] QB 972.

the right to a private life under Article 8 of the European Convention on Human Rights, whether it will withstand further testing is open to doubt.

II. THE CONTEXT OF *BONNARD v PERRYMAN*

Although the rule in *Bonnard v Perryman* is often applied as if it reflects an immutable principle, the central issue in the case itself arose in a particular historical context. The case occurred during, and as a result of, significant changes to the structure, powers and jurisdiction of English courts. Prior to 1854, a court exercising common law jurisdiction could not grant the equitable remedy of an injunction.[11] Thus, the possibility of an interim injunction to restrain an apprehended defamation simply did not arise. The Common Law Procedure Act 1854 conferred the power to grant injunctions on courts exercising common law jurisdiction. However, up until 1875, that power was used rarely.[12] As for courts exercising equitable jurisdiction before 1875, they were not able to grant injunctions for defamation because they did not exercise jurisdiction over claims in tort, like defamation,[13] but could, and did on occasion, grant injunctions where publications affected proprietary interests,[14] through causes of action such as 'trade libel' (or what would now be considered as malicious or injurious falsehood) and passing off. It was only after the passage of the Judicature Acts that the related issues of the jurisdiction of the High Court of Justice to grant an interlocutory injunction in a defamation claim and the proper approach to such relief arose directly for decision. The issues were not immediately settled; it took several years for judges of the High Court of Justice to adjust to the exercise of both common law and equitable jurisdiction. The line of authority dealing with these issues demonstrates judges grappling with the enlargement of their powers.[15] Even after the enactment of

---

[11] *Bonnard v Perryman* (n 1) 283 (Lord Coleridge CJ); *Monson v Tussauds Ltd* [1894] 1 QB 671, 692–93 (Lopes LJ). See also *Holley v Smyth* [1998] QB 726, 737 (Auld LJ); *Greene v Associated Newspapers* (n 10) 986.

[12] *Bonnard v Perryman* (n 1) 283 (Lord Coleridge CJ); *Monson v Tussauds Ltd* [1894] 1 QB 671, 693 (Lopes LJ). See also *Lennox v Krantz* (1978) 19 SASR 272, 275 (Zelling J); *Greene v Associated Newspapers* (n 10) 986. The first reported instance of this occurring appears to be *Saxby v Easterbrook* (1878) 3 CPD 339.

[13] *Gee v Pritchard* (1818) 2 Swans 402; (1818) 36 ER 670, 674 (Lord Eldon LC); *Martin v Wright* (1833) 6 Sim 297; (1833) 58 ER 605, 606 (Sir Lancelot Shadwell VC); *Clark v Freeman* (1848) 11 Beav 112; (1848) 50 ER 759, 761–62 (Lord Langdale MR); *Fleming v Newton* (1848) 1 HLC 363; (1848) 9 ER 797, 803 (Lord Cottenham LC); *Emperor of Austria v Day* (1861) 3 De G F & I 217; (1861) 45 ER 861, 870–71 (Lord Westbury LC). See also *Bonnard v Perryman* (n 1) 283 (Lord Coleridge CJ); *Collard v Marshall* [1892] 1 Ch 571, 577 (Chitty J); *Monson v Tussauds Ltd* [1894] 1 QB 671, 690 (Lord Halsbury), 692 (Lopes LJ). See further *Lennox v Krantz* (1978) 19 SASR 272, 275 (Zelling J); *Holley v Smyth* [1998] QB 726, 737 (Auld LJ); *Greene v Associated Newspapers* (n 10) 986.

[14] *Dixon v Holden* (1869) LR 7 Eq 488, 492 (Sir Richard Malins VC); *Thorley's Cattle Food Co v Massam* (1880) 14 Ch D 763, 773 (Sir Richard Malins VC). See also *Collard v Marshall* [1892] 1 Ch 571, 577 (Chitty J); *Monson v Tussauds Ltd* [1894] 1 QB 671, 690 (Lord Halsbury).

[15] *Saxby v Easterbrook* (1878) 3 CPD 339; *Thomas v Williams* (1880) 14 Ch D 864; *Quartz Hill Consolidated Gold Mining Co v Beall* (1882) 20 Ch D 501, 507 (Jessel MR); *Liverpool Household Stores Association v Smith* (1887) 37 Ch D 170.

the *Judicature Acts*, many judges who trained and practised in equity felt most comfortable granting an interlocutory injunction in a defamation case where the publication touched upon the plaintiff's property or trade.[16] The habits of mind cultivated and reinforced by training and practice were not readily discarded. The jurisdictional point awaited authoritative settlement. This was provided in *Bonnard v Perryman*.[17]

III. BONNARD v PERRYMAN

A. The Facts in *Bonnard v Perryman*

The rule in *Bonnard v Perryman* is so frequently invoked as a free-standing principle, without regard often being given to the factual context in which the case arose. Yet the facts in *Bonnard v Perryman* are fascinating. The case occurs towards the outset of finance reporting as a distinct genre of modern journalism. It highlights the potential for conflict of interest and corruption in financial journalism. The case also reflects the unpalatable reality of publicly acceptable expressions of anti-Semitism in late Victorian England.

Bonnard v Perryman concerned an article published in the 7 February 1891 edition of the weekly newspaper, the *Financial Observer and Mining Herald*. There had been a forestate of what was come in an issue of the same newspaper in the previous month:

> By the way, there appears a very peculiar concern between Marks, Campbell, and the gorgeous Mercantile and General Trust and Finance Company, Unlimited, located in the sumptuous offices in Broad Street Avenue, where the lovely Engel is on guard. We shall have a rare budget to say about this curious concern and those working the oracle.[18]

This teaser for the forthcoming article did not prepare the reader for the unpleasant, anti-Semitic nature of what was to be published. The 7 February 1891 article bore the headline:

The Fletcher Mills of Providence, Rhode Island.

The Providence and National Worsted Mills, Ltd.

A Jews' Den.

Marks' Promoting Vehicle.

---

[16] See, for example, *Riding v Smith* (1876) 1 Ex D 91, 93 (Kelly CB); *Saxby v Easterbrook* (1878) 3 CPD 339, 343 (Lindley J); *Thomas v Williams* (1880) 14 Ch D 864, 873 (Fry J). See also *Day v Brownrigg* (1878) 10 Ch D 294, 304 (Sir George Jessel MR), 305–06 (Thesiger LJ).

[17] *Lennox v Krantz* (1978) 19 SASR 272, 274 (Zelling J).

[18] *Bonnard v Perryman* (n 1) 270.

It commenced thus:

> In 1889 offices were taken at 143, Cannon Street, by a couple of Jews, named Gustave
> Richard Bonnard and Arthur H. Deakin, who styled themselves the Mercantile and
> General Trust. How they got into the offices we cannot understand, for they had
> not a sixpence in the world; the furniture was obtained on the hire system, and they
> often had to beg a lunch. They were, however, of a very enterprising nature, although
> young, and they were lucky enough to ingratiate themselves with the great Harry
> Hananel Marks by offering him inducements to puff the Sykes Brewery, which had by
> some means come into their hands.[19]

The article went on to suggest that Bonnard and Deakin, having acquired an
interest in their first brewery, were able to open a bank account and to acquire
an interest in the City of Baltimore United Breweries, the headquarters of which
were also located in Broad Street Avenue. It recorded that both breweries were
floated on the stock exchange. The article asserted that 'There was some very
shady work in this business' and that 'The plunder amounted to no less than
£58,000'.

Continuing in its anti-Semitic vein, the article then identified the other
principal backers of the enterprise in the following terms:

> In both these concerns they were greatly assisted by a Bernard Engel, a brother of a
> money-lender in Great Marlborough Street, who knew the corners in which shares
> could be pushed, and who also had a large Jewish connection. This Bernard Engel
> figures in Broad Street Avenue as D. Engel, and at times he has varied his name into
> Engle, Angle, and Eagle, to meet different phases of promoting and dodging.

> Success has so far crowned their shady deeds, and having such a wonderful engine as
> the *Financial News* at their disposal, on terms, we next find them at work, altogether,
> at the Broad Street Avenue, where they flourish as the Mercantile and General Trust
> Finance Company. This concern is composed of the following Jews: – Bernard Engel,
> Gustave Richard Bonnard, Arthur H. Deakin, Edmund Campbell, alias Callisher, a
> member of the Stock Exchange, Harry Hananel Marks.

The article then turned to examine the group's latest endeavour in promoting a company to the public, the Providence and National Worsted Mills Ltd.
It quoted from an article in the *New York Herald* describing the purchase of
two mills on Rhode Island by a syndicate led by Bonnard and 'Eagle', claiming
that these men were connected with the Bank of England. It then proceeded:

> If these gentlemen 'connected with the Bank of England' only made £58,000 over
> the Baltimore breweries, they appear to have a chance now of making far more over
> this deal. But when our readers have carefully considered what a wretched halo of
> picking and stealing surrounds the den in Broad Street Avenue, they will think twice
> before putting their hard-earned savings into the pockets of these gentry. The board
> of directors headed by Lord Suffield is a group of guinea pigs; but how such names

---

[19] Significant portions of the text of the article are reproduced at ibid, 270–71.

as Bircham & Co. for solicitors, and Sheppard, Pelly, Scott & Co. for brokers, have been obtained it is not for us to mention now. Suffice it to say they surely could not have known for whom they consented to work, and we look to a withdrawal of their names before the prospectus is issued.

In addition to its overt anti-Semitism, which is confronting to the modern reader's eye, the article is also notable for its criticism of Harry Hananel Marks. *Bonnard v Perryman* occurred in the media context of the emergence of finance journalism, at the height of Victorian capitalism. In this regard, the *Financial Observer and Mining Herald*, published, owned and edited by the first defendant, Charles W Perryman, was lagging behind, criticising the pioneer of the London daily financial newspaper, Harry Hananel Marks. By any measure, Marks was a colourful character. Son of the chief rabbi of the West London Synagogue, Marks went to the United States as a teenager. Spending over a decade there, Marks worked in newspapers in Texas, then spent five years at the *New York World*, finally ending up as the editor of the *Daily Mining News*. Returning to England, Marks became the proprietor and editor of the first London daily financial newspaper, the *Financial and Mining News* – a title which eventually merged with its principal rival to become the *Financial Times*.[20] The newspaper's reputation was decidedly mixed. On the one hand, it was an undoubted innovator, avoiding dullness and stuffiness, and introducing 'cross-headings, short paragraphs, and a breezy style which irritated competitors but appealed to financial sector professionals and their clerks'. It also became known for its crusading journalism, its investigative reporting uncovering significant corrupt corporate conduct, most notably its uncovering of corruption at the Metropolitan Board of Works.[21] On the other hand, the newspaper seemed to promote certain stocks through favourable coverage. In the absence of proper market regulation, there was ample scope for financial journalism to boost certain stocks (for covert profit in a variety of forms) or otherwise to distort financial markets.[22]

It was not, however, Marks who sued Perryman and the alleged newspaper printer, Clement Allen.[23] Bonnard and Deakin sued for libel, seeking £5,000 damages but also an injunction preventing the 'selling, circulating, or delivering, or communication' of the article itself or otherwise publishing imputations that they had engaged in fraudulent or dishonest conduct in relation to the promotion

[20] See D Kynaston, *The Financial Times: A Centenary History* (London, Viking, 1988) 4–5.

[21] As to the scandal surrounding the Metropolitan Board of Works, see G Clifton, *Professionalism, Patronage and Public Service in Victorian London: The Staff of the Metropolitan Board of Works* (London, Bloomsbury Academic, 2006) 142–59.

[22] 'Marks, Harry Hananel (1855–1916)', *Oxford Dictionary of National Biography*: www.oxforddnb.com/view/10.1093/ref:odnb/9780198614128.001.0001/odnb-9780198614128-e-47898.

[23] Both Perryman and Allen denied that Allen was the printer. See *Bonnard v Perryman* (n 1) 269–70.

or floating of the named breweries or mills or that they had bribed, suborned or conspired with the proprietors and editors of the *Financial News* or that they had engaged in stealing.[24] They swore affidavits denying that the allegations in the article were true. In particular, 'They denied specifically that they had any Jewish blood in them; that they had purchased their furniture on the hire system; and that they had any connection with Harry Hananel Marks'.[25] Perryman swore an affidavit that the allegations made against Bonnard and Deakin were true and that he would prove it at trial. He also swore that the bulk of the copies were already sold and circulated and the he had no intention of further printing or circulating the articles. However, Perryman had reprinted articles in the past. He also refused to give an undertaking that he would not sell any of the remaining 40 copies of the issue containing the article in suit.[26]

B. The Judgment at First Instance

The matter was heard by North J. At the outset of his judgment, his Lordship characterised the article thus:

> 'No one can read that article without seeing that it is one of a very serious character, that it directly affects and probably will affect the business of the Plaintiffs, and that it is an allegation which, unless it can be justified at the trial of the action, is one in which a jury would give the Plaintiffs very serious damages.'[27]

North J noted that Perryman's position was that nothing should be done about the article, as the jury was the proper tribunal of fact. However, his Lordship held that the issue before him was whether the publication should be allowed to continue until trial or whether it should be restrained by interlocutory injunction, and the determination of this issue required him to form a view about the article.[28]

North J treated the relevant principles to be governed by the Court of Appeal decision in *Quartz Hill Consolidated Gold Mining Company v Beall*.[29] His Lordship accepted that there was evidence of intention to publish the matter further.[30] He also accepted that there was evidence that the matter was untrue. Finally, he found that Perryman could not defend the publication on the basis of privilege because the newspaper article had not been published on

---

[24] ibid, 270.
[25] ibid, 272.
[26] ibid, 272–73.
[27] ibid, 274.
[28] ibid, 274–75.
[29] ibid, 275, citing *Quartz Hill Consolidated Gold Mining Company v Beall* (1882) 20 Ch D 501.
[30] ibid, 276.

a privileged occasion.[31] These were the three conditions North J identified emerging from Sir George Jessel MR's judgment in *Quartz Hill Consolidated Gold Mining Company v Beall* as relevant to the exercise of the jurisdiction to grant an interlocutory injunction in a defamation case. North J was unmoved by a 'floodgates' argument: that if the injunction were granted in this case, the courts would be filled with applications for similar relief.[32] His Lordship was satisfied that any jury, on the evidence before the court, would find the matter plainly defamatory and that a verdict to the contrary would be set aside as perverse. North J did concede that further evidence may be adduced at trial, which may alter this position.[33] North J granted the injunction against Perryman but did not think it necessary to restrain Allen.[34]

C. The Judgment of the Court of Appeal

Perryman appealed against the decision of North J to the Court of Appeal.[35] Giving the leading judgment, Lord Coleridge CJ, with whom Lord Esher MR, Lindley, Bowen and Lopes LJJ agreed, identified two issues arising on appeal. The first issue was whether the court had the jurisdiction to grant an injunction to restrain the publication of a libel, at all or before it had been determined to be defamatory. The second issue was, if such a jurisdiction existed, whether the court should exercise its discretion to grant such relief.[36] His Lordship noted that the former was a pure question of law, whereas the latter was fact-specific.

In relation to the issue of the existence of the jurisdiction for a court to grant an injunction to restrain the publication of defamatory matter, Lord Coleridge CJ was emphatic: 'the point is clear, and is settled by authority'. As such, his Lordship was 'unable to entertain any doubt' upon the point. He noted that the authorities on point were 'few and recent, for obvious reasons; but they are uniform, and they are clear'.[37] Lord Coleridge CJ noted that the effect of the Common Law Procedure Act 1854 was to confer the power on the courts of common law to grant an injunction in a defamation action and that the Judicature Act 1873 conferred this power on the Chancery Division of the High Court of Justice.

The real issue then was not whether the court had the jurisdiction to grant the interlocutory injunction but whether it should exercise its discretion to

---

[31] ibid, 277.
[32] ibid, 277.
[33] ibid, 278.
[34] ibid, 278–79.
[35] ibid, 279.
[36] ibid, 282.
[37] ibid, 283.

do so. What followed then is what has become known as 'the rule in *Bonnard v Perryman*'. Lord Coleridge CJ wrote:

> But it is obvious that the subject-matter of an action for defamation is so special as to require exceptional caution in exercising the jurisdiction to interfere by injunction before the trial of an action to prevent an anticipated wrong. The right of free speech is one which it is for the public interest that individuals should possess, and, indeed, that they should exercise without impediment, so long as no wrongful act is done; and, unless an alleged libel is untrue, there is no wrong committed; but, on the contrary, often a very wholesome act is performed in the publication and repetition of an alleged libel. Until it is clear that an alleged libel is untrue, it is not clear that any right at all has been infringed; and the importance of leaving free speech unfettered is a strong reason in cases of libel for dealing most cautiously and warily with the granting of interim injunctions.[38]

His Lordship went on to approve and adopt the following words of Lord Esher MR in the earlier Court of Appeal decision in *William Coulson and Sons v James Coulson and Co*:

> To justify the Court in granting an interim injunction it must come close to a decision upon the question of libel or no libel, before the jury have decided whether it was a libel or not. Therefore the jurisdiction was of a delicate nature. It ought only to be exercised in the clearest cases, where any jury would say that the matter complained of was libellous, and where, if the jury did not so find, the Court would set aside the verdict as unreasonable.[39]

Lord Coleridge CJ accepted that the impugned article unquestionably bore a defamatory character but concluded that only the jury could determine its impact upon the parties at trial. In relation to the defendant, his Lordship was not willing to find that the defence of justification was 'wholly unfounded'. In relation to the plaintiffs, he observed that the matter may turn upon their 'general character', which could not be properly determined on affidavit evidence on the hearing of a preliminary application but was properly an issue for the jury to decide at trial.[40] This was particularly important in relation to the assessment of damages. Lord Coleridge CJ stated that it was undesirable for the court to express a view on an interlocutory application when the jury at trial may only award nominal damages.[41] His Lordship concluded:

> Upon the whole we think, with great deference to Mr Justice North, that it is wiser in this case, as it generally and in all but exceptional cases must be, to abstain from interference until the trial and determination of the plea of justification.[42]

---

[38] ibid 284.
[39] ibid, 284, citing *William Coulson and Sons v James Coulson and Co* (1887) 3 TLR 846.
[40] ibid, 284.
[41] ibid, 284–85.
[42] ibid, 285.

So reasoned the majority. Kay LJ dissented. His Lordship agreed that the court had the jurisdiction to grant the injunction and that, ordinarily, the jurisdiction should be exercised sparingly. He departed from the majority in the application of the principles to the publication in question. Kay LJ was concerned by the 'coarse and abusive language' in which the article was written, from which his Lordship was prepared to infer that 'some personal feeling of spite or malignity against the Plaintiffs', rather than the pursuit of a public interest, was the actuating motive. The article's treatment of Marks and his position as a trade rival were the particular considerations weighing upon Kay LJ. His Lordship stated that:

> Some of the most serious allegations in the article are those by which the Defendant associates the Plaintiffs with a person whom he represents to be of infamous character. I know nothing whatever of that individual, except what appears in the evidence before us, and I have no means of judging whether the allegations made against him are true or false. It appears from another page in the same paper that since the 18th of February, 1890, the Defendant has been in the habit of publishing concerning this person accusations expressed in some of the strongest language of his well-furnished vocabulary. The individual so traduced is, it seems, the editor or owner of another financial paper published in London, called the *Financial News*, and the Defendant's paper states that the Defendant intends to repeat the article against him until some notice is taken of it by the London County Council, of which we are told this person is a member, the Incorporated Law Society, the Houses of Parliament, or the police. The article so published, and which the Defendant intends to repeat, calls the person denounced a city thief, a vulture, speaks of his swindles and his nefarious practices and says, amongst other choice phrases, that there is no phase of the criminal law that has not been scoffed at by him, and that fraud, conspiracy, burglary, and felony have been used to aid his schemes to despoil and hoodwink the public. Now, in the article complained of in this action, it is stated that the Plaintiffs have been lucky enough to ingratiate themselves with this person by offering him inducements to puff one of the companies which they promoted, and that the Mercantile and General Trust, which is the style under which the Plaintiffs are carrying on business, is composed of themselves, this man so vilified, and two other persons named Deakin and Campbell. These statements that the Plaintiffs are carrying on business in partnership in close association with a man who is described in this way as a swindler and a thief are undoubtedly calculated to damage the Plaintiffs extremely, if not to ruin them.[43]

Having determined that the matter was plainly defamatory and having expressed concern as to the publisher's motive, Kay LJ noted that the defendant intended to prove the matter was substantially true at trial. His Lordship was concerned by the state of the evidence in relation to the defence of justification.[44]

---

[43] ibid, 286.
[44] ibid, 286–88.

The defendant asserted his belief in the truth of what he had published but provided no grounds for that belief. Kay LJ was satisfied that there was a strong prima facie case that the statement was untrue.[45] His Lordship's concern about the state of the evidence and the strength of the publisher's defence of justification is an issue arising from the application of *Bonnard v Perryman*. Is it sufficient for a defendant merely to raise on an application for an interlocutory injunction an intention to justify the matter at trial or is something more required, even on an interlocutory application, bearing in mind the important role a defendant's intention to rely upon a defence of justification at trial can have in defeating an application for injunctive relief. Kay LJ then addressed the balance of convenience and found that it favoured the grant of the interlocutory injunction.[46] This was the approach of the minority, not only in this case, but also in the decided cases for over a century.

IV. THE RECEPTION AND APPLICATION OF *BONNARD v PERRYMAN*

Writing shortly after the decision was handed down, the *Law Quarterly Review* observed that the case was significant for establishing that the High Court of Justice had the jurisdiction to grant an injunction to restrain an alleged libel by virtue of what it described as 'the combined (and, it would seem, accidental) effect of the Common Law Procedure Act, 1854, and the Judicature Act, 1873'. Unlike some subsequent judges and commentators, the *Law Quarterly Review* was not perturbed by the decision's seemingly lax approach to the pleading of a defence of justification as a means of precluding the grant of an interlocutory injunction, observing that:

> It may be said that an unscrupulous defendant can always evade this jurisdiction by setting up the defence of justification on the pleadings and abandoning it at the trial. But this would be so hazardous a course that it is not likely to find favour even with unscrupulous libellers.[47]

Given that the issue of the proper approach to injunctive relief had been a difficult doctrinal problem that courts had grappled with for decades, it is unsurprising that the impact of the decision in *Bonnard v Perryman* was not immediately felt in the decided cases. There were some attempts to distinguish *Bonnard v Perryman*, or to accommodate the earlier approach within it. There was still a

---

[45] ibid, 288. Kay LJ's concern about the state of the evidence and the strength of the publisher's defence of justification has been an ongoing difficulty in the application of *Bonnard v Perryman*. See, for example, *National Mutual Life Association of Australasia Ltd v GTV Corporation Pty Ltd* [1989] VR 747, 754 (Ormiston J).
[46] *Bonnard v Perryman* (n 1) 288–89.
[47] 'Notes' (1891) 7 *LQR* 295, 300.

disposition to granting an injunction to restrain a defamatory publication that affected the plaintiff's property or trade.[48]

There was also judicial criticism of the decision. The most notable comment was provided in *Monson v Tussauds Ltd*.[49] In that case, the plaintiff was tried in Scotland for murder. The jury returned a verdict of 'Not proven'. Tussauds exhibited a waxwork figure of the plaintiff with the gun he allegedly used to shoot his victim. It was exhibited in a room with other waxwork figures of the other people convicted for, or suspected of committing, crimes. Leading off the room was the 'Chambers of Horrors', which included a recreation of the crime scene. The plaintiff sued for defamation and sought an interlocutory injunction restraining the exhibition, pending the trial.[50] At first instance, the injunction was granted.[51] Tussauds appealed against the decision. In his judgment, Lord Halsbury was critical of the reasoning in *Bonnard v Perryman* which sanctioned a restrictive approach to injunctive relief out of a concern that judges would pre-empt or even influence the jury's ultimate decision at trial. His Lordship stated:

> The jury will have upon the trial of the action to decide upon the question ultimately, and I have too high an opinion of the intelligence of juries to suppose that they would be influenced in their judgment if they learned that a judge or a Court thought that the continuance of an exhibition charged as libellous ought to be restrained until the matter came before them for decision. Indeed, it is a little singular to suppose, considering the controversies which used to arise before Mr Fox's Act, that a jury would on such a question be unduly influenced by an opinion of a judge or a Court.[52]

Later in his judgment, Lord Halsbury expressly engaged with *Bonnard v Perryman*. His Lordship accepted that, as a general proposition, a court should not grant an interlocutory injunction except in a clear case.[53] However, he was concerned that the court should not adopt an approach to injunctive relief which denied the express power to grant such relief under statute. Lord Halsbury observed as follows:

> If I were to understand the test suggested to be applicable to all cases, so that it practically excluded actions of libel from the operation of the Judicature Acts with respect to granting interlocutory injunctions, it would be to overrule the legislature – a power which is not possessed either by this or any other Court.[54]

---

[48] See, for example, *Collard v Marshall* [1892] 1 Ch 571, 577–78 (Chitty J); *Pink v Federation of Trades and Labour Unions Connected with the Shipping, Carrying, and Other Industries* (1892) 8 TLR 216, 217 (Kekewich J); *Pink v Federation of Trades and Labour Unions Connected with the Shipping, Carrying and Other Industries* (1892) 8 TLR 711, 712 (Kekewich J).

[49] *Monson v Tussauds Ltd* [1894] 1 QB 671.

[50] For a statement of the facts, see ibid, 675–76.

[51] ibid, 678 (Mathew J), 680 (Collins J).

[52] ibid, 685.

[53] ibid, 689.

[54] Ibid, 690.

In his Lordship's view, the instant case 'was a clear case of libel, and an equally clear case for the prompt interference of the Court to restrain it until the trial of the action'.[55] The concerns expressed in Lord Halsbury's judgment in *Monson v Tussauds Ltd* prefigure the concerns which exercised many Australian judges in the following century and beyond.

By contrast, in their separate judgments, Lopes and Davey LJJ also engaged with *Bonnard v Perryman*, in particular the statement that interlocutory injunctions should only be granted in defamation claims 'in the clearest cases'.[56] Both of their Lordships held that this was not an indefinite category but was explained and delimited by the judgment in *Bonnard v Perryman* itself, requiring that the matter should be plainly defamatory, such that any jury to the contrary would be set aside as unreasonable.[57] Lopes and Davey JJ treated *Bonnard v Perryman* as binding upon them and were more explanatory than critical of its effect.

Ultimately, the judges on appeal in *Monson v Tussauds Ltd* found that the interlocutory injunction granted by the court below had to be set aside because there was fresh evidence suggesting that the plaintiff may have consented to the exhibition.[58] As Lopes LJ observed:

> It is passing strange that a man who now asserts his anxiety to bury in oblivion the circumstances of the Ardlamont case should be found writing a pamphlet on that case, and, as he says, "on the impulse of the moment", announcing himself as a public lecturer on the same subject![59]

Whatever reservations may have been expressed about the correctness of *Bonnard v Perryman* in the first decade after its decision, it became well settled as the rule of practice in the twentieth century. Throughout the twentieth century, English courts reaffirmed the restrictive approach to injunctive relief in defamation claims sanctioned by *Bonnard v Perryman*.[60] In doing so, different judges identified slightly different rationales for *Bonnard v Perryman*.[61] In *Fraser v Evans*, Lord Denning MR acknowledged the importance of the jury as 'the constitutional tribunal' but expressly identified freedom of speech as the more significant justification for *Bonnard v Perryman*.[62] In *Herbage v Pressdram Ltd*,

---

[55] ibid, 690–91.

[56] *Bonnard v Perryman*, n 1, 284.

[57] *Monson v Tussauds Ltd* (n 49) 694 (Lopes LJ), 697 (Davey LJ).

[58] ibid, 691 (Lord Halsbury), 696 (Lopes LJ), 697–98 (Davey LJ).

[59] ibid, 696.

[60] See, for example, *Fraser v Evans* [1969] 1 QB 349, 360 (Lord Denning MR); *Hubbard v Vosper* [1972] 2 QB 84, 96–97 (Lord Denning MR); *Schering Chemicals Ltd v Falkman Ltd* [1982] QB 1, 18 (Lord Denning MR); *Khashoggi v IPC Magazines Ltd* [1986] 1 WLR 1412, 1414, 1416–17 (Sir John Donaldson MR).

[61] *Holley v Smyth* [1998] QB 726, 739 (Auld LJ).

[62] *Fraser v Evans* [1969] 1 QB 349, 360. For the expression of a similar view, see *Healy v Askin* [1974] 1 NSWLR 436, 441–42 (Lee J).

Griffiths LJ (as his Lordship then was) strongly endorsed *Bonnard v Perryman*, identifying the underlying rationale thus:

> These principles have evolved because of the value the court has placed upon freedom of speech and I think also upon the freedom of the press, when balancing it against the reputation of a single individual who, if wrong, can be compensated in damages.[63]

The proper juridical basis for *Bonnard v Perryman* was identified in slightly different terms again by the Court of Appeal in *Khashoggi v IPC Magazines Ltd*. Giving the leading judgment, Sir John Donaldson MR stated:

> The point is that *Bonnard v Perryman*, apart from its reference to freedom of speech, is based on the fact that the courts should not step in to defend a cause of action in defamation if they think this is a case in which the plea of justification might, not would, succeed.[64]

Bonnard v Perryman was reaffirmed again by the Court of Appeal in *Holley v Smyth*.[65] Having set out the rule in *Bonnard v Perryman*, Staughton LJ observed: 'That wholesome doctrine has often been acted on'.[66] This is so even where the defendant threatens to publish the truth about the plaintiff so as to extract money from the plaintiff as the price for not doing so.[67]

In *Holley v Smyth*, Auld LJ identified the rationale in *Bonnard v Perryman* in slightly different terms from those of Griffiths LJ in *Herbage v Pressdram Ltd*. Auld LJ observed that:

> From the earliest days of the courts' consideration of their power to grant interlocutory relief in libel cases they seem to have been guided by two associated notions, one of high principle and one of principle and practicality. The first is the importance of protecting the individual's right to free speech. The second is an acknowledgment that the judges should not, save in the clearest case, usurp the jury's role restraining at the interlocutory stage publication of a statement that the jury might later find to be no libel or true or otherwise defensible.[68]

Auld LJ then invoked the 'ringing tones' of Sir William Blackstone in his *Commentaries on the Laws of England* as to the balance that has been struck by the common law between freedom of speech and the protection of reputation. Blackstone famously wrote:

> The liberty of the press is indeed essential to the nature of a free state: but this consists in laying no *previous* restraints upon publications, and not in freedom from censure for criminal matter when published. Every freeman has the undoubted right to lay what sentiments he pleases before the public: to forbid this, is to destroy the

---

[63] *Herbage v Pressdram Ltd* [1984] 1 WLR 1160, 1162.
[64] *Khashoggi v IPC Magazines Ltd* [1986] 1 WLR 1412, 1417–18.
[65] *Holley v Smyth* [1998] QB 726.
[66] ibid, 730.
[67] ibid, 744 (Auld LJ), 746–50 (Staughton LJ).
[68] *Holley v Smyth* [1998] QB 726, 737.

freedom of the press: but if he publishes what is improper, mischievous, or illegal, he must take the consequence of his own temerity. To subject the press to the restrictive power of a licenser, as was formerly done, both before and since the revolution, is to subject all freedom of sentiment to the prejudices of one man, and make him the arbitrary and infallible judge of all controverted points in learning, religion, and government. But to punish (as the law does at present) any dangerous or offensive writings, which, when published, shall on a fair and impartial trial by adjudged of a pernicious tendency, is necessary for the preservation of the peace and good order, of government and religion, the only solid foundation of civil liberty. Thus the will of the individuals is still left free; the abuse only of that free will is the object of legal punishment.[69]

Even though the English authorities cast *Bonnard v Perryman* in terms of a rule, rather than a principle, and one which is restrictively applied, they still recognised that there remains a discretion to grant the injunction, given that it is an equitable remedy.[70]

Holley v Smyth confirms that the restrictive approach to injunctive relief is not displaced by the impropriety of the defendant's motive.[71] This follows from the principle that truth alone is a complete defence to defamation.[72] If the defendant tells the truth about the plaintiff, the defendant does no wrong to the plaintiff's reputation. A plaintiff is not entitled to a reputation he or she does not deserved. So telling the truth about the plaintiff does not so much damage the plaintiff's reputation as recalibrate it to its proper level.[73] The motive of the defendant in telling the truth about the plaintiff is irrelevant;[74] all that matters is whether the matter is objectively true or not. In so concluding, the Court of Appeal reinforces the notion that *Bonnard v Perryman* sanctions an approach to injunctive relief different from general equitable principles; under general equitable principles, an improper motive of the defendant would surely be a strong factor in favour of granting the plaintiff the injunctive relief he or she sought.[75]

The Court of Appeal returned yet again to *Bonnard v Perryman* in *Greene v Associated Newspapers Ltd*. The significance of this decision was that it was

---

[69] ibid, 737–38, citing Sir W Blackstone, *Commentaries on the Laws of England*, Vol IV (Oxford, Oxford University Press, 2016) 151–52. For a further citation of Blackstone in support of *Bonnard v Perryman*, see *Greene v Associated Newspapers* (n 10) 986.

[70] See, for example, *Holley v Smyth* [1998] QB 726, 731 (Staughton LJ), 743 (Auld LJ), 749 (Sir Christopher Slade).

[71] *Holley v Smyth* [1998] QB 726, 744 (Auld LJ), 746–50 (Sir Christopher Slade). Sir Christopher Slade (at ibid, 748), however, observed that the position might be different if the plaintiff alleges that the defendant's threatened publication amounted to the criminal offence of blackmail. See also *Crest Homes Ltd v Ascott* [1980] FSR 396, 398 (Lord Denning MR).

[72] *Sutherland v Stopes* [1925] AC 47, 62 (Viscount Finlay). See now Defamation Act 2013, s 2(1); Defamation Act 2005 (NSW) s 25 and the co-ordinate provisions in the other Australian States and Territories.

[73] *Rofe v Smith's Newspapers Ltd* (1924) 25 SR(NSW) 4, 21–22 (Street ACJ).

[74] *Holley v Smyth* [1998] QB 726, 744 (Auld LJ), 746–50 (Sir Christopher Slade).

[75] See further section V B below.

the court's first consideration of the status of *Bonnard v Perryman* after the commencement of the Human Rights Act 1998. After reviewing the line of authority, from *Bonnard v Perryman* to *Holley v Smyth*,[76] Brooke LJ, giving the judgment of the court, identified the multiple reasons underpinning *Bonnard v Perryman*:

> This is partly due to the importance the court attaches to freedom of speech. It is partly because a judge must not usurp the constitutional function of the jury unless he is satisfied that there is no case to go to the jury. The rule is also partly founded on the pragmatic grounds that until there has been disclosure of documents and cross-examination at the trial a court cannot safely proceed on the basis that what the defendants wish to say is not true. And if it is or might be true the court has no business to stop them saying it. This is another way of putting the point made by Sir John Donaldson MR in *Khashoggi v IPC Magazines Ltd* [1986] 1 WLR 1412, to the effect that a court cannot know whether the plaintiff has a right to his/her reputation until the trial process has shown where the truth lies. And if the defence fails, the defendants will have to pay damages (which in an appropriate case may includes (sic) aggravated and/or exemplary damages as well).[77]

His Lordship then considered whether the Human Rights Act 1998, s 12(3), affected *Bonnard v Perryman*. That sub-section provides that no injunctive relief affecting freedom of expression – a right protected by Article 10 of the European Convention on Human Rights – 'is to be granted so as to restrain publication before trial unless the court is satisfied that the applicant is likely to establish that publication should not be allowed'.

The proper construction of this sub-section, in the context of a claim for breach of confidence, had recently been the subject of consideration by the Court of Appeal and the House of Lords in *Cream Holdings Ltd v Banerjee*. The Court of Appeal assumed that *Bonnard v Perryman* was still good law.[78] The House of Lords did not deal with the issue, directly or indirectly.[79] Brooke LJ held that nothing in either of the judgments in *Cream Holdings v Banerjee* affected the practice in defamation cases relating to injunctive relief, with the particular considerations that attend it. Brooke LJ observed that: 'In a section of an Act of Parliament which is expressly concerned with the protection of freedom of expression and not undermining it, Parliament cannot be interpreted as having abrogated the rule in *Bonnard v Perryman* by a sidewind.'[80] His Lordship concluded that *Bonnard v Perryman* continued unaffected by the introduction of the Human Rights Act 1998.

---

[76] *Greene v Associated Newspapers* (n 10) 986–90.

[77] ibid, 990.

[78] ibid, 991. See *Cream Holdings Ltd v Banerjee* [2004] EWCA Civ 103, [2003] Ch 650, 678 (Arden LJ).

[79] *Greene v Associated Newspapers* (n 10) 991. As to the House of Lords decision, see *Cream Holdings Ltd v Banerjee* [2004] UKHL 44, [2005] 1 AC 253.

[80] *Greene v Associated Newspapers* (n 10) 991.

Greene v Associated Newspapers was decided shortly after the House of Lords decision in *Campbell v MGN Ltd*[81] – a landmark case in English privacy law. After the argument was heard, but before the judgment was handed down in *Greene v Associated Newspapers*, the House of Lords delivered its judgment in *In Re S*.[82] That case determined the proper approach to the balancing of competing rights under the European Convention on Human Rights when developing domestic law conformably with the Convention. In his speech, Lord Steyn stated that the proper approach to dealing with the interplay of competing rights under Articles 8 and 10 of the European Convention on Human Rights was as follows:

> First, neither article has *as such* precedence over the other. Secondly, where the values under the two articles are in conflict, an intense focus on the comparative importance of the specific rights being claimed in the individual case is necessary. Thirdly, the justifications for interfering with or restricting each right must be taken into account. Finally, the proportionality test must be applied to each.[83]

Brief reference is made to that decision at the end of the judgment in *Greene v Associated Newspapers*.[84] Since the decision in *Greene v Associated Newspapers*, the methodology sanctioned by the House of Lords in *In Re S* has become well established.[85] More importantly, misuse of private information has burgeoned.[86] Misuse of private information has itself, during the intervening period since *Greene v Associated Newspapers*, undergone a metamorphosis, from being an equitable cause of action for breach of confidence to its recognition as a freestanding tort.[87] Significantly, the primary remedy for misuse of private information is the injunction.[88] Moreover, since *Greene v Associated*

---

[81] *Campbell v MGN Ltd* [2004] UKHL 22, [2004] 2 AC 457.

[82] *In Re S* [2004] UKHL 47, [2005] 1 AC 593.

[83] ibid, 603.

[84] *Greene v Associated Newspapers* (n 10) 992–94.

[85] See, for example, *McKennitt v Ash* [2006] EWCA Civ 1714, [2008] QB 73, 91–92 (Buxton LJ); *Associated Newspapers Ltd v Prince of Wales* [2006] EWCA Civ 1776, [2008] Ch 57, 120–21 (Lord Phillips of Worth Matravers CJ); *Lord Browne of Madingley v Associated Newspapers Ltd* [2007] EWCA Civ 295, [2008] QB 103, 116–17 (Sir Anthony Clarke MR); *Mosley v News Group Newspapers Ltd* [2008] EWHC 1777 (QB), [2008] EMLR 20, 688–89 (Eady J).

[86] It is not possible to list all the decided cases in the now extensive case law on misuse of private information. Some landmark cases in the brief history of misuse of private information are *Douglas v Hello! Ltd* [2001] QB 967; *Campbell v MGN Ltd* [2004] UKHL 22, [2004] 2 AC 457; *Douglas v Hello! Ltd (No 3)* [2005] EWCA Civ 595, [2006] QB 125; *Vidal-Hall v Google Inc* [2015] EWCA Civ 311, [2016] QB 1003; *PJS v News Group Newspapers Ltd* [2016] UKSC 26, [2016] AC 1081.

[87] *Campbell v MGN Ltd* [2004] UKHL 22, [2004] 2 AC 457, 465 (Lord Nicholls of Birkenhead); *Vidal-Hall v Google Inc* [2015] EWCA Civ 311, [2016] QB 1003, 1028, 1031 (Lord Dyson MR and Sharp LJ). See generally B McDonald and D Rolph, 'Remedial Consequences of Classification of a Privacy Action: Dog or Wolf, Tort or Equity', in JNE Varuhas and NA Moreham (eds), *Remedies for Breach of Privacy* (Oxford, Hart Publishing, 2018) 239–63.

[88] H Fenwick and G Phillipson (eds), *Media Freedom under the Human Rights Act* (Oxford, Oxford University Press, 2006) 806–08. See also D Eady, 'Injunctions and the protection of privacy' (2011) 29 *Civil Justice Quarterly* 411.

Newspapers, the European Court of Human Rights has begun to recognise reputation as an aspect of the right to a private life under Article 8 of the European Convention on Human Rights.[89] The confluence of these developments means that *Bonnard v Perryman*'s conformity with the European Convention on Human Rights may need to be revisited. *Greene v Associated Newspapers* may not be reliably regarded as determinative of this issue.

V. ISSUES ARISING FROM *BONNARD v PERRYMAN*

A. Introduction

There have been two difficult issues which have arisen in the application of *Bonnard v Perryman*. The first may be regarded as settled. Indeed, as will become apparent, it was an issue which only arose acutely in particular jurisdictions. The issue was whether *Bonnard v Perryman* was the expression of a distinct rule for defamation claims or whether it was subject to the general equitable principles governing injunctive relief. Although this issue may now be regarded as settled, it may now also be moot. This is a potential consequence of the second difficult issue presented by *Bonnard v Perryman*, which is what is the proper approach to adopt to an application for an interlocutory injunction when a given set of facts discloses a cause of action in defamation and some other cause of action to which a less restrictive approach is taken. This issue has arisen periodically and has tended to be dealt with pragmatically, rather than satisfactorily from the perspective of principle. The issue is one which will only become more acute as the tension between the proper approaches to two causes of action continues to present itself: defamation and privacy.

B. Defamation as an Exception to the General Equitable Principles Governing Interlocutory Injunctions?

One significant doctrinal issue which emerged relating to the proper application of *Bonnard v Perryman* was its relationship to the general equitable principles governing injunctive relief. The general equitable principles governing injunctive relief were authoritatively laid down by the House of Lords in *American Cyanamid Co v Ethicon Ltd*.[90] In *American Cyanamid v Ethicon*,

---

[89] See, for example, *Radio France v France* (2005) 40 EHRR 29, 730; *Chauvy v France* (2005) 41 EHRR 29, 629–30; *Pfeifer v Austria* (2009) 48 EHRR 8, 183–84; *Karako v Hungary* (2011) 52 EHRR 36, 1045–46; *Axel Springer AG v Germany* (2012) 55 EHRR 6, 206. See generally T Aplin and J Bosland, 'The Uncertain Landscape of Article 8 of the ECHR: The Protection of Reputation as a Fundamental Human Right?' in A Kenyon (ed), *Comparative Defamation and Privacy Law* (Cambridge, Cambridge University Press, 2016) 265–90.

[90] *American Cyanamid Co v Ethicon Ltd* [1975] AC 396.

Lord Diplock rejected a range of formulations for what a plaintiff was required to prove on an application for an interlocutory injunction. His Lordship rejected threshold tests cast in terms of 'a probability', 'a prima facie case' or 'a strong prima facie case', instead preferring 'a serious question to be tried'.[91] Having established that, the issue then becomes whether the balance of convenience favours, or does not favour, the grant of the interlocutory injunction.[92] In determining such an application, the adequacy of damages as final relief needs to be considered.[93]

In most jurisdictions where *Bonnard v Perryman* has been applied, defamation is treated as a special case for the purposes of interim injunctions; the general equitable principles governing the grant of such relief are taken not to apply to defamation claims. This is reinforced by the designation of 'the rule in *Bonnard v Perryman*'.[94] This is the prevailing view in English case law.[95] Courts in New Zealand have likewise been comfortable with treating *Bonnard v Perryman* as an exception to the general equitable principles governing injunctive relief.[96] This also appears to be the position in Canada.[97] Not all jurisdictions are comfortable with treating a category of claim as an exception to general equitable principles. There have been differing views expressed about the issue in Hong Kong courts.[98] The jurisdiction where this issue has been most contentious, though, is in Australia.

---

[91] ibid, 407.

[92] ibid, 406.

[93] ibid, 408.

[94] See, for example, *McSweeney v Berryman* [1980] 2 NZLR 168, 175 (Barker J); *Fraser v Evans* [1969] 1 QB 349, 362 (Lord Denning MR) ('the salutary rule of law in libel'); *Healy v Askin* [1974] 1 NSWLR 436, 441–42 (Lee J) ('a stringent rule'); *Lennox v Krantz* (1978) 19 SASR 272, 279 (Zelling J) ('very stringent rules'); *Crest Homes Ltd v Ascott* [1980] FSR 396, 397 (Lord Denning MR), 398 (Stephenson LJ); *Holley v Smyth* [1998] QB 726, 743 (Auld LJ) ('The *Bonnard v Perryman* rule').

[95] See, for example, *Bestobell Paints Ltd v Bigg* [1975] FSR 421, 429–30 (Oliver J): 'There is an old and well established principle which is still applied in modern times and which is in no way affected by the recent decision of the House of Lords in *American Cyanamid Corporation v Ethicon* …'; *J Trevor & Sons v Solomon* (1978) 284 EG 779, 781 (Lord Denning MR), 781 (Roskill LJ); *Herbage v Pressdram Ltd* [1984] 1 WLR 1160, 1162 (Griffiths LJ); *Khashoggi v IPC Magazines Ltd* [1986] 1 WLR 1412, 1418 (Sir John Donaldson MR). See also *Holley v Smyth* [1998] QB 726, 745 (Auld LJ); *Greene v Associated Newspapers* (n 10) 989. Leading English texts on equity have no difficulty treating the approach to injunctive relief in defamation claims as a special category. See, for example, J Glister and J Lee, *Hanbury and Martin Modern Equity*, 21st edn (London, Sweet & Maxwell, 2018) [28-067]; J McGhee (ed), *Snell's Equity*, 33rd edn (London, Sweet & Maxwell, 2015) [18-062]. Contrast G H Brandis, 'Interlocutory Injunctions to Restrain Speech' (1992) 12 *Queensland Lawyer* 169, 173–76; I C F Spry, *The Principles of Equitable Remedies*, 9th edn (Sydney, Lawbook Co, 2014) 21–23; J D Heydon, M J Leeming and P G Turner, *Meagher, Gummow and Lehane's Equity: Doctrines and Remedies*, 5th edn (Sydney, LexisNexis Butterworths, 2015) [21-130].

[96] See, for example, *McSweeney v Berryman* [1980] 2 NZLR 168, 175 (Barker J); *Ron West Motors Ltd v Broadcasting Corporation of New Zealand (No 2)* [1989] 3 NZLR 520, 526 (Smellie J); *TV3 Network Services Ltd v Fahey* [1999] 2 NZLR 129, 132 (Richardson P).

[97] *Rapp v McClelland & Stewart Ltd* (1981) 128 DLR (3d) 650, 654 (Griffiths J), 34 OR (2d) 452.

[98] See, for example, *Target Newspapers Ltd v Narain* [1989] HKCA 242, [1989] 2 HKC 16, 19; *Poon Ying Hon v CCT Telecom Holdings Ltd* [2001] HKCFI 735, [40] (Leong J); *Chan v Ironwing*

For many decades in Australia, *Bonnard v Perryman* was accepted, in terms or in substance, as the applicable test for dealing with applications for interlocutory injunctions in defamation claims. The test regularly applied by Australian courts was that articulated by Walsh J in *Stocker v McElhinney (No 2)*.[99] The terms of the test were distilled from *Bonnard v Perryman*:

(1)   Although it was at one time suggested that there was no power in the court, under provisions similar to those contained in the *Common Law Procedure Act*, ss 176 to 179, to grant an interlocutory injunction, in cases of defamation, it is settled that the power exists in such cases.

(2)   In such cases, the power is exercised with great caution, and only in very clear cases.

(3)   If there is any real room for debate as to whether the statements complained of are defamatory, the injunction will be refused. Indeed, it is only where on this point, the position is so clear that, in the judge's view a subsequent finding by the jury to the contrary would be set aside as unreasonable, that the injunction will go.

(4)   If, on the evidence before the judge, there is any real ground for supposing that the defendant may succed upon any such ground as privilege, or of truth and public benefit, or even that the plaintiff if successful, will recover nominal damages only, the injunction will be refused.[100]

Zelling J in *Lennox v Krantz* described this statement as 'the *locus classicus* for Australia'.[101]

The straightforward application of *Bonnard v Perryman*, refracted through *Stocker v McElhinney (No 2)*, began to be questioned by Australian courts from the mid-1970s onwards. This occurred as part of a more fundamental reconsideration of general equitable principles governing applications for interlocutory injunctions. This broader issue has been contentious in Australia. As one outside observer noted, there had been a 'somewhat cool reception' by Australian courts to the House of Lords decision in *American Cyanamid v Ethicon*.[102] The leading Australian authority on the general equitable principles for granting injunctive relief was the High Court of Australia's decision in *Beecham Group Ltd v Bristol Laboratories Pty Ltd*.[103] In that case, the court, in a unanimous judgment, stated that, in all cases, the test for whether an interlocutory

---

Holdings Ltd [2001] HKCFI 1165, [3] (Poon J), [2001] 2 HKC 376; *Samba Engineering Ltd v Jet-Win Electrical Co Ltd* [2002] HKDC 248, [7] (Lin J); *Noble Spirit Ltd t/a Life Solutions v Wong Shu Yuen* [2011] HKCFI 418, [48] (Coleman J). However, see also *Cheng Chi v Chan Hok Man* [1984] HKCA 247, [1984] HKC 35, 41 (Roberts CJ); *Singh v Chinawal* [2013] HKCFI 1694, [20]–[25] (Leung J).

[99] *Stocker v McElhinney* [1961] NSWR 1043.

[100] ibid, 1048.

[101] *Lennox v Krantz* (1978) 19 SASR 272, 276. As to the application of the test by Australian courts, see, for example, *Royal Automobile Club of Victoria v Paterson* [1968] VR 508, 510 (McInerney J); *Healy v Askin* [1974] 1 NSWLR 435, 441 (Lee J).

[102] *McSweeney v Berryman* [1980] 2 NZLR 168, 173 (Barker J).

[103] *Beecham Group Ltd v Bristol Laboratories Pty Ltd* (1968) 118 CLR 618.

injunction should be granted was, first, whether the plaintiff had established a 'prima facie case, in the sense that if the evidence remains as it is there is a probability that the trial of the action the plaintiff will be held entitled to relief'[104] and, secondly, whether the balance of convenience favours, or does not favour, the grant of injunctive relief.[105] In relation to the threshold requirement of a 'prima facie case', the court observed that the nature of the rights involved and the practical consequences of the relief will affect the strength of the probability required to make out a prima facie case in any given set of facts.

The respective tests set out by the House of Lords in *American Cyanamid v Ethicon* and the High Court of Australia in *Beecham Group v Bristol Laboratories* – a 'serious question to be tried' versus a 'prima facie case' – appear in terms to be substantively different, with the latter imposing a higher threshold for injunctive relief than the former. The divergent articulations of the tests caused Australian courts some difficulty. Prior to the High Court of Australia's decision in *ABC v O'Neill*, it was a live issue as to whether the formulation of a 'prima facie case' or a 'serious question to be tried' was to be preferred, or whether they were, in substance, the same test.[106]

The other relevant aspect of context in which Australian courts began to question *Bonnard v Perryman* and *Stocker v McElhinney (No 2)* was what has been described as Australia's 'equity isolationism'.[107] The Judicature Acts were introduced into many Australian jurisdictions at a comparatively late stage.[108] This has fostered an insistence on doctrinal purity, most obviously manifested by the aversion to 'fusion' of common law and equity, which marks out Australian equity jurisprudence from the rest of the Commonwealth.[109]

The broad lines of authority have been characterised as the 'rigid' and the 'flexible' approaches. The flexible approach can be traced to the decision of Menhennitt J in *Gabriel v Lobban*.[110] In this case, his Honour began by deciding whether the plaintiff had a prima facie case for relief, explicitly applying *Beecham Group v Bristol Laboratories*.[111] In doing so, Menhennitt J held that he was required to consider not only defamatory meaning but also

---

[104] ibid, 622.

[105] ibid, 623.

[106] *Shercliff v Engadine Acceptance Corporation Pty Ltd* [1978] 1 NSWLR 729, 735–36 (Mahoney JA), cf *Castlemaine Tooheys Ltd v State of South Australia* (1986) 161 CLR 148, 153 (Mason ACJ).

[107] Hon Justice M Kirby, 'Overcoming Australia's equity isolationism' (2009) 3 *Journal of Equity* 1.

[108] Notoriously, New South Wales introduced the Judicature Acts reform almost a century after they were enacted in England. See Supreme Court Act 1970 (NSW) and Law Reform (Law and Equity) Act 1972 (NSW).

[109] J Edelman and S Degeling, 'Fusion: The interaction of common law and equity' (2004) 25 *Australian Bar Review* 195; J D Heydon, M J Leeming and P G Turner, *Meagher, Gummow and Lehane's Equity: Doctrines and Remedies*, 5th edn (Sydney, LexisNexis Butterworths, 2015) [2-130]– [2-400].

[110] *Gabriel v Lobban* [1976] VR 689.

[111] ibid, 690.

any available defences.[112] Having regard to the defences, his Honour was not satisfied that the plaintiff had established a prima facie case. He dismissed the application on that basis.[113] As an alternative, Menhennitt J also dealt with the application by reference to *Bonnard v Perryman* but reached the same outcome.[114] What is notable about the judgment is the centrality of *Beecham Group v Bristol Laboratories* at the expense of *Bonnard v Perryman*. In the subsequent three decades, there were a number of decisions, at first instance and by intermediate appellate courts, around Australia, adopting this 'flexible' approach to injunctive relief in defamation cases.[115]

Alongside this line of authority, there developed a line of authority sanction-ing the 'rigid' approach to interlocutory injunctions in defamation cases. The cases disclose a range of reasons for applying *Bonnard v Perryman*, rather than general equitable principles governing injunctive relief. For instance, in *Edelsten v John Fairfax & Sons Ltd*, Yeldham J held that he was still bound by deci-sions of the English Court of Appeal, to treat defamation as an exception to the general equitable principles for dealing with interlocutory injunctions.[116] More generally, there was an acceptance that the distinctive features of defamation as a cause of action, identified by *Bonnard v Perryman* and affirmed by *Stocker v McElhinney (No 2)*, justified treating defamation differently from other causes of action for the purposes of injunctive relief.[117]

Some judges changed their minds on the issue of the proper approach to injunctive relief in defamation cases. During the 1980s, Hunt J was the Defama-tion List in the Supreme Court of New South Wales. In *Church of Scientology of California Inc v Reader's Digest Services Pty Ltd*, Hunt J firmly rejected the submission that the High Court of Australia's decision in *Beecham Group v Bristol Laboratories* overruled 'the special exception in defamation cases' embodied in *Bonnard v Perryman*.[118] Eight years later, in *Chappell v TCN*

---

[112] Ibid, 690.

[113] ibid, 691, 693–94.

[114] ibid, 691–93.

[115] See, for example,*National Mutual Association of Australasia Ltd v GTV Corporation Pty Ltd* [1989] VR 747, 754 (Ormiston J): 'I cannot accept that the power of this court to grant interlocu-tory relief is so restricted ...' See also ibid, 763–65 (Fullagar, Hampel and McDonald JJ); *Jakudo Pty Ltd v South Australian Telecasters Ltd* (1997) 69 SASR 440, 442 (Doyle CJ): 'The grant of an interlocutory injunction, in my opinion, involves the application of equitable principles that are the same in all cases. The grant of interlocutory injunctions in respect of defamatory material is not the subject of principles unique to that area of the law'; *Australian Broadcasting Corporation v Hanson* (unreported, CA(Qld), App No 8716/97, 28 September 1998), 6 (de Jersey CJ).

[116] *Edelsten v John Fairfax & Sons Ltd* [1978] 1 NSWLR 685, 697.

[117] See, for example, *Healy v Askin* [1974] 1 NSWLR 435, 441–42 (Lee J); *Lennox v Krantz* (1978) 119 SASR 272, 276 (Zelling J); *Harper v Whitby* [1978] 1 NSWLR 35, 38 (Maxwell J); *Swimsure (Laboratories) Pty Ltd v McDonald* [1979] 2 NSWLR 796, 7999–8000 (Hunt J); *Edelsten v Australian Broadcasting Corporation* (1984) Aust Torts Reports 80-672, 68,821 (Hunt J); *Nationwide Publish-ing Pty Ltd v Furber* (1984) 3 FCR 19, 25 (Toohey and Fitzgerald JJ); *Lovell v Lewandowski* [1987] WAR 81, 91 (Kennedy J), 95–96 (Olney J); *Shapowloff v John Fairfax & Sons Ltd* [1980] 1 NSWLR 359n, 360 (Asprey J); *Shiel v Transmedia Productions Pty Ltd* [1987] 1 Qd R 199, 203 (Moynihan J).

[118] *Church of Scientology of California Inc v Reader's Digest Services Pty Ltd* [1980] 1 NSWLR 344, 350.

Channel Nine Pty Ltd, the same judge rejected emphatically the submission that defamation was a special exception to general equitable principles governing injunctive relief. His Honour emphasised this by referring throughout his judgment to the 'rule' in *Bonnard v Perryman*: for Hunt J, equitable principles, characterised by discretion and flexibility, should never be described as 'rules'.

The distinction between the 'rigid' and the 'flexible' approaches to injunctive relief in defamation claims in Australia was ultimately resolved by the High Court of Australia in *Australian Broadcasting Corporation v O'Neill*.[119] James O'Neill was a convicted child-killer, serving a life sentence in Risdon Prison in Hobart, Tasmania. Gordon Davie was a former police officer turned documentary film-maker. He had developed a theory that O'Neill was responsible for one of the greatest unsolved mysteries of modern Australia: the disappearance of the Beaumont children from Glenelg Beach in Adelaide, South Australia, on Australia Day, 1966. Davie earned O'Neill's trust, on the pretext that he was interested in the prisoner's insect breeding. Davie expounded his theory that O'Neill abducted and murdered the Beaumont children in a documentary called *The Fisherman*, which debuted at the Hobart International Film Festival. However, it was only when the national public broadcaster, the Australian Broadcasting Corporation ('the ABC'), scheduled its first television screening that O'Neill became concerned.

O'Neill applied to the Supreme Court of Tasmania for an interlocutory injunction to restrain the ABC's broadcast. At first instance, Crawford J found that the relevant test to be applied was the 'flexible' approach.[120] His Honour held that O'Neill had established a prima facie case of defamation. The defence of justification at the time in Tasmania required not only proof of substantial truth but also proof of public benefit.[121] Crawford J held that the ABC would find it difficult to establish the element of public benefit because, in his view, it amounted to more than 'trial by media'; it was 'conviction by media'.[122] His Honour found that the balance of convenience strongly favoured the grant of an interlocutory injunction because it was necessary to protect the individual from the power and influence of the media, and damages would not be an adequate remedy, as irreparable damage to O'Neill's reputation may occur if the broadcast proceeded.[123]

The ABC appealed to the Full Court of the Supreme Court of Tasmania. By majority (Blow and Evans JJ, Slicer J dissenting), its appeal was dismissed. Giving the leading judgment, Blow J found that there was no error of principle in the trial judge's approach. His Honour also endorsed the 'flexible' approach as the proper one to such applications.[124]

---

[119] *ABC v O'Neill* (n 9).
[120] *O'Neill v Australian Broadcasting Corporation* [2005] TASSC 26, [20]–[24].
[121] Defamation Act 1957 (Tas) s 15 (repealed).
[122] *O'Neill v Australian Broadcasting Corporation* [2005] TASSC 26, [28]–[29].
[123] ibid, [33]–[34].
[124] *Australian Broadcasting Corporation v O'Neill* [2005] TASSC 82, [75].

The ABC appealed to the High Court of Australia. By majority (Gleeson CJ, Gummow, Hayne and Crennan JJ, Kirby and Heydon JJ dissenting), its appeal was successful. In their joint judgment, Gummow and Hayne JJ (with whom Gleeson CJ and Crennan J agreed on this issue), were critical of both the 'rigid' and the 'flexible' approaches. The 'rigid' approach sought to transform a discretion into a rule;[125] the 'flexible' approach failed to give sufficient weight to the rights involved in defamation, namely the common law's long-standing commitment to freedom of speech and freedom of the press and its related aversion to prior restraint.[126] Their Honours concluded that general equitable principles applied – defamation was not a special case – but the way in which those principles applied would be informed by the nature of the cause of action.[127] Gummow and Hayne JJ, and Gleeson CJ and Crennan J in their separate joint judgment, found that the trial judge and the majority in the Full Court had erred as a matter of principle by failing to give adequate weight to freedom of speech, freedom of the press and the common law's aversion to prior restraint.

In his dissenting judgment, Kirby J held that the 'flexible' approach was the proper one for dealing with an application for injunctive relief in a defamation claim.[128] His Honour's principal concern was the need to protect unpopular litigants like O'Neill, to ensure that they were not treated as 'libel-proof'.[129] Given the rarity with which interlocutory injunctions are granted in defamation cases, it may be observed that O'Neill was in better position than most defamation plaintiffs, having actually obtained one at first instance.

In his dissenting judgment, Heydon J took an entirely different approach. His Honour undertook a comprehensive review of the jurisdiction of common law courts and equity courts to grant interlocutory injunctions for defamation claims, intimating that *Bonnard v Perryman* was wrongly decided.[130] His Honour also surveyed the declining use of the jury in defamation cases – one of the justifications advanced in support of *Bonnard v Perryman*.[131] Heydon J then critiqued the value ordinarily ascribed to freedom of speech, suggesting that the jurists usually invoked in support of the importance of freedom of speech engaged in overstatement.[132]

In point of principle, it is correct to state that, under Australian law, defamation is not a special case but general equitable principles apply to an application for an interlocutory injunction for this cause of action. However, given that, in the application of those general equitable principles, it is necessary to take

---

[125] *ABC v O'Neill*, n 9, 85.
[126] ibid, 86–88.
[127] *Ibid*, 68–69 (Gleeson CJ and Crennan J), 82 (Gummow and Hayne JJ).
[128] ibid, 103–06.
[129] ibid, 111–14.
[130] ibid, [188]–[209].
[131] ibid, [217]–[239].
[132] ibid, [252]–[268].

into account the particular features of defamation, the practical position under Australian law is that it is difficult to obtain an interlocutory injunction for defamation. In substance, then, the position under Australian law is the same as other Commonwealth jurisdictions.[133]

C. The Interaction between Approaches to Injunctive Relief for Defamation and Other Causes of Action

The other difficult doctrinal issue arising from *Bonnard v Perryman* is how the restrictive approach to injunctive relief in defamation interacts with the approach to injunctive relief in other causes of action. It has been said that, as a general proposition, 'a claim for mere loss of reputation is the subject of an action for defamation, and cannot ordinarily be sustained by means of any other form of action'.[134] Yet there are other causes of action at general law which can protect reputation, directly or indirectly. Malicious (or injurious) falsehood is a clear example of a cause of action which can be pleaded concurrently with defamation and can provide incidental protection for reputation.[135] Similarly, defamation is the obvious but not the only cause of action at general law seeking to impose liability for the publication of false statements. Again, malicious falsehood may be available on the facts; some jurisdictions, like the United Kingdom and Canada, permit the concurrent pleading of defamation and negligent misstatement;[136] some jurisdictions, like Australia, have a statutory cause of action for misleading or deceptive conduct,[137] which can overlap with defamation.[138] More broadly, a given set of facts may disclose a cause of action in defamation but also another cause of action, protecting another kind of interest. The province of defamation is not so exclusive.

Where a given set of facts discloses an arguable cause of action in defamation and some other cause of action, a difficult issue arises as to what the proper approach to injunctive relief should be. As *Bonnard v Perryman* makes clear, concerns about freedom of speech are central to the restrictive approach to injunctive relief in defamation. This is understandable, given that freedom of speech is one of the two interests protected by the tort of defamation, the other

---

[133] D Rolph, 'Showing Restraint: Interlocutory Injunctions in Defamation Cases' (2009) 14 *Media and Arts Law Review*, 255, 290.

[134] *Foaminol Laboratories Ltd v British Artid Plastics Ltd* [1941] 2 All ER 393, 399 (Hallett J).

[135] As to the relationship between defamation and injurious falsehood, see *Radio 2UE Sydney Pty Ltd v Chesterton* [2009] HCA 16, (2009) 238 CLR 460, 468–69 (French CJ, Gummow, Kiefel and Bell JJ).

[136] *Spring v Guardian Assurance Plc* [1995] 2 AC 296, 325 (Lord Goff of Chieveley), 325–27 (Lord Lowry), 334–37 (Lord Slynn of Hadley), 350 (Lord Woolf); *Young v Bella* (2006) 261 DLR (4th) 516, 529–30 (McLachlin CJ and Binnie J).

[137] Australian Consumer Law (Cth), s 18 and cognate provisions in the States and Territories.

[138] *Global Sportsman Pty Ltd v Mirror Newspapers Pty Ltd* (1984) 2 FCR 82, 86–87 *(per curiam)*.

being reputation.[139] Other causes of action are not directly concerned with freedom of expression, so understandably take a less restrictive approach to injunctive relief than defamation. The working test which has developed for negotiating the competing approaches to injunctive relief was distilled thus by Lightman J in *Service Corp International Plc v Channel Four Television Corp*:

> The rule prohibiting the grant of an injunction where the claim is in defamation does not extend to claims based on other causes of action despite the fact that a claim in defamation might also have been brought, but if the claim based on some other cause of action is in reality a claim brought to protect the plaintiff's reputation and the reliance on the other causes of action is merely a device to circumvent the rule, the overriding need to protect freedom of speech requires that the same rule be applied.[140]

There have been a number of other expressions of this test.[141] The difficulty with the test is that it is dependent upon the characterisation of the claimant's interests in the proceedings, as well as the ascertainment of the claimant's intention in relying upon particular causes of action. It does not provide guidance as to how a court is to determine what the nub of the claim is and whether the claimant's framing of his or her cause of action is a legitimate pursuit of an available claim or an impermissible attempt to subvert the restrictive approach to injunctive relief. It is dependent upon the facts, and is a matter of judicial impression. It seems to be more of a pragmatic, rather than a principled, test.[142]

This approach has been applied in cases involving the interaction between defamation and a wide variety of causes of action: malicious (or injurious) falsehood;[143] passing off;[144] trespass to land;[145] private nuisance;[146] unlawful interference with contractual relations;[147] conspiracy;[148] copyright

---

[139] *Lange v Australian Broadcasting Corporation* (1997) 189 CLR 520, 589 (*per curiam*); *Dow Jones & Co Inc v Gutnick* [2002] HCA 56, (2002) 210 CLR 575, 599 (Gleeson CJ, McHugh, Gummow and Hayne JJ).

[140] *Service Corp International Plc v Channel Four Television Corp* [1999] EMLR 83, 89–90.

[141] See, for example, *Fraser v Evans* [1969] 1 QB 349, 362 (Lord Denning MR); *Woodward v Hutchins* [1977] 2 All ER 751, [1977] 1 WLR 760, 764 (Lord Denning MR); *Swimsure (Laboratories) Pty Ltd v McDonald* [1979] 2 NSWLR 796, 800 (Hunt J); *Church of Scientology of California Inc v Reader's Digest Services Pty Ltd* [1980] 1 NSWLR 344, 350–51 (Hunt J); *Edelsten v Australian Broadcasting Corporation* (1984) Aust Torts Reports 80-672, 68,822 (Hunt J); *Gulf Oil (Great Britain) Ltd v Page* [1987] Ch 327, 333–34 (Parker LJ); *Microdata Information Services Ltd v Rivendale Ltd* [1991] FSR 681, 688 (Griffiths LJ); *McKennitt v Ash* [2008] EWCA Civ 1714, [2008] QB 73, 100 (Buxton LJ).

[142] D Rolph, 'Irreconcilable Differences? Interlocutory Injunctions for Defamation and Privacy' (2012) 17 *Media and Arts Law Review* 170, 182.

[143] *Swimsure (Laboratories) Pty Ltd v McDonald* [1979] 2 NSWLR 796; *Kaplan v Go Daddy Group Inc* [2005] NSWSC 636; *Beechwood Homes (NSW) Pty Ltd v Camenzuli* [2010] NSWSC 521.

[144] *Sim v H J Heinz Co Ltd* [1959] 1 All ER 547, [1959] 1 WLR 313; *Brabourne v Hough* [1981] FSR 79.

[145] *Brighten Pty Ltd v Nine Network Australia Pty Ltd* [2009] NSWSC 319.

[146] *Animal Liberation (Vic) Inc v Gasser* [1991] 1 VR 51.

[147] *Microdata Information Services Ltd v Rivendale Ltd* [1991] FSR 681.

[148] *Gulf Oil (Great Britain) Ltd v Page* [1987] Ch 327; *Femis-Bank (Anguilla) Ltd v Lazar* [1991] Ch 391.

infringement;[149] and trade mark infringement.[150] In some instances, the interlocutory injunction based on the alternative cause of action has been granted;[151] in other instances, it has not.[152]

Until recently, the issue of conflicting approaches to injunctive relief in defamation and other causes of action arose only intermittently. However, the tension is likely to become more acute, as a consequence of the development of the tort of misuse of private information. Interim injunctions are readily granted in privacy claims. There are a number of reasons for this. The tort of misuse of private information had its origins in the equitable cause of action for breach of confidence. The means selected by courts in the United Kingdom to accommodate the requirements of Article 8 of the European Convention on Human Rights was to extend and adapt breach of confidence. When dealing with causes of action for breach of confidence, courts have always been predisposed to grant interim injunctions to preserve the subject matter of the proceedings. Once the confidentiality of the information has been lost, the subject matter of the proceedings has been destroyed before any trial has occurred.[153] A similar approach is adopted in relation to privacy. Courts are predisposed to grant interim injunctions in privacy claims because privacy, once invaded, cannot be restored.[154]

This observation is often linked to the assertion that privacy differs from defamation in this respect, because reputation can be adequately vindicated by an award of damages.[155] The efficacy of an award of damages for defamation should not be overstated. Once published, defamatory matter cannot be unpublished. What is striking, though, about the majority judgment in *Bonnard v Perryman* is that it does not seek to justify the restrictive approach to injunctive relief by invoking the adequacy of damages for defamation. Few subsequent judgments seek to explain the rationale of *Bonnard v Perryman* in this way.[156]

---

[149] *Western Front Ltd v Vestron Inc* [1987] FSR 66; *Service Corp International Plc v Channel Four Television Corp* [1999] EMLR 83.

[150] *Bestobell Paints Ltd v Bigg* [1975] FSR 421; *Boehringer Ingelheim Ltd v Vetplus Ltd* [2007] FSR 29.

[151] See, for example, *Swimsure (Laboratories) Pty Ltd v McDonald* [1979] 2 NSWLR 796; *Gulf Oil (Great Britain) Ltd v Page* [1987] CH 327; *Animal Liberation (Vic) Inc v Gasser* [1991] 1 VR 51; *Microdata Information Services Ltd v Rivendale Ltd* [1991] FSR 681; *Kaplan v Go Daddy Group Inc* [2005] NSWSC 636.

[152] See, for example, *Bestobell Paints Ltd v Bigg* [1975] FSR 421; *Brabourne v Hough* [1981] FSR 79; *Western Front Ltd v Vestron Inc* [1987] FSR 66; *Femis-Bank (Anguilla) Ltd v Lazar* [1991] Ch 391; *Service Corp International Plc v Channel Four Television Corp* [1999] EMLR 83; *Tillery Valley Foods v Channel Four Television* [2004] EWHC 1075 (Cth); *Brighten Pty Ltd v Nine Network Australia Pty Ltd* [2009] NSWSC 319.

[153] As Sir John Donaldson MR remarked in *Attorney-General v Newspaper Publishing Ltd* [1988] Ch 333, 358, 'confidential information is like an ice cube ... Give it to the party who has no refrigerator ... and by the time of trial you just have a pool of water.'

[154] *Mosley v News Group Newspapers Ltd* [2008] EWHC 1777 (QB), [2008] EMLR 20, 736 (Eady J); *Cooper v Turrell* [2011] EWHC 3269 (QB), [102] (Tugendhat J).

[155] *Mosley v News Group Newspapers Ltd* [2008] EWHC (QB), [2008] EMLR 20, 736 (Eady J).

[156] For a rare instance of this, see *Jakudo Pty Ltd v South Australian Telecasters Ltd* (1997) 69 SASR 440, 442–43 (Doyle CJ).

The primacy of freedom of speech is usually identified as the principal justification for *Bonnard v Perryman*, not the effectiveness of remedies for defamation. The basis of *Bonnard v Perryman* is then a principled one, but if those principles change, *Bonnard v Perryman* will need to be revisited.

The differential approach to injunctive relief in defamation and privacy is novel, understandably given that the misuse of private information has only been recognised as a cause of action within the last two decades. The distinction has been invoked, though, to avoid a fundamental rethinking of the viability of *Bonnard v Perryman* after the enactment of the Human Rights Act 1998. In *McKennitt v Ash*, Longmore LJ observed that:

> The question in a case of misuse of private information is whether the information is private not whether the information is true or false. The truth or falsity of the information is an irrelevant inquiry in deciding whether the information is entitled to be protected and judges should be chary of becoming side-tracked into that irrelevant inquiry.[157]

The suggestion is that defamation turns upon a dichotomy of truth or falsity, whereas misuse of private information turns upon a dichotomy of whether the information is private or not, and, implicitly, that these dichotomies do not intersect, let alone clash.

A similarly minimalist approach to the tension between defamation and privacy for the purposes of injunctive relief was adopted by Tugendhat J in *Terry v Persons Unknown*.[158] His Lordship outlined the 'limited classes of cases' in which there might be an overlap between defamation and privacy:

> The first group of cases, where there is no overlap, is where the information cannot be said to be defamatory (e.g. *Douglas v Hello!* and *Murray*). It is the law of confidence, privacy and harassment that are likely to govern such cases. There is a second group of cases where there is an overlap, but where it is unlikely that it could be said that protection of reputation is the nub of the claim. There are cases where the information where the information would in the past have been said to be defamatory even though it related to matters which were involuntary e.g. disease. There was always a difficulty in fitting such cases into defamation, but it was done because of the absence of any alternative cause of action. There is a third group of cases where there is an overlap, but no inconsistency. There are cases where the information relates to conduct which is voluntary, and alleged to be seriously unlawful, even if it is personal (e.g. sexual or financial). The claimant is unlikely to succeed whether at an interim application or (if the allegation is proved) at trial, whether under the law of defamation or the law of privacy. The fourth group of cases, where it may make a difference what law governs, is where the information relates to conduct which is voluntary, discreditable, and person (e.g. sexual or financial) but not unlawful (or not seriously so). In defamation, if the defendant can prove one of the libel defences,

---

[157] *McKennitt v Ash* [2006] EWCA Civ 1714, [2008] QB 73, 102.
[158] *Terry v Persons Unknown* [2010] EWHC 119 (QB), [2010] EMLR 16.

he will not have to establish any public interest (except in the case of Reynolds privilege, where the law does require consideration of the seriousness of the allegation, including from the point of view of the claimant). But if it is the claimant's choice alone that determines that the only cause of action which the court may take into account is misuse of private information, then the defendant cannot succeed unless he establishes that it comes within the public interest exception (or, perhaps, that he believes that it comes within that exception).[159]

The tension between defamation and privacy for the purposes of injunctive relief cannot be avoided or minimised indefinitely. A threatened publication can readily implicate a claimant's reputation and privacy. This is unsurprising, given that reputation is in essence the claimant's public self – what other people think of him or her[160] – whereas privacy obviously protects the claimant's private self. They are both dignitary interests, and different aspects of the claimant's persona. The test of identifying the nub of the claim will not always work in practice. In *Terry v Persons Unknown*, the claimant's failure to give evidence was critical to Tugendhat J's conclusion that the essence of the claim was the protection of reputation, not privacy. However, what if the claimant had given evidence of his personal distress about the threatened publication? Would the claimant's subject evidence be determinative of the issue as to whether his privacy was the nub of the claim? If that were the case, it would be quite straightforward for claimants to avoid the restrictive approach to injunctive relief in defamation.

Beyond the practical reality that a publication may readily touch upon a person's reputation and privacy, reputation and privacy are now, as a matter of law, inextricably linked. Historically, the common law drew a distinction between an individual's dignitary interests, protecting reputation highly through the tort of defamation but providing no direct, general protection of privacy. The recent recognition of misuse of private information has helped overcome this anomalous bifurcation of dignitary interests. More than that, the relationship between reputation and privacy under English law has now been enmeshed. Reputation is now considered an aspect of the right to a private life under Article 8 of the European Convention on Human Rights[161] – a position which has been acknowledged by the United Kingdom Supreme Court.[162] The consequences of this recognition, though, have not yet been fully explored by English courts. The inversion of the relationship between reputation and privacy, treating privacy as the primary right and reputation as the subsidiary one should cause a rethinking of defamation law, including the rule in *Bonnard v Perryman*.

---

[159] ibid, 424–25. See generally T Aplin et al, *Gurry on Breach of Confidence: The Protection of Confidential Information*, 2nd edn (Oxford, Oxford University Press, 2012) [5.67]–[5.69], [18.43]–[18.44].

[160] *Plato Films Ltd v Speidel* [1961] AC 1090, 1138 (Lord Denning).

[161] See above n 89.

[162] *In re Guardian News and Media Ltd* [2010] UKSC 1, [2012] 2 AC 697, 717. (Lord Rodger of Earlsferry JSC).

The fact that reputation and privacy are treated as aspects of the same human right will make it difficult in the future to maintain differential approaches to injunctive relief for defamation and privacy.

VI. REVISITING *BONNARD v PERRYMAN*

The continuing viability of *Bonnard v Perryman* has been questioned by a number of leading academic commentators, from a variety of perspectives. According to a leading media law text, 'it is very doubtful whether the survival of the common law priority for freedom of speech is compatible with the modern jurisprudence of Convention rights'.[163] According to a leading human rights text, *Bonnard v Perryman* is incompatible with the European Court of Human Rights' jurisprudence, particularly on the right to reputation as an aspect of the right to a private life, and the Court of Appeal's attempt in *Greene v Associated Newspapers* to reconcile these common law and human rights streams of reasoning cannot stand. The learned authors conclude that 'the rule in *Bonnard v Perryman* must give way to a proper proportionality analysis'.[164]

There is some indication that judges are willing to revisit the soundness of *Bonnard v Perryman*. Recently, in *Taveta Investments Ltd v Financial Reporting Council*, Nicklin J stated:

> Respectfully, however, I have serious reservations as to whether setting the bar so high is still correct or can be justified.
>
> i)   Although the principle from *Bonnard v Perryman* has been approved, post-Human Right Acts 1998, by the Court of Appeal in *Greene v Associated Newspapers* [2005] QB 972, one of the bases of doing so was that the determination of meaning (so often the heart of a defamation claim) was reserved to the jury ([57]). The Court distinguished the authority of *In re S (A Child)*, stressing '*the distinction between a defamation claim (where the claimant's right to a reputation has been put in issue and the issue cannot be effectively resolved before the trial) and a case which raises direct issues of privacy or confidentiality.*' [79]–[81].
>
> ii) Since the decision in *Greene*, the right to trial by jury in defamation claims has been removed (s. 11 Defamation Act 2013). A key plank of the justification for retaining the rule in *Bonnard v Perryman* has therefore gone ...
>
> iii) Application of the rule in *Bonnard v Perryman* ... gives a presumptive priority to Article 10 (freedom of expression) right over Article 8 (including the right to reputation). It has been held in private law litigation that such presumptive priority is not justifiable, being inconsistent with the jurisprudence of the

---

[163] N A Moreham and M Warby (eds), *Tugendhat and Christie: The Law of Privacy and the Media*, 3rd edn (Oxford, Oxford University Press, 2016) [8.65].

[164] R Clayton and H Tomlinson, *The Law of Human Rights*, 2nd edn (Oxford, Oxford University Press, 2009) [15.28].

ECHR: *Douglas v Hello! Ltd* [2011] QB 967 [133], [135] *per* Sedley LJ, approved by the House of Lords in *Campbell v MGN Ltd* [2004] 2 AC 457, [55] *per* Lord Nicholls; [111] *per* Lord Hope; [138]–[139] *per* Baroness Hale and in *In re S (A Child)* [17] *per* Lord Steyn. The authorities identify the correct test whenever Article 10 and Article 8 interests conflict as that in *In re S (A Child)* [17] and the test to be applied at the interim stage as that provided by s. 12 Human Rights Act 1998.[165]

Beyond the removal of the jury from defamation trials and the methodology concerning the balancing of competing rights under the Human Rights Act, there is a more fundamental reason of principle that the rule in *Bonnard v Perryman* may need to be rethought. Two of the major related justifications for *Bonnard v Perryman* were the common law's commitment to freedom of speech and the need to avoid undue interference with freedom of speech by prior restraint, particularly where what is published may turn out to be true. In *Fraser v Evans*, Lord Denning MR identified the policy underlying *Bonnard v Perryman* as being 'the importance in the public interest that the truth should out'.[166] At the time *Bonnard v Perryman* was decided, and up until recently, the policy of the law was that it was in the public interest to speak the truth about a person. However, the policy of the law has decisively changed. It is now wrong to publish true but private information about a person. It is no longer possible to assert that there is an unalloyed public interest in speaking the truth about a person. The protection of privacy as a human right will eventually necessitate a reconsideration of *Bonnard v Perryman*. Not all landmarks stand for ever.

---

[165] *Taveta Investments Ltd v Financial Reporting Council* [2018] EWHC 1662 (Admin), [97].
[166] *Fraser v Evans* [1969] 1 QB 349, 360.

3

Byrne v Deane *(1937)*

BARBARA McDONALD

> *But he who gave the game away*
> *May he byrnn in hell and rue the day.*
> 'The law of defamation has loaded the word 'publish' with a gloss
> which would seem bizarre to all but the *cognoscenti*'[1]

I. INTRODUCTION

'THE ESSENCE OF tortious defamation lies in the communication of the disparaging statement to someone other than the person defamed.'[2] This communication is known as 'publication', yet the term as used in defamation law has a meaning very different to the wider meaning in every day speech: publication to one person is sufficient.[3] There is no set form of publication: it must simply come about 'by some means',[4] any means in fact by which meaning can be conveyed. '[A] statue, a caricature, an effigy, chalk marks on a wall, signs, or pictures may constitute a libel.'[5]

---

[1] *Tom & Bill Waterhouse Pty Ltd v Racing New South Wales* (2008) 72 NSWLR 577, [26] Palmer J.

[2] C Sappideen and P Vines, *Fleming's Law of Torts*, 10th edn (Sydney, Lawbook Co, 2011) [25.90]. For a detailed analysis of the law on publication, see generally, D Rolph, *Defamation Law* (Sydney, Lawbook Co, 2016) ch 8; A Mullis and R Parkes, *Gatley on Libel and Slander*, 12th edn (London, Sweet & Maxwell, 2013) ch 6.

[3] *Tom & Bill Waterhouse Pty Ltd v Racing New South Wales* (2008) 72 NSWLR 577, [26] Palmer J.

[4] *Webb v Bloch* [1928] HCA 50, (1928) 41 CLR 331 [2] (Isaacs J).

[5] *Monson v Tussauds Ltd* [1894] 1 QB 671, 692. A libel is a defamatory statement in permanent form. Slander comprises a defamatory publication in transient form, eg speech. The distinction used to be more important than it is today, as at common law libel was actionable per se and damage was presumed, while slander required proof of special damage. However, modern statute law renders the distinction irrelevant to liability, and the term 'defamation' is routinely now used to connote both forms. See further A Mullis and R Parkes, *Gatley on Libel and Slander*, 12th edn (London, Sweet & Maxwell, 2013) [1.5].

While publication to one person other than the plaintiff is sufficient for liability, there may be multiple publications and thus, at common law, multiple causes of action, each with its own limitation period. In the digital age, every download of a statement is treated as a discrete publication,[6] rendering liability for internet defamation potentially expansive, except where legislation such as the Defamation Act 2013 (UK) provides for a first or single publication rule.[7]

Further, it is an established principle that republishing or repeating what a third party has said or done will itself be a publication and found a separate cause of action.[8] Eighty years ago, *Byrne v Deane*[9] was notable for a related issue: can a person be liable in defamation for *failing to remove* a statement of a third party? In other words, can a person be a publisher 'by omission'? At the time, Slesser LJ in the Court of Appeal noted that holding the defendant, Mrs Deane, to have published the statement in question extended the evidence of publication further than in any prior case he could discover.[10]

In the 1930s, courts were concerned primarily with what we would today call hard copy[11] or tangible publications in one form or another: in *Byrne v Deane*, a notice on a club's walls. Some previous cases had concerned a sign on a fence;[12] or a placard on a roadway to which the defendant, seated on a stool smoking a pipe, continually pointed attracting the attention of passers-by;[13] or some disparaging object fixed on a person's door.[14]

However, today the decision of *Byrne v Deane* is routinely applied in a very different context. One of the most contentious issues in defamation law in the digital age is whether a person or entity can be liable for failing to remove a defamatory publication posted online by another person. Defendants range from website hosts with constant control and supervision of a site which allows third-party comments, to automated social media platforms hosting thousands or even millions of users, to internet service providers and internet search engines using algorithms to create hyperlinks and autocues.

Defamation is not, of course, the only context in which the courts have had to determine the liability of one person for failing to supervise or prevent, or protect a victim from, the conduct of others. Generally, liability for a pure omission in tort will be exceptional. It is separate from the imposition of vicarious liability, and from the legal attribution of one person's conduct to another.

---

[6] *Dow Jones & Co Inc v Gutnick* [2002] HCA 56, (2002) 210 CLR 575.

[7] Defamation Act 2013 (UK), s 8.

[8] Rolph, *Defamation Law* (2016) [8.60]–[8.70].

[9] *Byrne v Deane* [1937] 1 KB 818, [1937] 2 All ER 204.

[10] ibid 834 (Slesser LJ).

[11] *Loutchansky v Times Newspapers Ltd [No 2]* [2001] EWCA Civ 1805, [2002] 2 WLR 640 [55].

[12] *Byrne* (n 9) 824 (Slesser LJ), citing *De Libellis Famosis* (1605) referred to in 5 Coke 125a.

[13] *Hird v Wood* (1894) 38 SJ 234.

[14] *Byrne* (n 9) 824 (Slesser LJ), citing *Halliwood's Case* (1601) referred to in 5 Coke 125b.

The liability for failure to supervise third parties or prevent their conduct, or for failing to protect a victim from the acts of third parties, is a personal liability. Before a person can come under such an onerous liability, he or she must be in some exceptional or special relationship either with the perpetrator or the victim, usually voluntarily undertaken, or have created or increased the risk of damage occurring.[15] Or it may be, exceptionally, that a legal duty is treated as non-delegable, giving rise to a personal liability if the delegate is negligent.[16] However, as a general rule, the common law does not impose a liability on one person for the torts of third parties. As Lord Toulson recently observed in *Michael v Chief Constable of South Wales Police*:[17]

> English law does not as a general rule impose liability on a defendant (D) for injury or damage to the person or property of a claimant (C) caused by the conduct of a third party (T): *Smith v Littlewoods Organisation Ltd* [1987] AC 214, 270 ... The fundamental reason ... is that the common law does not generally impose liability for pure omissions. It is one thing to require a person who embarks on action which may harm, others to exercise care. It is another matter to hold a person liable in damages for failing to prevent harm caused by someone else.

Further, the issue of liability, in the digital and internet age, for a publication initiated by a third party, is not confined to defamatory publications. It arises also – whether in civil or criminal contexts – in relation to publications of privacy-invading material, pornography, copyright infringements, seditious material and the like. Some jurisdictions have provided limited 'safe harbour' protection from liability by legislation, usually in the context of specific types of wrongs.[18] Usually safe harbour protection applies only when the entity did not know of the content of the offending publication. Safe harbour provisions are directed at overall liability once it is proved that the entity was a publisher. Publication remains a threshold issue, determined usually by the common law.

Knowledge of the communication, or lack of it, may be critical to a finding of publication by a defendant. In cases involving positive conduct, publication is generally not in contention because it may be clear that the defendant intended to communicate a statement: to speak or sing words, to engage in conduct such as gesturing or miming,[19] to print or text or post words, to display an installation or statue,[20] to post or print images, photographs or cartoons.[21]

---

[15] *Council of the Shire of Sutherland v Heyman* [1985] HCA 41, (1985) 157 CLR 424 [11]–[12] (Brennan J). See also *Goldman v Hargrave* [1966] HCA 42, (1966) 115 CLR 458 (PC); *Modbury Triangle Shopping Centre v Anzil* [2000] HCA 61, (2000) 205 CLR 254.
[16] *Woodland v Essex County Council* [2013] UKSC 66, [2014] 1 AC 537.
[17] *Michael v The Chief Constable of South Wales Police* [2015] UKSC 2, [2015] AC 1732, [97].
[18] See, eg, Broadcasting Services Act 1992 (Cth), Sch 5, cl 91. See also Rolph (n 2) [14.60].
[19] *Bishop v New South Wales* [2000] NSWSC 1042 [1]–[4] (Dunford J): teacher sued over a mime at a school assembly.
[20] *Monson v Tussauds Ltd* [1894] 1 QB 671.
[21] Rolph (n 2) [8.50].

Tobin quotes Starkie from 1832 that 'it is sufficient if the defendant be the partial instrument of communication either by assisting in its original construction or subsequent promulgation'.[22]

Publication may occur inadvertently: an open postcard[23] or note or telegram[24] can be read by someone through whose hands it passes.[25] Dictating a letter addressed to the plaintiff to a secretary or typewriter will do.[26] The requirement of publication is clearly satisfied by the defendant's voluntary, positive conduct, with the defendant either knowing or being deemed to know of the risk that communication to a third party could occur.[27]

An email or letter *mistakenly* sent to the wrong addressee is more problematic: here, there is positive conduct on the part of the sender but the publication itself may be characterised as accidental or non-voluntary. There is some authority[28] that such a mistaken or accidental communication is not treated as publication, given it was not intended and as long as the communication to the unintended recipient could not have been foreseen by the sender.[29]

At this point, it is important to distinguish the issue of publication of a statement from the issue of liability for its defamatory content. These two issues seem to get conflated in some discussions about the relevance of a defendant's knowledge.[30] At common law, once publication is proved, liability for defamation is strict: there is no fault requirement. A defendant is prima facie liable simply because he or she has published – that is, communicated – the statement which is in law defamatory. Liability does not depend on proof that the defendant intended to defame the plaintiff or that he or she was negligent and ought to have known of the defamatory nature of the statement. (However, once it is proved that the defendant published the statement and is prima facie liable, the

---

[22] R Tobin, 'Publication and Innocent Dissemination in the Law of Defamation; Adapting to the Internet Age' (2016) 27 *New Zealand Universities Law Review* 102, 108, citing T Starkie, *Law of Slander, Libel, Scandulum Magnatum and False Rumours* (1832, reprinted Colorado, Fred B Rothman, 1997) 171.

[23] *Sadgrove v Hole* [1901] 2 KB 1.

[24] *Williamson v Freer* (1874) 9 LR CP 393.

[25] *Gomersall v Davies* (1898) 14 TLR 430 (plaintiff's foreman opened letter in course of business).

[26] *Pullman v Walter Hill & Co Ltd* [1891] 1 QB 524, 527 (Lord Esher MR).

[27] Rolph (n 2) [8.90].

[28] See *Thompson v Australian Capital Television Pty Ltd* (1996) 186 CLR 574, 594 (Gaudron J).

[29] *R v Paine* (1696) 5 Mod R 163, 87 ER 584, 587 per curiam: 'It is true, the delivering it by mistake is no publication.' See also C Sappideen and Vines, *Fleming's Law of Torts* (2011) [25.120]; Rolph (n 2) [8.100]; Tobin, 'Publication' (2016) 105, citing *Sadgrove* (n 23) and the 'rather odd decision' of *Theaker v Richardson* [1962] 1 WLR 151 (CA) (defendant found liable where sealed letter sent to plaintiff was opened and read by her husband, as this was held foreseeable). *cf Huth v Huth* [1915] 3 KB 32 (not foreseeable that butler would open unclosed envelope); *Gomersall* (n 25) 431 (AL Smith LJ). For a humorous attempt to reconcile these older cases on methods of sending a defamatory letter with a risk of publication to a third party, see *Tom & Bill Waterhouse Pty Ltd v Racing New South Wales* (2008) 72 NSWLR 577, [25] Palmer J.

[30] *Tamiz v Google Inc* [2013] 1 WLR 2151 [26] (Richards LJ).

defendant may be able to put forward the defence of innocent dissemination, either at common law[31] or under statute.)[32]

Byrne v Deane illustrates that proof of the defendant's knowledge is critical to the issue of publication where there is no positive conduct by the defendant. As we will see, publication by omission at common law depends on proof that the defendant actually knew of the presence of the statement and, having the power to do so, deliberately failed to take reasonable steps to remove it within a reasonable time. Liability in defamation for publication by omission is thus fault-based.[33]

II. *BYRNE v DEANE*: THE CASE

Seaford Head Golf Club is a picturesque golf club on the edge of the Sussex coastline, hundreds of feet above sea level, with stunning vistas across Seaford Bay and the South Downs to the white chalk cliffs of the Seven Sisters and even to Brighton in the distance. The website of the modern-day club describes its course as 'steeped in recent and ancient history', having been constructed in 1887 on the site of an ancient Saxon camp, and used as a strategic post in World War II.

Like all golf clubs, Seaford Golf Club no doubt had its controversies. Raising sufficient funds to keep the fairways and facilities in good condition is a perennial problem. Hard decisions have to be made by those charged with administration. Golf players – amateur as well as professional – take their game seriously and like members of all clubs are not slow to voice their opinions on club matters.

In the 1930s, this club, renowned for its scenic green fairways, found itself mired in litigation. All because of an anonymous poem posted on the club noticeboard.

The club was, at that time, owned by the defendants, Robert and Aletta Deane, who served as directors and Mrs Deane also as secretary. The plaintiff, Edmund Byrne, was a member of the club. A problem arose after an unknown informer gave police a tip-off that the club had a number of (presumably illegal or unlicensed) automatic gambling 'diddler' machines, whose owners gave the

---

[31] As discussed in *Godfrey v Demon Internet Ltd* [1999] EWHC 244 (QB), [2000] 3 WLR 1020 (Morland J).

[32] Defamation Act 1996 (UK), s 1; Defamation Act 2005 (NSW), s 32, and equivalents in the State Uniform Defamation Acts.

[33] This is somewhat consistent with other contexts in which the law of tort draws a distinction, in terms of strict liability or fault-based liability, between positive acts and omissions. In the law of private nuisance: a defendant is not liable for *failing to* abate a nuisance on his or her land unless he or she knew or ought to have known of its existence and failed to take reasonable care to abate it. See further *Goldman v Hargrave* [1967] 1 AC 645 (PC) and *Fleming's Law of Torts* (n 2) 508–11.

club-owners a percentage of the profits. The day after the police notified the club to remove the machines, the following typewritten 'doggerel verse'[34] was posted on the wall where the machines has stood for the previous three years:

> For many years upon this spot
>
> You heard the sound of a merry bell
>
> Those who were rash and those who were not
>
> Lost and made a spot of cash
>
> But he who gave the game away
>
> May he byrnn in hell and rue the day.
>
> —*Diddleramus*[35]

Mr Byrne was incensed that the poem stated or implied that he had reported the presence of the machines to the police, that he was disloyal and underhand, that his conduct was deserving of the greatest censure, that he was a person devoid of all true sporting spirit, and that he was a person unfit for others to associate with and who should be ostracised.

Further, he blamed the defendants: he claimed they had published or caused to be published the defamatory words to other members of the club. The defendants admitted that they had seen the notice but denied having written or put it up. Mrs Deane, as secretary, said that she was responsible for any notices posted in the club and would have removed the verse if she had thought it harmful, but she said she thought one member was 'poking fun' at another.[36]

The trial judge found the verse defamatory and that the defendants, having complete control of the club, had approved the continued publication of it.

The appeal dealt with two questions, both described as difficult by Greer LJ and also as questions on which reasonable minds could differ:[37]

(1) Was the statement – literally or by innuendo – defamatory of the plaintiff?
(2) Was it published by either or both of the defendants?

The Court of Appeal was divided on these issues.

As to whether the notice was defamatory, two judges, Slesser and Greene LJJ, reversed the trial judge, holding that the words were not capable of being defamatory. They dealt only with the meaning, to be drawn from the notice, that the plaintiff had given information to the police about the unlawful act of having gambling machines, or that he was 'an informer'. They held that

---

[34] *Byrne* (n 9) 819.

[35] In fact, the poem said 'burn in hell' on the top typed copy over a blacked-out word, but the words 'byrnn in hell' could be seen on the carbon copy underneath.

[36] *Byrne* (n 9) 820.

[37] ibid 827.

this meaning was not capable of being held to be defamatory, no matter how trivial or morally lacking in culpability was the offence. The standard to be applied was that of 'right-thinking men', not that of the criminal class who might take a different view of informers. Scottish cases taking a different view of the defamatory quality of such statements were not to be followed (Greene LJ)[38] or impliedly doubted (Slesser LJ).[39]

Greer LJ had held that the notice was defamatory, but delivered an addendum to his earlier judgment, to make it clear that if the only meaning that could be drawn from the notice was that the plaintiff had reported an unlawful act to the police, he would have agreed with them.[40] However, he had rested his judgment that the notice was defamatory on the innuendo implicit in it that the plaintiff Byrne had been guilty of underhand disloyalty to his fellow club members.[41] While this aspect of the decision in *Byrne v Deane* is interesting, as is any case dealing with whether an allegation, defamatory from the perspective of a minority group, is capable of being defamatory at law by reference to the hypothetical ordinary reasonable reader,[42] this chapter will concentrate on the second issue.

On the second issue, of publication, there was agreement by all three judges that Mrs Aletta Deane had published the statement, and agreement by Greer and Greene LJJ only that Mr Robert Deane had also published it. Mrs Deane's liability rested mainly on her position as club secretary, who by Rule 12 of the Club Rules was given power over any notice or placard in the club:

> Rule 12: No notice or placard, written or printed, shall be posted in the club premises without the consent of the secretary.[43]

Undoubtedly Mrs Deane, as secretary of the club, was entitled to take down the notice. Therefore, by allowing it to remain 'she was a consenting party to the defamatory statement'.[44] But Greer LJ also stressed that as proprietors of the club, and lessees, both defendants were the occupiers of the club – 'the walls are their walls'[45] and 'they allowed the defamatory statement to be put up and to remain in a position where it could be read by anyone'.[46] He concluded:

> In my judgment the two proprietors of this establishment by allowing the defamatory statement, if it be defamatory, to rest on the wall and not to remove it,

---

[38] ibid 841.
[39] ibid 833.
[40] ibid 841.
[41] ibid 831.
[42] *Readers Digest Services Pty Ltd v Lamb* [1982] HCA 4, (1982) 150 CLR 500. cf *Hepburn v TCN Channel Nine Pty Ltd* [1983] 2 NSWLR 682, dealing with sectional attitudes. See also *Radio 2UE Sydney Pty Ltd v Chesterton* [2009] HCA 16, (2009) 238 CLR 460, 467 (French CJ, Gummow, Kiefel and Bell JJ), criticising the requirement that the ordinary reasonable reader be 'right-thinking'.
[43] *Byrne* (n 9) 819.
[44] ibid 829.
[45] ibid.
[46] ibid.

with the knowledge that they must have had that by not removing it it would be read by people to whom it would convey such meaning as it had, were taking part in the publication of it.[47]

Greene LJ also drew no distinction between the two defendants in terms of publication:

They were entitled as proprietors to remove the trespassing article from the walls ... they had ample power, notwithstanding the position and rights of the committee, to remove something from their property the presence of which could not be justified under the rules.[48]

He noted that publication is a question of fact and must depend on the circumstances in each case. He rejected any general principle that publication could only occur by a positive act. Failure to remove a statement may or may not be publication depending on the facts. The test to be applied is as follows: by not removing the defamatory matter did 'the Defendant really make himself responsible for its continued presence'[49] where a third party had put it? In this case, the defendants, *being easily able to remove it*, and '*knowing that members of the club when they came into the room would see it* ... must be taken to have elected deliberately to leave it there ... they were consenting parties to its continued presence'[50] (emphasis added).

While agreeing with the majority about Mrs Deane's liability, Slesser LJ, in obiter, would have excused Mr Deane from liability on the basis that he had given up control either to his wife or to her in conjunction with the Club Committee.[51]

It will be noted that not just the knowledge of the defendants but also their ability to remove the notice easily, 'involving no trouble whatsoever',[52] were both key factors in the judges' decisions as to publication. Greene LJ distinguished a situation where 'to remove it would require very great trouble and expense'.[53]

Further, the conclusion of the judges in finding publication by either or both defendants was that, by failing to remove the statement, they were to be taken to have consented to or adopted or endorsed the statement. The concept of adopting a statement is redolent of the concept, and basis of liability, in another tort: a person will be taken to have adopted a nuisance by making use of it or taking advantage of it. In nuisance law, that is treated as equivalent to a positive act of misfeasance, of creating a nuisance, leading to strict liability.[54]

---

[47] ibid 830, emphasis added.
[48] ibid 837.
[49] ibid 838.
[50] ibid.
[51] ibid 836.
[52] ibid 838 (Greene LJ).
[53] ibid.
[54] *Sedleigh-Denfield v O'Callaghan* [1940] UKHL 2, [1940] AC 880.

III. *BYRNE v DEANE* AS PRECEDENT:
PARTICIPATION IN PUBLICATION IN THE MODERN WORLD

Byrne v Deane is routinely cited in both specialised defamation and general torts textbooks, treatises and case books as a leading authority on the issue of publication in defamation law. This chapter will not attempt a comprehensive analysis of the current state of the law on publication in the internet age,[55] but a brief survey of recent case law illustrates how the concepts set out by the Court in the 1930s in *Byrne v Deane* in relation to publication have both continuing and renewed relevance today.

In the case law since *Byrne v Deane*, courts have continued to emphasise the need for the defendant to have had *actual knowledge* of the defamatory matter before he or she can be found to have published it by omission. So, it was held in *Urbanchich v Drummoyne Municipal Council* that a transport authority can only be found to have published third-party posters in bus shelters if it had actual knowledge of their presence and the power and opportunity to remove them and had failed to do so within a reasonable time, leading to proof or at least an inference that it had consented to, approved of or adopted the defamatory matter 'as its own'.[56] Importantly, constructive knowledge – that is, knowledge which would have been gained if one had made reasonable enquiries – was rejected as sufficient for publication by the New Zealand Court of Appeal, following both *Byrne v Deane* and *Urbanchich*.[57]

> The actual knowledge test ... makes the liability risk of a Facebook page host no greater than that of an organiser of a public meeting – another appropriate analogy.[58]

Until the advent of the internet, the vast majority of defamation cases were not concerned with issues of publication. The *act* of publication by a defendant

---

[55] Readers are rather directed to an authoritative and comprehensive treatise and numerous articles on the subject. Rolph (n 5) [8.180] et seq; P Milmo, WVH Rogers, R Parkes, C Walker and G Busuttil (eds), *Gatley on Libel and Slander,* 11th edn (London, Sweet & Maxwell, 2008); M Collins, *The Law of Defamation and the Internet,* 3rd edn (Oxford, Oxford University Press, 2010) ch 5; J Ireland, 'Defamation 2.0: Facebook and Twitter' (2012), 17 *Media and Arts Law Review* 53; D Rolph, 'Publication, Innocent Dissemination and the Internet After *Dow Jones & Co Inc v Gutnick*' (2010) 33 *UNSWLJ* 562; R Turner, 'Internet Defamation Law and Publication by Omission: A Multi-Jurisdictional Analysis' (2014) 37 *UNSWLJ* 34; Tobin (n 22); M Hafeez-Baig and J English, 'The Liability of Search Engines Operators in Defamation: Issues Relating to Publication and Qualified Privilege' (2017) 24 *Torts LJ* 218, considering *Google Inc v Duffy* [2017] SASCFC 130 (4 October 2017).

[56] *Urbanchich v Drummoyne Municipal Council* (1999) Aust Torts Reports 81-127, 69, 193 (Hunt J). See also *Rana v Google Australia Pty* Ltd [2013] FCA 60 [51]. cf *Vaa v Brooker* [2017] NSWDC 300 (defamatory poster with photograph of plaintiff and word 'THIEF!' in window of shop owned by defendant, held not liable). See also *Hellar v Bianco* (graffiti about plaintiff on tavern lavatory wall) (1952) 244 P 2d 757, the Court of Appeal of California citing *Byrne v Deane* ay 759–60.

[57] *Murray v Wishart* [2014] 3 NZLR 722, [2014] NZCA 461 [136]–[143].

[58] ibid [144].

was usually deliberate, just as the place or places of publication were also obvious. Even broadcasting did not challenge the commonly understood concept of publication, although syndicated broadcasting[59] did raise the possibility of publication by subordinate distributors who might be given some common law[60] or statutory protection if they could be bring themselves within the defence of 'innocent dissemination'[61]: innocent in the sense that the broadcasting distributor was in most cases as unaware of the defamatory content of the publication as other subordinate or secondary publishers, such as newsagents, libraries or bookshop owners, might be when selling or lending papers, magazines and books hot off the press.

The internet has changed the profile of defamation cases. There are many examples of defamation against people who have acted positively by publishing emails, tweets, posts on social media sites.[62] However, many cases not involving the original or primary publisher now require courts to deal with online publication as a contentious threshold issue.

The case law illustrates how the common law, in the absence of overriding legislation, must apply fundamental concepts to a wide variety of ever-changing social conditions and factual situations involving new technologies. The simple concept of publication by communication, while suitable perhaps before the twentieth century advent of radio and television when communications were physically limited, may now be too broad in its application in the internet age.[63] For example, in *Dow Jones & Co Inc v Gutnick*,[64] the High Court of Australia applied to internet publications the same common law principles set out in a case brought by the Duke of Brunswick in 1849[65]: that every publication of a defamatory statement founds a new cause of action.[66] In *Loutchansky v Times Newspapers Ltd (No 2)*, the Court of Appeal refused to substitute an internet single publication rule instead of the general multiple publication rule, rejecting a submission that the latter rule was incompatible with Article 10 of the European Convention of Human Rights, noting that 'the change of the law of defamation for which the Defendant contends is a radical one'.[67] The multiple

---

[59] *Thompson v Australian Capital Television Pty Ltd* [1996] HCA 37, (1996) 186 CLR 574.

[60] *Godfrey* (n 31) [27] (Morland J), citing *Day v Bream* (1837) 2 Mood & R 54, 174 ER 212.

[61] Rolph (n 5) [14.20]–[14.50]. See also Defamation Act 1996 (UK), s 1(1), considered in detail, together with prior case law on publication, in *Godfrey* (n 31). Of course, it does not necessarily follow that those who are unable to avail themselves of the defence will be treated as publishers at common law.

[62] *Cairns v Modi* [2012] EWCA Civ 1382, [2013] 1 WLR 1015, [30]–[41]; *McAlpine of West Green v Bercow* [2013] EWHC 1342 (QB); *Murray* (n 57); *Mickle v Farley* [2013] NSWDC 295.

[63] Rolph (n 5) [8.30].

[64] *Dow Jones* (n 6).

[65] *Duke of Brunswick v Harmer* (1849) 14 QB 185, 117 ER 75.

[66] See now the single publication rule in Defamation Act 2013 (UK), s 8. A single publication rule is adopted in most states of the United States: E Barendt, J Bosland, R Craufurd-Smith and L Hitchens, *Media Law: Text, Cases and Materials* (London, Pearson, 2014) 390.

[67] *Loutchansky* (n 11) [76]. See also *Times Newspapers Limited (Nos 1 and 2) v United Kingdom* App nos 3002/03 and 23676/03 (ECtHR, 10 March 2009).

publication rule is obviously problematic, not least for issues relating to juris-diction, applicable law, limitation periods and damages, but it is consistent with the notion of publication as a bilateral not a unilateral concept.[68] These cases illustrate that courts will feel bound to take a similar approach to those taken in previous conditions when dealing with modern examples of publication. They do not feel free simply to make up new rules depending on the facts of a case and are wary of being accused of engaging in 'judicial legislation'. Generally only parliament will change long-established principles, unless a particular principle or application is seen to be inconsistent with a broader development in the common law. Yet legislators also struggle to keep up with or ahead of technological change, preferring to enact legislation that is general in applica-tion, rather than targeted at specific situations.

On the issue of whether publication by a defendant has occurred, the problem of course is deciding whether a modern example involving the internet is truly analogous with the facts of a prior decision. The problem is huge: in *Tamiz v Google Inc*, it was noted that over 250,000 words were added to Google Inc's blogs alone every minute.[69] The wide variation in technologies and the wide array of actors and entities involved in internet defamation – users, platforms, gateways, publishing services, internet service providers, search engines – means that only some examples will involve passive publication or publication by omission and thus be analogous with our starting point *Byrne v Deane*. As the Court in *Byrne v Deane* emphasised, ultimately publication by a defendant is a matter of fact. Judges have to decide whether on the evidence the facts are capable of supporting a conclusion by the court or the jury, if there is one, as to publication. Because facts vary from case to case, much of the disagreement may actually be contained in obiter dicta, but this does not lessen the potential for confusion wrought by conflicting judicial views.

We now turn to look at various categories of cases raising the issue of publi-cation on the internet of material originally composed or posted by third parties.

A. Hyperlinks to Content Composed by Others

One would have thought that a person deliberately communicating a hyper-link to another site which contains defamatory material is voluntary positive

---

[68] *Dow Jones* (n 6) 600 [26] (Gleeson CJ, McHugh, Gummow and Hayne JJ). For example, a statement in a foreign language is only published when capable of being understood by a recipient: *Jones v Davers* (1596) Cro Eliz 496, 78 ER 747. See also *Crookes v Newton* [2011] 3 SCR 269, [55] (Deschamps, J): 'publication has two components: (1) an act that makes the defamatory information available to a third party in a comprehensible form, and (2) the receipt of the information by a third party in such a way that it is understood'.

[69] *Tamiz v Google* [2013] EWCA Civ 68, [2013] 1 WLR 2151 [16] (Richards LJ): 'the judge noted inter alia that it was virtually impossible for Google Inc to exercise editorial control over the content of the blogs it hosts, which in the aggregate contain more than half a trillion words, with 250,000 new words added every minute'.

conduct which on ordinary principles would be treated as publication.[70] However, whether that is so will depend on the circumstances and context of the hyperlink. That was the view of Beech-Jones J in *Visscher v Maritime Union of Australia (No 6)*[71] where the MUA had included in an article on its website a hyperlink to a defamatory article in the *Cootamundra Herald*. Looking at the surrounding story on the MUA website, Beech-Jones J noted that readers were urged to read the 'full story' in the *Cootamundra Herald* article. By doing this, the MUA had clearly accepted responsibility for the publication, its actions amounting to adoption or promotion of the content of the newspaper article.[72] The Supreme Court of Canada took a different view in *Crookes v Newton*,[73] with some recognition that they were departing from established principles. Abella J:

> The internet cannot, in short, provide access to information without hyperlinks. Limiting their usefulness by subjecting them to the traditional publication rule would have the effect of seriously restricting the flow of information and, as a result, freedom of expression … Only when a hyperlink presents content from the hyperlinked material in a way that actually repeats the defamatory content, should that content be considered to be 'published' by the hyperlinker. Such an approach promotes expression and respects the realities of the Internet.[74]

McLachlin CJ and Fish J, while agreeing in the dismissal of the plaintiff's appeal, took a different approach, holding that publication of a defamatory statement via a hyperlink should be found only if the text indicates agreement, adoption or endorsement of the content of the hyperlinked text.[75] Deschamps J also agreed with the result, but suggested 'a more nuanced approach to revising the publication rule' which would see any reference, by hyperlink or other means, as an act of publication if the actor deliberately makes the defamatory information readily available to a third party in comprehensible form.[76]

In contrast to those who call for a new approach to publication, Beech-Jones J in *Visscher* warned of the futility, in an age of fast developing technology, of judges trying to forge technology-specific principles:[77]

> Generally, any attempt to a craft a legal principle specific to the internet or world wide web should be undertaken with caution. It runs a significant risk of having the principle undermined by changes to the manner in which users conform with the internet or the web's protocols.

---

[70] Barendt et al, *Media Law* (2014) 399, citing Milmo et al, *Gatley* (2008) 6.34.
[71] [2014] NSWSC 350.
[72] [30].
[73] *Crookes* (n 68).
[74] ibid [36]–[42].
[75] ibid [48].
[76] ibid [59].
[77] *Visscher v Maritime Union of Australia (No 6)* [2014] NSWSC 350, [28].

B. Website Hosts Aware of the Material Posted

Perhaps the most straightforward category comprises those cases where a website host has become aware of a post by a third party, either through its own perusal or through being made aware of the post by the victim, the media or some other person.

The Court of Appeal in *Tamiz v Google Inc*[78] drew an analogy with the circumstances of *Byrne v Deane*. Google was held liable in relation to a defamatory post on a blog hosted by Google's 'Blogger.com' service where Google had been notified and had not removed the post for more than a month. Overturning the decision of Eady J at first instance,[79] which had rested on Google's passive role as a platform provider, Richards LJ in the Court of Appeal, with whom Lord Dyson MR and Sullivan LJ agreed, held that *after notification*, Google was arguably a publisher: Google not only provided but controlled the Blogger service; it 'plainly facilitates publication of the blogs (including the comments posted on them)'.[80] Further, similarly to the defendants in *Byrne v Deane*, Google had failed to remove the defamatory matter within a reasonable time after being notified of its presence. Richards LJ stated that he was led to take a different view from that of Eady J by the decision of the Court of Appeal in *Byrne v Deane*:[81]

> [Certain] features bring the case in my view within the scope of the reasoning in *Byrne v Deane*. Thus, if Google Inc allows defamatory material to remain on a Blogger blog after it has been notified of the presence of that material, it might be inferred to have associated itself with, or to have made itself responsible for, the continued presence of that material on the blog and thereby to have become a publisher of the material Mr White QC submitted that the vast difference in scale between the Blogger set-up and the small club-room makes such an inference unrealistic and that nobody would view a comment of a blog as something with which Google Inc had associated itself or for which it had made itself responsible by taking no action to remove it after notification of a complaint. Those are certainly matters for argument but they are not decisive in Google Inc's favour at this stage of proceedings, where we are concerned only with whether the claimant has an arguable case against it as a publisher of the comments in issue.[82]

In the New Zealand case of *Murray v Wishart*, a Facebook page operator was held liable for statements posted by third parties on its site where it had actual knowledge of the statements and had failed to remove them within a reasonable time. The Court of Appeal drew a close analogy with the facts in *Byrne v Deane* and followed the same approach.[83]

---

[78] *Tamiz* (n 69) [34]. See also *Davison v Habeeb* [2011] EWHC 3031 (QB), [2012] 3 CMLR 104.
[79] *Tamiz v Google Inc* [2012] EWHC 449 (QB), [2012] EMLR 595.
[80] *Tamiz* (n 69) [25]. See also *Davison v Habeeb* (n 68).
[81] *Tamiz* (n 69) [27].
[82] ibid [34].
[83] *Murray* (n 57) [129], [144].

C. Internet Service Providers

The second category comprises those cases which concern internet service providers (ISPs) rather than website hosts. The first United Kingdom case on the liability of ISPs was *Godfrey v Demon Internet Ltd*,[84] in which the defendant was found liable but on the basis that it was more than a mere ISP: it also provided a news server on which it hosted content; it had been requested and had failed to remove the defamatory material.

By contrast, three ISPs were found *not* to be publishers in the case of *Bunt v Tilley*.[85] They were described by Eady J, on the facts, as mere passive facilitators, like a postal service or a telephone company, rather than as publishers.[86] He held that, for the ISP to be treated as a publisher, 'there must be knowing involvement in the process of publication of the relevant words'.[87] One does wonder if this is consistent with the situation of bookshops and libraries which have traditionally been held to be publishers, as Morland J in *Godfrey v Demon Internet Ltd* recounts.[88] But this observation perhaps rather only shows that bookshops and libraries were too strictly treated in the past. The law did respond to the harshness of their position by formulating the innocent dissemination defence for 'subordinate publishers',[89] but perhaps it had been too ready to treat them as publishers in the first place.

D. Internet Search Engines

The third category has proved the most contentious worldwide in recent times. These cases concern internet search engines, such as those operated by Google or Yahoo!. Search engines are designed to find, collate and provide access to matter for their users. The underlying matter may well be defamatory. While the use of search engines has become universally commonplace, they are also the bane of people who would rather that some details of their lives – past fame, unwanted images, prior convictions or scandals, rumours, possible shady associations – are not exposed to all and sundry at the touch of a fingertip.

---

[84] *Godfrey* (n 31).
[85] *Bunt v Tilley* [2006] EWHC 407 (QB), [2007] 1 WLR 124.
[86] ibid [36]–[37].
[87] ibid [23].
[88] *Weldon v 'The Times' Book Co Ltd* (1911) 28 TLR 143; *Vizetelly v Mudie's Select Library Ltd* [1900] 2 QB 170; *Bottomley v FW Woolworth & Co Ltd* (1932) 48 TLR 521. Morland J goes on to contrast the position in the United States, not just because of the impact of the First Amendment to the US Constitution, but also a recent federal statute, the Communications Decency Act (47 USC #230): '#230 creates a federal immunity to any cause of action that would make service providers liable for information originating from a third-party user of the service': *Zeran v America Online Inc* (1997) 129 F 3d 327, 330 (Wilkinson CJ).
[89] *Emmens v Pottle* (1885) 16 QBD 354.

Much attention has been given to privacy claims and a so-called right for true facts 'to be forgotten'[90] but many of the internet cases are based on defamation where the claimant will rely on the presumed falsity[91] of the slur and put the defendant to proof of truth.

There is now significant disagreement between first instance courts in England and Wales, Victoria and New South Wales as to whether a search engine can be held to have published defamatory matter.[92] Because of the nature of search engines, the cases tend to deal with instant results or responses to searches, that is, responses of which the search engine entity would not – or possibly even could not – have specific knowledge in advance. A recent appeal to the High Court of Australia has not resolved the issue because the appeal was only in relation to a strike-out application and the Court held that the question of publication as a matter of fact depended on the evidence to be presented at a full hearing after discovery.[93]

In *Bunt v Tilley*,[94] Eady J had likened ISPs to providers of telephone services. In *Metropolitan International Schools Ltd v Designtechnica Corporation*,[95] Eady J dealt directly with the issue of Google as a search engine. The plaintiff sued Google for an automated search result that directed the enquirer to defamatory matter posted on Designtechnica's online forum. Eady J held that the search engine was merely a conduit, similar to those providing infrastructure. Again, as he had done in relation to ISPs, Eady J drew a distinction between publishers and mere passive facilitators, the search engine falling within the latter.[96]

However, in a 2012 claim brought by Trkulja against Google Inc[97] in the Victorian Supreme Court, Beach J took a different view to that of Eady J on the role of search engines. Beach J held that it was open to a jury to decide that Google was a publisher *even before Google had any notice* from anybody acting on behalf of the plaintiff[98] that its search engine results generated and disseminated defamatory material. While Google had established automated systems, those systems had acted in the way Google intended, a point that Beach J said Eady J had appeared to overlook.[99] The performance of the function

---

[90] Most recently in *NT 1 & NT 2 v Google LLC* [2018] EWHC 799 (QB), [2018] WLR(D) 225.

[91] *Age Company Ltd v Elliott* [2006] VSCA 168, (2006) 14 VR 375 [15] (Ashley JA). See also Rolph (n 5) [9.40].

[92] See D Rolph, 'The Ordinary, Reasonable Search Engine User and Defamatory Capacity of Search Engine Results in *Trkulja v Google Inc*' (2017) 39 *Sydney LR* 601.

[93] *Trkulja v Google LLC* (2018) 356 ALR 178, [39].

[94] *Bunt* (n 85) [5]–[17].

[95] [2009] EWHC 1765 (QB), [2011] 1 WLR 1743 [36]–[47].

[96] ibid [51].

[97] *Trkulja v Google Inc LLC (No 5)* [2012] VSC 533 (Beach J).

[98] ibid [18]: Beach J noted that before it received notice, Google could be treated as an *innocent* disseminator for the purposes of the statutory defence.

[99] ibid [27].

of Google's algorithm could help establish that Google was a publisher. Google did not appeal against the decision of Beach J.

Kaye J had come to a similar conclusion in an action brought by the same plaintiff against Yahoo! Inc in the same year.[100] Trkulja was awarded a total of A$425,000 in the two cases.

In *Bleyer v Google* in 2014,[101] McCallum J in the New Wales Supreme Court disagreed with Beach J's view of the English authorities and with any assertion that as a matter of law a search engine may be a publisher before it is put on notice of the defamatory matter. Her Honour emphasised the lack of any human input in the operation of the algorithm during an internet search.

In 2017 in *Google Inc v Duffy*, the Full Court of the Supreme Court of South Australia rejected an appeal by Google against the finding of the trial judge that Google had published search results which defamed the plaintiff. The search results included hyperlinks to the original articles and extracts which were sufficient to inform the reader of their defamatory content. The Full Court preferred the analysis of Beach J in the 2012 case discussed above[102] to that of Eady J in *Bunt v Tilley*[103] or the Court of Appeal in *Tamiz v Google Inc*.[104] The three judgments spanning 171 pages contain a bewildering analysis, none more so than a statement by Hinton J that the elements of the tort of defamation differ depending on whether the defendant is either a primary or subordinate publisher.[105] With respect, this is not correct: for both, publication by the defendant must be proved and once proved, liability is strict but subject to available defences. His Honour appears to be confusing the elements of the tort with the question of ultimate liability which depends on both proven elements and available defences.

The High Court of Australia recently allowed an appeal from the decision of the Victorian Court of Appeal in *Google Inc v Trkulja*, reinstating the trial judge's decision. The trial judge had held, inter alia, that it was strongly arguable that Google was a publisher of its search engine results.[106] The High Court's judgment is as much about the proper judicial approach to strike out applications as it is about the issues in contention. Google had applied to have the plaintiff's latest statement of claim set aside, on the grounds that it had no real prospect of success. Google argued that the relevant words were not capable of being defamatory of the plaintiff, that Google was not a publisher

---

[100] *Trkulja v Yahoo! Inc LLC* [2012] VSC 88 (Kaye J). The defamatory slurs were that he was a criminal connected to Melbourne's criminal underworld.

[101] *Bleyer v Google* [2014] NSWSC 897, (2014) 88 NSWLR 670.

[102] *Trkulja v Google Inc LLC (No 5)* [2012] VSC 533.

[103] *Bunt* (n 85).

[104] [2012] EWHC 449.

[105] *Google Inc v Duffy* (2017) 129 SASR 304, 460 [578].

[106] *Google Inc v Trkulja* [2016] VSCA 333, (2016) 342 ALR 504, on appeal from *Trkulja v Google Inc* [2015] VSC 635 (17 November 2015) (McDonald J). See generally Rolph (n 92).

and that Google should have a common law immunity from liability on the basis of public interest. McDonald J at first instance dismissed the application, rejecting Google's submissions on all three points. On the issue of publication, he emphasised, in contrast to McCallum J in *Bleyer*, the human input into the *creation* of the algorithm.[107] The Court of Appeal allowed an appeal against McDonald J's dismissal of the application, agreeing with Google's submission that Trkulja's claim had no reasonable prospects of success. However, the basis for the Court's decision was that, applying the test of the 'ordinary reasonable user of such a site'[108] the material was not capable of being held to convey any of the pleaded imputations. This would have been enough on its own to uphold the appeal, but the Court of Appeal went further and also stated that Google *should* be treated as a publisher:

> [O]n first principles, ... a search engine, when it publishes search results in response to a user's enquiry, should be accounted a publisher of those results – [including] autocomplete predictions. It is a participant in a chain of distribution of material.[109]

In allowing the appeal, the High Court was critical of the Court of Appeal for giving a purportedly final determination in a summary dismissal application, without the benefit of discovery, a defence and full evidence. The High Court held that:

> McDonald J [at first instance] was correct to hold that *it is strongly arguable* that Google's intentional participation in the communication of the allegedly defamatory results to Google search engine users supports a finding that Google published the ... results. Properly advised, that was all that the Court of Appeal needed to say on the subject.[110]

The High Court briefly commented on the issue of publication, noting that while 'in point of principle, the law as to publication is tolerably clear', it is the application of that law to the particular facts of the case which tends to be difficult, especially in a novel context such as internet search engines.[111] With respect, this latter observation is an understatement, with the practical difficulty of reconciling conflicting decisions as to application calling into doubt the first.

However, one welcome point made by the High Court was its rejection of any need for the plaintiff to plead that the defendant was a 'primary' or

---

[107] Rolph (n 92) 604.

[108] *Google Inc* (n 106) [390].

[109] ibid [348]. The Court also noted at [353] that '(a)ssuming that it is correct to say that a search engine is a secondary publisher of search results of the kind in issue in this matter, we think that an innocent dissemination defence will almost always, if not always, be maintainable in a period before notification of an alleged defamation.'

[110] ibid [38], emphasis added.

[111] ibid [39].

'secondary' publisher of the defamatory material,[112] saying 'all degrees of participation in the publication are publication'[113] and quoting Isaacs J in *Webb v Bloch:*[114]

> The term *published* is the proper and technical term to be used in the case of libel, *without reference to the precise degree* in which the defendant has been instrumental to such publication; since, *if he has intentionally lent his assistance as to its existence for the purpose of being published*, his instrumentality is evidence to show a publication by him.[115]

The only relevance of a defendant being a subordinate publisher is where it wishes to rely on the statutory defence of innocent distribution or the similar defence at common law. The distinction is not one to be drawn when deciding whether the defendant is a publisher in the first place.[116]

It is not only the results of an internet search that raise the issue of publication. Plaintiffs have also complained of the autocomplete predictions which are compiled automatically from terms that other users have used. Some of the case law shows how the two issues of publication and the conveying of defamatory meaning can be interwoven. This seems best illustrated by this statement by Blue J at first instance *Duffy v Google Inc*, a statement endorsed by the Victoria Court of Appeal in *Google Inc v Trkulja:*[117]

> The ordinary reasonable person reading the autocomplete predictions would understand that *they are neither a statement by Google nor a reproduction by Google of a statement by someone else* ... Rather they comprise a collection of words that have been entered by previous searchers when conducting searches.[118]

It is certainly difficult to see how Google can at the same time be taken to have published another person's statement while it cannot be taken to have reproduced it for the purposes of conveying meaning. Rolph argues that there is a 'degree of artificiality in suggesting that they are wholly discrete elements' and implies that it should not be readily assumed, or merely the subject of obiter dicta, that a search engine is a publisher, concluding that the issue needs careful argument and analysis as a matter in contention between parties.[119] The High Court's decision affirms this view.

---

[112] A distinction made both by the Supreme Court of Victoria Court of Appeal in this case at *Google Inc v Trykulja* [350], [357], by the Supreme Court of South Australia Full Court in *Google Inc v Duffy* [2017] SASFC 130.

[113] *Google Inc* (n 106) [40].

[114] (1928) 41 CLR 331.

[115] ibid 363-364 quoting Folkard, *The Law of Slander and Libel*, 5th edn (1891) at 439 (second and third emphasis added by Isaacs J).

[116] ibid.

[117] *Google Inc* (n 106) [393].

[118] *Duffy v Google Inc* [2015] SASC 170, (2015) 125 SASR 437 [375], emphasis added.

[119] Rolph (n 92) 610–11.

E. Internet Hosts and the like who are Unaware of the Relevant Material Posted by Third Parties

It appears that there is not yet a case example in a last possible category: of a website or social media host being found to have published a post originally posted by a third party where the host is not aware of the post and it occurs without any intervention by the host. The internet cases mentioned in the first category, such as *Tamiz v Google*,[120] just like the earlier 'hard copy' cases such as *Byrne v Deane* and *Urbanchich v Drummoyne Municipal Council*,[121] have been at pains to emphasise that the host becomes liable only once it has actual knowledge of the post *and* has failed to remove the post within a reasonable time.

Before that point, the position of the host is, according to the Court of Appeal in *Tamiz v Google*, neither a primary nor a secondary publisher. However, the Court's reasoning on this point is, with respect, open to the criticism that it has used the criteria for the defence of innocent dissemination which is directed, not at publication, but only at the issue of fault or lack of it once publication has been established:

> There is a long-established line of authority that a person involved only in dissemination is not to be treated as a publisher unless he knew or ought by the exercise of reasonable care to have known that the publication was likely to be defamatory: *Emmens v Pottle* (1885) 16 QBD 354, 357-358; *Vizetelly v Mudie's Select Library Ltd* [1900] 2 QB 170, 177-180; *Bottomley v FW Woolworth and Co Ltd* (1932) 48 TLR 521 ... Since it cannot be said they Google Inc either knew or ought reasonably to have known of the defamatory comments prior to notification of the Appellant's complaint, that line of authority tells against viewing Google Inc as a secondary publisher prior to such notification.[122]

With respect, this line of authority cited does not determine the issue of whether someone is a publisher.[123] As Morland J pointed out in *Godfrey v Demon Internet Ltd*,[124] the defendants in the cases to which the Court of Appeal referred were all held able to rely on what was in substance a defence of *innocent* dissemination, not one of non-dissemination.[125] Tobin shows that there was both ambiguity in the judgments and unease among the judges about the precise basis of the early decisions.[126]

The Victorian decisions in cases on search engines, discussed above, must be causing concern to websites and social media hosts: if an internet search engine

[120] *Tamiz* (n 69).

[121] *Urbanchich* (n 56).

[122] *Tamiz* (n 69) [26].

[123] See further the discussion by Ribeiro PJ in *Oriental Press Group Ltd v Fevaworks Solutions Ltd* [2013] 5 HKC 253, [2013] HKFCA 47, [31], [53].

[124] *Godfrey* (n 31) [22]–[23].

[125] A point also noted by the New Zealand Court of Appeal in *Murray* (n 57) [127].

[126] Tobin (n 22), 110 ff.

can be found to have published matter regardless of knowledge of whatever matter a search will elicit or what search terms may be autocompleted due to previous users' searches, it may be difficult to see why website hosts should be treated more leniently. Are they active distributors like the hosts of a television show or talkback radio show who encourage and invite postings by third parties or rather mere passive facilitators like a telephone company[127] or the club in *Byrne v Deane*, before it became aware of the statement or matter posted, without permission, on its walls? In *Oriental Press Group Ltd v Fevaworks Solutions Ltd*, the Court of Final Appeal in Hong Kong certainly did not see a popular internet discussion platform host as analogous to the defendants in *Byrne v Deane*, on whom the defamatory matter was forced. Ribeiro PJ saw the internet host as clearly an active participant in the publications of its users by their conduct in setting up, encouraging use of and monitoring the platform.[128] Yet it could not possibly know in advance what was to be posted on a wide range of topics. Imposing liability on an entity where it cannot know in advance what material will be communicated seems at odds with the notion of publication as a voluntary exercise. Other judges, including Eady J in the High Court, the members of the Court of Appeal in *Tamiz v Google* and McCallum J in the Supreme Court of New South Wales in *Bleyer* seem, with respect, to take a more practical and workable approach to the issues of publication on the internet.

Knowledge of publication should continue to be the basis on which defamation liability for publication by omission or arising out of the acts of third parties should rest on those who control spaces and means of communications (knowledge in this context does not require knowledge of the defamatory nature of the communication or material: that would be confusing the issue of publication with the issue of fault). Frankly, any other basis for imposition of publication is as unworkable in the virtual sphere as it would be in the physical sphere, and more so. Once an internet entity is alerted to potentially defamatory material, it has a choice: take appropriate action to remove it or face liability for leaving it there.

IV. CONCLUSION

There are several notable aspects to *Byrne v Deane* and its reception in the law since it was decided. First, the decision can be accurately described as landmark in that it went further than any prior decision on the issue of publication and opened up the possibility of more extensive liability for defamation. Secondly, two judges in the Court of Appeal decided the issue of publication without

---

[127] *Anderson v New York Telephone Company* (1974) 35 NY 2d 746.
[128] *Oriental Press Group Ltd v Fevaworks Solutions Ltd* [2013] 5 HKC 253, [2013] HKFCA 47 [50]–[55].

reference to a single prior case on the issue of publication, while the other judge referred to only one case: such was the novelty of the fact situation with which the Court was dealing.[129] Thirdly, the judges set out the relevant legal principles in terms of unambiguous clarity, general application and broad utility for the social and technological conditions of the time. Fourthly, the correctness of the principles in their application to the facts of the case has never been doubted. And finally, the principles set out by the Court have shown themselves to be of perennial and lasting utility and relevance, even in social and technological conditions that would have sounded like science fiction in 1937. However, *Byrne v Deane* was in essence a case of omission, if anything, on the part of the defendants. No relevant active conduct by the defendants was involved, save their acting as managers and secretary of the golf club. Most of the modern internet cases involve some underlying conduct by the defendants. The question is usually whether that conduct meets the minimum requirement for active participation in the publication.

We will finish by a tentative attempt at summing up on the law on publication as it now stands:

(1) If the defendant has engaged in deliberate positive conduct which has played some part in the communication of *particular* material to a third party, it will be considered a publisher. This is a matter of fact and it will be necessary for a court to decide whether a defendant's role was one of deliberate participation in the communication of particular material or merely one analogous to the provision of infrastructure or means of transfer or communication, such as a telephone line or an internet service. If the defendant has no control or means of control of the particular material then it will not be considered a publisher.

(2) That participation may come about merely by hyperlinking to another source if this is seen as endorsing, calling attention to, adopting or accepting responsibility for the material. In the absence of the highest appellate authority, there is still uncertainty and disagreement in Australia and England as to whether liability will rest on a search engine which creates results by the operation of algorithms without any human input into the collation of those particular results. The mere fact that the algorithm works as intended by its creators and employers may or may not be sufficient.

(3) Where the defendant has not engaged in any positive action in relation to the particular material, the defendant will only be treated as a publisher if it knows or ought to know of its existence and it has either adopted the material or, having the power and reasonable ability to do so, has failed to remove the material within a reasonable time. *Byrne v Deane* continues to be authority on this point.

---

[129] *Hird* (n 13).

(4) Whether it has engaged in positive conduct or become liable for publication by omission due to its negligent failure to remove, the publisher may be able to rely on the defence of innocent dissemination if it is a subordinate publisher and fulfils the requirements of the relevant common law or statutory defence.

The history of the common law of defamation shows that the courts have occasionally had to develop pragmatic responses to new social phenomena and new forms of communication. Instant internet communication, with its underlying mining, aggregation and analysis of world wide data is, in the main, of great social benefit. In the absence of legislation to deal with liability or appropriate safe harbours, courts should be wary of using superficial factual analogies with older cases which may lead them to apply rules formulated in a very different technological context to new situations where a more modern approach is required. However, any technology-specific principles must be consistent with the fundamental principles that underpin legal responsibility.

4

Kemsley v Foot *(1952)*

JASON BOSLAND*

I. INTRODUCTION

A N ESSENTIAL ELEMENT of the common law defence of fair comment to defamation is the requirement that protected comment must have a sufficient factual basis.[1] A comment will only be considered 'fair' if it is one that an honest person could hold based on facts that the defendant is able to prove to be true[2] or on alleged facts published on an occasion of privilege.[3] Given that the right to comment is seen as a fundamental aspect of the right to freedom of speech,[4] the concept of fairness has been construed liberally: a comment will be considered fair irrespective of how prejudiced, exaggerated or obstinate it might be,[5] or how rudely or offensively it might be expressed.[6] Importantly, while the facts upon which a comment is based must have existed at the time of publication,[7] only enough facts need be proven true (or shown to be protected by privilege) so as to establish to the satisfaction of the trier of fact

---

* Associate Professor, Melbourne Law School, University of Melbourne; Director, Centre for Media and Communications Law (CMCL), University of Melbourne. The author would like to thank the staff of the Melbourne Law School's Law Research Service, especially Robin Gardner and Louis Ellis, for their generous assistance locating sources.
    [1] See, eg, *Hunt v Star Newspaper Co Ltd* [1908] 2 KB 309, 320 (Fletcher Moulton LJ). Note, in the United Kingdom, the common law defence of fair comment has been abolished and replaced with a statutory defence called honest opinion: Defamation Act 2013, s 3(8). The common law defence continues to operate in most common law jurisdictions.
    [2] See, eg, *London Artists Ltd v Littler* [1969] 2 QB 375, 391 (Lord Denning MR); *Orr v Isles* [1965] NSWR 677, 698 (Taylor J).
    [3] See, eg, *Brent Walker Group plc v Time Out Ltd* [1991] 2 QB 33, 45 (Bingham LJ); *Joseph v Spiller* [2011] 1 AC 852, 858.
    [4] *Brent Walker Group plc v Time Out Ltd* [1991] 2 QB 33, 44; *Lyon v Daily Telegraph* [1943] KB 746, 753 (Scott LJ).
    [5] *Merivale v Carson* (1887) 20 QB 275, 280 (Lord Esher MR); *Silkin v Beaverbrook Newspapers Ltd* [1958] 2 All ER 516, 518; *Tse Wai Chun v Cheng* [2000] HKCFA 86, [79].
    [6] David Rolph, *Defamation Law* (Lawbook Co, Pyrmont, 2016) 283.
    [7] *Cohen v Daily Telegraph Ltd* [1968] 1 WLR 916, 919–20 (Lord Denning MR).

that a comment was an objectively fair one.[8] The touchstone of fairness in this sense is where the law has chosen to draw the line between a claimant's right to the protection of his or her reputation and a commentator's right to freely express his or her views on matters of public interest.

The issue considered by the House of Lords in the landmark 1952 case of *Kemsley v Foot*[9] was whether, in addition to the defendant having to plead particulars of true or privileged facts to establish a comment's fairness,[10] the law also imposes a further requirement that the factual basis of a comment be included in the defamatory publication itself. It was already well established that sometimes the facts underpinning a comment will need to be explicitly or implicitly set out to enable a reader to identify a statement as one of comment as opposed to a 'bare' allegation of fact.[11] Thus, an otherwise factual statement may be treated as comment where an ordinary, reasonable recipient would understand it as a 'conclusion or deduction come to by the speaker from other facts stated or referred to' in the publication.[12] The distinction between fact and comment, however, was not the issue in *Kemsley v Foot*, with the parties agreeing that the statement was properly characterised as comment. The question, instead, was whether a requirement exists, independently of the fact/comment distinction, to set out the factual basis of a comment and, if so, the specificity with which such facts must be stated.[13] The plaintiff, Kemsley, argued that the facts must be sufficiently identified to *enable recipients to assess the validity or fairness of the comment for themselves.*[14]

It is important to note at the outset that the fair comment defence originated in cases involving the review of public works, such as plays, books and sporting spectacles.[15] Even prior to *Kemsley v Foot*, it had long been accepted, at least implicitly, that the specific facts used to justify a review do not need to be set out in the matter complained of.[16] All that the defence requires is that the subject

---

[8] Note, a defamation trial in England and Wales is now conducted by judge alone unless ordered otherwise: Defamation Act 2013, s 11.

[9] *Kemsley v Foot* [1952] AC 345 (*Kemsley v Foot*).

[10] See, eg, *Aga Khan v The Times Publishing Co* [1924] 1 KB 675, 682–83.

[11] See, eg, *O'Brien v Marquis of Salisbury* (1889) 54 JP 215, 216 (Field J); *Hunt v Star Newspaper Co* [1908] 2 KB 309, 319 (Fletcher Moulton LJ).

[12] *O'Brien v Marquis of Salisbury* (1889) 54 JP 215, 216 (Field J).

[13] *Kemsley v Foot* (n 9), 354 (Lord Porter).

[14] In the House of Lords, Kemsley argued that the reader should be able to assess the 'validity' of the comment: ibid 348. In the Court of Appeal, however, Kemsley argued that it is the 'fairness' of the comment that the reader should be able to assess: *Kemsley v Foot* [1951] 2 KB 34, 36 (*Kemsley v Foot* CA). To the extent that there is a difference between validity and the potentially narrower question of fairness, this was not noted in the House of Lords.

[15] See, eg, *Dibdin v Swan and Bostock* (1793) 1 Esp 28, 170 ER 269; *Tabart v Tipper* (1808) 1 Camp 349, 170 ER 981; *Carr v Hood* (1808) 1 Camp 355, 170 ER 983. For a history of the defence of fair comment, see Paul Mitchell, *The Making of the Modern Law of Defamation* (Hart, Oxford, 2005) ch 8.

[16] *Kemsley v Foot* CA (n 14), 42 (Somervell LJ), 50 (Birkett LJ). For early 'review' cases where this is clear, see, eg, *Carr v Hood* (1808) 1 Camp 355, 170 ER 983; *McQuire v Western Morning News Co* [1903] 2 KB 100. See, also, *Telnikoff v Matusevitch* [1992] 2 AC 343, 361 (Lord Ackner).

matter of the comment is referred to – for example, by the title of the play, book, or other artistic work that is the subject of review.[17] This, of course, makes sense given the obvious difficulties in having to describe a work or dissect it into its relevant parts.[18] Furthermore, while reference to the subject matter will in some cases enable the recipient to consult the work and assess whether the comment is fair,[19] in other cases – particularly where the work is ephemeral[20] or where the review successfully deters recipients from dedicating time, effort and money to see, read or hear the work[21] – recipients may never be in a position to assess the fairness of the review for themselves.

The defence of fair comment, however, is not limited to the review of public works. At least since the 1838 case of *Cooper v Lawson*,[22] it has been recognised that it also extends to the protection of comment upon all matters of public interest, including the conduct of public, and sometimes private, persons.[23] Given the early recognition of the wide ambit of the fair comment defence, it is remarkable that it was not until well over 100 years later in *Kemsley v Foot* that the English courts were asked to directly address the question of whether outside of the review context the underlying factual basis of a comment must be stated in the matter itself,[24] an issue that is clearly fundamental to the operation of the defence. The delay is all the more remarkable given the central role that fair comment is said to play in protecting freedom of speech in defamation law and the fact that the issue raises, as we shall see, important questions that turn on the very justifications for the defence.

Shortly following the decision in *Kemsley v Foot*, it was asserted in a brief case note that the House of Lords had 'clarified satisfactorily' the point.[25] However, history has proven this to be an overly optimistic assessment of the case. As it turned out, the manner in which the House of Lords resolved the issue in *Kemsley v Foot* meant that the case did not present an ideal opportunity to pronounce a principle of general application outside of the review context. Consequently, as I explain in this chapter, apparent ambiguity in the leading speech given by Lord Porter seems to have led to differing opinions amongst

---

[17] AJE Jaffey, 'The Right to Comment' in JW Bridge (ed) *Fundamental Rights* (London, Sweet & Maxwell, 1973) 60, 67.

[18] See, eg, *Channel Seven Adelaide Pty Ltd v Manock* [2007] HCA 60, (2007) 232 CLR 245, 279–80 (Gummow, Hayne and Heydon JJ); *Telnikoff v Matusevitch* [1992] 2 AC 343, 361 (Lord Ackner).

[19] See, eg, *Thornton v Telegraph Media Group Ltd* [2009] EWHC 2863 (QB), [44] (Gray J).

[20] *Joseph v Spiller* [2010] UKSC 53, [2011] 1 AC 852, 884 (Lord Phillips of Worth Matravers PSC).

[21] *Kemsley v Foot* CA (n 14), 42 (Somervell LJ).

[22] *Cooper v Lawson* (1838) 8 Ad & E 746, 112 ER 1020. See, also, *Turnbull v Bird* (1861) 2 F & F 508, 175 ER 1163; *Campbell v Spottiswoode* (1863) 3 B & S 769, 176 ER 188. As to the latter case, see ch 1.

[23] See, eg, *Wason v Walter* (1868) LR 4 QB 73, 93 (Cockburn CJ).

[24] The issue had been directly considered in South Africa: *Roos v Stent and Pretoria Printing Works Ltd* [1909] Transvaal LR 988.

[25] R L Sharwood, 'Tort – Defamation – Facts Need Not be Included in Statement When Fair Comment is Pleaded' (1953) 6 *Res Judicatae* 22, 24.

English judges as to the nature and extent of the 'underlying fact' requirement and has certainly led to inconsistent treatment between England and other common law jurisdictions.

II. *KEMSLEY v FOOT*: FACTUAL BACKGROUND
AND DECISION OF THE COURT OF APPEAL

The facts of *Kemsley v Foot* are relatively simple. The plaintiff was Lord Kemsley, a press baron with a vast stable of daily, weekly and Sunday newspapers. His most notable masthead was the *Sunday Times*, which, along with some of his other newspapers, reflected the 'complacent conservatism and Victorian certitudes' of Kemsley himself.[26] The unwavering anti-Labour editorial policy of his newspapers, like that employed by the popular tabloid titles owned by the Rothermeres, was the source of significant hostility between Kemsley and Labour back-benchers and ministers and played a central role in the establishment of the 1947–49 Royal Commission into the regulation of the press.[27] Lord Kemsley's antipathy for the left led to numerous libel skirmishes with key Labour figures, of which *Kemsley v Foot* is one example.[28] Kemsley sued in relation to an article written by Michael Foot, a Labour MP and prominent twentieth-century political writer and journalist.[29] The article appeared under the headline 'Lower than Kemsley' in the *Tribune* newspaper, a weekly democratic socialist newspaper founded in 1937 by a group of left-wing Labour MPs, including Sir Stafford Cripps and George Strauss. The *Tribune* was established to give Labour and left-leaning socialist parties a unified voice against the conservative National Government of the day[30] and no doubt the press barons, including Lord Kemsley, who supported it. In the article Foot was highly critical of the *Evening Standard*, a newspaper with which Kemsley had no association, for publishing an article suggesting that the Secretary of State for War, John Strachey, was a supporter of communism. According to the House of Lords, it was at least arguable that the headline inferred that the 'Kemsley Press is of a low and undesirable quality and that Lord Kemsley is responsible for its tone'.[31]

---

[26] Adrian Smith, 'Berry, (James) Gomer, first Viscount Kemsley (1883–1968), newspaper proprietor', *Oxford Dictionary of National Biography* (Oxford University Press, Oxford, 2008), www.oxforddnb.com/view/10.1093/ref:odnb/9780198614128.001.0001/odnb-9780198614128-e-30731.

[27] ibid.

[28] ibid.

[29] Kenneth Morgan, 'Foot, Michael Mackintosh (1913–2010), journalist, politician, author' *Oxford Dictionary of National Biography* (Oxford University Press, Oxford, 2016), www.oxforddnb.com/view/10.1093/ref:odnb/9780198614128.001.0001/odnb-9780198614128-e-102722.

[30] Paul O'Flinn, 'Orwell and *Tribune*' (1980) 6 *Literature and History* 201, 205.

[31] *Kemsley v Foot* (n 9) 354–55 (Lord Porter).

The defendants sought to defend the headline by pleading fair comment. The facts relied upon in the defendants' pleadings to support the defence consisted of excerpts from Kemsley's newspapers, allegations as to how they were 'inaccurate or untruthful', along with examples of their 'tone and impropriety of their method of dealing with news'.[32] On the application of Kemsley, Parker J struck out these pleadings on the basis that they disclosed no reasonable defence. The defendants then appealed Parker J's decision to the Court of Appeal. Kemsley argued, as he did before Parker J, that the fair comment defence was unavailable because the headline, although conceded to be comment, was 'bare' or 'naked' comment – that is, none of the facts upon which the comment was alleged to be based were set out, nor were they referred to, in the defamatory matter complained of. As a result, it was said to be impossible for a reader to judge whether the comment was fair.[33] The defendants contended that such a proposition, at least as a general statement of principle, was 'too wide' and that the application of the fair comment defence to a comment where the supporting facts were common knowledge, like the one in dispute, did not require any underlying facts to be expressly set out.[34]

The Court of Appeal allowed the appeal and reinstated the fair comment defence. In separate judgments, Somervell and Birkett LJJ (with each of whom Jenkins LJ agreed) held that the comment, being concerned with the person responsible for the way in which a newspaper presents news, was to be treated as analogous to a review or criticism of a play or book, or some other work submitted to the public domain for comment.[35] Somervell LJ remarked:

> [The] cases show that in criticizing something put before the public, as in a play or a book, for its approval or disapproval, the defence is, or at any rate may be, open although there are no citations or examples by reference to which the reader can judge the fairness of the comment.[36]

On the facts, it was therefore enough that the subject matter – Kemsley's press – was made clearly apparent to the reader.[37]

Outside of the review context, Somervell and Birkett LJJ both went on to assert that facts underlying a comment may not need to be set out where such facts are already in the public domain. As Somervell LJ said:

> The act or acts of a public man, unlike a play after its first night, or a book just published, may be both undisputed and under such vigorous discussion at the moment that what might in form seem to be a bare comment might to any reader be plainly referable to that act or acts.[38]

[32] ibid 346.
[33] *Kemsley v Foot* CA (n 14) 37.
[34] ibid 36.
[35] ibid 45–46 (Somervell LJ), 52 (Birkett LJ).
[36] ibid 42 (Somervell LJ), 52 (Birkett LJ).
[37] ibid 51–52 (Birkett LJ).
[38] ibid 42, 51 (Birkett LJ).

Cases involving notorious or well-known facts, however, were distinguished from cases where the facts had received no prior publicity. Thus, Somervell LJ suggested that the defence might not be available 'unless the facts relied on were substantially set out or indicated'.[39] Birkett LJ came to the same conclusion, although he acknowledged from the outset that it may not be possible to 'lay down any rule of universal application'.[40]

III. *KEMSLEY v FOOT*: DECISION OF THE HOUSE OF LORDS

Kemsley appealed the decision to the House of Lords. He argued, in essence, that the analogy between the headline and the review cases relied upon by the Court of Appeal should be rejected since the headline focused on the conduct of Kemsley and was not confined to the quality or contents of his newspapers.[41] It was contended that, outside of the review context, a different principle therefore applied: 'one is not entitled to comment on the conduct of a public man unless one sufficiently identifies the facts on which the comment is based *so that the reader may form an opinion as to the validity of the comment*'.[42]

In making the argument, Kemsley placed reliance upon the following passage from Fletcher Moulton LJ's judgment in *Hunt v Star Newspaper Co Ltd* (*Hunt v Star*):

> The law as to fair comment, so far as is material to the present case, stands as follows. In the first place, comment in order to be justifiable as fair comment must appear as comment and must not be so mixed up with the facts that the reader cannot distinguish between what is report and what is comment ... The justice of the rule is obvious. *If the facts are stated separately and the comment appears as an inference drawn from those facts, any injustice that it might do will be to some extent negatived by the reader seeing the grounds upon which the unfavourable inference is based* ... In the next place, in order to give room for the plea of fair comment *the facts must be truly stated*. If the facts upon which the comment purports to be made do not exist the foundation of the plea fails.[43]

In the 1909 South African decision in *Roos v Stent and Pretoria Printing Works Ltd*[44] (*Roos v Stent*), this passage was said to be authority for the proposition that the fair comment defence will not be available where the underlying facts are not stated or referred to in the publication.[45] Two justifications for

---

[39] ibid 43 (emphasis added); see, also similar comments by Birkett LJ, 51.
[40] ibid 51.
[41] *Kemsley v Foot* (n 9) 349–50 (Lord Porter).
[42] ibid 348.
[43] [1908] 2 KB 309, 319–21.
[44] [1909] Transvaal LR 988.
[45] ibid 999 (Innes CJ), 1009–10 (Smith J). Note, however, that Somervell LJ in the Court of Appeal was clearly sceptical that this interpretation of Fletcher Moulton LJ's statement could be supported: 'Fletcher Moulton LJ was referring to cases where comment and fact are intermingled in the words

the requirement were subsequently offered by Innes CJ: 'Because it is impossible to know whether the comments are fair unless we know what the facts are; and because the public must have an opportunity of judging the value of the comments'.[46] Based on *Hunt v Star* and *Roos v Stent*, Kemsley argued that the plea of fair comment was 'not open to the defendants here since the facts on which they allege the article to be comment are neither stated nor referred to therein'.[47]

The defendants, for their part, maintained that the criticism pertained to how Kemsley's newspapers were conducted and that, since the newspapers were widely read, the subject matter of the criticism was readily identified to the reader. The law, they argued, does not require the expression of any further facts beyond the subject matter of the criticism[48] and it certainly does not impose a burden upon a publisher to ensure that the reader be placed in a position to judge for themselves the fairness of the comment in question or, indeed, whether they agree with the conclusions of the commentator.[49] It was argued that *Hunt v Star* did not intend to establish such a rule.[50]

The House of Lords unanimously dismissed the appeal. Lord Porter, with whom the remainder of the court agreed, rejected the distinction that Kemsley sought to draw between criticism of his newspapers and criticism of him personally. He held that fair comment directed at works submitted to the public domain is not limited to criticism of the work; it extends to criticism of the producer in their capacity *as producer*.[51] According to Lord Porter, in the present case:

> Kemsley is held up as worthy of attack on the ground that he is a newspaper proprietor who prostitutes his position by conducting his newspapers or permitting them to be conducted in an undesirable way. In this sense the criticism does not differ from that which takes place when what is called literary criticism comes into question.[52]

His Lordship held that criticism of a newspaper is no different from criticism of any other work,[53] and like the Court of Appeal, held that criticism of such work will amount to fair comment if the subject matter – the work – is indicated.[54]

This finding meant that it was unnecessary for Lord Porter to consider whether the need to specify the underlying facts of a comment, rather than the subject matter, applied outside of the review context. Nevertheless, he proceeded

---

complained of, but Rose Innes CJ extracted a general principle, whether it be right or wrong, from that sentence': *Kemsley v Foot* CA (n 14) 44.

[46] ibid 998 (Innes CJ).

[47] *Kemsley v Foot* (n 9) 348.

[48] ibid 350–51 (Lord Porter).

[49] ibid 351.

[50] ibid 352.

[51] ibid 355–56.

[52] ibid 355.

[53] ibid.

[54] ibid.

to set out what is presented as a general principle applicable to all forms of comment, not just review cases. He said that while the fair comment defence does not require the setting out of *all* of the defendant's underlying facts,[55] the 'question ... in *all* cases is whether there is a *sufficient substratum of fact stated or indicated in the words* which are the subject-matter of the action'.[56] Lord Porter then said that his view was 'well expressed' in the following passage from the sixth edition of *Odgers on Libel and Slander*, which is necessary to set out in full:

> Sometimes, however, it is difficult to distinguish an allegation of fact from an expression of opinion. It often depends on what is stated in the rest of the article. If the defendant accurately states what some public man has really done, and then asserts that 'such conduct is disgraceful', this is merely the expression of his opinion, his comment on the plaintiff's conduct. So, if without setting it out, he identifies the conduct on which he comments by a clear reference. In either case, the defendant *enables his readers to judge for themselves how far his opinion is well founded*; and therefore, what would otherwise have been an allegation of fact becomes merely a comment. But if he asserts that the plaintiff has been guilty of disgraceful conduct, and does not state what that conduct was, this is an allegation of fact for which there is no defence but privilege or truth.[57]

As we shall see, the significance of the apparent 'rule' expounded by Lord Porter[58] – and what he precisely meant by it – has been the source of 'speculation'[59] and contradictory treatment in subsequent case law. There are two main interrelated points of ambiguity: what meaning did Lord Porter attribute to the term 'substratum of fact', and when will such a substratum be deemed sufficient? In particular, does Lord Porter's approval of the passage from *Odgers* indicate that, outside of the review context, readers should be given a sufficient account of the facts to enable them to make their own assessment of the validity or value of the comment? Lord Oaksey, who delivered a short concurring opinion, was perhaps less ambiguous in expressing his view of the law. He said that 'It is not ... a matter of importance that the reader should be able to see *exactly* the grounds of the comment',[60] and that 'It is sufficient if the *subject* which ex hypothesi is of public importance is sufficiently and not incorrectly or untruthfully stated'.[61] However, even on Lord Oaksey's explanation, the

---

[55] ibid 357 (Lord Porter), 361 (Lord Oaksey). See, also, *London Artists Ltd v Littler* [1969] 2 QB 375, 391 (Lord Denning MR).

[56] *Kemsley v Foot* (n 9), 356 (Lord Porter) (emphasis added).

[57] W Blake Odgers and Robert Ritson, *Odgers on Libel and Slander*, 6th edn (Stevens & Sons, London, 1929) 166–67.

[58] The principle was described as a 'rule' by Bingham LJ in *Brent Walker Group plc v Time Out Ltd* [1991] 2 QB 33, 44. See, also, Sharwood (n 25) 23.

[59] Raymond E Brown, *Brown on Defamation: Canada, United Kingdom, Australia, New Zealand, United States*, 2nd edn (Toronto, Thomson Reuters Canada, 2017) [15-56].

[60] *Kemsley v Foot* (n 9) 361 (Lord Oaksey) (emphasis added).

[61] ibid (emphasis added).

question remains: when will the statement of the 'subject' of the comment be considered 'sufficient' and sufficient for what?

Before we move to consider the subsequent treatment of *Kemsley v Foot*, it is necessary to highlight three further points enunciated by Lord Porter. First, Lord Porter said that the underlying facts can be implied, in which case, only the subject matter of the comment will need to be indicated.[62] Importantly, he said that in such cases: '[T]he inquiry *ceases to be* – Can the defendant point to *definite assertions of fact* in the alleged libel upon which comment is made? and *becomes* – Is there *subject-matter* indicated with sufficient clarity to justify comment being made?'[63]

It is at least clear from Lord Porter's judgment that the relevant facts can be implied where they are well known. Indeed, on one reading of Lord Porter's speech,[64] the notoriety of Lord Kemsley and his newspapers was an alternative basis upon which he may have resolved the appeal. He said that it was 'at least arguable that the words directly complained of imply as a matter of fact that Lord Kemsley is in control of a number of known newspapers and that the conduct of those newspapers is in question'.[65] Thus, the defendant was entitled to make the argument:

> We have pointed to your press. It is widely read. Your readers will and the public generally can know at what our criticism is directed. It is not bare comment; it is comment on a well-known matter, much better known, indeed, than a newly printed book or a once-performed play.[66]

But what is unclear from Lord Porter's speech is whether facts can *only* be implied, as indicated by the Court of Appeal, where they are well-known or notorious. Or, can they also be implied where they have simply been put into the public domain or where they are easily accessible, or perhaps even where the publication merely implies that they exist?

Second, in line with the view that not all of the individual facts used to justify the fairness of a comment need be set out in the publication itself, Lord Porter made the point that if the defendant elects to expressly set out in the defamatory matter the facts upon which a comment is based, *all* such facts must be proven to be true.[67] The failure to prove one such fact will see the defence fail. It is implied in Lord Porter's speech and expressly confirmed by Lord Oaksey that this is what is meant by the frequent reference in the cases, including in *Hunt v Star*,

---

[62] ibid 357 (Lord Porter).

[63] ibid (emphasis added).

[64] See, eg, the interpretation of this aspect of *Kemsley v Foot* by the High Court of Australia in *Channel Seven Adelaide Pty Ltd v Manock* [2007] HCA 60, (2007) 232 CLR 245, 279–80.

[65] *Kemsley v Foot* (n 9) 357 (Lord Porter).

[66] ibid.

[67] ibid 357–58. This was modified by the Defamation Act 1952, s 6, which has recently been repealed by the Defamation Act 2013, s 3(8).

to facts underpinning a comment having to be 'truly stated':[68] thus, while the facts need not be set out in full, any facts which are stated must not be *untruly stated*.[69] However, where some or all of the facts relied upon by the defendant to establish a comment's fairness are contained only in the defendant's pleaded particulars (ie where they are extraneous to the publication), no such requirement exists. Instead, all that is required is that enough particularised facts be proven to be true in order to meet the fairness test.[70]

Third, and finally, Lord Porter noted that the main support relied upon by Kemsley for the argument that the underlying facts must be stated was based on the observations of Fletcher Moulton LJ in *Hunt v Star* (quoted above). However, having found that the defendants' reference to Kemsley was a sufficient identification of the subject matter of the comment, Lord Porter dismissed the suggestion that the decision in *Hunt v Star* (or any other case) warranted a different conclusion. He did this on the basis that Fletcher Moulton LJ in *Hunt v Star* was not asked to consider 'whether the facts must be set out in full or whether a reference to well known or easily ascertainable facts was a sufficient statement of those relied on'.[71] Instead, Lord Porter said that the focus of Fletcher Moulton LJ's judgment was distinguishing fact from comment and setting out the principle that the facts pleaded by the defendant must be sufficient to justify the fairness of the comment made upon them.[72] Notably, Lord Porter's treatment of *Hunt v Star* as being confined to the distinction between fact and comment, although probably correct, is confounding given that the passage from *Odgers* relied upon by him to assert the underlying fact requirement seems to be equally focused on the issue of distinguishing fact from comment.[73]

IV. RECEPTION OF LORD PORTER'S 'RULE'

I have already mentioned that the factual basis of a comment will sometimes need to be stated or indicated to enable a statement to be understood by the

---

[68] See, eg, *Hunt v Star Newspaper Company Ltd* [1908] 2 KB 309, 319 (Fletcher Moulton LJ).

[69] *Kemsley v Foot* (n 9), 357–58 (Lord Porter), 361 (Lord Oaksey). See, also, *Kemsley v Foot* CA (n 14) 47–48 (Birkett LJ).

[70] *Kemsley v Foot* (n 9) 358 (Lord Porter). See, also, *London Artists Ltd v Littler* [1969] 2 QB 375, 392–93 (Lord Denning MR).

[71] *Kemsley v Foot* (n 9), 358–60.

[72] ibid 360.

[73] However, there is no contradiction if one adopts Eady J's conclusion in *Lowe v Associated Newspapers Ltd* [2006] EWHC 320 (QB), [2007] QB 580 that Lord Porter's use of the passage from *Odgers* was to emphasise the need to set out a 'sufficient substratum to enable readers to recognise that the words complained of consisted of comment rather than fact' (at 597): see below n 103 and accompanying text.

recipient as comment rather than fact.[74] Historically at least, some cases took this further by declaring that, with the exception of reviews of public works, a statement can *only* qualify as comment if the factual basis of the comment is disclosed by the commentator, or at least is otherwise known or easily ascertained by the person to whom the comment is published.[75] This led to the somewhat strained conclusion that a bare comment, despite being readily identifiable as an inference or conclusion derived from undisclosed facts, can never qualify as comment.[76] Irrespective of whether such per se exclusion from the ambit of comment was or remains correct,[77] following *Kemsley v Foot* it became firmly established for both courts and commentators that the need to state or indicate the underlying facts of a comment operates as a separate rule or element of the defence.[78] Thus, reflecting the language used by Lord Porter, the position was summarised in *Duncan & Neill on Defamation* as follows:

> It is a *necessary ingredient* of fair comment that the comment shall be based on facts which are either *stated by the commentator or indicated by him with sufficient clarity* to enable the reader or listener to ascertain the matter on which the comment is being made.[79]

This passage, which relies on *Kemsley v Foot* as authority, was approved by Bingham LJ in *Brent Walker Group Plc v Time Out Ltd.*[80] More recently,

---

[74] *Cooper v Lawson* (1838) 8 Ad & E 746, 112 ER 1020; *O'Brien v Marquis of Salisbury* (1889) 54 JP 215, 216 (Field J); *Hunt v Star Newspaper Co Ltd* [1908] 2 KB 309, 319 (Fletcher Moulton LJ).

[75] See, eg, *Crawford v Albu* 1917 AD 102, 105; *Goldsbrough v John Fairfax & Sons Ltd* (1934) 34 SR (NSW) 524, 532; *Pryke v Advertiser Newspapers Ltd* (1984) 37 SASR 175, 192 (King CJ): 'A statement can be regarded as comment as distinct from allegation of fact *only* if the facts on which it is based are stated or indicated with sufficient clarity to make it clear that it is comment on those facts' (emphasis added). See, also, Mitchell, *Modern Law of Defamation* (2005) 179 (discussing *O'Brien v Marquis of Salisbury* (1889) 54 JP 215); *Joseph v Spiller* [2010] UKSC 53, [2011] 1 AC 852, 882–83. See, also, *Orr v Isles* [1965] NSWR 677, where Taylor J said (at 698): 'It is rarely possible in a practical sense to comment without stating the facts or otherwise bringing them to the mind of the person who will read the comment. So that to say that a person is to have a right of fair comment on matters of public interest, necessarily contemplates that he is either expressly or by reference to other matter going to state facts, unless his comment be on matters that are notorious'.

[76] *Joseph v Spiller* [2010] UKSC 53, [2011] 1 AC 852, 859, 882–83 (Lord Phillips of Worth Matravers PSC). On this view, the statement 'on the basis of what I know, Jones is a thief', while clearly an inference, will not be considered comment: see Alistair Mullis and Richard Parkes (eds), *Gatley on Libel and Slander*, 12th edn (London, Sweet & Maxwell, 2013), 433 [12.9].

[77] See, eg, *Lowe v Associated Newspapers Ltd* [2006] EWHC 320 (QB); [2007] QB 580, where Eady J (at 599) appeared to accept that a 'bald comment' could be considered comment provided it is possible to understand it as an inference. Note, also, that doubts about such a rule were expressed in *Joseph v Spiller* [2010] UKSC 53, [2011] 1 AC 852, 859, 883.

[78] See, however, *Roos v Stent and Pretoria Printing Works Ltd* [1909] Transvaal LR 988, 1000, where Innes CJ appeared to treat the need to state the facts as a separate question from whether the words are comment: 'Applying that principle to the words complained of, *if these words are comment at all ... they are certainly not comment upon facts stated or referred to in the article*' (emphasis added).

[79] Colin Duncan, Brian Neill and Richard Rampton, *Duncan & Neill on Defamation*, 2nd edn (London, Butterworths, 1983) 58, [12.05] (emphasis added).

[80] [1991] 2 QB 33, 39–40.

courts in England,[81] Australia,[82] Canada,[83] Hong Kong[84] and New Zealand[85] have embraced modern formulations of the fair comment defence that treat the requirement to state or indicate the underlying facts as a standalone element. Thus, although sometimes expressed in different ways, such formulations typically require that the following elements be established: (1) the statement must be comment and not fact; (2) the comment must be on a matter of public interest; (3) the facts upon which the comment is based must be true or protected by privilege; (4) such facts must be sufficiently stated or referred to; and (5) the comment must be fair.[86]

As indicated above, the contentious aspect of *Kemsley v Foot* centres on how Lord Porter's rule applies to cases that do not involve the review of public works and where the facts are not notorious – in other words, non-notorious fact cases. Two divergent interpretations of the rule have emerged in the case law. One interpretation insists, as had been contended by Kemsley in *Kemsley v Foot*, that the facts in support of a comment must be stated or indicated to such a degree that the reader or listener is able to assess the fairness of the comment for themselves. This 'restrictive' approach has been adopted by the High Court of Australia[87] and the Supreme Court of Canada,[88] and was endorsed by Lord Nicholls in two significant appellate decisions – *Reynolds v Times Newspapers Ltd*[89] (House of Lords) and *Cheng v Tse Wai Chun* (Court of Final Appeal of Hong Kong).[90] Thus, in the latter case, in setting out the essential elements of the fair comment defence, Lord Nicholls of Birkenhead said:

> [T]he comment must explicitly or implicitly indicate, at least in general terms, what are the facts on which the comment is being made. *The reader or hearer should be in a position to judge for himself how far the comment was well founded.*[91]

In the important House of Lords case of *Telnikoff v Matusevitch*, on the other hand, Lord Ackner embraced a much more 'liberal' interpretation of Lord Porter's rule.[92] In his dissenting judgment, he made the observation in

---

[81] *Joseph v Spiller* [2010] UKSC 53; [2011] 1 AC 852, 886 (Lord Phillips).
[82] *Channel Seven Adelaide Pty Ltd v Manock* [2007] HCA 60, (2007) 232 CLR 245, 268–70 (Gummow, Hayne, and Heydon JJ). See, also, *Petritsis v Hellenic Herald Pty Ltd* [1978] 2 NSWLR 174, 181 (Reynolds JA); *Orr v Isles* [1965] NSWR 677, 697 (Taylor J).
[83] *WIC Radio Ltd v Simpson* [2008] 2 SCR 420, 446 (McLachlin CJ, Bastarache, Binnie, Deschamps, Fish, Abella, and Charron JJ, delivered by Binnie J).
[84] *Cheng v Tse Wai Chun* (2000) 3 HKLRD 418, 425 (Lord Nicholls of Birkenhead).
[85] *Mitchell v Sprott* [2002] 1 NZLR 766 (CA), 773.
[86] See, eg, *Spiller v Joseph* [2011] 1 AC 852, 858 (Lord Phillips of Worth Matravers PSC).
[87] *Channel Seven Adelaide Pty Ltd v Manock* [2007] HCA 60, (2007) 232 CLR 245.
[88] *WIK Radio Ltd v Simpson* [2008] 2 SCR 420, 445–46 (McLachlin CJ, Bastarache, Binnie, Deschamps, Fish, Abella, and Charron JJ, delivered by Binnie J).
[89] *Reynolds v Times Newspapers Ltd* [2001] 2 AC 127, 201.
[90] *Cheng v Tse Wai Chun* (2000) 3 HKLRD 418, 425, 429, 431.
[91] ibid 425.
[92] *Telnikoff v Matusevitch* [1992] 2 AC 343.

direct reliance upon *Kemsley v Foot* that 'the defence of fair comment is not based on the proposition that every person who reads a criticism should be in a position to judge for himself'.[93] As discussed in the following section, the liberal approach has prevailed in two relatively recent cases in England: *Lowe v Associated Newspapers Ltd* and *Joseph v Spiller*.

V. THE LIBERAL INTERPRETATION IN ENGLAND

A. *Lowe v Associated Newspapers Ltd*

In 2008, Rupert Lowe, the then chairman of Southampton Football Club, brought defamation proceedings in respect of an article published in the *Evening Standard*, a newspaper owned by Associated Newspapers Ltd. The allegations, broadly speaking, were twofold: the first related to his poor treatment of a former club manager, while the second was that he had obtained ownership of the club 'by underhand and dishonest means'.[94] The claimant challenged the newspaper's fair comment defence on the basis that the 'welter of alleged facts' sought to be relied upon by the defendant in defending the allegations were not referred to or indicated in the article.[95] The argument, in essence, was that the dicta of Lord Nicholls in *Reynolds* and *Cheng* require that *all* supporting facts be referred to in the matter *so that the reader can judge the comment for themselves*.[96] Any facts not referred to in the article must therefore be struck from the defendant's pleaded particulars.

Eady J rejected the claimant's challenge to the defendant's pleadings and largely adopted the defendant's submissions on the state of the law. He held that *Reynolds* and *Cheng* are clearly inconsistent with the conclusion in *Kemsley v Foot* that not all facts pleaded in the defendant's particulars are required to be indicated in the comment.[97] Eady J's conclusion in this regard is undoubtedly

---

[93] ibid 361. On a related matter, Lord Keith in *Telnikoff v Matusevitch* said (at 354), directly relying upon *Kemsley v Foot*, that 'where the words complained of are clearly to be recognised as comment, and the subject matter commented on is identified, *then the subject matter must be looked at to determine whether the comment is fair*' (emphasis added). This, of course, is a mischaracterization of what was said in *Kemsley v Foot*. Lord Porter was clear that it is not the subject matter of the comment as expressed in the comment that is relevant for the purpose of assessing fairness, it is the fairness of the comment judged against *true (or privileged) facts*. Some such facts might be contained in the defamatory matter itself, while others may be 'extraneous' to the matter and appear only in the defendant's pleaded particulars: see *Kemsley v Foot* (n 9) 358.

[94] *Lowe v Associated Newspapers Ltd* [2006] EWHC 320 (QB), [2007] QB 580 (QB), 584.

[95] ibid 588.

[96] ibid 594–95.

[97] ibid 595–96. This, of course, assumes that Lord Nicholls in *Reynolds* and *Cheng* required that *all* pleaded facts be set out in the matter. In *Channel Seven Adelaide Pty Ltd v Manock* [2007] HCA 60, (2007) 232 CLR 245, Gummow, Hayne and Heydon JJ said that Lord Nicholls 'did not assert any proposition of that kind' and therefore the 'principal object of the attacks' on his approach in *Lowe* proceeded upon a 'false issue' (at 273–74).

correct and it is perhaps surprising that the issue was litigated as a contentious point given the clear direction in *Kemsley v Foot*.[98] Eady J then went on to say that an approach 'more consonant' with the right to freedom of speech under article 10 of the European Convention on Human Rights and Fundamental Freedoms,[99] and one which is reflected in the judgment of Lord Porter in *Kemsley v Foot*, focuses on 'subject matter': 'comment may be made, *if the matter is already before the public*, without setting out the facts on which the comment is based – provided the subject matter of the comment is plainly stated'.[100] At least as far as the substratum of fact underpinning a comment is well known or notorious, this is indeed an accurate interpretation of Lord Porter's decision in *Kemsley v Foot*.

Given that the underlying facts in *Lowe v Associated Newspapers Ltd* were already before the public and were well known,[101] Eady J did not expressly offer an opinion on the controversial issue of whether simply indicating the subject matter of a comment would be sufficient where the substratum of fact is *not notorious*. This was left to the Supreme Court in the case of *Joseph v Spiller*. However, before turning to consider that case, it is important to highlight that two related aspects of Eady J's judgment suggest that, in his opinion, the restrictive approach in such a case would not apply. First, he rejected that Lord Porter's statement regarding the 'sufficient substratum of fact' in *Kemsley v Foot* stands as authority for the proposition that the underlying facts must always be stated in the comment. Rather, he said that in using the language 'sufficient substratum of fact stated or indicated', 'his Lordship had in mind a sufficient substratum to enable readers to *recognise that the words complained of consisted of comment*'.[102] This is evident, according the Eady J, from Lord Porter's reliance on the passage from *Odgers*, which, in his view, was confined to the issue of distinguishing fact from comment.[103] Second, without reference to authority in support of his position, he concluded that there is no requirement that readers, viewers or listeners should be placed in a position to judge the comment for themselves. Rather, he observed that 'It is difficult to see why it should matter whether a reader agrees; *what matters is whether he or she can distinguish fact from comment*'.[104] On this approach, it seems that the underlying fact element is effectively collapsed into the antecedent question of whether the allegation is fact or comment.

---

[98] See, eg, Thomas Gibbons, 'Demonstrating a Factual Basis for Fair Comment: *Lowe v Associated Newspapers*' (2006) 11 *Communications Law* 29.

[99] Opened for signature 4 November 1950, 213 UNTS 222 (entered into force 3 September 1953).

[100] *Lowe v Associated Newspapers Ltd* [2006] EWHC 320 (QB), [2007] QB 580 (QB) 596.

[101] ibid 596.

[102] ibid 597 (emphasis added).

[103] ibid.

[104] ibid 600 (emphasis added).

B. *Joseph v Spiller*

The application of the rule to cases involving facts that are not notorious or well known was authoritatively resolved in UK law in *Spiller v Joseph* – a case which may itself qualify for 'landmark' status[105] – where the Supreme Court adopted a similar but not identical approach to the one suggested by Eady J in *Lowe v Associated Newspapers Ltd.* An entertainment booking agency and one of its directors sought to defend as fair comment an allegation posted on the booking agency's website that the claimants, the members of musical groups The Gillettes and Saturday Night at the Movies, were 'grossly unprofessional and untrustworthy'.[106] The question for the Supreme Court was whether the defendants had sufficiently referred to the fact that the claimants had breached their contract with the agency as the material fact upon which the comment was based.

The facts of *Joseph v Spiller* provide a useful illustration of the practical difference between the restrictive and liberal approaches. On the former, the defendants would have been required to include in the publication details of the contract and its alleged breach (ie the precise terms of the contract and the conduct of the plaintiff that was said to constitute the breach), so that the reader could 'evaluate whether the breach justified the comment'.[107] On a liberal interpretation, on the other hand, only the broad subject matter – the fact of the breach – would need to be referred to. Given the importance of the distinction, Associated Newspapers Ltd and others intervened, arguing that the proposition expressed by Lord Nicholls in *Reynolds* and *Cheng* could not be reconciled with the decision in *Kemsley v Foot*.

Lord Phillips of Worth Matravers PSC, who gave the lead judgment, held that there was no authority available to him that 'put in doubt the fact that the defence of fair comment required *the facts* upon which the comment was made to be stated or identified in or from the publication'.[108] In apparent contrast to the view of Lord Porter,[109] he held that such a requirement was implicit in the passage from Fletcher Moulton LJ's judgment in *Hunt v Star* (set out above).[110] He said, however, that where comment is in the form of the review of public works or where the underlying facts are already in the public domain, Lord Nicholls's proposition that recipients should be placed in a position to judge the comment for themselves was clearly inconsistent with

---

[105] Brian Pillans, 'A Storm in a Teacup or a Landmark Case? *Joseph v Spiller*' (2011) 16 *Communications Law* 31.
[106] *Joseph v Spiller* [2010] UKSC 53, [2011] 1 AC 852, 862 (Lord Phillips of Worth Matravers PSC).
[107] ibid 889.
[108] ibid 883 (emphasis added).
[109] See above nn 71–72 and accompanying text.
[110] *Joseph v Spiller* [2010] UKSC 53, [2011] 1 AC 852, 868 (Lord Phillips of Worth Matravers PSC).

Kemsley v Foot and should not be followed.[111] Lord Phillips dismissed any suggestion that a different conclusion was warranted based on Lord Porter's endorsement of the statement in *Odgers* that identifying the facts enables readers to judge the comment for themselves. Relying upon the dicta of Lord Ackner in *Telnikoff v Matusevitch*, he said that it is 'fallacious to suggest that readers will be able to form their own views of the validity of the criticism on a matter merely because in the past it was placed in the public domain'.[112] According to Lord Phillips, all that is required, as apparently made clear in *Kemsley v Foot*, is that the *subject matter* of the comment be identified.[113] Unfortunately, Lord Phillips's analysis does not address the point that where the facts are notorious or well known, readers *will be* in a position to judge the comment for themselves; indeed, this may explain why Lord Porter held that specifying the subject matter alone in such circumstances will be sufficient. If this is correct, then there may in fact be no inconsistency between *Kemsley v Foot* and the statements of Lord Nicholls in *Reynolds* and *Cheng* in cases where the underlying facts are matter of general public knowledge.

Lord Phillips then proceeded to ask the question: 'what of the case where the subject matter of the comment is not within the public domain, but is known only to the commentator or to a small circle of which he is one?'[114] In light of the ability of the 'man in the street to make public comment about others' without a reader having access to information to enable them to evaluate such comment, he held that applying Lord Nicholls's proposition would rob the defence of 'much of its efficacy'.[115] He said that the authorities to which he had referred, including *Kemsley v Foot*, 'emphasised repeatedly that the comment should identify the *subject matter* on which it is based'.[116] However, it is clear that by 'subject matter', Lord Phillips was referring to the need to identify 'the general nature of the facts'.[117]

Importantly, Lord Phillips said that the requirement to identify the subject matter, or general facts, was *not* to enable the reader to assess the validity of the comment or to judge it for themselves. All that is required is that the recipient be able to 'identify at least in general terms what it is that has led the commentator to make the comment, so that the reader can understand *what the comment is about* and the commentator can, if challenged, explain by giving particulars'.[118] Lord Phillips said that any suggestion to the contrary in Fletcher Moulton LJ's opinion in *Hunt v Star* was merely obiter, despite his acceptance of that case as

---

[111] ibid 884–85.
[112] ibid 884.
[113] ibid.
[114] ibid 885.
[115] ibid.
[116] ibid.
[117] ibid.
[118] ibid 886 (emphasis added).

authority for the need to state or refer to the underlying facts in the matter. He also said that no fair comment defence had ever 'failed on the ground that the comment did not identify the subject matter on which it was based with sufficient particularity to enable the reader to form his own view as to its validity'.[119] Remarkably, Lord Phillips did not address the possibility that Lord Porter's endorsement of *Odgers* might have been intended to impose such a requirement where comment is based on non-notorious facts.

Lord Phillips said that 'a fair balance must be struck between allowing a critic the freedom to express himself as he will and requiring him to identify to his readers why it is that he is making the criticism'.[120] However, if the need to identify, at least in general terms, the underlying facts of a comment is *not* to enable recipients to judge it for themselves – and is not, therefore, about extending to the subject of the defamatory comment the 'fairness' that such a standard is said to provide – then what is the purpose of the underlying fact requirement? The need to state what the comment is about, broadly speaking, undoubtedly ensures that the reader is provided with a modicum of context for the comment and an indication of what prompted the commentator to make the comment.[121] As pointed out by David Mangan, in reference to Lord Phillips's decision in *Joseph v Spiller*:

> In mandating a line be drawn for the reader between the opinion and the facts upon which it is based, there is an inherent call for responsibility. The spirit which the requirement gives rise to is public discourse; that is, permitting the free discussion so long as context is provided.[122]

However, Lord Phillips did not expressly embrace the need for recipients to be aware of the broad facts as an element of responsibility in expressing public opinion and contributing to public discourse. Instead, he related the need to the other elements of the defence. Thus, he said that the justification for the defence is 'the desirability that a person should be entitled to express his views freely about a matter of public interest'[123] and that 'if the subject matter of the comment is not apparent from the comment this justification for the defence would be lacking'.[124] Furthermore, he said that the requirement that the comment must be based on true facts is 'better enforced' if the factual basis of the comment has to be identified in the matter itself.[125] Apart from observing that it 'may be thought desirable', albeit for unspecified reasons,

---

[119] ibid 885.
[120] ibid 886.
[121] See, eg, David Mangan, 'An Argument for the Common Law Defence of Honest Opinion' (2011) 16 *Communications Law* 140, 144–45.
[122] ibid 144.
[123] *Joseph v Spiller* [2010] UKSC 53, [2011] 1 AC 852, 885.
[124] ibid.
[125] ibid.

that commentators should be required to identify the 'general nature of the facts',[126] it is difficult to see what independent role Lord Phillips considered the underlying fact requirement as playing in the fair comment defence. Indeed, on Lord Phillips's account, it appears to exist merely to ensure that the other elements of the defence are properly adhered to.

VI. THE RESTRICTIVE INTERPRETATION

In contrast to the UK Supreme Court's decision in *Joseph v Spiller*, the Australian and Canadian courts have adopted a much more burdensome interpretation of the underlying fact requirement.[127] In these jurisdictions, the courts have held that in cases where the underlying facts are not notorious, the facts in support of a comment must be stated to such an extent that an ordinary reasonable recipient is in a position to assess the comment for themselves. This understanding of the underlying fact requirement and the meaning of Lord Porter's judgment in *Kemsley v Foot* has been most closely analysed by the High Court of Australia in the case of *Channel Seven Adelaide Pty Ltd v Manock*.

A. *Channel Seven Adelaide Pty Ltd v Manock*

Dr Colin Manock, a forensic pathologist, brought defamation proceedings in relation to a short promotional advertisement for a forthcoming episode of a popular current affairs television programme called *Today Tonight*. According to Manock, the advertisement carried the meaning that he had 'deliberately concealed evidence' in the trials of Henry Keogh, who was twice tried for the 1994 murder of Anna-Jane Cheney. The defendant television station pleaded fair comment but Manock sought to have the particulars of the defence struck out on the basis, inter alia, that the underlying facts in support of the comment were not sufficiently stated or indicated in the words that were spoken (although they were later set out in the episode of the programme itself). Indeed, the defendant's promotion did not indicate or refer to *any* underlying facts, and it could not be argued that they were notorious.

---

[126] ibid.

[127] For the position in Canada, see *WIC Radio Ltd v Simpson* [2008] 2 SCR 420, 446 (McLachlin CJ, Bastarache, Binnie, Deschamps, Fish, Abella, and Charron JJ, delivered by Binnie J). Note the Court did not directly cite *Kemsley v Foot*. Instead, the Court cited *Gatley on Libel and Slander* for the proposition, which cites *Kemsley v Foot*: see Patrick Milmo and WVH Rogers (eds), *Gatley on Libel and Slander*, 10th edn (London, Sweet & Maxwell, 2004), 298 [12.12]. Note, also, the same position prevails in South Africa, although this was established prior to the decision in *Kemsley v Foot*: see, eg, *Roos v Stent and Pretoria Printing Works Ltd* [1909] Transvaal LR 988, 999–1000, 1010; *Crawford v Albu* 1917 AD 102, 126–27; *The Citizen v McBride* 2011 (4) SA 191 (CC).

i. Majority decision

In their joint majority reasons in *Manock*, Gummow, Hayne and Heydon JJ followed the approach of the High Court's earlier decision in *Pervan v North Queensland Newspaper Co Ltd* ('*Pervan*').[128] Gleeson CJ adopted the same approach in separate reasons. Relying on Lord Porter's judgment in *Kemsley v Foot*, the majority in *Pervan* said that the fair comment defence:

> [I]s not lost by the absence of the facts on which the comment is based provided ... [they are] ... sufficiently indicated or notorious to *enable persons to whom the defamatory matter is published to judge for themselves how far the opinion expressed in the comment is well founded.*[129]

To qualify as fair comment, it was said that 'the reader must be able to judge for himself or herself whether it is *fair*'.[130] It is clear that the joint majority in *Manock* saw this finding as consistent with the above quoted passage from *Odgers*, as endorsed by Lord Porter in *Kemsley v Foot*, where the need for recipients to assess the comment is explicitly referred to.[131] They said that based on *Pervan*, as supported by *Odgers*, 'a sufficient linkage between the comment alleged and the factual material relied on' to enable such an assessment can appear in one of three ways: the facts can be (1) expressly stated, (2) referred to, or (3) notorious.[132]

The defendant in *Manock* argued, however, that the adoption of such a restrictive approach misconstrued the decision in *Pervan*. Instead, it pressed for a broad interpretation of *Pervan* and *Kemsley v Foot*, based on the dissenting view of McHugh J in *Pervan*. In particular, it was argued that McHugh J's dissent was not inconsistent with the majority judgment in *Pervan* and therefore could be used to illuminate the majority's reasoning in that case.[133] The defendant argued that McHugh J's approach was based on his view that Lord Porter's reference in *Kemsley v Foot* to 'subject matter' was not confined to review cases or where the underlying facts were notorious. Thus, McHugh J, who (erroneously in my view) equated 'substratum of fact' with 'subject matter' rather than 'individual facts',[134] said (citing *Kemsley v Foot*):

> The defence is available even though the publication does not state or indicate the facts which form the basis of the comment. As long as the *subject-matter* of the comment is identified, the defendant is entitled to the benefit of the defence of fair comment if he or she is able to prove one or more facts which will justify the comment.[135]

---

[128] *Pervan v North Queensland Newspaper Co Ltd* (1993) 178 CLR 309.
[129] ibid 327.
[130] ibid.
[131] *Channel Seven Adelaide Pty Ltd v Manock* [2007] HCA 60; (2007) 232 CLR 245, 271–72.
[132] ibid 272.
[133] ibid 278.
[134] *Pervan v North Queensland Newspaper Co Ltd* (1993) 178 CLR 309, 340.
[135] ibid (emphasis added).

The defendant in *Manock* further relied upon McHugh J's dissenting judgment to reject the specific proposition that the recipient must be placed in a position to judge the value or fairness of the comment for themselves. It was argued that while Lord Porter quoted the relevant passage from *Odgers* containing the sentence that setting out the facts enables the reader to assess the comment, McHugh J had pointed out in *Pervan* that later statements made by Lord Porter could not be reconciled with aspects of that passage.[136] According to the defendant, it therefore followed that Lord Porter could not have intended to endorse that particular sentence from *Odgers*.[137]

The joint majority in *Manock* rejected the defendant's reliance upon McHugh J's broad interpretation of *Kemsley v Foot*. This was for a number of reasons. First, the comments of McHugh J in *Pervan* were held to be dicta.[138] This was because the case turned on the requirements of s 377(8) of the Queensland *Criminal Code*, which, unlike the view of the majority in *Pervan*,[139] McHugh J saw as differing from the common law.

Second, it was said that even if McHugh J's judgment could be read as embracing the principle that in all cases only the *subject matter* need be stated or referred to, which they doubted,[140] they rejected that Lord Porter intended such a broad principle. Thus, they said that Lord Porter 'did not suggest that the principle relevant to plays and spectacles extended to all publications'.[141] Furthermore, such an approach, which in their view would have 'changed the fair comment defence from one of fair comment on facts indicated and accurately stated into one of fair comment on indicated topics of public interest',[142] was not anywhere endorsed in the majority reasons in *Pervan*.[143] In addition, they said that it is clear that the majority in *Pervan*, contrary to the approach of McHugh J, were 'using the expression "substratum of fact" to mean "facts"' and not subject matter.[144]

Finally, they rejected the defendant's argument based on Lord Porter's purported lack of endorsement of the relevant sentence in the passage from *Odgers*. They held that whatever Lord Porter's view in *Kemsley v Foot*, it could not be said that the majority in *Pervan* did not cited the passage with approval, particularly given that it is 'supported by much other authority',[145] including *Hunt v Star*, *Reynolds* and *Cheng*.

---

[136] McHugh J said (at 345) that 'Although Lord Porter said that he found his view "well expressed" in the long extract from *Odgers*, the later passages in his speech – which I have quoted – make it plain that his Lordship was not saying that the fact which justify the comment must be placed before the reader. Quite the contrary': ibid 345.

[137] *Channel Seven Adelaide Pty Ltd v Manock* [2006] HCA 60, (2007) 232 CLR 245, 281.

[138] ibid 279.

[139] *Pervan v North Queensland Newspaper Co Ltd* (1993) 178 CLR 309, 327.

[140] *Channel Seven Adelaide Pty Ltd v Manock* [2007] HCA 60, (2007) 232 CLR 245, 282.

[141] ibid 280.

[142] ibid 282.

[143] ibid.

[144] ibid.

[145] ibid 281.

ii. Dissenting Opinion of Kirby J

In dissent, Kirby J criticised the reliance in the joint reasons on a 'close textual analysis'[146] of *Kemsley v Foot* on the basis that Australian courts are not bound to follow decisions of the House of Lords, 'which was never part of the Australian judicial hierarchy'.[147] Nor, according to Kirby J, was the High Court bound by the approach in *Pervan*; because *Pervan* was concerned with the Queensland *Criminal Code* and not the defence of fair comment under the common law, the majority decision in that case did not answer the 'exact problem' arising in *Manock*.[148] Moreover, the facts at issue in *Pervan* were vastly different from those in *Manock*. Given the lack of binding authority and the novelty of the point, at least for Australia's apex court, Kirby J decided to resolve the issue by reference to broader consideration of 'legal policy and principle'.[149]

Kirby J accepted that the 'general principle' emerging from the case law is that in order 'to be "fair" in a legal sense, a "comment" must sufficiently *identify* the facts on which it is based so that the recipient of the publication may form his or her own view about the comment'.[150] However, in applying this general principle, Kirby J endorsed the dissenting reasoning of McHugh J in *Pervan* and said that the principle that fair comment can be based on facts extraneous to the publication extended beyond cases involving the review of plays and sporting spectacles and the like.[151] Therefore, the question according to Kirby J was whether the facts underpinning the comment in *Manock* were 'sufficiently identified' in the promotion by reference to the future time and place where viewers could watch the full episode of *Today Tonight* to hear the facts and, in turn, judge the comment for themselves.

In answering this question, Kirby J said that changes in communication technologies meant that limited reliance could be placed on previous authorities. *Pervan* was concerned with publication in a newspaper rather than via a brief television promotion;[152] moreover, *Kemsley v Foot* was decided and *Odgers* was published well before television developed into the mass medium of communication that it is today.[153] Thus, he said:

> Because [the fair comment] defence is very important to the maintenance of free expression in Australian society, it is essential that the understanding of the ambit

---

[146] ibid 303.
[147] ibid 302–03.
[148] ibid 303–04.
[149] ibid 306–07.
[150] ibid 304. This, of course, misstates the law. The question of the fairness of a comment, in a legal sense, can be based on facts included or referred to in the publication or on facts extraneous to the publication, or a combination of both: see above nn 67–70 and accompanying text. Also, fairness in a legal sense is not judged by reference to whether the recipient agrees or does not agree with the comment: see above nn 3–8 and accompanying text.
[151] ibid 305–06.
[152] ibid 306.
[153] ibid.

of the defence at common law should keep pace with (and be relevant to) the new technology by which comment is now often published.[154]

Given that many new modes of communication tend to 'place a high premium on brevity', he said that the 'practical availability' of the defence would be destroyed if a publisher were always required to set out 'all relevant facts that a recipient would need to judge the "fairness" of the comment'.[155] To remove the availability of the defence on the basis of such a universal rule would amount to so serious an erosion of the right to freedom of expression that it should be rejected. Instead, he said that in the context of 'abbreviated electronic communications', it is not unreasonable for facts to be treated as sufficiently identified if they can be accessed 'conveniently and with reasonable promptness' by a recipient of the comment.[156] On the facts at issue in *Manock*, Kirby J held that it was open to a trier of fact to find that such a test was satisfied.

VII. CONCLUDING COMMENTS

Lord Walker of Gestingthorpe in *Joseph v Spiller* described the House of Lords decision in *Kemsley v Foot* as an 'important milestone' in the development of the law of fair comment.[157] Given the legal significance of the case, it is extraordinary that Lord Porter's judgment has led to such wildly differing interpretations as to the meaning of the underlying fact requirement. Indeed, the distance between the restrictive and liberal approaches could scarcely be further apart. This raises the obvious question: what interpretation *should be* given to the rule set out in *Kemsley v Foot*? This necessitates an examination of what purpose the rule is designed to serve and, perhaps more importantly, how such a purpose fits within the broader role of the fair comment defence in defamation law.

For example, if one takes a particularly 'speaker-centric' view of the fair comment defence, it may be that the liberal interpretation is sufficient. Provided recipients can understand the statement as comment and are able to identify what the comment is broadly about, it may not matter whether a recipient can judge the comment for themselves. It might be thought that the victim of the defamatory comment will receive adequate protection of their reputational interests by virtue of the fact that the statement is recognisable as the commentator's mere opinion (rather than an authoritative statement of fact)[158] and because the defendant is required to prove at trial that the comment has a true

---

[154] ibid 307.
[155] ibid 307.
[156] ibid 309.
[157] *Joseph v Spiller* [2010] UKSC 53, [2011] 1 AC 852, 890 (Lord Walker).
[158] For a discussion of the nature of comment in this sense, see Eric Descheemaeker, 'Mapping Defamation Defences' (2015) 78 *Modern Law Review* 641, 653–57.

(or privileged) factual basis and that it satisfies the criterion of 'fairness'. Alternatively, the fair comment defence might be seen as grounded in promoting a particular type of speech: that of reasoned and responsible debate.[159] If so, to achieve this goal it might be a necessary precondition of the defence that the reader be able to assess the precise reasoning of the commentator so that the recipient can both evaluate the comment and make their own contribution to the debate.

Of course, a detailed examination of such normative considerations is beyond the scope of this chapter. Suffice to say that it is unfortunate that none of the cases discussed above has either directly or adequately addressed the fundamental connection between the justifications for the fair comment defence and the content of the underlying fact rule, whichever interpretation of the rule has been adopted. Indeed, Lord Phillips in *Joseph v Spiller*, as I have explained, was content to link the rule to the other elements of the defence, while the Australian High Court in *Manock* adopted the restrictive interpretation without any sustained critical reflection on *why* it is necessary that readers be able to judge the comment for themselves. It is only once the courts engage with a detailed evaluation of the foundations of the defence, beyond sweeping statements about freedom of speech, that the nature and extent of Lord Porter's rule can be properly established.

---

[159] See, eg, Jaffey, 'The Right to Comment' (1973) 67–68; Mitchell (n 15) 176, 179; Mangan, 'Common Law Defence' (2011) 144–45.

5

Lewis v Daily Telegraph *(1964)*

ERIC BARENDT

I. INTRODUCTION

THE DETERMINATION OF meaning is often the most crucial issue in a libel case, for it is necessary to resolve questions of meaning before it can be ruled, for example, whether the relevant words defamed the claimant and whether the defendant has proved their truth in order to make out a defence of justification or of honest opinion. The decision of the House of Lords in *Lewis v Daily Telegraph* (reported under the name *Rubber Improvement Ltd v Daily Telegraph*[1]) is without doubt the leading modern ruling on the approach courts should take to resolve meaning issues, though, as will be explained later, its significance has been a little eclipsed by some recent rulings of the English courts. *Lewis* was also a very important ruling on the assessment of damages. The jury had made what can only be regarded as extravagantly large awards of damages to the plaintiffs,[2] Lewis and Rubber Improvement Ltd, of which he was chairman. Both the Court of Appeal and the House of Lords found the damages excessive and would on that ground alone have ordered a new trial, though they took that course principally because the trial judge had given an inadequate direction to the jury on the meaning of the defamatory material.

It is important when assessing the importance of the Law Lords ruling in *Lewis* to appreciate that at the time of the proceedings – the early 1960s – and indeed until recently most libel actions in England, as in other common law jurisdictions, were subject to trial by jury. It has been for the jury to determine what the words mean and whether the defendant had made out a good defence, while the role of the judge was to determine whether the words were capable of bearing the meanings alleged by the parties. The jury also assessed the damages

---

[1] [1964] AC 234 (*Lewis*).
[2] The term 'plaintiffs' is used, as it was current at that time in English law. They are now 'claimants'.

to be awarded a successful plaintiff. The rulings in *Lewis* concerned the terms of the directions given by the judge, Salmon J, to the jury on the meaning of the words in two newspaper articles, and to a lesser extent the ability of appellate courts to control jury awards of damages. But *Lewis* has been followed in libel cases tried by a judge without a jury, so this change in the mode of trial does not affect the significance of the decision – though it does mean that the terms of the judgments in the House of Lords now read rather oddly, at least in England where trial by jury has in effect been abolished by recent legislation.[3]

II. THE LEGAL BACKGROUND

Courts have long wrestled with questions of meaning.[4] The leading decision was that of the House of Lords towards the end of the nineteenth century in *Capital and Counties Bank Ltd v Henty and Sons*,[5] which was much discussed in the litigation in *Lewis*. The defendants, a firm of brewers, had informed their customers that they would no longer accept cheques drawn on the plaintiff bank after a row between them and the branch of the bank in Chichester. By a majority of 4:1 the House ruled that the words were not capable of bearing a defamatory meaning. The test was whether reasonable men, to whom the publication was made, would be likely to understand it in a defamatory sense.[6] It would be wrong to infer from the words used in the circular to the brewer's customers that the bank was about to collapse, even though it seems that a number of account-holders had drawn that inference and withdrawn their accounts. Whatever the merits of the actual decision on the facts in this case (see section V A below), the approach of the House of Lords in *Henty* was followed in a number of subsequent cases.[7] That approach was refined and developed by the House of Lords in *Lewis* in a novel context.

Henty concerned the natural and ordinary meaning of the words used in the allegedly defamatory material. But in some instances apparently innocuous words may take on a defamatory meaning because of some extrinsic facts or circumstances which are known to the readers (or viewers) who are likely to have access to them. The classic example is that of the publication of an article reporting that a man entered a certain house; this apparently harmless report bears a defamatory meaning for those who know that the house is a brothel.[8]

---

[3] Defamation Act 2013, s 11 removed the presumption of jury trial for libel and slander cases.

[4] For an historical account of interpretation in libel law, see P Mitchell, *The Making of the Modern Law of Defamation* (Oxford, Hart, 2005) ch 3.

[5] *Capital and Counties Bank Ltd v Henty and Sons* (1882) 7 App Cas 741.

[6] ibid 745, per Lord Selborne, LC. Lord Blackburn at 772 said the court should ascribe the meaning to the words in which they would be understood by ordinary persons.

[7] See, for example, *Nevill v Fine Art and General Insurance Co Ltd* [1897] AC 68, HL; *English and Scottish Co-operative Properties Mortgage and Investment Society Ltd v Odhams Press Ltd* [1940] 1 KB 440, CA; *Turner v MGM Pictures Ltd* [1950] 1 All ER 449, HL.

[8] See the speech of Lord Devlin in *Lewis*, n 1 above, at 278.

This is known as an *innuendo* meaning; it provides a separate cause of action from that arising from the publication of words understood as defamatory in their natural and ordinary meaning. The plaintiff (now in England the claimant) must plead and prove the extrinsic facts which are relied on to constitute an innuendo.[9] An innuendo meaning must be distinguished from the implications which may be drawn from the words used in the article, a distinction made most sharply by the Court of Appeal in *Grubb v Bristol United Press*,[10] a decision reached just two weeks before its own ruling in *Lewis* (see section III B below). Although *Lewis* did not itself raise a real innuendo meaning, there was much discussion in it, particularly in Lord Devlin's speech in the House of Lords, of the difference between innuendoes and inferences from the natural and ordinary meaning of words; an understanding of this difference is therefore necessary to appreciate the significance of the ruling in *Lewis*.

III. THE *LEWIS* CASE

A. The Facts and the Parties

On 23 December 1958, two large circulation London newspapers, the *Daily Telegraph* and the *Daily Mail*, published similar reports on their front pages to the effect that the City of London Fraud Squad 'are inquiring into the affairs of Rubber Improvement Ltd', the chairman of which 'is Mr John Lewis, former Socialist MP' for Bolton. There were similar dramatic headlines to the reports, 'INQUIRY ON FIRM BY CITY POLICE' in the *Daily Telegraph*, 'FRAUD SQUAD PROBE FIRM' in the *Daily Mail*. The *Daily Telegraph* report, but not that in the *Daily Mail*, made it clear that the investigation had been requested after criticisms of the chairman's statement and the accounts by a shareholder at the recent company meeting. (The shareholder might have been the source for the newspapers' reports, though they might have alternatively have emanated from a police leak.[11]) The company and John Lewis immediately brought libel actions against the two newspapers; their actions against each newspaper were consolidated, so there were two proceedings, one against the *Daily Telegraph* and one against the *Daily Mail*, the latter being heard a few days after the former.

John Lewis had been a Labour MP for Bolton from 1945 to 1951, when that constituency was represented by two MPs, and then MP for Bolton West

---

[9] Following changes to pleading rules which were made on the recommendation of the Porter Committee on the Law of Defamation, Cmd 7536 (1948) 165–66.

[10] *Grubb v Bristol United Press Ltd* [1963] 1 QB 309.

[11] Lewis said in evidence he had been told by the *Daily Telegraph* City editor that the report must have come from 'one of the crime boys': *The Times*, 19 July 1961, 5. Also see Holroyd Pearce LJ in the Court of Appeal: *Lewis v Daily Telegraph Ltd* [1963] 1 QB 340, 378.

from 1950 to 1951. In 1951 he lost the constituency to the Liberal candidate, Arthur Holt. He had been Parliamentary Private Secretary to the Postmaster General for a few months in 1950, but otherwise his political career seems to have been relatively undistinguished. He had, however, been a leading rubber technologist, and was the inventor of a number of rubber substitutes which had been widely used in the Second World War.[12] The Rubber Improvement company had been established by his father; the *Daily Telegraph* report stated it had authorised capital of £1 million, while the *Daily Mail* referred to 'the £4,000,000 group' whose shares had recently declined sharply in value. Lewis had also been a Steward of the British Boxing Board of Control for a number of years, and owned a racehorse, perhaps unusual activities for a Labour MP.[13] The political journalist, Alan Watkins, in his book on the unsuccessful libel action brought by another Labour MP, Michael Meacher, against *The Observer*, described Lewis as a litigant with 'a vindictive disposition'.[14] On the other hand Neville Faulks, the leading counsel for the two newspapers in the libel actions, clearly had some respect for Lewis without finding him an entirely sympathetic character.[15]

The two newspapers involved in the litigation were then (and are now) strong supporters of the Conservative party, so it is perhaps unsurprising that they reported this story of an investigation into the affairs of a company whose chairman was a former Labour MP, and that he was described as a 'Socialist'. But there was no suggestion that the newspapers acted out of any particular hostility to Lewis; moreover, there were no issues of malice for the courts to resolve.

B. The Cases in the High Court and the Court of Appeal

The cases were heard in July 1961 before Salmon J and two juries. The plaintiffs argued that the words in the reports meant that the affairs of the company were conducted fraudulently or dishonestly, or in such a way that the police suspected their affairs were so conducted. Against that interpretation of the words, the defendants contended that they meant only that the police were investigating the company, and that on this understanding the allegation was true. In their view the words could not bear the meanings put forward by the plaintiffs. It was argued, in the jury's absence, in the action against the *Daily Telegraph*[16]

---

[12] Information provided by *The Times House of Commons Guide for 1950*, 90 and *Who's Who of British MPs* Vol IV, 216.

[13] See the description of Lewis by Sir Neville Faulks in his memoir, *A Law unto Myself* (London, William Kimber, 1978) 104. Chapter 12 of this book is devoted to the *Lewis* case.

[14] *A Slight Case of Libel: Meacher v Trelford and others* (London, Duckworth, 1990) 22.

[15] See n 13 above.

[16] In the *Daily Mail* case the defendant did not argue that the innuendo meaning should be struck out.

that the plaintiffs' extended meaning involved an innuendo and should be withdrawn from the jury, but this contention was rejected by Salmon J.[17] He ruled that it was unnecessary for the plaintiffs in this case to have pleaded an innuendo meaning, but no harm had been done to the defendants by its pleading; this complex issue is considered fully in section IV C below.

The first question for the jury was simply whether it found for the plaintiffs or for the defendants on the issue of meaning: did the words imply, as the plaintiffs argued, guilt or suspicion, or only report an inquiry into the company's affairs? This was essentially a matter for the jury; indeed Salmon J's direction stated his view that a jury decision was the only proper way of determining how the ordinary man and woman would understand a newspaper report of this kind. Secondly, if the jury found for the plaintiffs on the question of meaning, then it must determine how much to award them. If, on the other hand, it found that the words meant only that an inquiry was under way, it was for the defendant newspaper to justify that story.

After deliberating for nearly two hours the jury in the *Daily Telegraph* action asked for evidence of movements in the share value of Rubber Improvement Ltd as a result of the newspaper report, but the judge indicated that no evidence had been called on the matter. After a further 20 minutes the jury returned a verdict for the plaintiffs, awarding Lewis £25,000 and the company £75,000.[18] The jury in the action against the *Daily Mail* heard two days later was informed by the plaintiffs' counsel of the awards in the earlier action; it reached the same verdict and awarded Lewis £17,000 and the company £100,000.[19] The jury might have made a more generous award to the company in this case, because there was evidence before it, in contrast to that available to the jury in the earlier proceedings, that there had been a decline in the company's share value subsequent to the newspaper reports. Moreover, the *Daily Telegraph* had published the following day a statement by John Lewis on its report, but the *Daily Mail* had not. The total of the two jury awards to the plaintiffs was therefore £217,000, equivalent now to a sum of over £4,550,000 – a quite phenomenal figure understandably found excessive by the appellate courts.

The Court of Appeal upheld the defendants' appeals and ordered new trials.[20] Two members of the Court, Holroyd Pearce LJ[21] and Havers J, held that the judge should have ruled that the words could not be understood to suggest the plaintiffs were guilty of fraud; that allegation raised an innuendo which should not have been left to the jury, nor was it a reasonable implication of the words in the newspaper reports. Davies LJ took a different line.

---

[17] See the full summary of the pleadings and the argument before Salmon J in the report of the House of Lords decision: *Lewis*, n 1 above at 238–41.

[18] See the report in *The Times,* 20 July 1961, 5.

[19] For a report of the *Daily Mail* proceedings, see *The Times,* 22 July 1961, 4.

[20] *Lewis v Daily Telegraph Ltd* [1963] 1 QB 340 (*Lewis* CA).

[21] Subsequently as Lord Pearce he was a member of the House of Lords.

He would have agreed with the judge that the words could be understood as amounting to an allegation of fraud, though he did not think the direction to the jury was sufficiently precise. But all three members of the Court of Appeal ruled that a new trial should be ordered on the assessment of damages, which were clearly excessive in view of the absence of cogent evidence of real financial loss as a result of the reports.[22] On this point also the jury had not been given an adequate direction. Holroyd Pearce LJ was particularly blunt: the damages awarded by the jury were 'divorced from reality'.[23]

C. The Decision of the House of Lords

The Lords heard the plaintiffs' appeal over nine days in December 1962, and unanimously dismissed it in March 1963. The Court of Appeal's order for a new trial was therefore confirmed. Four members of the House – Lords Reid, Jenkins,[24] Hodson and Devlin – agreed with the majority of the Court of Appeal that the words in the report were not capable of being understood as imputing guilt, though they might be understood as alleging suspicion of fraud. As Lord Reid put it, an ordinary man 'not avid for scandal' would not infer guilt from reading that a police inquiry was taking place.[25] The trial judge's direction to the jury was therefore inadequate; he should have told it that the reports could not be understood to allege guilt. Lord Morris of Borth-y-Gest dissented from the majority on this question of meaning, without disagreeing from its view that a proper direction should always be given by the judge to the jury on the interpretation of the words. In his opinion some reasonable readers might have taken the view that the words meant there was an inquiry because of some fraud or dishonesty occasioning it; a 'fair-minded reader would assume that a responsible newspaper would also be fair in its reporting', and would not have dared to publish the story unless there was some basis for thinking that there had been fraud or dishonesty.[26] The coherence of the majority approach to the meaning of the language used in a defamation case and the significance of the disagreement between the judges on its interpretation are explored later in this chapter; see section IV A and section V below.

The House of Lords was however unanimous on the other point in the appeal; a new trial must be ordered as the damages awarded by the jury were 'far too high',[27] 'excessive',[28] or in Lord Devlin's robust phrase 'ridiculously

---

[22] There was no allegation by either of the plaintiffs of special damages, which must be pleaded and proved.

[23] *Lewis* CA, n 20 above, 375.

[24] Lord Jenkins was unable to be present for the decision and Lord Reid reported that he concurred: *Lewis* (n 1) at 262.

[25] ibid n 1 at 260.

[26] ibid 268–69.

[27] ibid 260 per Lord Reid.

[28] ibid 269 per Lord Morris, at 276 per Lord Hodson.

out of proportion to the injury suffered'.[29] The sums awarded by the juries in the two actions were indeed, as already mentioned, phenomenal. There was no substantial evidence that the publication of the reports had been responsible for any loss. Lord Reid made a number of points about the awards of damages,[30] the first of which was that they must have been made on the erroneous assumption that the reports did allege actual guilt; they could not possibly stand if at most suspicion of the offence were alleged. Secondly, a clear direction to each jury should have been given to consider how far the loss suffered by the plaintiffs was to be attributed solely to the libellous report with which it was concerned, rather than as a joint result of the two reports.[31] This was in effect required by section 12 of the Defamation Act 1952, which enables a defendant to give evidence in mitigation of damages that the plaintiff has already received an award, or has taken proceedings, in respect of the publication of words to the same effect as those for which the action was brought. A clear direction was needed to achieve the object of the statutory provision to prevent the over-compensation of a plaintiff successful in two actions based on very similar publications.

Lord Reid's third point was that the juries should have been directed to make an allowance for the income tax which the plaintiffs would have had to pay on any income (or in the company's case profits) lost as a result of the reports, for which libel damages might be awarded.[32] This principle would not apply to general damages intended to vindicate a successful plaintiff's reputation or to compensate for injured feelings. Lord Reid pointed out that a company is not entitled to compensation for injured feelings, but insofar as compensation had been awarded it for loss of profits its taxation position should be considered.[33] Otherwise a corporate body which wins a libel action would be overcompensated, for it would recover a capital sum which had been assessed without regard to the fact that tax would have been paid on the income which it represented. The extravagant sums awarded to Rubber Improvement Ltd (£75,000 and £100,000) would hardly have been awarded if the jury had taken account of the tax it would have paid on its profits.

It is appropriate at this point to comment briefly on the significance of *Lewis* with regard to the control of jury awards of damages in libel cases. The decision of the House of Lords (and the earlier ruling of the Court of Appeal) on the award of damages attracted at the time as much scholarly attention as their rulings on meaning.[34] Before the 1990s it was very unusual indeed for an

---

[29] ibid 287.

[30] Lords Morris and Hodson made the same points more briefly: ibid 269–70 and 276–77 respectively.

[31] ibid 261.

[32] The House of Lords applied the principle in *British Transport Commission v Gourley* [1956] AC 185, a personal injuries case.

[33] *Lewis* (n 1) at 262.

[34] See the notes by A Samuels, 'Excessive Damages for Defamation' (1963) 79 *Law Quarterly Rev* 489, and on the Court of Appeal decision, AL Armitage (1962) *Cambridge Law Journal* 158.

appellate court to interfere with jury awards.[35] The practice was to intervene only if the award was so excessive that no jury could reasonably have made it.[36] The Court of Appeal confirmed this position shortly after *Lewis,* when it held it should order a new trial when an award was wholly irrational; but it ordered a new trial in this case when the plaintiff had been awarded £9,000, a very modest sum in comparison with the awards to Lewis and Rubber Improvement Ltd.[37] The ruling in *Lewis* on damages was cited by two members of the court.[38] More recently the Court of Appeal in England has acquired power under legislation to vary a jury award as an alternative to the more cumbersome and expensive procedure of ordering a new trial.[39] Lord Reid's dictum that corporations may not recover damages for injury to feelings has been followed, so that they cannot recover the aggravated damages which may be awarded successful libel claimants who have suffered further distress as a result of the way in which the defendant has conducted its case.[40] On these points as well as on the application to defamation cases of the requirement to take account of taxation in assessing damages, *Lewis* was an important ruling, which influenced the development of this area of law.

D. The Aftermath

Following the litigation Rubber Improvement Ltd went into liquidation and disputes arose between Lewis and the liquidator with regard to their respective liability for the costs of the appeals to the Court of Appeal and House of Lords which had been ordered by the House.[41] In June 1963 the actions were set down for rehearing. Shortly afterwards, Lewis applied for an order deconsolidating his action from that of the company, while the newspaper defendants applied to have the actions against them consolidated into one action. Lewis's application was rejected, but the defendants' application for a comprehensive consolidation was granted; these orders were upheld by the Court of Appeal. The only difference between the claims concerned damages: Lewis claimed general damages, while the company liquidator would claim special damages for loss of business. It was clearly more convenient to resolve all the issues in a single trial.[42]

A settlement of the claims was eventually reached in December 1964 about six years after the publication of the offending reports. Under it Lewis

---

[35] See Mitchell (n 4) 53–56. Gatley. *Libel and Slander*, 5th edn (London, Sweet and Maxwell, 1960), para 1202 pointed out that a new trial was seldom ordered.

[36] *Praed v Graham* (1889) 24 QBD 53, CA.

[37] *McCarey v Associated Newspapers (No 2)* [1965] 2 QB 86.

[38] ibid 102 per Pearson LJ, at 111 per Willmer LJ.

[39] Courts and Legal Services Act 1990, s 8.

[40] *Collins Stewart Ltd v The Financial Times Ltd* [2006] EMLR 5, [2005] EWHC 262 (QB), Gray J, 31.

[41] *Lewis* (n 1) at 262. The costs of the abortive trial were to await the result of the new trial.

[42] *Lewis v Daily Telegraph (No 2)* [1964] 2 QB 601.

received £6,000 from each newspaper, a total sum equivalent to over £250,000 today. The claim of Rubber Improvement was settled at £5,000 from each defendant, a drastic reduction from the fantastic sums awarded by the juries. The newspapers paid the costs of the actions and waived the costs of the appeals due to them under the order of the House of Lords.[43] This settlement was apparently reached without the advice of counsel.[44]

IV. THE ASCERTAINMENT OF MEANING IN *LEWIS*

Lewis is a landmark case because of the approach of the House of Lords to the ascertainment of meaning. The most important aspect of this approach is the elaboration of the 'ordinary man' test which had been formulated in earlier cases and its application to the facts of the case. But two other aspects merit discussion: the distinction drawn by the Law Lords between an allegation of suspicion and the repetition of a rumour, and their treatment of innuendo meanings.

A. Interpretation by the Ordinary Man

Lord Reid began by saying that in libel cases the question was what the words meant to the ordinary man. He elaborated this traditional approach in the following well-known passage:[45]

> The ordinary man does not live in an ivory tower and he is not inhibited by a knowledge of the rules of construction. So he can and does read between the lines in the light of his general knowledge and experience of worldly affairs.

Leaving aside innuendo meanings (which Lord Reid himself did not discuss) the question was what an ordinary man would take to be 'the natural and ordinary meaning of the words'. But that expression concealed the fact that there are two elements to an ordinary meaning: there is the plain literal meaning of the actual words, and there are inferences which can properly be drawn from them. Often the defamatory sting lies in the inference which can be drawn from the words, as here from the report that the police were making an inquiry into the affairs of the company.

While it is for the jury to determine the meaning of the words, the judge must rule whether they are capable of bearing the meanings attributed to them.[46] The judge should consider the most damaging meaning ordinary people, neither

---

[43] *The Times,* 18 December 1964, 4.
[44] According to Neville Faulks's memoir (n 12) at 110.
[45] *Lewis* (n 1) at 258.
[46] Lord Reid on this point followed the earlier decisions of the House of Lords in *Capital and Counties Bank v Henty* (n 5) and *Nevill v Fine Art & Insurance Co Ltd* (n 7).

unduly suspicious nor very naïve, would put on the words, and by implication exclude from the jury's consideration any more extreme interpretation. At this point Lord Reid imagined a discussion between members of the public – a hypothetical jury – of the newspaper reports in this case. Doubtless some readers would say that if the fraud squad were involved, then the people looked into must be guilty, but others would respond that they should not jump to conclusions and should wait for the result of the inquiry.[47] He concluded that the ordinary man, 'not avid for scandal', would not infer guilt from the report and the judge should have directed the jury in those terms. The paragraphs in the report might mean suspicion, but they could not be read to imply guilt.

Lords Hodson and Devlin took the same approach as Lord Reid to the ascertainment of meaning, both generally and in the context of this case. In a libel case the meaning of the words was a question of fact, not of law, and the ordinary man cannot be expected to adopt the same approach as a lawyer construing a contract or other legal document. Lord Hodson said that to infer guilt from the report would be to take two steps by drawing an inference of guilt from the inference of suspicion. That would be quite unreasonable.[48] Lord Devlin agreed. Laymen are more inclined than lawyers to draw implications from the words, and are especially prone to do this when they are derogatory.[49] However, while the statement that an inquiry was under way could give the impression that there were grounds for suspicion, it could not convey the further impression of guilt.[50] On the other hand, while sharing the general approach of the majority to the ascertainment of meaning,[51] Lord Morris, as has been explained, took the view that the ordinary reader of the reports might well have derived an impression of guilt from the newspaper reports. This is perhaps a more realistic view of the impressions formed by the ordinary man on reading an article. Lord Reid's approach is open to criticism, as will be discussed later.

B. Suspicion and Rumour

An argument strongly pressed by the plaintiffs' counsel, Helenus Milmo, QC before the House was that the 'rumour' principle meant that any reporting of a suspected offence had to be treated as an allegation that the offence had been committed, and therefore could only be justified by showing that the offence had in fact been committed.[52] Under this principle, usually now known as the

---

[47] *Lewis* (n 1) at 259–60.
[48] ibid 274. The High Court of Australia has also held that it is wrong to draw an inference of guilt from an inference of suspicion: *Mirror Newspapers Ltd v Harrison* (1982) 149 CLR 293, at 298–300 per Mason J.
[49] *Lewis* (n 1) at 277.
[50] ibid 285–86.
[51] ibid 264–65.
[52] *Lewis* (n 1) at 260. Helenus Milmo became a High Court judge in 1964.

'repetition rule',[53] the spread of a rumour that X has committed fraud is tantamount to making the allegation that X is guilty of fraud. It is no defence for, say, a newspaper defendant to argue that it is merely reporting the rumour; it must prove the truth of the facts alleged in the rumour.

The argument was rejected by the House of Lords. Lords Hodson and Devlin dealt with it fully. The former said that rumour and suspicion differ essentially from one another. While the spread of a rumour amounted to a republication of a libel, there is a clear difference between the report of a suspicion and an allegation of actual guilt.[54] For Lord Devlin, this was not a case of repetition or rumour. Even if it was to be treated as a rumour case, it remained necessary to find out what the rumour was about: suspicion or guilt. There was a difference between a rumour of suspicion and a rumour of guilt. The plaintiffs' argument was really an attempt to collapse the distinction between an allegation of suspicion and one of guilt, which could not be accepted in this case where there was no mention in the report of any ground for suspicion other than the fact of the police inquiry.[55]

There can be little quarrel with this aspect of the reasoning of the House of Lords which has never been seriously challenged. The rumour principle (or repetition rule) is perhaps itself a rather artificial principle of construction; many ordinary readers might think there is a difference between an allegation in a newspaper that X is guilty and the dissemination by it of a rumour that X is guilty. The principle may be too well established to be challenged, but it was right not to extend it to blur the distinction between a report of suspicion and an allegation of actual guilt.

C. Innuendo Meanings

The most complex aspect of the House of Lords ruling in *Lewis* was its treatment of innuendoes. The difficulty arose because the plaintiffs' pleading could be read as raising the allegation of guilt as an innuendo meaning, but no extrinsic facts had been pleaded or proved to support an innuendo.[56] Salmon J had rejected the defendants' argument that no innuendo should be left to the jury for it to consider; but in his view no innuendo was necessary and he left the jury to consider whether the words in the report could be understood to allege guilt in their ordinary and natural meaning. The Court of Appeal ruled he had been wrong not to withdraw the innuendo meaning from the jury or give it any directions on the matter.[57]

---

[53] This term has been usual since the decision of the Court of Appeal in *Stern v Piper* [1997] QB 123.

[54] *Lewis* (n 1) at 274–75.

[55] ibid 283–85.

[56] See the argument of Neville Faulks, QC before the House of Lords, ibid 251.

[57] *Lewis* CA (n 20).

Three Law Lords considered at some length the possibility of an innuendo meaning in the case. Lord Morris was inclined to agree with the Court of Appeal that in the absence of extrinsic facts to support an innuendo, the judge should have directed the jury that he was not leaving any innuendo meaning for it to consider. But this omission did not matter if, as in this case, the meanings in the pleaded innuendo did not go any further than the ordinary and natural meaning of the words used in the reports. So it was really quite unnecessary for the judge to have told the jury anything about innuendo meanings or even to use the word at all.[58] Lord Hodson was very clear on the issue. The plaintiffs' pleading had blurred the distinction between 'true' and 'false' innuendoes. The former required the pleading and proof of the extrinsic facts which supported the innuendo, while the latter amounted only to inferences from the actual words. The problem was that the plaintiffs' pleading had raised, or had purported to raise, a true innuendo, but was unsupported by any extraneous facts. It should not have been left to the jury.

Lord Devlin devoted much of his long concurring speech to points about innuendoes and their pleading. He disliked the description 'false' innuendo, for it showed a regrettable divergence between legal and popular usage of the term 'innuendo'. He preferred to describe an innuendo which constitutes a separate cause of action and which must be supported by evidence of extrinsic facts as a 'legal' innuendo. Ideally in defamation actions the pleading should clearly set out the possible meanings in three separate paragraphs: the plain meaning of the words, the implications or inferences which may be drawn from these words as a 'popular' innuendo, and the secondary meaning or 'legal' innuendo with particulars of the facts and other matters which support it.[59] He thought it was desirable to plead a popular innuendo clearly, in fairness to the defendant who would then know the plaintiffs' case on meaning. But the House was not ruling that such pleading was necessary. He did not agree with the Court of Appeal that a new trial should be ordered merely because the judge had failed to direct the jury about the innuendo meanings. Salmon J had left it in substance to consider whether the report raised a popular innuendo, although in form the plaintiffs' case appeared to raise a legal innuendo; the jury was not in any way misled by the failure to issue a clear direction on innuendo meanings.[60]

While the discussion of innuendoes in *Lewis* is rich and complex, particularly in Lord Devlin's speech, it was of relatively little significance for the decision. The key point was the judge's failure to give a proper direction to the jury about the natural meaning of the words, not his omission to exclude the innuendo meaning. But *Lewis* confirmed the distinction which had recently been drawn

---

[58] *Lewis* (n 1) 263–65.
[59] *Lewis* (n 1) 277–83, and in particular 280–81.
[60] ibid 283.

by the Court of Appeal in *Grubb*[61] between true (or legal) innuendoes on the one hand, and false (or popular) innuendoes on the other. There was some disagreement about the appropriate nomenclature, but none about the substance of the matter; *Lewis* did not raise a real or genuine innuendo meaning.

V. THE RECEPTION OF *LEWIS*

A. Early Critical Reaction

The approach taken by the House of Lords in *Lewis* was followed immediately at the highest level. The Privy Council adopted it in an appeal from New South Wales six months later.[62] Interestingly its advice was given by Lord Morris who had dissented from the House of Lords decision. Lord Reid himself elaborated on the ordinary man test in *Morgan v Odhams Press Ltd*,[63] where the question was whether the plaintiff had been referred to in a tabloid article about the kidnap of a girl involved in a doping scandal. Although the article did not name the plaintiff, he could sue as some readers knew the girl had been staying with him voluntarily before the article was published; it was immaterial whether or not they believed the allegation of kidnapping was true. Lord Reid said that if the courts were to follow *Lewis*, and adopt the 'ordinary man' test, some loose thinking must be accepted. The ordinary reader did not formulate reasons and formed a general impression of an article, though one could expect him to look at it again before coming to a conclusion.[64] Lord Guest expected rather more from the ordinary reader; he must have rational grounds for believing that the allegation of kidnapping referred to the plaintiff.[65] With Lord Donovan, he dissented from this odd decision which applied the ordinary man test to the question whether the material identified the plaintiff.

The approach taken to the ascertainment of meaning in *Lewis* was strongly approved in 1975 by a Committee examining the reform of libel law, chaired by Sir Neville Faulks.[66] The ordinary sensible reader test provided the 'classic statement of the current law', an encomium followed by a long quotation from Lord Reid's speech.[67] The Committee defended the test against the charge that it might not reflect how actual readers understood the words used in the relevant material. In its view the test provided the best guide to the actual readers' understanding. Further, it would be wrong to allow the introduction of

---

[61] n 10 above.
[62] *Jones v Skelton* [1964] NSWR 485.
[63] *Morgan v Odhams Press Ltd* [1971] 1 WLR 1239.
[64] ibid 1245.
[65] ibid 1261.
[66] Report of the Committee on Defamation, Cmnd 5909 ('Faulks Committee Report'). Sir Neville Faulks, leading counsel for the newspapers in *Lewis*, had become a High Court judge in 1963.
[67] ibid para 93.

evidence how various readers had actually understood the words, as that would inevitably add to the length and cost of defamation proceedings.[68]

A more serious charge against the ordinary man test had been made a few years earlier by Diplock LJ (as he then was) in his judgment in the Court of Appeal's decision in *Slim v Daily Telegraph Ltd*.[69] In this case, the plaintiffs were a solicitor who had previously been clerk to Hammersmith Council and the factory for which he now worked. They brought libel proceedings in respect of remarks in letters to the *Daily Telegraph* which could be interpreted to mean that they had brought improper pressure on Hammersmith Council to establish a right of way for the factory's vehicles on a path by the Thames. The action was heard by Paull J without a jury; he ruled that words in the letters did bear the meaning alleged by the plaintiffs – they meant that Slim was not fit to remain a solicitor and that the factory had been guilty of improper conduct – and awarded them damages. The defendants' appeal was successful, partly on the ground that the letters should not be read to imply that Slim had behaved unprofessionally; all they meant was that he was acting on behalf of his new employer, which was legitimately trying to establish a right of way for its vehicles.[70]

Lewis was fully considered, particularly by Diplock LJ in a sustained critique of the approach of defamation law to the elucidation of meaning. That approach showed the 'artificial and archaic character of the tort of libel'.[71] Everyone outside the law knows that words mean different things to different people, yet libel law persisted in an illusory search for a single right meaning. But *Lewis* itself conceded that reasonable people might draw different inferences from the words used – in *Lewis* itself either the inference of suspicion of fraud or the lesser meaning that a police inquiry was investigating fraud. The best way of finding out how the words were understood would be to hear evidence from those to whom they had been published. But that was not permitted, except in legal innuendo cases where evidence was tendered of the extrinsic facts which gave the words a special meaning. So the jury, or as in this case the judge, had to decide what was the single right meaning of words which could reasonably be read to bear different meanings.[72]

The single meaning rule, under which one meaning must be ascribed by the trier of fact to the words used, has sometimes been criticised as artificial.[73] It was never examined, or even referred to, in *Lewis*, though it was surely implicit in the search for the natural and ordinary meaning of the language in the

---

[68] ibid paras 102–03.

[69] *Slim v Daily Telegraph Ltd* [1968] 2 QB 157 (*Slim*).

[70] The alternative ground was that even if the words did bear the meanings alleged by the plaintiffs, they amounted to fair comment on a matter of public interest.

[71] *Slim* (n 69) 171.

[72] ibid 171–72.

[73] See Sedley LJ in *Ajinomoto Sweeteners Europe v Asda Stores Ltd* [2010] EWCA Civ 409, [2011] QB 497, CA, and A Scott, '*Ceci n'est pas une pipe*': the autopoietic inanity of the single meaning rule' in AT Kenyon (ed), *Comparative Defamation and Privacy Law* (Cambridge, CUP, 2016) 40.

newspaper reports. Diplock LJ was in effect suggesting that the courts' allowance in that case for the reasonableness of drawing different inferences from the reports undermined the single meaning rule. But that is not correct. The ascription by a jury of a particular meaning to the relevant words does not mean that other conclusions would necessarily be unreasonable, though those that are unreasonable must be excluded by the judge. The meaning ascribed to the words by the jury is the single right meaning. The Faulks Committee was probably right to reject Diplock's criticism of the single meaning rule when it concluded that any alternative approach to the ascertainment of meaning would be disadvantageous.[74] It had also rejected as impracticable his idea that the actual readers of a report should give evidence on how they understood it.[75]

Another judgment in *Slim v Daily Telegraph Ltd* was given by Salmon LJ, who was the trial judge in *Lewis*. It began with the observation that the decision of the House of Lords in that case (and other recent decisions) had not made rationalisation of libel law any easier. He agreed with Lord Devlin's recommendation that a plaintiff's pleadings should set out separately the indirect meanings, or inferences to be drawn from the words used. That would be fairer to the defendant than leaving him in the dark about the meanings alleged by the plaintiff.[76] Salmon LJ's most interesting remarks came at the end of his judgment.[77] As a judge used to construing legal documents, he was aware of the difficulty a court faces when trying to discover the meaning which an ordinary layman would attribute to the words in a newspaper report. *Lewis* showed the difficulties in determining what words are capable of meaning to the ordinary reader – an implicit reference perhaps to the disagreement in the Lords between Lord Morris and the other members of the House, with Davies LJ in the Court of Appeal and Salmon LJ himself as the trial judge having taken the same view as Lord Morris. Finally, he noted, the principles for determining meaning had never been better formulated than they had been in the old *Henty* case,[78] but had never been worse applied. The words in the circular were held not to be capable of meaning that the bank was in financial difficulty, but they caused a run on the bank whose customers were ordinary men.

B. Recent English Authority

The principles in *Lewis* have continued to be applied by the English courts in the last 25 years. But they are prepared to apply them flexibly as shown by the judgment of Sir Thomas Bingham, MR (as he was then) for the Court of Appeal in *Skuse v Granada Television Ltd*.[79] The question was how the words

[74] Faulks Committee Report, n 65 above, para 103.
[75] See n 68 above.
[76] *Slim* (n 69) 184.
[77] ibid 187.
[78] See section II, at n 5 above.
[79] *Skuse v Granada Television Ltd* [1996] EMLR 278 *(Skuse)*.

in a television programme about the trial of the Birmingham Six convicted of bombing public houses in the city should be interpreted: did they mean that the plaintiff, a forensic scientist who had given crucial evidence at the trial had negligently misrepresented the results of the tests he had conducted or only, as Brooke J had ruled, that there were reasonable grounds to suspect that the plaintiff had been careless. The Court of Appeal allowed the plaintiff's appeal from this ruling on meaning. Sir Thomas quoted the passage from Lord Devlin's speech in *Lewis* pointing out that laymen are more inclined than lawyers to read derogatory implications into words.[80] The key point in this case was that, while in *Lewis* the distinction between an allegation of fault or wrongdoing and reasonable suspicion of it may have been warranted, it was not one which would occur to 'the ordinary reasonable viewer of this hard-hitting, arresting, quickly-moving television programme'.[81]

The principles in *Lewis* were in contrast strictly applied by the Court of Appeal in a case concerning a newspaper report that a police sergeant had killed himself after being asked to provide information about former colleagues who had been accused of peddling drugs.[82] The report stated that eight officers were alleged to have been involved in this offence and had been transferred to other police stations during the investigation. The plaintiffs, five of the eight officers concerned, contended that the ordinary meaning of the newspaper article was that they were guilty of drug dealing and the police sergeant had killed himself to avoid having to confirm their involvement. Hirst LJ for the Court of Appeal quoted extensively from Lord Reid's 'now classic statement' of the ordinary man test.[83] The decision of the House of Lords in *Lewis* that the reference to a fraud inquiry might be understood to impute reasonable suspicion, but not actual guilt of the offence should be followed here. The reference to the police sergeant's suicide did not affect this conclusion, for it could be interpreted in a number of ways, for example, that he had been suffering from depression. Reference was made to Lord Reid's imaginary conversation between members of the public reading a newspaper report.[84] This report could not be interpreted as alleging actual guilt.

The same approach was taken by the Court of Appeal in further libel litigation arising from these facts.[85] Here it considered the relationship of the decision in *Lewis* to the repetition rule, and followed the distinction drawn by the House of Lords between an allegation of suspicion and the spread of rumour.[86] *Lewis* made clear that in the context of the report of an investigation

---

[80] ibid 286 (and *Lewis* (n 1), 274 for Lord Devlin's speech).
[81] *Skuse* (n 79) 290.
[82] *Mapp v News Group Newspapers Ltd* [1997] EMLR 397 (*Mapp*).
[83] ibid 400, quoting Lord Reid in *Lewis* (n 1) at 258. David Hirst had been junior counsel for the newspapers in *Lewis*.
[84] *Mapp* (n 82) 405–06.
[85] *Bennett v News Group Newspapers Ltd* [2002] EMLR 39 (*Bennett*).
[86] See section IV B above.

or inquiry there were three possible levels of meaning; that an inquiry was under way, that there were reasonable grounds for suspicion, and that the persons concerned were guilty. There were three corresponding levels of justification; the defendant could not justify an allegation of suspicion by reporting a rumour, rather he had to point to facts which justified the suspicion.[87] This last point was confirmed by the Court of Appeal in *Chase v News Group Newspapers Ltd*,[88] though the case is most noteworthy for the remarks of Brooke LJ about the sting of a libel. The sting might mean that the claimant had committed a serious act such as murder, or it might mean that there are reasonable grounds to suspect that he has committed that act. 'A third possibility is that they may mean there are grounds for investigating whether he/she has been responsible for such an act.'[89] These different meanings have become known as 'Chase level 1', 'Chase level 2', and 'Chase level 3', largely replacing the taxonomy of meaning elaborated in *Lewis*.[90]

Nevertheless *Lewis* was the first case in which the difference between various levels of meaning had clearly been recognised.[91] The levels of meaning formulated in *Chase* did not really add much to the House of Lords ruling; indeed, they may have confused the position. As Sedley LJ has recognised, the distinction between the second and third categories (reasonable grounds for suspicion, and grounds for an investigation) is a fine one, and may be hard to apply.[92] *Lewis* itself is probably not responsible for this difficulty. The *Chase* formulation identifies the third possible meaning, as 'grounds for investigating' whether an offence has been committed, which may indeed be hard to differentiate on the facts from reasonable grounds for suspicion. But the least damaging meaning in *Lewis* was that the newspaper articles simply reported that an inquiry was under way, a meaning which could be easily justified by the defendants. The ruling of the House of Lords should not be blamed for any problems in distinguishing between the levels of meaning identified in *Chase*.

C. Criticism from Australia

The 'ordinary reasonable reader' test has often been adopted in Australia. In a leading New South Wales ruling,[93] Hunt J formulated the test in terms strikingly similar to those used by Lord Reid in *Lewis*: the 'ordinary reasonable reader

---

[87] *Bennett* (n 85) [16]–[22].

[88] *Chase v News Group Newspapers Ltd* [2003] EMLR 11.

[89] ibid at 45.

[90] See *King v Telegraph Group Ltd* [2004] EWCA Civ 613, [2004] EMLR 23, CA; *Charman v Orion Publishing Group Ltd* [2007] EWCA Civ 972, [2008] 1 All ER 750, CA; *Curistan v Times Newspapers Ltd* [2008] EWCA Civ 432, [2009] QB 231, CA.

[91] See *Jameel v Times Newspapers Ltd* [2004] EWCA Civ 983, [2004] EMLR 31, [10] and [18].

[92] ibid [18], quoting Simon Brown LJ in *Jameel v Wall Street Journal Europe SPRL* [2003] EWCA Civ 1694, [2004] EMLR 6, [19]–[20].

[93] *Farquhar v Bottom* [1980] 2 NSWLR 380, 386.

does not ... live in an ivory tower. He can, and does, read between the lines'. Such a reader is a layman, not a lawyer, and is more willing than a lawyer to draw inferences from the words used. The judge cited *Lewis* as authority no fewer than six times. As in England,[94] the test has been applied flexibly, so greater latitude may be afforded radio and television listeners and viewers to form a general impression from the material in a programme than would usually be allowed the readers of a printed article.[95] The High Court of Australia has held, following *Lewis*, that a newspaper report which does no more than state that a person has been arrested and charged with a criminal offence is not capable of bearing the imputation that he is guilty or probably guilty of that offence.[96]

But the test has been subject to some criticism, particularly from Kirby J in two judgments in the High Court of Australia. In *Chakravarti v Advertiser Newspapers Ltd*,[97] he suggested the tribunal of fact, whether judge or jury, really made its own subjective decision on the meaning of the words, though the ordinary reasonable reader test provided a check on its decision: would the reasonable recipient of the material have understood it in the same way as the tribunal? Kirby J took his criticism further in a more recent High Court ruling. The 'ordinary reasonable reader' test was a fiction which should now be discarded altogether. The test enabled the tribunal to attribute to fictitious reasonable readers its own understanding of meaning for which it should take responsibility.[98]

The criticism is perhaps unwarranted. Of course juries, and now in England judges, decide the meaning of words in defamation cases. But that is a trite proposition. The important question is what test or standard they should use when they approach the issue: are they entitled to adopt the meaning which they would themselves ascribe to the words, or that which they consider would be ascribed by the ordinary man coming across their publication. In principle the latter approach is right, for in defamation cases a fundamental question is whether the words injure the reputation of the plaintiff in the estimation of the community. Their meaning therefore must be that which would be ascribed by ordinary members of that community.

It is difficult for judges to put themselves in the shoes of ordinary readers or viewers, as Salmon LJ admitted in his judgment in the *Slim* case.[99] Juries are much better placed than judges to understand how a text or programme would be understood by the average reader, listener or viewer, and that is a strong argument for allowing questions of meaning to be resolved by juries rather than by judges. But judges can, and do, resolve questions of meaning by the

---

[94] See *Skuse* (n 78 above).
[95] *Amalgamated Television Services Ltd v Marsden* (1998) 43 NSWLR 158, CA(NSW).
[96] *Mirror Newspapers Ltd v Harrison* (n 48).
[97] *Chakravarti v Advertiser Newspapers Ltd* (1998) 189 CLR 519.
[98] *Favell v Queensland Newspapers Pty Ltd* [2005] HCA 52, (2005) 221 ALR 186, [23]–[24].
[99] See text at n 76 above.

ordinary man (or reader) test as it was formulated in *Lewis*. All the English cases discussed in the previous subsection (section V B) concerned appeals from rulings by judges on the meaning of words; the Court of Appeal had no difficulty in following the approach taken by the House of Lords in *Lewis*.

A more pertinent criticism would be that courts rarely take a realistic approach to the ascription of meaning by ordinary readers and viewers. Ordinary people reading a newspaper (or now more likely playing with their smartphone) on the bus from Clapham probably are more inclined to infer guilt from a report of an inquiry than a lawyer would. For them there really is no smoke without fire. The dissent of Lord Morris in *Lewis* may therefore better reflect the approach of typical newspaper readers to the reports of a police inquiry than the majority speeches which drew a sharp distinction between an allegation of suspicion and one of guilt. The 'ordinary man' test in *Lewis,* as applied in that case and later cases, is open to the criticism that it takes too rosy a view of the assessments made by ordinary readers and viewers.[100] But this point is quite different from the critique offered in the High Court of Australia by Kirby J.

VI. CONCLUSION

Is then *Lewis* a landmark case in defamation law, or in what sense is it a landmark case? There can of course be room for argument about what constitutes a landmark case.[101] If a decision must radically reshape an area of the common law or establish a new principle of liability to be a landmark case, *Lewis* would not qualify for the accolade. The 'ordinary' or 'reasonable' man or reader test had been established 80 years earlier by the House of Lords in its ruling in *Henty*,[102] which Lord Reid himself regarded as 'The leading case'.[103] But *Lewis v Daily Telegraph* elaborated the conception of the 'ordinary man' in defamation law, establishing him as neither naïve nor unduly suspicious, and as certainly not living in an ivory tower. The ordinary man's general approach to the understanding of a newspaper report of a police inquiry was clarified, as were the differences between the spread of a rumour and an allegation of suspicion and between true and false or (for Lord Devlin) legal and popular innuendoes. On all these points *Lewis* is unquestionably the leading modern defamation case. It was also an important ruling on the assessment of damages, although on this

---

[100] See AK Antoniou and D Akrivos. 'Indecent Images and Defamatory Meaning in Late Modern Societies: Taking Ordinary Reasonable Readers Outside Their Ivory Towers' (2017) 9 *Journal of Media Law* 155.

[101] See, for example, reflections in the essays of SH Bailey and K Hughes in *Landmark Cases in Public Law* (Oxford, Hart, 2017) at 39–40 and 183–84.

[102] *Capital and Counties Bank Ltd v Henty & Sons* (n 5).

[103] *Lewis* (n 1), 259.

topic it is significant as a precursor of the modern law, at least in England and Australia, on the control of extravagant jury awards and now the transfer of entitlement to award them to the judge.[104]

The point on which *Lewis* is most clearly a landmark case is its drawing of distinctions between different levels of meaning, which in the context of the case itself was responsible for the House of Lords decision to uphold the Court of Appeal's order for a new trial. Lines must be drawn between the report of a police inquiry, an allegation of suspicion, and an allegation of guilt. So in *Lewis* the short report in the two newspapers of a police fraud inquiry could not be understood as amounting to an allegation of guilt. The distinction between these three levels of meaning is now very well established in English law, although, as noted in the previous section of the chapter, they are these days known as 'Chase level 1', 'Chase level 2', and 'Chase level 3' after a recent ruling of the Court of Appeal.[105] But the foundation for that ruling had been laid 40 years earlier in *Lewis v Daily Telegraph*. The distinctions between these levels of meaning may be too sharply drawn and may not always realistically reflect how ordinary people actually understand reports in a tabloid or on social media. But the criticism does not detract from the significance of this landmark ruling.

---

[104] For the transfer in Australia of the assessment of damages to the judge, see D Rolph, *Defamation Law* (Sydney, Thomson Reuters, 2016) [15.20].
[105] See the text at nn 88–89 above.

6

New York Times v Sullivan *(1964)*

DAVID PARTLETT*

I. INTRODUCTION

MY COLLEAGUES IN this volume probably had some difficulty in deciding the leading case in defamation jurisprudence. As an American the choice is easy: *New York Times v Sullivan* remade the law of defamation in the USA. It marked a radical departure from the law that remained, since the Revolution in 1786, hand in hand with the rest of the common law world.[1] Suddenly, in what seems like warp speed, the law turned on its axis and made what was acceptable and routine into something that had to be scotched from the fabric of American law. Law that had, by common law accretion, been accepted over centuries was cast into outer darkness, criticised as anathema to the free speech principles of the First Amendment of the United States Constitution. Doctrine conventionally accepted that there was no First Amendment protection for defamatory speech.[2] This conformed with the acceptance of rules of law at the founding of the United States and assumptions about the federal system that vested the States with sovereignty over the common law of torts.[3] It shared the Republican tenets of the place of the jury and precepts of the First Amendment as binding governments exercising their powers.[4] The idea of State action still inhabited the hearts of judges and

---

* Asa Griggs Candler Professor of Law, Emory University School of Law.

[1] An outstanding historical treatment is in R Helmholz, *Introduction to Select Cases on Defamation to 1600* in R Helmholz (ed), *The Publications of the Selden Society*, Vol 101 (London, Selden Society, 1985).

[2] See *Chaplinsky v New Hampshire* 315 US 568, 571–72 ('There are certain well-defined and narrowly limited classes of speech, the prevention and punishment of which have never been thought to raise any Constitutional problem. These include the lewd and obscene, the profane, the libelous, and the insulting or 'fighting' words'); *Beauharnais v Illinois* 343 US 250, 266 (1952) (holding that 'libelous utterances' are not 'within the area of constitutionally protected speech.').

[3] *Erie Railroad Co v Tompkins* 304 US 64 (1938).

[4] *Heart of Atlanta Motel v United States* 379 US 241 (1964). As *New York Times v Sullivan* shows judicial enforcement was sufficient state action. See *Shelly v Kramer* 334 US 1 (1948) (holding that a racially restrictive land covenant was a state action).

commentators, even as the Civil War Constitutional Amendments – the 14th in particular – incorporated the Bill of Rights protections into constitutional interpretation to bind State governments in addition to the federal government.[5]

In this discussion I will set forth the historical background of the case and then discuss its limitations as the law and society have changed and developed over the past almost 55 years.

II. HISTORY AND SOCIETY: CIVIL RIGHTS AND THE PURPOSES OF DEFAMATION LAW

To understand how this judicial revolution happened, it is necessary to view the case in its social context. There is a national context that had been evolving since World War II. In the South, the power bases of the Southern white establishment were eroded to be replaced by populist politicians who took advantage of the sense of outrage of the working class. Race-baiting had great salience. At the national level it seemed intolerable that a war that in retrospect had been fought, in part, to eradicate the Nazi policies of racial supremacy should find a home in the American South and pockets of the large cities of the North. Many African-Americans who fought in the war came home to Jim Crow. A civil rights movement led by Dr Martin Luther King among others led mass movements. This would not have mattered greatly except that simultaneously the media age came to maturity and television screens showed the abuse of demonstrators in Birmingham and Selma, Alabama, among others. Integration of schools in the South, as in Little Rock, Arkansas, was opposed by the State governments – necessitating the deployment of the National Guard. This too led to violence. In Birmingham, a black church was bombed, killing four young girls. Medgar Evers, the black civil rights leader who led the NAACP in Mississippi, was murdered in his front garden in 1963. It took until 1994 for his murderer to be convicted and incarcerated. Freedom riders from the North taking buses into the Southern states rode as integrated passengers exercising their constitutional rights in interstate travel. The use of the law to lift the oppressive hand of Jim Crow was widely employed as part of the King credo of peaceful change. Southern states banned the NAACP to prevent legal representation in voting rights and desegregation in public facilities.[6]

In addition to the daily reports of these and other incidents, the United States was enmeshed in the war in Vietnam that was proving to be intractable and wearing on the national psyche. The civil rights movement fueled reactions to the war in Vietnam that resulted in mass protests later in the decade and

---

[5] See *Palko v Connecticut* 302 US 319 (1937); *Adamson v California* 332 US 46 (1947).

[6] See generally, T Branch, *Parting the Waters: America in the King Years 1954–63* (New York, Simon & Schuster, 1989); G Roberts and H Klibanoff, *The Race Beat: The Press, the Civil Rights Struggle, and the Awakening of a Nation* (New York, Knopf, 2006);

in the early 1970s. Again, the media played a large part in fueling the protest movements. Middle-class assumptions about America's role in the world and its anti-communist credo came under fire. The Vietnam War too had class and race dimensions as service was avoided by many of the well-off sectors of society. President Lyndon Johnson's war on poverty was mired in the social ructions and the fiscal shortfalls of a financially ruinous war.[7]

A. The Law of Defamation in the South

One would assume that an arcane corner of tort law would be immune to these vexations. The litigation shows how a systematic deprivation of rights and control of the levers of power can subvert the equal protection of the law. The famous *Brown* decision, which declared that separate schools were inherently unequal, was designed to demolish the racial segregation of schools.[8] The Southern states, however, engaged in a deliberate tactic of obstruction to thwart the Court's edict. A well-known example is massive resistance in Virginia which placed state and local governmental barriers in the way of desegregation.[9] The courts were in the vanguard in breaking down these barriers through use of structural injunctions.[10] Resentment against federal action grew as the Supreme Court struck down segregationist practices and law. In an area of the country that had not seen the benefits of the economic growth fostered by the end of World War II, there was a widely held feeling that Southerners and Southern culture were not understood, and arrogantly so, by a Northeastern elite that was perfectly framed by that 'liberal' news organ: the *New York Times (NYT)*.

Local norms compete with national norms in tort law.[11] Thus, if the doctrines of the intentional torts are examined, local expectations of interhuman interaction are usually adopted to promote the social co-operation.[12] To arm a child with a hunting rifle and expect a standard of care is viewed differently in Arkansas than it is elsewhere, where the tradition of hunting is not accepted as a usual rite of passage. Ideas of honour in the South are sacrosanct, leading to assumptions as to what would constitute the tort of assault.[13] Assumed consent

---

[7] Robert A Caro, *The Years of Lyndon Johnson: The Passage of Power* (New York, Vintage, 2013).

[8] *Brown v Cnty Bd of Education* 186 SC 325 (1938). For a full treatment see M Klarman, *Brown v. Board of Education And The Civil Rights Movement* (New York, Oxford University Press, 2007).

[9] For an assessment of the Court's initial vacillation, see Robert A Burt, *Brown's Reflection* (1994) 103 *Yale LJ* 1483.

[10] *Missouri v Jenkins* 515 US 70 (1995) (holding by a majority that the District Court's longstanding desegregation order and specific recent order for the school district to be reformed into a magnet school ought to be re-examined).

[11] Cristina Carmody Tilley, *Tort Law Inside Out* (2017) 126 *Yale LJ* 1242, accessible at: www.yalelawjournal.org/article/tort-law-inside-out.

[12] ibid.

[13] *Purtle v Shelton* 474 SW2d 123 (Ark 1971).

will vary according to local norms, although they may merge into national norms where consent to sexual conduct is under examination, as in the #MeToo movement.[14]

The roots of defamation are found in the mists of early English history. They are community-based. In a static society, as is found in medieval society, reputation carried a critical value. The ecclesiastical courts first established a jurisdiction on defamation. The invention of the printing press was a singular event in energising liabilty. In an immobile society an individual's livelihood and social life depended on establishing a reputation for probity and honesty. This social function of liability and therefore protection from words that would tend to make an individual an outcast or pariah was an essential ingredient in one's dignity. Citizens of nation states in the modern world, at least in industrialised societies, may still see reputation as possessing great value in a commercial sense – as a kind of property. But dignity as a member of a community plays a lesser role.[15] Mobility means that one can escape. It allows new lives to be established. Take convicts transported to the colony of New South Wales, as I can attest to in my family tree. The great disruption, as mentioned, coincided with the invention of the printing press. Government became insecure with the greater possibility of seditious libel. The ecclesiastical courts lost jurisdiction with libel – written defamation – finding a home in the notorious Star Chamber where the notion of actionability per se upon a showing of defamatory meaning was born. Eventually both slander and libel were brought within the common law courts, but the origins of the actions still held sway from their graves. It was in this form that the causes of action were transplanted to the North American colonies and regarded as one of the rights of 'Englishmen'. In any originalist interpretation, they were existent and taken to form and be part of the law at the revolution and on the adoption of the Constitution.

The transplantation was to fit within the varied tapestry of American society. As Hall and Urofsky point out in their book on *Sullivan*, the South was an honour society where reputation had strong dignitary and communitarian roots.[16] The duel held sway in the South for a longer time than in the North and the defamation liability could be viewed as way of reducing social violence.

[14] The American Law Institute is presently engaged in the task of drafting the *Restatement (Third) of the Law of Torts: Intentional Torts*. On the defence of consent it has taken close account of the current concerns about consent to sexual acts and crafted language that takes account of power differential between persons. See, *Restatement of Torts* § 15. The degree to which actual consent can be presumed is closely examined: ibid.

[15] See Robert C Post, 'The Social Foundations of Defamation Law: Reputation and the Constitution' (1986) 74 *Calif L Rev* 691. See also David Rolph, *Reputation, Celebrity, and Defamation Law* (Aldershot, Ashgate, 2008) (discussing reputation in terms of property and honour and in the context of social and technological change).

[16] KL Hall and MI Urofsky, *New York Times v. Sullivan: Civil Rights, Libel Law, And The Free Press*, (Lawrence (Ka), University of Kansas Press, 2011) (citing Post, 'The Social Foundations of Privacy' (1989)).

The North was much more market-oriented and saw reputation as a property right within a more mobile society. In the South, a code of honour was seen as an organising principle of an ordered society. New aggressive political actors took advantage of the waning hold of the old elites imbued with noblesse oblige.[17] If a lawyer from London or Sydney had reviewed the 1964 Alabama defamation law on the books, it would be familiar. The tests for defamatory meaning are the same: the presumption of falsity and damages at large prevailed. Even the role of the jury is familiar considering that the jury persisted in defamation actions in England and New South Wales for a considerable time beyond its decline in those jurisdictions in other forms of civil litigation. The idea of protecting 'good men' in public from false and vicious vilification was a common theme. It is possible to imagine that American law, even without First Amendment scrutiny, would have developed along the lines of other common law jurisdictions to give greater leeway to free speech. Furthermore, the American courts would have taken closer note of other courts in adopting more flexible remedies and reducing the reliance on damages, particularly punitive damages. But that train has long left the station. The quick demise of defamation was a cause for celebration of most and, crucially, a victory for civil rights. But that victory in civil rights has come at a cost, as I will argue below.

B. The Fateful Litigation

It all started in Montgomery, the capital city of Alabama and a citadel of the old South. In the early 1960s, the control of local government fell into the hands of followers of the Ku Klux Klan, who condemned the old velvet-gloved elite. Fundamentalist Baptists and Methodists took a dislike to a more tolerant and entitled elite. The city became more racially segregated in its housing. The power of African-American voters had increased, but the attitudes of a new class of white politicians, unleashed from moderating influences of the old white class, pushed heavily and harshly for maintenance of Jim Crow policies in public bussing in the city. It was in Montgomery that Rosa Parks famously took her seat in the white section of the bus, beginning the bus boycott that polarised the city. The 26-year-old Martin Luther King was named president of the Montgomery Improvement Association (MIA). King's home was bombed and a law suit was filed to desegregate the bus service. The law suit was commenced in federal court, which was more welcoming than state courts. The business community,

---

[17] See R White, *The Republic for Which It Stands: The United States during Reconstruction and the Gilded Age, 1865–1896,* 1st edn (New York, Oxford University Press, 2017) 188–92 (describing the intimidation in the South wrought by the Ku Klux Klan); MJ Klarman, *From Jim Crow To Civil Rights: The Supreme Court And The Struggle For Racial Equity,* 1st edn (New York, Oxford University Press, 2006) (describing the growing force of farmers and the KKK in driving African Americans away from exerting hard-won freedoms).

the police commissioner, and his segregationist allies turned to the state courts seeking a criminal indictment under an Alabama Anti-Boycott statute. A grand jury returned indictments against 89 African-Americans, 24 of whom were ministers. Tensions in the city were exacerbated by Northern press coverage of the boycott. The MIA eventually prevailed at law with the US Supreme Court in *Gayle v Browder*, mandating that segregation stop on the Montgomery buses.[18] For the white hardliners, this was another insult following on the heels of the school desegregation cases. The law was trending one way while the politics went the other, with electoral victories that turned on the racists' cries. In 1958, John Patterson was elected governor of Alabama, defeating George Wallace. Employing the rhetoric of 'unalloyed racism',[19] Patterson defeated George Wallace and cementing the latter to an electoral path and tactic that he would, he declared, 'never be out-niggered again'.[20] Patterson succeeded in obtaining a court order banning the NAACP from the state and by copying Virginia's massive resistance to school desegregation, thwarted other federal court orders for desegregating public facilities by mandating all 13 city parks and the city zoo to be sold.

LB Sullivan entered centre-stage in 1959. He had worked episodically in the private and public sectors, taking care to establish himself as a reliable lieutenant. He was elected police commissioner by painting the incumbent as weak on crime and social activists, and promised fair enforcement of the law. Any plans along those lines were disrupted by the arrival in Montgomery of the 'sit-in movement' that had begun in Greensboro, North Carolina, and had swept through the South. Lunch counters had been segregated throughout the South, and sit-ins were an effective public expression that such practices were unacceptable. The Northern press, including the NYT, sent correspondents to the South to report on these protests. In Montgomery, students from the all-black Alabama State College sought service at a lunch counter in the basement of the County Court House. They were thrown out and the Governor then ordered their expulsion from the College. This led to a march of about 800 students on the State House. The Governor and Sullivan decided to employ unofficial intimidation by allowing the KKK to beat demonstrators while the police stood idly by. The attackers were not punished despite the fact that many were easily identifiable. On 29 March 1960, a full-page ad was published in the NYT entitled 'Heed Their Rising Voices'.[21] Northern supporters of Martin Luther King and the civil rights movement in the South paid for the ad – its purpose to generate

[18] 352 US 903 (1956).

[19] Hall and Urofsky, *New York Times v. Sullivan* (2011) 10.

[20] He was to apologise for this toward the end of his life. See, Rick Bragg, *30 Years Later, Wallace Apologizes to Marchers*, NYT 11 March 1995, accessed at: http://articles.baltimoresun.com/1995-03-11/news/1995070104_1_marchers-montgomery-wallace (last viewed 14 June 2018).

[21] 'Heed Their Rising Voices,' NYT, 29 March 1960. accessed at: www.archives.gov/exhibits/documented-rights/exhibit/section4/detail/heed-rising-voices.html.

Northern support for the movement both in attitude and money. To add to its appeal, it sought to create a strong appeal to citizens in the North from those in South who had been downtrodden. It listed outrages in the Montgomery and was endorsed by worthy Northern public figures, such as Eleanor Roosevelt, Sidney Poitier, Marlon Brando, and by four Alabama ministers: Ralph Abernathy, Solomon Seay, Fred Shuttlesworth and Joseph Lowery. The publishers did not consult these ministers before using their names as endorsers. The ad, for context, followed a forceful editorial in the *NYT* some ten days earlier where Congress was urged to 'heed their rising voices', advocating peaceful disobedience, support for Dr King, and civil rights legislation in Congress.[22]

The format, the assertions and the venue were directed to maximise the impact to the message and to generate support. As an equal and opposite reaction, all those factors would elicit a full-throated response from the state of Alabama and the city of Montgomery. The affront was to be told what to do – how to handle its problems – by a newspaper that hailed from, and was an organ of, the establishment Northeast. Politicians and police at the highest ranks felt the sting. The paper had little circulation in the state of Alabama – only 390 on an average day and 2,500 on a Sunday – and only 35 copies circulated in Montgomery County. While offence was taken by the few citizens who had noticed and read the ad, Merton Ronald Nachman, an astute Harvard-trained lawyer and leading defamation attorney in Alabama, read it with a gimlet eye. He saw that the ad contained a number of factual misstatements and, although not explicitly naming Sullivan, it could be interpreted as referring to him implicitly.[23] To use actions in defamation against newspapers fit within a strategy to employ the law to attack the civil rights movement. For example, Governor Patterson had directed state revenue authorities to charge Dr King with tax evasion,[24] and *NYT* reporters seeking to cover civil rights in Alabama found a hostile environment restricting their capacity to report.[25]

On 19 April 1960, the three police commissioners, including Sullivan, filed a defamation suit against the *NYT* and the four clergy, seeking $500,000 against each. The clergy had been added to assure that jurisdiction could be asserted by the Alabama courts. As a result of reports of riots and police action in Birmingham, Alabama, three city commissioners there, including 'Bull' Connor, filed similar suits. Even more suits were brought – another by Governor Patterson, seeking $1m in damages. In all, damages in excess of $6m had been initiated. The *NYT* was not then the wealthy institution it is today. The weight of these

---

[22] Above n 19.

[23] Hall and Urofsky (n 11) 24–26.

[24] For a description of the prosecution by Alabama and the equital by a jury of 12 white men see: Why Justice Matters: The Income Tax Trial Of Martin Luther King, Jr', www.forbes.com/sites/kellyphillipserb/2018/01/15/why-justice-matters-the-income-tax-trial-of-dr-martin-luther-king-jr.

[25] Hall and Urofsky (n 11) 89 (describing the tale of a *NYT* 'stringer' that arrived in Birmingham only to have friends take him aside to warn him of the danger posed by police and thus return back to Atlanta).

damages, together with the prospect of success of the plaintiffs and those trailing later, posed a real threat to the financial integrity of the *NYT*.

C. The Alabama Courts

From the outset this was not a simple defamation suit – the civil rights background made all the difference. The accumulation of suits was designed to punish the *NYT*. The law up to that time stood with the plaintiffs. The determination of factual questions rested in the jury, the sympathies of which were firmly in favour of the plaintiffs. The juries were not racially diverse and, indeed, the court room was racially segregated. In the reporting of the case, African-American lawyers were referred to as 'Lawyer [...]', while white lawyers were dubbed 'Mr'. The best, albeit mundane, chance for the *NYT* was to establish that the Alabama courts had no jurisdiction. For this, the paper could rely on the fact that it had a miniscule circulation in the state and very little revenue derived from its sales there. The Judge Jones in the trial court, who had played a strong hand in having the case heard in his court, wrote the book on Alabama pleadings.[26] The *NYT* attorney meticulously followed the black letter in filing a limited appearance to quash the pleadings. On both the necessary connections with the state and the appearance, the judge found against the *NYT* and held that the court had jurisdiction. The judge with experience in defamation actions ran the trial tightly but regularly, and at every turn he ruled in favour of the plaintiffs.

Once jurisdiction was established, the salient matters were identification and defamatory imputation. In addition, there was the issue of damages that were at large with the jury. Evidence was adduced that persons reading the ad concluded it referred to Sullivan. It was held that this was a reasonable conclusion given his involvement with city policing. Evidence showed that some of the assertions in the ad were factually incorrect. It established too that the *NYT* had not gone through a rigorous vetting of the ad to ensure it was wholly factually correct. In Alabama, as in some other States, the burden in getting evidence to the jury was light; it is the 'bare scintilla' of evidence rule.[27] The judge applied this to overrule the defendant's objections of precluding evidence going to the jury.

---

[26] Walter Burgwyn Jones, through his writings a 'son of the south', was the author of *Alabama Practice Forms: An Authoritative and Comprehensive Treatment of Jurisdiction, Pleading, and Procedure in the State Courts of Alabama* (St. Paul, West Pub Co, 1947). See also A Lewis, *Make No Law: The Sullivan Case and the First Amendment* (New York, Vintage, 2011).

[27] The burden of proving sufficient evidence to go to the jury has been the subject of considerable comment after the US Supreme Court's decision in *Ashcroft v Iqbal*, 556 US 662 (2009) (requiring under Fed R Civ 8(a)(2) 'demands more than an unadorned, the -defendant-harmed-me accusation. ... To survive a motion to dismiss, a complaint must contain sufficient factual matter, accepted as true, to state a claim to relief that is plausible on its face').

The jury's role was fulsome given that liability was strict. Plaintiffs, as the common law stated, did not have a burden of proving fault. The plaintiff merely had to prove that the *NYT* published the ad and that it was 'of and concerning' the plaintiff. The jury had the province of determining whether the imputation was defamatory, in that it tended to make other members of the community shun and avoid the plaintiff and hold him in low esteem. The jury was given wide discretion in setting damages that could include compensatory and, in addition, punitive damages for contumelious disregard for the plaintiff's rights.[28]

The jury was duly charged and returned in two hours with its verdict. Seven months after the ad was published, the jury in Montgomery awarded the requested $500,000 (about $4m in today's dollars) to LB Sullivan. It was then on to the appeal to the Alabama Supreme Court.

No one was in suspense about the conclusion of the Alabama Supreme Court. Other cases proceeded at the same time. In *New York Times v Connor*, 1961 the 5th Circuit Court of Appeals in Atlanta held that the paper could not be sued in Alabama for reporting on the conduct of the police in riots in Birmingham.[29] This was but a small apostrophe in the success of plaintiffs in defamation proceedings in the State. The state courts had been recalcitrant in the face of federal court rulings. In *Sullivan*, the *NYT* attorney bravely relied on the First Amendment, but was preempted by bland citation of the previous and well-established law that the First Amendment does not protect libellous speech. The court affirmed the holding in the trial court. It was, however, vital that counsel for the *NYT* raised the First Amendment argument before the court for this allowed the argument to be made before the US Supreme Court and, as we will see, enabled the constitutional law issue to form the centrepiece of the appellants' brief and the Court's subsequent holding.

D. Onto the United States Supreme Court

Much was at stake in the civil rights movement. The ambit and application of defamation law carried potential with other legal tactics to stifle the movement. It would deter news media running stories or even having reporters in the South to witness and write reports. Cometh the hour, cometh the man. In this case it was two men – Herbert Wechsler a distinguished Columbia Law School professor, counsel for *NYT*, and Justice William Brennan of the US Supreme Court. Both rose to the challenge of elevating the First Amendment to new heights

---

[28] From a stance over 50 years distant, one could point out that the small circulation of the ad in Montgomery would diminish damages. *Dow Jones & Co Inc v Gutnick* (2002) 210 CLR 575 (Austl).

[29] *New York Times Co v Connor*, 365 F 2d 567 (5th Cir 1966). Judge Tuttle presided. He was a champion of civil rights sitting in Atlanta. The 11th Circuit Court of Appeals jurisdiction was later carved out of the 5th. See also A Emanuel, *Elbert Parr Tuttle: Chief Jurist Of The Civil Rights Revolution* (Athens (Ga), University of Georgia Press, 2011).

to safeguard civil rights. Both persuaded the remainder of the Justices to hew this new line. Both added lustre to the Court's central role in guarding constitutional rights. Both gave an impetus to the Congress enactment of the Civil Rights legislation. For writers in tort law, the watershed for the law of defamation law in the United States was built. That law then enters a new orbit outside that of other common law jurisdictions.[30]

The appeal to the Supreme Court of the United States was the by way of writ of *certiorari*. The basis was that important constitutional issues are at stake and that the lower court failed to take them into account and apply them correctly. Wechsler was an experienced advocate before the Court and was revered as a leading scholar in constitutional law and federal courts. He carried the intellectual heft to move the Court to new frontiers. Wechsler asked four questions that he submitted merited the Court's attention:

> Whether, consistently with the guarantee of freedom of press in the First Amendment as embodied in the Fourteenth, a state may hold libelous *per se* and actionable by an elected City Commissioner, without proof of special damage, statements critical of the conduct of a department of the City Government under his jurisdiction which are inaccurate in some particulars.

> Whether there was sufficient evidence to justify, consistently with the guarantee of freedom of the press, the determination that statements, naming no individual but critical of the Police Department under the jurisdiction of the respondent as an elected City Commissioner, were defamatory as to him and punishable as libelous per se.

> Whether an award of $500,000 as 'presumed' and punitive damages for libel constituted, in the circumstances of this case, an abridgement of freedom of the press.

> Whether the assumption of jurisdiction [in this case] transcended the territorial limitations of due process, imposed a forbidden burden on interstate commerce or abridged freedom of the press.[31]

The summation of his argument he pithily presented as:

> The decision [of the Supreme Court of Alabama] gives scope and application to the law of libel so restrictive of the right to protest and to criticize official conduct that it abridges the freedom of the press.[32]

In particular he cited the 1798 Sedition Act. This Act, adopted to protect the fledgling republic, required the showing of a purpose to bring the 'official into contempt or disrepute' while the claim in defamation assumes the intent

---

[30] David Partlett, '*New York Times v. Sullivan* at Fifty Years' in A Kenyon (ed), *Comparative Defamation and Privacy Law* (Cambridge, Cambridge University Press, 2016) 58.
[31] Brief of Petitioner at 2, *New York Times v Sullivan*, No 39, 1963 WL 105891 (US) (Appellate Brief) (1963).
[32] ibid 32.

to defame.[33] The Act exacted criminal consequences, but the civil action here had a potential of equal force in the level of damages and thus deterrent that could be meted out. Wechsler put his argument squarely under the First Amendment and the chilling effect that liability would entail for free speech. To be sure, civil rights was a critical backdrop. The argument for the clergymen was taken separately and argued by another consummate lawyer, IH Wachtel, who more pointedly couched his argument in the clothes of civil rights. Wachtel had been inspired by Dr King and volunteered to represent the clergymen who were found liable and had their possessions executed upon partially to cover the award of damages. They were regarded as legitimate defendants because, although they had not known they would be named as endorsers of the ad, they had not acted in a timely fashion in disassociating themselves from it.

The Court notified all the parties and the clerk of the Supreme Court of Alabama that it granted *certiorari* on 7 January 1963. The cases were *New York Times v Sullivan*[34] and *Abernathy et al v Sullivan*[35]. Wechsler set to work drafting the brief that was to dominate his time over the remainder of the year. Serendipitously, he was on sabbatical in the spring semester and freed up time when he deferred taking up the post of Executive Director of the American Law Institute.[36] Wechsler spent the summer in steamy New York City rather than his usual haunts on Cape Cod with his family. The brief covered 112 pages – far beyond the allowable pages now prescribed. It was extremely thorough. It wove history and case law together to drum home the theme that the First Amendment protected political speech. This had been the case from the outset, he urged, showing that the 1798 Sedition Act was unconstitutionally infirm, although the court had not passed on it. To protect public officials from criticism was anathema to the role of free speech in the republic.[37] The press must be free to publish material critical of public officials, like LB Sullivan. It followed that the use of libel by the Alabama courts abridged free speech essential in a democracy.

Importantly, Wechsler utilised an idea that was to be attractive to the Court. He quoted *Roth v United States*[38] that constitutionally protected expression was driven by a desire to enhance democracy, designed 'to assure unfettered interchange of ideas for the bringing about of political and social changes desired by the people'.[39] Using the analogy of the limits of the contempt power where judges could not have an unbridled power to protect their reputations, by the same token, public officers have no immunity from libel suits where in

---

[33] W Bird, *Press and Speech Under Assault: The Early Supreme Court Justices, the Sedition Act of 1798, and the Campaign Against Dissent* (New York, Oxford University Press, 2016).

[34] *New York Times v Sullivan* 376 US 254 (1964).

[35] *Abernathy v Sullivan* 371 US 946 (1963).

[36] He held the post for 21 years, steering the Model Criminal Code to its adoption.

[37] See Post (n 15) 724 (discussing the American Constitutional character of the relationship between public officials and the people).

[38] *Roth v United States* 354 US 476 (1957).

[39] ibid 484.

their official communications they defame private citizens. The brief filed in *Abernathy* contained little law in comparison, but attacked the racist influences of the court process. It was the Wechsler brief that was a tour de force in quiet but persuasive advocacy, resetting the law of defamation. Oral argument was set for 4 January 1964. This was the activist Warren Court that had begun dismantling Jim Crow and had decided cases that articulated a strong liberal agenda in respect to civil rights generally from school prayer to access to contraceptives.[40]

Oral argument did little to change views but it did vent the issue of how an alternative test sensitive to the First Amendment could be formulated. Wechsler knew he had to thread a needle between the absolutist views of Justices Black and Douglas, that 'no law' in the terms of the First Amendment, meant that Congress was prohibited from regulating speech, and the common law doctrinal approach of Justice Harlan who had reverence for settled common law and had a firmly held fidelity for federalism.[41] The brief covered, for example, the standard to be adopted in reviewing the jury's finding of fact. Traditionally great deference under the Seventh Amendment, guaranteeing trial by jury, was to be given to those findings. Wechsler proposed a stronger test and greater judicial oversight on review. This was adopted by Justice Brennan, allaying Harlan's fear that hostile state courts could adopt interpretations to bypass constitutional requirements of 'actual malice'.

After oral argument, the Justices gather in conference to discuss the case and a vote is taken.[42] All the justices in *Sullivan* spoke in favour of reversing the Alabama court, but they had different ideas on the reasoning to adopt. The Chief Justice, if in the majority, by convention may choose to write the Court's opinion or may delegate to another. The opinion to bring the court together and declare the law in a convincing way would have to exhibit the highest juristic skills, married to subtle and persuasive lobbying. In their time on the Court, the Chief Justice formed a strong bond with Justice Brennan. Thus came the second man equal to the hour. There was to be no narrow opinion; the Court was to create law for a brave new world.

Brennan's first draft to his final draft drew heavily from Wechsler's brief. But it was no mere cutting and pasting. First, he had to answer the argument that the case was a private lawsuit and that the State had not acted. State action is necessary to base a claim of protection of constitutional guarantees. The State courts administered the courts and this was, in the Court's view, sufficient state action. This was a step beyond the usual concept that state action is the executive or legislative exercise of powers. Next, he concluded that the ad was

---

[40] See *Brown v Board of Education* 347 US 483 (1954); *Gideon v Wainwright* 372 US 335 (1963); *Griswold v Connecticut* 381 US 479 (1965).

[41] S Stern and S Wermeil, *Justice Brennan: Liberal Champion* (New York, Houghton Mifflin Harcourt Publishing Company, 2010) 225.

[42] S Shapiro et al, *Supreme Court Practice*, 10th edn (Bloomberg, 2013).

political, rather than commercial speech, that traditionally drew less protection. This, although not apparent at first, is a large step. It allows the court to apply the strong test of compliance to First Amendment principles that would be applied to acts of governmental fiat. Thus, from this point on, a balance of interests in defamation between reputation and free speech is not adequate. Political speech is too precious to be left to such balancing, particularly seeing that the common law restricts the breathing space of publishers – a point that Wechsler made forcefully in his brief and that is much discussed in later case law and commentary. This led to heart of the opinion. The long tradition of the First Amendment was to fear more the risk of self-censorship than the impact on others of speech that may be faulty. Before the emergence of the First Amendment as the right 'that rules them all',[43] Holmes and Brandeis promoted its centrality early in the twentieth century.[44] One cannot gainsay the power of this aspect of the decision is the eloquence of the language. It speaks to aspirations of freedom and good government of the republic. Wechsler's stifling summer locked up with books and assistants was worth it. It was replete with rich rhetorical veins that Brennan tapped. Within the Court it struck its mark. It was clear that other justices would wish to go farther in protecting speech, but the words brought them to concur. Justices Black and Goldberg would have preferred categorically to deny any action in libel by a public official in his public conduct. The actual malice formula, preserving a right in an official who can prove show actual malice, preserved sufficient liability to gain Justice Harlan's concurrence although it lost Justice Goldberg who only concurred in the result.[45]

The Court, in the run-of-the-mill case, would have remanded the case to the state court but in this case decided it should pre-empt the state court by deciding the issue that the plaintiff had not reached the necessary threshold of proving that the ad was published with actual malice.

---

[43] JRR Tolkien, *The Lord of the Rings*, 2nd edn (New York, Houghton Mifflin Company, 1966) (In Tolkien's allegory, the ring, like the invocation of the First Amendment, has wonderful magical powers.)

[44] See T Healy, *The Great Dissent: How Oliver Wendell Holmes Changed His Mind – And Changed The History Of Free Speech In America* (New York, Metropolitan Books, 2013) (describing how Holmes and Brandeis shifted the prism of analysis). Healy, at 370, discussing the influence of Holmes's dissent in *Abrams v United States* 250 US 616, 624 (1919), rightly says that it influences deeply: '[Holmes's] metaphor of the marketplace of ideas and his concept of "clear and present danger" have worked their way into our collective consciousness, becoming part of our language, our view of the world, and our identity as a nation'. See also GE White, 'Justice Holmes and the Modernization of Free Speech Jurisprudence: The Human Dimension' (1992) 80 *Calif L Rev*391 (discussing the Holmes-Brandeis-Hand relationship); L Barnett Lidsky, 'Nobody's Fool: The Rational Audience as First Amendment Ideal' (2010) *Illinois L Rev* 799, 813 (reasoning that 'radical speakers', like the defendants in *Abrams*, do not create a clear and present danger by urging their audience to take action: 'Justice Holmes' opinion rests on faith in rational deliberation as an antidote to violence').

[45] Stern and Wermeil, *Justice Brennan* (2010) 225–26.

Thus ended the litigation in the case that launched the new American law of defamation. It was a cause Lewis said for 'dancing in the streets'.[46] The acclaim derived from the victory for civil rights and the declamation of the centrality of free speech in the constitutional jurisprudence of the country. The First Amendment's free speech clause appeared from the closet in full bloom to dominate constitutional discourse and to affect not only the law of defamation but also the law of privacy and other communication torts.[47] As I have written elsewhere it was a juggernaut leading to free speech as the key determinative value. This depended on the notion of the marketplace of ideas that found its way as the central rational. It described a process of arriving at truth. It could through that market process protect the freedoms of citizens.

As for the common law the sweeping holding left much to be decided. This is why we tend to describe the law not just as the holding in *NYT v Sullivan* but also of its progeny – later cases that have struggled to accommodate the demands of the First Amendment with the interests protected at common law. Defamation practice became constitutional law practice. Specialists in defamation law and its intricacies, as Merton Nachman was an example, have been replaced by those who are adept in constitutional law theory.[48]

E. An American Defamation Orbit

From that January day in 1964, defamation law in the US shot into a different orbit. Its kinship with other common law jurisdictions was severed. In consequence, the developments over the last 50 years in other common law jurisdictions have been ignored. Reforms that could have moderated the extent of damages and promoted alternative remedies beyond damages have not been seriously considered. This distance has been increased in the last decade with a US Supreme Court determined to hew a path that does not draw on fellow democracies when constitutional matters are salient. I have written that *NYT v Sullivan* had an initial influence in courts around the world, ensconcing free speech as a critical element in defamation liability rules.[49] But it must be said that influence is less now with the Supreme Court's singular approach that discounts other interests. The singularity of the free speech interest is put into relief in

[46] A Lewis, '*New York Times v. Sullivan* Reconsidered: Time to Return to "The Central Meaning of the First Amendment"' (1983) 83 *Colum L Rev* 603; H Kalven, '*The New York Times Case: A Note on 'The Central Meaning of the First Amendment*" 1964 *Sup Ct Rev*191.
[47] See D Partlett, 'Remedies for Breach of Privacy: A Study of a Different Hedgehog' in J Varuhas and N Moreham (eds), *Remedies for Breach of Privacy*, (Oxford, Hart Publishing, 2018).
[48] D Rolph, 'Vindicating Reputation and Privacy' in AT Kenyon (ed), *Comparative Defamation and Privacy Law* (Cambridge, Cambridge University Press, 2016) 291–308. Contrast the fustian specialty defamation bars in London, Melbourne and Sydney.
[49] D Partlett, '*New York Times v. Sullivan* at Fifty: Defamation in Separate Orbits' in Kenyon (ibid) 58.

the saga played out in English courtrooms where actions were brought against Americans who had published defamatory material in England. Congress was outraged sufficiently to pass legislation against the enforcement of judgments. Editorials in American newspapers bemoaned this 'libel tourism' pointing to the lack of freedoms in England.[50] The outcry was sufficient to commission a select committee and prompt the English Parliament to pass legislation requiring a showing of closer connections to England. Whatever can be said about this libel tourism episode, one thing is clear. The absorption of *NYT v Sullivan* into the fabric of American society is deep and pervasive. It is hard to imagine any case law in the rest of the world that has left such a mark; that has become a talisman of faith in the constitutional system. Its ties with the Civil Rights movement and its towering rhetoric have fuelled the public influence of the case.[51] To be sure, the standing of the case rests heavily on the institution that gained greatly. The press was given room to make errors that harm people. It was given an exalted status and an unparalleled soap box. The economics of running the business of the press was given a huge financial break.[52] No longer was exposure to liability for defamation a major item on the balance sheet.[53]

III. THE UNEVEN PATH POST-*SULLIVAN*

The Court left much to be determined in constitutionalising the tort. What should happen in cases where the plaintiff is not a public officer? What if the plaintiff is a private citizen? If the publication is not of public concern? If the imputation is not one of fact? Who bears the burden of proving falsity? Is fault required to be proved by the plaintiff in all defamation actions? Should the law move beyond the dichotomy between public officials and figures to have protection turn on the public importance of the speech?

Development of the law depended on federal courts and the Supreme Court. State courts which deal with the common law on a daily basis reflecting local norms are excluded. This of course reflects the holding in *NYT v Sullivan* that deprives defamation actions of the jury's grounding in local norms and understandings. In addition, the judges on federal courts and the Supreme Court are

---

[50] See D Partlett, 'The Libel Tourist and the Ugly American: Free Speech in an Era of Modern Global Communications' (2009) 48 *University of Louisville Law Review* 629. Courts have struggled with multijurisdictional defamation. See *Haaretz.com v Goldhar* 2018 SCC 28 (Canadian Supreme Court adopting a *forum non conveniens* argument in rejecting jurisdiction where the ties to Canada were not significant and even though plaintiff was in the jurisdiction, ie Ontario).

[51] See R Tsai, *Eloquence and Reason: Creating a First Amendment Culture* (New Haven, Yale University Press, 2008).

[52] See R Weaver, D Partlett et al, *The Right To Speak Ill: Defamation, Reputation And Free Speech* (Durham (NC), Carolina Academic Press, 2006).

[53] D Logan, 'Libel Law in the Trenches: Reflections on Current Data on Libel Litigation' (2001) 87 *Virginia Law Review* 503 (reporting on the paucity of cases that are successful).

generally steeped in public law, possessing little experience with private law. Recall that Justice Harlan, with experience in private legal practice and in the government sphere, voiced concern in *Sullivan* in the whorl of internal debate among the Justices about preserving the common law tradition. But that sentiment is one rarely heard nowadays.[54]

Beyond the doctrinal and judicial policy challenges, the issue subsequently not well examined is whether the case fostered a destructive public dialogue that erodes the foundations of the exchange of ideas pressed by the court as the foundation of its finding. The 'background', stated Justice Brennan, was the 'profound national commitment to the principle that debate on public issues should be uninhibited, robust and wide open, and that it may well include vehement, caustic, and sometimes unpleasantly sharp attacks on government and public official'.[55] Such speech is the 'essence of self-government'.[56] Even the most vile, outrageous, speech is to be tolerated to provide a 'breathing space' to freedoms protected under the First Amendment. The reasoning is adopted by the Court in *Snyder v Phelps*,[57] in rejecting a tort action in intentional infliction of emotional distress brought by the plaintiffs who were subjected to picketing near the funeral of their son who had been killed in Iraq. The Westboro Baptist Church had a *modus operandi* of visiting funerals of fallen soldiers to push their message that God hated America because its government tolerated homosexuals. The Court found that speech was capable of inflicting great harm. But Chief Justice Roberts intoned that as 'a Nation' the path has been chosen not to punish the speaker. This was because public debate on matters of public concern is not to be stifled. Justice Alito was the lone dissenter observing the narrowness of the tort and the private figure status on the plaintiffs. The plaintiff's status had stemmed from *NYT v Sullivan*, and the Court's willingness to lumber those with public status with the sling and arrows of harsh and wounding speech on the basis of the voluntary assumption of public official and figures of putting up with the 'heat in the kitchen'. Furthermore, those persons had a greater ability to fight back in the market place of ideas.

Snyder also accepts that the cost of hurtful speech is to be borne by individuals. This flouts a basic element of justice that the good of many should not be put at the feet of the few. If a liability rule is to be jettisoned for a public purpose those who are to be protected by the rule ought in justice be able to claim compensation against the public who are so benefitting. The public are

---

[54] A hollow ring of it is found in some of the originalist interpretation where the justice will strive to determine the law at the time of the constitution's framing. See Justice Scalia's support of the jury role in determining punitive damages: *State Farm Mutual Auto Ins Co v Campbell* 538 US 408 (2003). See generally, A S Krishnakumar and V Nourse, 'The Canon Wars' (2019) 97 *Texas Law Review* (forthcoming).

[55] *New York Times Co v Sullivan* 376 US 254, 270 (1964).

[56] *Garrison v State of Louisiana* 379 US 64, 74–75 (1964).

[57] 562 US 443 (2011).

represented by government. To give an example drawn from the application of the defence of necessity, destruction of property to save a city from conflagration ordered by an official is justifiable and thus is a good defence to any tort action. However, this leaves the issue that the social contract ought to compensate those harmed property-owners.[58]

Furthermore, the holding fails to understand that tort law is not simply a regulatory regime. It bespeaks also community values of autonomy and protection of the vulnerable. The law had long regarded that persons at funerals were particularly vulnerable.[59]

The other issue in giving room for errors concentrates on but one dimension of public speech; its increase in quantum. An equal matter is the quality of public speech. Careful speakers who commit errors are tarred with the brush of those who are completely careless of the truth of their utterances. As the Supreme Court recognizes in *Dun & Bradstreet, Inc v Greenmoss Builders*,[60] in respect of private information, a credit report, was actionable in defamation absent a showing of actual damage. The commercial value of accuracy loomed large in enforcing a stricter liability. The liability exposure would be priced into the product, resulting in an optimal level of accurate information. It is liability that acts as a guarantee. It is axiomatic that the provider of the report is in the better position to check on accuracy. The rule encourages reliance and therefore sound business decisions.

The market for public information is a far cry from the purely private commercial information in private information. Accuracy is sought after, and is mainly delivered, via demonstrated reputations for full, fair and accurate, reporting. This is why in *NYT v Sullivan* the plaintiff highlighted the shoddy checking of the information in the advert. Leading newspapers like the *NYT* and the *Washington Post* trade on their integrity. Magazines like the *New Yorker*[61], the *Economist*, and *Atlantic Monthly* are motivated likewise. In broadcasting, National Public Radio seeks to attain the same status. Reputations are hard-won, but are delicate. Political attack and disinformation of them are favoured by political forces seeking to create chaos and advance agendas through populist movements. In a world of asymmetric information, consumers, citizens, come to distrust all media not being able to discern reliable reporting from false reporting. The reliability of all reportage is diminished. The public falls back then on tribal instincts in reaching conclusions about public matters. Media manipulators hold sway. It is attractive to support wide-open robust speech, but erroneous speech crowds out reliable speech as 'lemons' in the car market crowd out good,

---

[58] See *Surocco v Geary* 3 Cal 69 (1853). See also F Schauer, 'Uncoupling Free Speech' (1992) 92 *Columbia L Rev* 1321, 1339–43.

[59] D Partlett, 'Tort Liability and the American Way: Reflections on Liability for Emotional Distress' (1997) 45 *American Journal of Comparative Law* 171.

[60] 472 US 749 (1985).

[61] *Masson v New Yorker Magazine Inc* 501 US 496 (1991).

reliable cars.[62] The fear, scotched in the *NYT v Sullivan* case, that 'good men' would be dissuaded from entering public life is real.[63] The quality of speech and the preparedness of persons to enter the field of politics is a major issue in modern democracy. Civic republicanism depends on voices in the town hall meeting to assist the community in deciding who should govern and what rules should apply to the community, as Meiklejohn persuasively showed.[64] But, the ideal of the New England town hall, where information asymmetries are absent, is far from the din of modern American politics, where asymmetries are ubiquitous. It is this marketplace of ideas that also fails, as I now suggest.

A. The Uncertain Foundations: The Market Place Fiction

It fit nicely within laissez-faire ideology to conceptualise free speech as an evolutionary process that through market testing maximises the chances of truth emerging. For a democracy, this was like Adam Smith's invisible hand at work. In the New England town hall, views would be aired and rational debate would drive toward truth.

This premise found such powerful champions as Holmes[65] and Brandeis.[66] The marketplace of ideas, sitting at the centre of *NYT v Sullivan*, is much repeated and often misused. This is a most important matter.[67] Does competition of the most robust and vehement type, although it makes us uncomfortable, serve a higher purpose of exposing truth through the fire of contending views? If this is true, and if democracy is made the stronger for it, the fulsome interpretation of the First Amendment ought to be upheld. For our purposes, the press ought to be unfettered and, perhaps, an even greater scope ought to be afforded public speech. Here lie the epistemological problems.

Two points are salient. Why is it that free speech has attained a trumping power when the interests it is protecting, say liberty or democracy, are not seen as standing on their own feet? There are other rights that may play as important a role in sustaining the ultimate value.[68] It may be tactically justifiable to

---

[62] The cost of dishonesty, therefore, lies not only in the amount by which the purchaser is cheated; the cost also must include the loss incurred from driving legitimate business out of existence. See G Akerlof, 'The Market for 'Lemons': Quality Uncertainty and the Market Mechanism' (1970) 84 *Quarterly Journal of Economics* 488.

[63] Baron Bramwell in *Derry v Peek* rightly saw that too wide a liability for fraud would chase out the reasonably honest leaving the rogue: (1889) 14 App Cas 337, 58 LJ.CH 864.

[64] R Krotoszynski Jr, *The First Amendment In Cross Cultural Perspective, A Comparative Legal Analysis Of The Freedom Of Speech* (New York, NYU Press, 2006).

[65] See *Abrams v United States* 250 US 616, 624 (1919) (Holmes J, dissenting).

[66] See *Whitney v California* 274 US 357, 372 (1927) (Brandeis J, concurring).

[67] It has not fared well in contemporary commentary. See, eg, A Goldman and J Cox, 'Speech, Truth, and the Free Market for Ideas' (1996) 2 *Legal Theory* 1.

[68] See F Schauer, 'Free Speech on Tuesdays' (2015) 34 *Law and Philosophy* 119; Opinion, B Ackerman, 'Dignity Is a Constitutional Principle', *New York Times*, 30 March 2014, at SR5, http://nyti.ms/1hKKIVx (championing human dignity as a base constitutional value). For a powerful

employ a powerful version of free speech, but that does not make it philosophically sound.[69] The recitation of an express right must signal that the right, as part of a wider right, was absent or threatened especially. That makes the right historically contingent and its form will vary in time and place. Thus, to punish speech denying the Holocaust is understandable in Europe but not in the United States. To criticise European laws prohibiting such denial under First Amendment grounds fails to attend to the historic grounding of the prohibition.

What is more, the rhetoric of the marketplace implants unfortunate elements of laissez-faire ideology that allow anti-regulatory assumptions to be translated as accepted versions of constitutional free speech rights. In accepting the metaphor, under the view that the right is to protect an audience or listener's rights, the US Supreme Court assumes the truth-producing powers of the 'free market'. Thus, the Court relies on the free market to strike down not only campaign financing restrictions in *Citizens United*[70] and *McCutcheon*,[71] but also the dissemination of false information on military decorations in *Alvarez*.[72] Such a market also is available to those traduced by defamatory imputations, even private persons it is supposed under *Phelps*.[73] Like the abandoned *Lochner*[74] decision that threw its lot in with laissez-faire freedom of contract under substantive due process, the First Amendment rhetoric marginalises the role of government and the common law.

In the second place, the rhetoric of truth production through the operation of the free market flies in the face of research showing that the public, receiving information, is not composed of rational actors. The listener rights theory is premised on the assumption that individuals faced with a range of competing information on topics may rationally sift through that information and come to conclusions that, when grossed across a population, will express truth. Research reported by Glaeser and Sunstein shows that persons faced with truth that does not fit their preconceived ideas and persuasions will reject the truth.[75]

---

rejoinder to the all-encompassing First Amendment see, J Waldron, *The Harm In Hate Speech* (Cambridge (Ma), Harvard University Press, 2012). Compare F Abrams, *The Soul Of The First Amendment* (New Haven, Yale University Press, 2017).

[69] See Schauer (ibid) 122.

[70] *Citizens United v Federal Election Commission* 558 US 310 (2010). For a criticism on the policy plane see, R Hasen, *Plutocrats United: Campaign Money, The Supreme Court, & The Distortion Of American Elections* (New Haven, Yale University Press, 2016).

[71] *McCutcheon v Federal Election Commission* 572 US 185 (2014).

[72] *US v Alvarez*, 567 US 709, 132 S Ct 2537 (2012). See also T Joo, 'The Worst Test of Truth: The 'Marketplace of Ideas' as a Faulty Metaphor' (2014) 89 *Tulane L Rev* 383. First Amendment jurisprudence may justify the protection either in the rights of the speaker (an exercise in autonomy) or in the rights of the audience or listener (the sustenance of democratic values or republican ideals). Republican theory may base certain rights in protecting ideals of citizens' participation. See A Roberts, 'A Republican Account of the Value of Privacy' (2014) 14 *European Journal of Political Theory* 320.

[73] *Snyder v Phelps* 562 US 443, 131 S Ct 1207 (2011).

[74] *Lochner v NY* 198 US 45 (1905).

[75] See E Glaeser and C Sunstein, 'Does More Speech Correct Falsehoods?' (2014) 43 *Journal of Legal Studies* 65.

For example, people given a mock news article, where President Bush defends the Iraq War by citing the risks of weapons being passed to terrorists, were given the Duelfer Report,[76] which documented the lack of weapons of mass destruction in Iraq. Those people were then asked on a five-point scale their agreement with the statement that Iraq had 'an active weapons of mass destruction program'.[77] Noting the subjects' political ideology, one finds a remarkable result. Liberals shifted modestly to disagree while for conservatives, there was a significant shift to agreeing with the statement. In other words, the correction backfired.[78]

Cognitive explanations may encourage people to cling to false information. To change one's views leads to uncertainty in how one views the world, which comes at a cost in accessing memories. Glaeser and Sunstein base an explanation on what they label 'asymmetric Bayesianism'.[79] A speaker conveys the information, and the identity of that speaker is critical. The speaker may be interested in persuading to a viewpoint or independent. Given that listeners have preconceptions, information is filtered as to conform to a preexisting, settled view of the world. The authors state that 'corrections may backfire if people have strong antecedent convictions and understand purported corrections of those convictions as evidence that those convictions must be right'.[80] Alternatively, the authors also model the 'memory boomerang,' which, in the face of an asserted fact, acts to surface a host of lost memories that were the basis of forming a contrary view. Those past memories, now recalled, will move a person to reject the new information. The argument holds that the only speaker who is likely to shift these antecedent convictions is the 'surprising validator', the speaker who is representative of the ingrained view but takes the other unexpected view. The surprising validator has special credibility in counteracting asymmetric Bayesianism.[81] Rather than a competition convincing listeners of truth, the authors find that the most convincing vehicle is the opinion of a person

---

[76] C Duelfer, *Comprehensive Report of the Special Advisor to the DCI on Iraq's WMD* (Washington, DC, Central Intelligence Agency, 2004), www.cia.gov/library/reports/general-reports-1/iraq_wmd_2004.

[77] See Glaeser and Sunstein (n 75).

[78] The authors cite similar studies. In recent research about immunisation, parents given scientific facts about the dangers of immunisation still persist in believing falsehoods about connections to autism. B Nyhan, J Reifler, S Richey and G L Freed, 'Effective Messages in Vaccine Promotion: A Randomized Trial' (2014) 133 PEDIATRICS DOI: 10.1542.

[79] See Glaeser and Sunstein, 'More Speech' (2014).

[80] ibid 77.

[81] An example that should have worked in this way was a story floated by President Trump that the Obama Administration had planted a 'spy' in the Trump campaign: S Davis, 'Ryan Says There's "No Evidence" the FBI Informant Spied on Trump's Campaign', NPR (6 June 2018). The FBI gave a confidential briefing to both sides of politics. Rep Trey Goudy, a strong supporter of the President, and a 'surprising validator' gave an interview to Fox News in which he stated that no such thing had happened and that the FBI had acted correctly in protecting Americans. Still the conspiracy theory lived and was repeated.

with a similar and shared worldview who vouches for the truth. Dan Kahan has shown through exhaustive empirical research that perceptions of risks arising in socially contested areas like gun control, disposal of nuclear wastes and climate change, are mediated by values rather than scientific fact.[82]

Similarly, the new behaviouralism in social sciences has alerted us to the limits of the rational actor model of human actions. Humans are decision-makers that are energy-conserving. They depend on shortcuts to make decisions that are usually good enough, but which break down in contexts where tough rational thought is called for.[83] The ordinary person relies on certain decision-making heuristics to get by. This is a problem, as Paul Horwitz points out: 'Much of our current free speech jurisprudence is based on the assumption that the government should not regulate speech because, in an unregulated marketplace, people will be perfectly capable of responding rationally to speech'.[84] Distinguished commentators like Lyrissa Lidsky concede the flaws but urge that it is a noble model, serving the purpose of guarding against the dangers of overweening government.[85] Another argument in rescue of the possible emergence of truth is that humans evolved to make and evaluate arguments. One would assume they show biases in order to make persuasive arguments. This would be the reason for resistance to truthful statements.[86] If one believes in the veracity of an idea or fact, one is more convincing and persuasive. Yet, these arguments cannot be pursued here. What is plain is that the First Amendment will be under attack as rotten in its foundations. Like Lidsky's contention, the repair work will take the form of treating the marketplace as a theoretical construct – a metaphor – for a principle that eschews government regulation as dangerous to the democracy, to the rights of the public audience and to the speakers in the public forum. One cannot ground this in behaviour, but rather in faith. The sceptic Holmes never thought truth would emerge. Everything in his world was up for grabs.

These qualifications on the marketplace support a judicial role in correcting error. If a validator has a role in correcting falsehoods, it would seem that the process of defamation liability is a powerful tool. The truth of the facts is subjected to independent review through court proceedings. May this 'non-market' process be an effective vehicle to convey the truth? If listeners often

---

[82] DM Kahan, H Jenkins-Smith and D Braman, 'Cultural Cognition of Scientific Consensus' (2011) 14 *Journal of Risk Research* 147.

[83] See D Kahneman, *Thinking Fast And Slow* (New York, Farrar, Strauss and Giroux, 2011).

[84] P Horwitz, 'Free Speech as Risk Analysis: Heuristics, Biases, and Institutions in the First Amendment' (2003) 76 *Temple L Rev* 1. See also P Horwitz, 'The First Amendment's Epistemological Problem' (2012) 87 *Washington L Rev* 445. For a comprehensive listing of the role of the marketplace device/metaphor see DE Bambauer, 'Shopping Badly: Cognitive Biases, Communications, and the Fallacy of the Marketplace of Ideas' (2006) 77 *University of Colorado L Rev* 649.

[85] Lidsky, 'Nobody's Fool' (2010).

[86] See D Westen, *The Political Brain: The Role Of Emotion In Deciding The Fate Of The Nation* (New York, Public Affairs, 2008) (neuroscience establishing that political choices are driven by emotional portions of the brain, thus people may vote against their objective self-interests).

agree with courts when they support a worldview, say, in support of the Second Amendment, will those listeners be more amenable when the court speaks to truth that does not conform to the preconceived beliefs? Since defamation litigation is centred on the truth of allegations, would the courts as an institution play a powerful part in correcting mistaken information? The courtroom as a neutral and trusted forum for dispute resolution and diversion of warring camps has great advantage.[87]

It has been recognised in the academic literature that the traditional approach in the marketplace of ideas lacks substance at least as framed by the courts. The theories of cognitive science have undermined the presumptions of rational debate. As Julie Seaman in an elegant paper submits, the theoretical ground is now taken with what is known as the Argumentative Theory of Reasoning (ATR).[88] As she says, the theory 'posits that the function of human reason is not – as in the classical view – to find the "right" or "true" or "best" answer; rather, the function of reason is to make and win arguments'.[89] Seaman employs the insights of 'crowd theory', however, to argue that the participation of many tends to better decisions and development of knowledge. She ventures that the reasoning of Justice Brennan in *NYT v Sullivan* and the Chief Justice in *Snyder* confirm the notion that speech is for persuasion and not a honing of views to objective truth. Thus, the room to err, even unreasonably in the actual malice test, draws greater numbers to issues of public interest and allows room for wide arguments. All this would itself be persuasive if the listener or group could rationally discern strong and weak arguments. To be sure in a perfect debating society a deliberative process may lead to better decisions. But in the clamorous world of shouted and accelerated opinion and false fact, much more likely is the dismal conclusion that arguments that fit preconceived worldviews will be accepted and other conflicting views or evidence discounted.[90] The paper is nevertheless important deploying a sophisticated scientific theory in rescuing Sullivan from the reliance on the 'market place of ideas' rationale. One thing is for sure – the marketplace metaphor as traditionally couched has lost its mojo. And in the end a process under traditional defamation law, as modified for example under *Reynolds v Times Newspapers Ltd* in the UK[91] or *Lange v Australian Broadcasting Corporation* in Australia,[92] would allow juries greater scope to weigh arguments may be more efficacious than the court's *NYT v Sullivan* turn.

---

[87] For a general argument about the power of tort litigation in generating information see Alexandra Lahav, *In Praise of Litigation* (New York, Oxford University Press, 2017) 56–83.

[88] J Seaman, 'Winning Arguments' (2017) 41 *Law and Psychology Review* 1 (2017).

[89] ibid (citing H Mercier and D Sperber, 'Why do Humans Reason? Arguments for an Argumentative Theory' (2011) 34 *Behavioral and Brain Science* 57).

[90] See Kahan et al, 'Cultural Cognition' (2011).

[91] [2001] 2 AC 127. As to this case, see ch 9.

[92] (1997) 189 CLR 520.

One conclusion follows from this discussion: the cacophony of voices in the public marketplace will *not* tack public debate toward truth. Further, the very metaphor may be biased against reasonable regulation and the use of liability rules to balance rights in speech. Moreover, as I propose to canvass in the next part, the assumptions about the production of public information are frozen in an era past, that of major news outlets and are not reflective of modern technology and methods by which citizens garner information about the world around them.

IV. PUBLIC INFORMATION: THEN AND NOW

Whether it is progeny of *NYT v Sullivan* or other courts in the Anglo-American tradition, the desire to draw on journalistic standards has been fraught. In a context of traditional publications, the standards are clearer. For example, to vet stories and seek comment from those traduced is articulated in the *Reynolds v Times Newspapers*[93] test and found to be critical in the application of *Lange v ABC*.[94] In post-*NYT v Sullivan* law the inquiry focuses on proof of 'actual malice'. This approach places a heavy burden on the plaintiff to show reckless-ness by producing 'obvious reasons to doubt the veracity of the informant or the accuracy of his reports'.[95] The difficulty in applying the standard can be seen in *Masson*,[96] which also highlights the nature of the publication and the standard of journalism to be expected. That will be a constant issue with online publications and the expectations that are made on accuracy. Even the use of the term 'journalist' now creates problems.[97] Costless entry to the blogosphere has set up different expectations. Additionally, the privacy concerns are grave given that electronic media remains retrievable well past its date of publish.[98] So the question is posed: how do we establish any kind of reliability in public discourse? Is that a forlorn hope that used to be relevant when we could talk about responsible journalism? Or perhaps it is that the press carries the impri-matur of reliability even more strongly, given that there is so much dross around.

Can this be asserted in an era when information is frictionless and where celebrity is the coin of the realm? Where the citizen depended on newspapers and a restricted electronic media, it may rightly be said that a liability rule may

---

[93] Above n 91.

[94] Above n 92.

[95] *St Amant v Thompson*, 390 US 727, 732 (1968).

[96] *Masson v New Yorker Magazine* 501 US 496 (1991).

[97] See KHF Kwok, 'Liability of Online Service Providers for Defamatory Content: The Case of Online Discussion Forums' (2014) 130 *LQR* 206; ASY Cheung, 'Liability of Internet Host Providers in Defamation Actions: From Gatekeepers to Identifiers', University of Hong Kong Faculty of Law Research Paper No 2014/013, 2014 http://ssrn.com/abstract=2428566.

[98] DJ Solove, *The Future of Reputation: Gossip, Rumor, and Privacy on the Internet* (New Haven, Yale University Press, 2007).

be targeted effectively to restrain publication. And perhaps the chill would be real. The world of blogs, of instantaneous communications, is distinguishable from this model. Google, Yahoo!, and others have powers that can range beyond the nation state. These private entities are the norm entrepreneurs and much of the action involves nation states attempting to regulate or engage their activities. Here I contend that *NYT v Sullivan* joins the leading English case of *Reynolds v Times Newspapers* in presenting a quaint version of the world set in aspic. To be sure, the traditional press still has power, but it is in competition with new and rapidly evolving ways in which the public receives its information.[99]

The classic model for journalism acting as the fourth estate was the investigative journalist, who bravely garnered information, tracked down its reliability, and published it fearlessly. The *Washington Post's* stories about Watergate are usually cited as the exemplar.[100] Certainly the *Pentagon Papers* case[101] emboldened the press to intrude on government secrecy, even where national security was claimed. This precedent has given the *NYT* in particular space and freedom to publish when the press elsewhere has been crimped by government prerogatives.[102] The test for false information that should not be protected has been acceptable standards of journalistic and press behaviour.[103]

The dawn of the internet era brought opinions that at last citizens, for the good of society, could involve themselves in national and international marketplaces of ideas. The benefits of this for participatory democracy were it was urged, obvious.[104] But the potency of false facts and trolls at the hands of bad actors have banished high hopes to the hopeless land of naivete. Even worse, it has usurped the role of responsible press in mediating debates and bringing

---

[99] See D Partlett and B McDonald, 'International Publications and Protection of Reputation: A Margin of Appreciation but not Subservience' (2011) 62 *Alabama L Rev* 477, 483. Ironically, it is traditional press that ought to invite a quality-ensuring defamation liability rule as an efficient means of differentiating its product from that of blogs and other electronic evanescent information.

[100] The reporting made the careers of Bob Woodward and Carl Bernstein. 'Deep Throat,' whose identity was eventually revealed, fed the story to them and it did not require the kind of in-depth research that is often claimed as the marker of this journalism. See generally D Von Drehle, 'FBI's No. 2 Was 'Deep Throat': Mark Felt Ends 30-Year Mystery of The Post's Watergate Source', *Washington Post*, 1 June 2005. www.washingtonpost.com/politics/fbis-no-2-was-deep-throat-mark-felt-ends-30-year-mystery-of-the-posts-watergate-source/2012/06/04/gJQAwseRIV_story.html.

[101] *NY Times v US*, 403 US 713 (1971).

[102] Note the *Guardian's* compunctions and reliance on the *NYT's* greater legal freedoms in the Snowden disclosures. See L O'Carroll, 'Guardian partners with New York Times over Snowden GCHQ files', *The Guardian*, 23 August 2013, http://gu.com/p/3t98j; Editorial, 'British Press Freedom Under Threat', *NY Times*, 14 November 2013 www.nytimes.com/2013/11/15/opinion/british-press-freedom-under-threat.html?smid=pl-share.

[103] See A Lewis, '*New York Times v. Sullivan* Reconsidered: Time to Return to 'The Central Meaning of the First Amendment'' (1983) 83 *Columbia L Rev* 603 (arguing that *NYT v Sullivan* has been insufficiently protective of free speech).

[104] J Balkin, 'Digital Speech and Democratic Culture: A Theory of Freedom of Expression for the Information Society' (2004) 79 *NYU L Rev* 1 (arguing for a citizens' participation theory of in the digital age; seeing that the digital age increases the possibility of a truly democratic culture.).

reliable information to the marketplace as I expressed above in the analogy of the market for lemons.

Attention has turned to the spreading of misinformation online. Take for example conspiracy theories. In an article by Del Vicario et al,[105] the authors show that homogeneity and polarisation are the main determinates for cascading information on the intenet. Using quantitative analysis, the authors find the spreading of misinformation inspiring conspiracy theories wherein cascades of users cluster around stories that support personal beliefs and worldviews. This was used to great effect in the last American Presidential election.

A product of the naïve early years is section 230 of the *Communications Decency Act 1996* (US). The section provides that: 'no provider or user of an internet computer service shall be treated as the publisher or speaker of any information provided by another information content provider'.

Congress, intruding into the common law republication rule, accordingly granted internet service providers (ISPs) immunity from liability for publishing false or defamatory material if the information is given by another party.[106] In *Reno v American Civil Liberties Union*,[107] the United States Supreme Court lauded the vital role of the networks' 'vast demographic fora'.[108] The internet was described as a 'dynamic multifaceted category of communication'.[109] The court extolled the virtues of Facebook and social media. A broad, robust protection has been afforded ISPs. For ISPs the section has become a new safe harbour, their *NYT v Sullivan* in statutory form. Some have even argued that the immunity is mandated by the First Amendment under the seminal case.[110] It follows that false news such as the Pizzagate internet story about Hillary Clinton running a child prostitution ring in Washington, DC, could not have been actionable despite its obvious falsity.[111] It should be noted that to hope that the posters of material are subject to liability is fatuous – such persons or entities usually evaporate in the mists of cyberspace.

It is a long trail from Montgomery in the oppressive heat of 1960 to the 2016 Presidential Election. The shadow is also long of the case that constitutionalised the law of defamation. The faith in maximal free speech has given birth to a place of free expression that carries great capacity to injure individuals and divide people to the detriment of democracy.

---

[105] M Del Vicario et al, 'The Spreading of Misinformation Online', *Proceedings of the National Academy of Sciences of the United States* (2018).

[106] *Carafano v Metrosplash.com Inc* 339 F3d 1119 (9th Cir 2003).

[107] 521 US 844 (1997).

[108] ibid 895.

[109] ibid 896.

[110] Note, 'Section 230 as First Amendment Rule' (2018) 131 *Harvard L Rev* 2017.

[111] EM Savino, Case Comment, 'Fake News: No one is Liable and that is a Problem' (2017) 65 *Buffalo L Rev* 1101.

V. CONCLUSION

The common law draws on the ancient history of experience of peoples who have, on the whole, deeply valued their lives under the rule of law.[112] The shortcomings of the human condition reflected in the politics of the time will sometimes subvert laws and institutions designed to accord civil rights. This was to occur during Reconstruction in the American South after the Civil War.[113] It was to well up in the 1960s as African-Americans asserted their constitutional rights.[114] The great case came at an hour when two men made a difference. The opinion of the court was truly pathfinding, but perhaps too iconic. Time and chance happeneth to all men and it does to cases.[115] Fifty-four years later we can look upon the case in its defamation aspect as a curate's egg. Bits are good bits are bad or at least not as resilient as we would have hoped on that January day in 1964. But society has changed and renewal is called for. There is a green light across the water and 'so we beat our boats against the current borne back ceaselessly into the past'.[116]

---

[112] R Tombs, *The English and Their History* (New York, Alfred Knopf, 2014).
[113] White, *The Republic for Which It Stands* (2017) 325–84.
[114] Klarman, *From Jim Crow To Civil Rights* (2006) 236.
[115] *Ecclesiastes* 9:11.
[116] F Scott Fitzgerald, *The Great Gatsby* (1925).

7

Uren v John Fairfax & Sons Pty Ltd *(1966)*

MARK LUNNEY*

I. INTRODUCTION

IN FEBRUARY 1963 Ivan Skripov, First Secretary of the Soviet Embassy in Australia, was declared *persona non grata* by the Australian government and was given a week to leave the country.[1] Skripov was a KGB officer who had arrived in Australia in 1959 to re-establish the Soviet Embassy after it was disbanded in the wake of the Petrov affair in 1954.[2] Skripov's connections to a number of Australian politicians, primarily from the left, was the context for articles in the press in early 1963 connecting the left-wing Federal member for Reid, Tom Uren, with Skripov, for which he sued for defamation. By the time the litigation finished six and a half years later, Skripov was the Soviet ambassador to Uganda and his attempt to destabilise Australian democracy had long been forgotten. But, no doubt unexpectedly for Skripov, his work did contribute to a challenge of another kind to orthodoxy: the nature of the relationship of the High Court of Australia and the Judicial Committee of the Privy Council. Throughout the 1960s, the High Court began to openly decline to follow decisions of superior English courts, including the House of Lords. While the decision of the High Court to reject the limits on awards

* Professor, University of New England, Australia; Visiting Professor, Dickson Poon School of Law, King's College London; Visiting Professor, University College, London. Thanks are due to Professor Paul Mitchell for his comments on an earlier draft.

[1] Skripov was exposed by a covert operation organised by the Australian Security Intelligence Organisation (ASIO) which involved the use of a double agent: D Horner, *The Spy Catchers: The Official History of ASIO 1949–1963: Vol 1* (Sydney, Allen & Unwin, 2014) 540–59.

[2] Petrov was a Russian diplomat who was stationed in Australia and defected in 1954. Amidst protests in Sydney, his wife, in the company of Russian security service personnel, was placed on a plane to be taken back to the Soviet Union but she was later removed from the plane by ASIO officers when it landed in Darwin. The events triggered a controversial federal Royal Commission on Espionage. See further R Manne, *The Petrov Affair: politics and espionage* (Sydney, Pergamon Press, 1987).

of exemplary damages in tort actions (including defamation) set out by Lord Devlin in *Rookes v Barnard*[3] was not the first time the High Court had declined to follow a House of Lords decision, it was the first time the Privy Council had the opportunity to comment on the practice. In allowing diversity between the positions in Australia and England, the Privy Council not only drew attention to the competing rationales for awards of exemplary damages but also established a new framework for the relationship between the common law and its application in non-English jurisdictions.

II. BACKGROUND

Tom Uren was elected as the Australian Labor Party (ALP) candidate for the federal seat of Reid in the 1957 federal election in Australia. Uren was from a working class background and had been a prisoner of war of the Japanese during the Second World War, enduring horrendous conditions while working on the Burma railway.[4] His entry into politics also required him to navigate the factional minefield that was the New South Wales branch of the ALP which he did with considerable political skill.[5] His life history up to the time of the defamatory publications in 1963 suggested both that he would not take kindly to someone questioning his patriotism and that he would be willing to fight to clear his name. Subsequent events proved this to be only too true, and whatever the legal ramifications of the court proceedings, they were only possible due to Uren's dogged persistence to clear his name of charges that were particularly hurtful to someone who had paid a high price in the service of his country.

In Uren's view, the allegations made against him were part of an Australian McCarthyism that took root in Australian politics after the Petrov affair in 1954 and was exacerbated by the alleged spread of communism in south-east Asia. Uren always believed, with some justification as was later revealed, that the basis of the allegations made against him came from the Australian Security Intelligence Organisation (ASIO). Three days after Skripov had been declared *persona non grata*, the *Sun-Herald* newspaper, owned by the Fairfax publishing family, published an article by Elwyn Spratt with the headline: 'LABOR LINK WITH RED SPY – CANBERRA CHARGE'. The second edition contained an identical article with a different headline: 'SPY DUPED LABOR MPs'. The underlying article alleged that allegations were shortly to be made in the federal parliament that two Labor MPs had been unsuspectingly provoked by Ivan Skripov to ask questions in federal parliament about the new, highly secret communications base the United States was building in Northwest Cape in Western Australia. Although the article had referred to two MPs rather than Uren by name, Uren had

---

[3] [1964] AC 1129 (*Rookes*).
[4] T Uren, *Straight Left* (Sydney, Random House, 1994) ch 3.
[5] ibid chs 6–7.

asked questions about the facility to the members of the government mentioned in the article and it was conceded by counsel at the trial of the action that the imputations could be taken as referring to Uren[6] and no further 'reference to the plaintiff' point was taken throughout the long history of the proceedings.[7]

In fact, allegations of this nature had been made in the Melbourne newspaper *The Age* in July 1962 although they had, apparently, not come to Uren's notice at the time.[8] The inspiration for the later article seems to have been comments in Parliament by the Liberal member for Ballarat, George Erwin, on 29 November 1962, suggesting that three federal Labor MPs, including Uren, had been inspired by Skripov to ask questions on sensitive foreign policy issues and had been briefed for foreign policy debates.[9] When Skripov was expelled from Australia, the *Sun-Herald* speculated that the matter would be raised again in Parliament, a speculation highlighted by the presence on the front page of a picture of Skripov and news of his deportation. The *Sun-Herald's* confidence seems quickly to have evaporated: while advertisements for the Sunday edition with the headline were advertised on television the previous night, by the third edition of the paper on the Sunday the article and associated headlines had been dropped and the following week an apology to the members (who were not named) was printed. But the *Sun-Herald's* competitor, the *Sunday Telegraph*, became aware of the article shortly after it was published, and in some of its later editions it printed a very similar story, with the headlines 'Spy Used Labor Men as "Pawns"' and 'Did Russian Spy Dupe A.L.P men?'. In cross examination in his action against Australian Consolidated Press Ltd (ACP), the publisher of the *Sunday Telegraph*, Uren claimed that the paper had 'stolen' the article from the *Sun-Herald*,[10] and even the editor of the *Sunday Telegraph* (who had written the article) agreed that the *Sun-Herald* piece was the inspiration for the article.[11] The result was that Uren had choices as to who to sue for publishing the alleged libel and he chose to sue both newspapers.

III. THE TRIALS

The action against ACP was heard first in February and March 1964. To bolster Uren's case, his barrister, the irrepressible Clive Evatt QC,[12] had advised Uren

---

[6] *Sydney Morning Herald (SMH)*, 1 May 1964, 6.

[7] Nor was it argued in Uren's case against Australian Consolidated Press where the allegation was that 'some' Labor MPs had been inspired to ask questions. Although lack of reference to Uren was pleaded it was not argued at trial: see *SMH*, 25 February 1964, 6; 6 March 1964, 6; 7 March 1964, 12.

[8] Uren (n 4) 138.

[9] *Hansard*, House of Representatives, 29 November 1962, 2820–21. Counsel for Australian Consolidated Press claimed that the 'guts' of their similar article in the *Sunday Telegraph* came from Erwin's speech: *SMH*, 6 March 1964, 6.

[10] *SMH*, 28 February 1964, 10.

[11] *SMH*, 5 March 1964, 9.

[12] Younger brother of former High Court judge, Federal Attorney General and Leader of the ALP Opposition in the federal parliament in the 1950s, Dr HV Evatt.

when initially consulted to see if there were any other libellous publications that could be included in the action against ACP. Uren found two others, one an editorial in the *Daily Telegraph* on the eve of the 1961 federal election and the other an article in the weekly *The Bulletin*[13] by Alan Reid, a well-known political journalist with historic Labor connections but who by 1961 was working for ACP and its conservative owner, Sir Frank Packer. The allegations in these publications were not as serious – Uren himself admitted he would not have sued on them on their own – and it was the gravamen of the Skripov allegations, common to both the Fairfax and ACP publications, that prompted the actions.[14]

The ACP trial was a lusty affair before a common jury of 12.[15] Apart from pleading the general issue, ACP relied on a statutory defence of qualified privilege available under the law of New South Wales. The conduct of Clive Evatt, Uren's counsel, was the subject of merited criticism on appeal: there is little doubt that he did transgress the boundaries of acceptable conduct in arguing his client's case.[16] Counsel for the defendant's tactics were also questionable: Uren was kept in the witness box for four days,[17] being asked questions 'in places of an acid nature'[18] that 'reached the uttermost bounds of relevancy, if it did not transgress them'.[19] But some things were clear: the trial judge, Collins J, had ruled that the Skripov allegations could not give rise to the imputation that Uren was a traitor. Despite this, Collins J left the question of exemplary damages to the jury. Perhaps because the reasons were not available, and in the absence of reliance on it by either counsel, the direction was not in accord with the recent observations of Lord Devlin in *Rookes*. Rather, the jury were told that it could award exemplary damages

> where the conduct of the defendant merits punishment, and this could only be considered to be so where its conduct has been malicious; that it has shown what has been described as contumelious disregard for the rights of the plaintiff, here, of the plaintiff's right to enjoy the reputation that he possesses.[20]

---

[13] Founded in 1880, *The Bulletin* was influential in advocating for Australian federation. It was bought by ACP in 1961, merged with another publication, and became a news magazine. It ceased publication in 2008.

[14] Uren (n 4) 140. In fact, the allegations made by Erwin in Parliament may have been the indirect result of earlier comments made by Reid involving Skripov and another Labor member of the House of Representatives, Bert James: R Fitzgerald and S Holt, *Alan the Red Fox Reid: Pressman Par Excellence* (Sydney, UNSW Press, 2010) 149–50.

[15] A detailed account of the trial is provided in G Fricke, 'The Member for Reid and the Russian Spy' in *Libels, Lampoons and Litigants: Famous Australian Libel Cases* (Melbourne, Hutchinson, 1984) 34–37.

[16] *Uren v Australian Consolidated Press Ltd* (1965) 65 SR (NSW) 271, 281–99 (Walsh J).

[17] Uren (n 4) 140.

[18] *Uren v Australian Consolidated Press Ltd* (1965) 65 SR (NSW) 271, 312 (Wallace J).

[19] *Australian Consolidated Press Ltd v Uren* (1966) 117 CLR 185, 202 (Windeyer J).

[20] *Uren v Australian Consolidated Press Ltd* (1965) 65 SR (NSW) 271, 300 (Walsh J), quoting from Collins J's summing up to the jury.

The jury returned verdicts for Uren: £5,000 for the first publication, £10,000 for the second and £15,000 for the two editions of the *Sunday Telegraph* containing the Skripov allegations (about AU $825,000 in 2018).

The action against Fairfax went to trial with a jury of 12 in late April. Although defences had apparently been pleaded, at the commencement of the trial these were withdrawn and an offer of an apology in open court together with the payment of Uren's costs was made and rejected. Fairfax had earlier offered, in March, to print an apology naming Uren as his identity was revealed as being caught by the publication in the ACP trial but this too had been rejected.[21] The result was that the trial was solely on the question of damages and the operation of various statutory provisions that could reduce or eliminate Fairfax's liability.[22]

Exemplary damages were at the forefront of the arguments in the trial but they revealed the ambiguity at the heart of these awards that *Rookes* had tried to address. Although ruling that the articles could not found an imputation that Uren was a collaborator, the trial judge, Maguire J, ultimately rejected Woodward's submission for Fairfax that the case was not one for exemplary damages.[23] Unlike in the ACP case, counsel for the defendant cited *Rookes* in support of his claim that exemplary damages were not available. Maguire J rejected counsel's argument that *Rookes* prevented exemplary damages from being awarded in this case. He directed the jury that exemplary damages could be awarded by way of example and discouragement and told the jury to consider the seriousness of the libel, the surrounding circumstances (such as the absence of any check as to the accuracy of the story so as to make it a 'reckless proceeding'), the reckless disregard of the plaintiff's right to have his reputation preserved unsullied, and that the libel was published with the intent of increasing sales, circulation and profit.[24] It is difficult to know whether this final consideration was in recognition of Lord Devlin's second category in *Rookes* as Evatt for Uren in both his opening and closing addresses had stressed that Uren was fighting against 'this' type of journalism, journalism that was no doubt commercially inspired but was objectionable not only for that reason. What is clear is that this factor, even if it was meant to reflect Lord Devlin's second category, was not an independent limitation. It was simply one of a number

---

[21] Fairfax's primary argument at the trial seems to have been that damages should be reduced to reflect Uren's failure to accept an apology: *SMH*, 1 May 1964, 6; 5 May 1964, 10.

[22] Defamation Act 1958 (NSW), s 22 (apology and payment of damages into court); s 24 (evidence in mitigation of previous recovery of damages in respect of other defamatory publications to the same effect as matter sued upon). Maguire J ruled that s 22 was not admissible as no payment into court had been made but rejected arguments that s 24 did not apply because of technical compliance failures with regulations for printing and publishing newspapers: *SMH*, 2 May 1964, 5.

[23] *SMH*, 5 May 1964, 10.

[24] *Uren v John Fairfax & Sons Pty Ltd* (1965) 65 SR (NSW) 223, 233 (Herron CJ, citing Maguire J at trial).

of factors to consider in determining whether an exemplary award would be available. The jury returned a verdict of £13,000 (AU $360,000 in 2018) for Uren.

IV. EXEMPLARY DAMAGES AT THE TIME OF *UREN*

Exemplary (or punitive damages as they were sometimes called) were a well-established facet of the law of damages for torts by the early 1960s. Their origins remain shrouded in some mystery but almost certainly they derived from the Roman notion of *injuria*, reflected in early English law through the medieval statutes allowing for multiple damages awards for proscribed conduct and through compensation mechanisms which attached to conduct which was 'wrongful', pre-dating a firm distinction between tort and crime.[25] Mitchell notes that from the eighteenth century the conduct of the defendant was something that could be taken into account to increase awards of damages in a wide variety of torts, including defamation. In his view, one explanation for the concern with the method in which the damage was inflicted was the analogy with Roman law's separate delict of *injuria* which rendered actionable contemptuous conduct towards another.[26]

Injuria seems also to have been the basis of Salmond's description of exemplary damages in the first edition of his textbook on torts in 1907 but with a particular slant. His explanation of vindictive damages (which he noted were otherwise called exemplary damages) was that they provided a solatium for insult or injury, beyond any material loss suffered by the plaintiff. Salmond recognised that it was said that such awards were made to punish the defendant but thought the better view was that they were a solatium for wounded dignity and feelings, 'as a remedy for *injuria*, in the sense in which Roman lawyers used that term'.[27] The connection with Roman law is evident in his statement that such awards were only available for conscious wrongdoing in contumelious disregard of another's rights, *contumelia* being the Latin word used to describe the kind of conduct actionable under the delict.[28] It is tempting to think that the *contumelia* would obviate the need to prove distress and humiliation but in practice no doubt counsel wanted to play up these elements in appeals to the jury to maximise any award of damages (as Evatt did in the Uren trials). But there was also sufficient doubt as to the place for 'compensating' feelings in a defamation action for defendant's counsel in the Fairfax trial to argue that no compensation could be granted for hurt feelings.[29]

---

[25] J Taliadoros, 'The Roots of Punitive Damages at Common Law: A Longer History' (2016) 64 *Cleveland State Law Review* 251.

[26] P Mitchell, *The Making of the Modern Law of Defamation* (Oxford, Hart, 2005) 66.

[27] J Salmond, *The Law of Torts* (London, Stevens & Haynes, 1907) 102.

[28] ibid; Mitchell (n 26) 67.

[29] *SMH*, 30 April 1964, 6.

The ambiguity surrounding the concept is found in tort texts from the late nineteenth century up until the time of *Rookes* in 1964. Later editors of Salmond,[30] and through various editions of Addison,[31] Clerk & Lindsell,[32] Pollock,[33] and Winfield,[34] and in related texts on damages,[35] the original text was either ambiguous, or, if originally clear, became convoluted when judicial decisions forced subsequent editors to be less definitive. For example, the author of the 13th edition of *Salmond* in 1961, RFV Heuston, was perhaps more equivocal than Salmond about the legal position but was more certain on the normative question. Heuston maintained Salmond's view that exemplary damages constituted a solatium but recognised the authorities were not quite so clear-cut.[36] Although the punitive element could not be entirely excluded, he thought it was anomalous to the compensatory aim of tort law. While noting that the authorities drew no distinction between 'aggravated' and 'exemplary' damages, he argued that the former was the correct expression where compensatory damages were at large and the latter where damages were awarded to reflect disapproval of the defendant's conduct.[37] This was consistent with the relative newcomer to the tort text scene, JG Fleming, who seemed to unequivocally if briefly accept that exemplary damages served a purely punitive function, something he disliked given his view that the primary function of tort law was compensation.[38] But where was the boundary to be drawn? While Pollock saw the analogy of exemplary damages with *injuria*, he refers to both 'exemplary' and 'aggravated' damages as describing these kind of damages, and for 'gross' defamation added that 'there it is rather that no definite principle of compensation can be laid down than that damages can be given which are distinctly not compensatory'.[39] While this looks like an affirmation of a punitive principle, the comment must be read in light of his introductory statement that

---

[30] RFV Heuston, *Salmond on the Law of Torts*, 13th edn (London, Sweet & Maxwell, 1961) 737–39.

[31] L Cave, *Addison on Torts*, 5th edn (London, Stevens and Sons, 1879) 72; W Gordon and W Griffith, *Addison's Law of Torts*, 8th edn (London, Stevens and Sons, 1906) 49–50.

[32] J Clerk, F Lindsell, T Hollis Walker, *The Law of Torts*, 2nd edn (London, Sweet & Maxwell, 1896) 113; W Wyatt-Paine, *Clerk and Lindsell on Torts*, 7th edn (London, Sweet & Maxwell, 1921) 143; AL Armitage et al (eds), *Clerk and Lindsell on Torts*, 12th edn (London, Sweet and Maxwell, 1961) para 358.

[33] F Pollock, *The Law of Torts*, 7th edn (London, Stevens & Sons, 1904) 185–86. The text remained the same in the 12th edn (F Pollock, *The Law of Torts* (London, Stevens & Sons, 1923) 189.

[34] P Winfield, *A Textbook of the Law of Tort* (London, Sweet and Maxwell, 1937) 153; JA Jolowicz and T Ellis Lewis, *Winfield on Tort*, 7th edn (London, Sweet and Maxwell, 1963) 96.

[35] H McGregor, *Mayne and McGregor on Damages*, 12th edn (London, Sweet & Maxwell, 1961) paras 207, 212.

[36] *cf* his view in 1960 that exemplary damages were awarded to mark disapproval of the defendant's conduct: 'The Law of Torts in 1960' (1961) 6 *Journal of the Society of Public Teachers of Law* (ns) 26, 29.

[37] RFV Heuston, *Salmond on the Law of Torts*, 13th edn (London, Sweet & Maxwell, 1961) 737–39.

[38] JG Fleming, *The Law of Torts*, 2nd edn (Sydney, Law Book Co of Australasia, 1961) 2, 560.

[39] F Pollock, *The Law of Torts*, 7th edn (London, Stevens & Sons, 1904) 186.

exemplary damages were awarded where damages could not be assessed by any numerical rule so that 'juries have been not only allowed but encouraged to give damages that express indignation at the defendant's wrong rather than a value set upon the plaintiff's loss'. While such damages were not strictly compensatory as the injury they compensated had no monetary substitute, it is not clear that these awards were not compensatory in the wider sense of compensating for an intangible loss. In one sense, the opprobrium of the proscribed conduct was being used as a surrogate to value the non-pecuniary loss of the plaintiff.[40]

A different approach was taken by Street in his text on the law of damages, published in 1962. Street recognised the dispute over the nature of exemplary awards but did not argue conclusively as to which of the competing views was to be preferred. Recognising the arguments against purely punitive awards, he noted that the countervailing arguments in their favour were essentially pragmatic. After listing a number of these, he stated that 'in the present state of knowledge, one cannot say whether exemplary damages are desirable'.[41] The basic question was the practical usefulness of exemplary damages and 'no amount of theorising can provide an answer' to the question of the effectiveness of punitive awards in achieving the ends said to justify them.[42] While the point was perceptive, Street's views were of limited use to a court struggling to determine the judicial boundaries of awards of exemplary damages. The legal issue was the *nature* of awards that had been characterised as exemplary – something on which Street provided no definitive conclusion – and only once this had been clarified could questions as to their efficacy be addressed.

Little help was gained from the Anglo-Australian periodical literature. For example, while a 1929 historical study of exemplary damages for defamation in the *Australian Law Journal* seems to conclude that exemplary damages could extend beyond compensatory damages, even broadly construed,[43] it is sufficiently ambiguous for Julius Stone to have later claimed it in support of his (contrary) view that compensatory aggravated damages broadly conceived coincided completely with exemplary awards so that the latter were unnecessary.[44] Writing in 1963, Alec Samuels suggested at the start of his article that damages in defamation could have three components: for pecuniary or non-pecuniary injury, for the conduct of the defendant, and exemplary damages by way of a deterrent.[45] The 'conduct of the defendant' category seems to have been for

---

[40] ibid 185.

[41] H Street, *Principles of the Law of Damages* (London, Sweet & Maxwell Limited, 1962) 36.

[42] ibid.

[43] LFS Robinson, 'Exemplary Damages in Defamation' (1929) 3 *Australian Law Journal* 250; (1930) 3 ALJ 292, 294.

[44] J Stone, 'Double Count and Double Talk: The End of Exemplary Damages' (1972) 46 *Australian Law Journal* 311, 319, fn 50.

[45] A Samuels, 'Problems of Assessing Damages for Defamation' (1963) 79 *LQR* 63, 63–64.

conduct that contemporaries would have seen as attracting aggravated damages yet later Samuels argued that exemplary damages ought to be 'an assessment of the injury suffered by the plaintiff in particularly humiliating circumstances'.[46] How this fitted with his earlier categories was not explained, but the dearth of assistance to judges is evidenced by Windeyer J's favourable reference to the article in the Fairfax appeal in the High Court (albeit in support of the 'muddle the matter is in'[47]). Even where there were definitive statements, these were not always supported by an analysis of the authorities.[48]

One reason for the lack of clarity as to the juridical basis for awards of exemplary damages lay in its practical irrelevance. The vast majority of cases where the issue was relevant were defamation cases where the mode of trial was almost exclusively by jury. A jury verdict in favour of a plaintiff did not distinguish between compensatory, aggravated and punitive components of the award. As Lord Atkin pointed out in one of the few English cases to consider exemplary damages prior to *Rookes*, the punitive factor could not be separated from some known non-punitive factor[49] which made it difficult for appellate courts to decide questions solely on the nature of any exemplary award. This explains why the authors of a contemporary edition of Winfield detailed the limits of appellate review of jury verdicts in the section on exemplary or vindictive damages: what was important was the overall award the jury made, not any dissection of its constituent parts.[50]

V. *ROOKES v BARNARD* AND THE BANCO COURTS OF NEW SOUTH WALES

By the time the appeals were heard in the *Uren* cases the implications of *Rookes* for exemplary awards were clear. The details of *Rookes* are not relevant for present purposes – the case itself involved intimidation, not defamation – but in the course of his speech, Lord Devlin (with whom the other members of the House agreed) imposed limits on when awards of exemplary damages could be made in tort actions. Apart from where these awards were recognised by statute, only where there was 1) oppressive, arbitrary or unconstitutional action by servants of the government, or 2) where the defendant's conduct was calculated by him to make a profit for himself which might exceed the damages payable to the plaintiff, would such awards be allowed.[51] Lord Devlin was aware that these restrictions went beyond anything previously recognised in existing law.[52]

---

[46] ibid 76. There is no reference to aggravated damages in the article.
[47] *Uren v John Fairfax & Sons Pty Ltd* (1966) 117 CLR 118, 149.
[48] PS James, 'Measure of Damages in Contract and Tort – Law and Fact' (1950) 13 *MLR* 36, 38.
[49] *Ley v Hamilton* (1935) 153 LT 384, 386.
[50] JA Jolowicz and T Ellis Lewis, *Winfield on Tort*, 7th edn (London, Sweet and Maxwell, 1963) 96–97.
[51] *Rookes* [1964] AC 1129, 1226.
[52] ibid 1226.

The speech also recognised a strict divide between aggravated damages, which were compensatory, and exemplary damages, which attached solely to the conduct of the defendant and were punitive.[53] However, it was also recognised that awards of damages that compensated, including aggravated damages, could themselves have a punitive effect, giving rise to a potential concern of the double counting of a punitive element where both aggravated and punitive damages were awarded.[54]

The status of *Rookes* in Australia was an important issue when Fairfax and ACP appealed the jury verdicts in favour of Uren to the Full Court of the Supreme Court of New South Wales. The Fairfax appeal was heard and decided first,[55] and one of the general grounds of appeal related to aggravated and exemplary damages. In considering this ground the court was required to decide whether Lord Devlin's restrictions on exemplary awards applied in Australia. Several cases in both the High Court of Australia and the Supreme Courts of the states had upheld awards of exemplary or punitive damages in a wider range of situations than allowed for in *Rookes*. In *Whitfield v De Lauret & Co*,[56] a tort action involving unlawful interference with contractual performance, Knox CJ recognised a distinction between compensatory and exemplary damages, suggesting the later was only awarded 'in cases of conscious wrongdoing in contumelious disregard of another's rights'.[57] In the same case Isaacs J noted that from 'a very early period exemplary damages have been considered by very eminent Judges to be punitive for reprehensible conduct and as a deterrent'.[58] Isaacs J reiterated this view in *Herald & Weekly Times Ltd v McGregor*.[59]

While these cases were from the 1920s, later examples into the 1960s existed where Australian courts had assumed that exemplary damages could be awarded outside the categories of *Rookes*.[60] As a decision of the House of Lords, *Rookes* was not technically binding on Australian courts but from early in the High Court's history it had accepted as a matter of comity that it should follow decisions of the House of Lords.[61] This was reiterated in 1943 in

---

[53] ibid 1221.

[54] ibid 1228. The point is made more explicitly by Lord Hailsham of St Marylebone LC in *Broome v Cassell & Co* [1972] AC 1027, 1076. For criticism see J Stone, 'On the Liberation of Appellate Judges: How Not to Do It' (1972) 35 *MLR* 449.

[55] *Uren v John Fairfax & Sons Pty Ltd* (1965) 65 SR (NSW) 223. Other grounds related to the award being excessive and improper admission of evidence.

[56] *Whitfield v De Lauret & Co* (1920) 29 CLR 71.

[57] ibid 77.

[58] ibid 81.

[59] *Herald & Weekly Times Ltd v McGregor* (1928) 41 CLR 254, 266.

[60] *Triggell v Pheeney* (1951) 82 CLR 497; *Williams v Hursey* (1959) 103 CLR 30; *Fontin v Katopodis* (1962) 108 CLR 177. For state courts see *George v Truth & Sportsman Ltd* (1926) 26 SR (NSW) 595; *Guest v Ravesi* (1927) 27 SR (NSW) 449; *Mutch v Sleeman* (1929) 29 SR (NSW) 125; *Smith v Commonwealth Life Assurance Society Ltd* (1935) 35 SR (NSW) 552; *Proprietary Schools of Western Australia Ltd v The Crown* [1943] WAR 37; *Guise v Kovelis* (1946) 46 SR (NSW) 419.

[61] *Brown v Holloway* (1909) 10 CLR 89, 102–03 (O'Connor J); *Davison v Vickery's Motors Ltd* (1925) 37 CLR 1, 13–17 (Isaacs J).

Piro v W Foster & Co Ltd where the High Court affirmed that Australian courts (including itself) should follow decisions of the House of Lords in preference to a contrary decision of its own.[62] But this affirmation of imperial loyalty in a time of war came under pressure in the very different post-war world, and in 1963, in *Parker v R*,[63] Dixon CJ on behalf of the court declared that it would no longer consider itself bound to follow decisions of the House of Lords that were contrary to opinions and judgments of the High Court. But the precise effect that the declaration in *Parker* had on both the *Piro v Foster* rule and earlier Privy Council authority[64] suggesting House of Lords decisions were binding in 'colonial courts' was still uncertain, particularly for state courts, when the Uren litigation was before the New South Wales courts.[65]

The Full Court divided on whether it was required to follow *Rookes*. The majority of Herron CJ and Walsh J gave the *Parker* declaration a limited scope[66] and would have followed *Rookes* in preference to the earlier, contrary Australian authority. Wallace J disagreed, holding that a wide view of *Parker* was in line with modern trends.[67] He pointedly noted that no Australian cases had been cited in *Rookes* because it was not contemplated by the House of Lords that its decision would automatically effect High Court decisions on the issue. But the difference between the judges made no difference on the facts: even though Herron CJ and Walsh J found that the case did not fall within Lord Devlin's second category,[68] all members of the court held that even on the pre-*Rookes* Australian law, there was no evidence which would justify an award of exemplary damages being left to the jury[69] and a new trial limited to damages was ordered. While there were some different issues in the ACP appeal, the members of the Full Court approached the *Rookes* question in the same way they had in the Fairfax appeal.[70]

---

[62] *Piro v W Foster & Co Ltd* (1943) 68 CLR 313.

[63] *Parker v R* (1963) 110 CLR 610.

[64] *Trimble v Hill* (1879) 5 App Cas 342; *Robins v National Trust Company* [1927] AC 515.

[65] The decision of the High Court in *Skelton v Collins* (1966) 115 CLR 94, that other courts in Australia should follow the decision of the High Court in cases of clear conflict with a House of Lords decision, was not available to the Full Court, it being delivered after the judgments in the appeals: I Renaud, 'Uren v John Fairfax & Sons Pty Ltd; Australian Consolidated Press v Uren' (1968) 6 *Melbourne University Law Review* 439, 442. It was also suggested this applied to conflicting dicta issued by the High Court as well as formal decisions: 'A Three Part Fugue' (1966) 40 *Australian Law Journal* 69, 70.

[66] *Uren v John Fairfax & Sons Pty Ltd* (1965) 65 SR (NSW) 223, 247 (Herron CJ), 254 (Walsh J).

[67] ibid 268. His view was implicitly supported in a contemporary comment on the case: 'Parker's Case: A Cloud or a Beacon?' (1965) 39 *Australian Law Journal* 150.

[68] *Uren v John Fairfax & Sons Pty Ltd* (1965) 65 SR (NSW) 223, 255 (Walsh J). Herron CJ (248) agreed with Walsh J on this point.

[69] *Uren v John Fairfax & Sons Pty Ltd* (1965) 65 SR (NSW) 223, 234–35 (Herron CJ); 259 (Walsh J), 271 (Wallace J).

[70] *Uren v Australian Consolidated Press Ltd* (1965) 65 SR (NSW) 271. There were 77 grounds of appeal dealing primarily with the conduct of the trial.

VI. *UREN* IN THE HIGH COURT

Both *Uren* cases were appealed to the High Court. As the ACP appeal was heard first, arguments over the effect of *Rookes* were primarily made in that appeal[71] but the *Fairfax* judgment was delivered first ensuring its place as the leading authority.[72] While members of the court disagreed over whether a new trial should be ordered, all five judges held that *Rookes* did not represent the law in Australia and that the pre-existing law on when an award of exemplary damages could be made applied.[73] A number of themes supporting this conclusion can be discerned in the judgments.

First, all judges noted that *Rookes* was contrary to the previously accepted position in Australia as to when exemplary damages could be awarded. McTiernan J, for example, thought it would be 'injudicious' for the court to limit the scope of exemplary damages which had been established by earlier authority of the court.[74] Along the same lines as Wallace J in the Full Court, Taylor J also noted that in *Rookes* 'no account was taken of the development of the law in Australia where exemplary damages could be made in a much wider variety of cases'.[75] Moreover, the Australian authority was based on the recognised law of England on exemplary damages prior to *Rookes*. Taylor J's review of many of the authorities discussed by Lord Devlin led him to the conclusion that the categories in *Rookes* were not justified either upon principle or authority.[76]

Second, several members of the court critiqued Lord Devlin's first and second categories. The most powerful critique in this respect was from Taylor J. He found difficulty in determining the meaning of 'government' for the purpose of someone being a servant of the government, a matter of considerable importance in Australia because of the role of government entities in trade and commerce (such as banking, shipping and aviation). If servants of these entities were caught, it was difficult to see why persons performing similar roles in the private sector should be excluded from exemplary awards.[77] There was also the problem of what 'unconstitutional' meant in the context of a written constitution where it was perfectly possible for an unconstitutional act to be committed in good faith but be unconstitutional because it was held later to be beyond power. Taylor J opined that this was not what was meant – some flagrant and deliberate violation of a fundamental principle of the constitution

---

[71] *Australian Consolidated Press Ltd v Uren* (1966) 117 CLR 185.

[72] *Uren v John Fairfax & Sons Pty Ltd* (1966) 117 CLR 118.

[73] Members of the court variously described the conditions of the pre-existing law that justified an award as conscious conduct that demonstrated a contumelious disregard for the plaintiff's rights, that was reprehensible, that was malicious, wilful or disclosed fraud, violence, cruelty or insolence or the like: ibid 122 (McTiernan J), 143 (Menzies J), 154 (Windeyer J), 158 (Owen J).

[74] ibid 123.

[75] ibid 138.

[76] ibid 139.

[77] ibid 132.

was required[78] – but even the possibility of such conduct being caught lent support to his criticisms. The second category was for Taylor J equally problematic:

> I am quite unable to see why the law should look with less favour on wrongs committed with a profit-making motive than upon wrongs committed with the utmost degree of malice or vindictively, arrogantly or high-handedly with a contumelious disregard for the plaintiff's rights.[79]

A third theme is the rejection of Lord Devlin's statement that his treatment was designed to remove, or at least reduce, the anomaly of exemplary damages being imposed in civil cases. As Menzies J put it, 'What the House did was not to remove an anomaly but, for reasons of policy, to limit what was regarded as an anomaly to cases "in which an award of exemplary damages can serve a useful purpose"'.[80] To the extent that Lord Devlin was trying to remove an anomaly, Owen J thought this was 'a task I would have thought was one for the legislature rather than for the courts'.[81] And Taylor J argued that, far from removing any anomaly, the introduction of the categories would introduce others.[82]

While McTiernan, Taylor, Menzies and Owen JJ left no doubt as to their disapproval of *Rookes*, a different tone was taken in the characteristically thoughtful judgment of Windeyer J. The powerful critique of his brethren is absent; rather, Windeyer J's focus was on rejecting any simplistic notion of a strict divide between the compensatory function of tort law and its possible function in deterring faulty behaviour (in the broad sense of fault) as expressed through an award of exemplary damages. The close links in the past between tort and crime might make for modern anomalies but the anomalies had roots 'too deep for them to be easily uprooted'.[83] If there was any criticism of *Rookes*, it was as much for its attempt to draw a strict division between compensatory aggravated damages and punitive exemplary damages than for the categories. Assessing damage to reputation could not be measured as a tangible thing and the wide variety of matters held to be relevant in determining quantum 'mean that the amount of a verdict is a product of a mixture of inextricable considerations'.[84] While the conduct and motive of the defendant might play no role in the harm the plaintiff suffered, these factors had always been important in assessing damages. What *Rookes* had done was to do produce more distinct terminology between aggravated and exemplary damages but how far 'the different labels denote concepts really different in effect may be debatable'.[85]

---

[78] ibid 135.
[79] ibid 138.
[80] ibid 147.
[81] ibid 160.
[82] ibid 139.
[83] ibid 150.
[84] ibid.
[85] ibid 152. While the specific issue in *Uren v John Fairfax* involved exemplary damages, Windeyer J's comments on the nature of an award of compensatory damages in a defamation

Unlike other members of the court, Windeyer J spent little time on Lord Devlin's two categories: he did not discuss the first, and thought the second was capable of a broad interpretation. In the end, he rejected *Rookes* as limiting awards for forms of wrongdoing that had previously been the subject of awards in the High Court. But while he doubted the practicality of a clear line between aggravated and exemplary damages, he valued *Rookes*' attempt to make one as highlighting the need for exceptional conduct – beyond a jury's mere disapproval of the conduct – before an award of exemplary damages could be justified.[86] Applying this standard, he joined with Taylor and Owen JJ to find that, even on the pre-*Rookes* law, there was no evidence which supported leaving the question of exemplary damages to the jury and the decision of the Full Court was upheld. The same approach to *Rookes* was adopted in the ACP appeal which was delivered immediately after.[87]

The immediate response to the High Court's approach to *Rookes* was positive albeit the grounds of approval differed in Australia and England. Samuels praised the 'characteristically robust examination of judicial principle' of the High Court and, whilst recognising it did not solve all problems associated with awards of exemplary damages, welcomed the return to 'sound general principle' represented by the decision.[88] Conversely, the note on the case in the *Australian Law Journal* was as enthusiastic for the method adopted by the High Court as for the result. The wide approach taken to the *Parker* discretion and the explicit weighing of policy factors in determining the appropriate law for Australia was considered 'very desirable'.[89] However, one important question remained. If the High Court was willing to adopt a broad view of its discretion to reject decisions of the House of Lords, what would the Privy Council do when faced with an appeal from a High Court decision which had rejected a decision of the House of Lords? The issue became live when in July 1966 the Privy Council granted leave to appeal in the ACP case.[90] Some argued that the decision to grant leave was linked to the Practice Statement delivered by the Appellate Committee of the House of Lords in June 1966 declaring that henceforth it would not consider itself bound by its own previous decisions.[91] One commentator noted

---

action have been extremely influential. They were cited with approval by a subsequent High Court of Australia (*Carson v John Fairfax & Sons Ltd* (1993) 178 CLR 44) and, together with the later case, are the most cited authorities for the assessment of damages in defamation cases in Australia (*cf John v MGN Limited* [1997] QB 586).

[86] *Uren v John Fairfax & Sons Pty Ltd* (1966) 117 CLR 118, 153.

[87] (1966) 117 CLR 185. By a 4:1 majority, a new trial generally on all counts was ordered, it being considered that there was insufficient evidence even under the pre-*Rookes* law to leave exemplary damages to the jury on every count and that the awards on individual counts were excessive.

[88] A Samuels, 'Exemplary Damages – Restoration of Sound Fundamental Principle' (1967) 30 MLR 213.

[89] 'A Three Part Fugue' (n 65).

[90] The Fairfax case settled after the High Court appeal: Uren (n 4) 141–42.

[91] E St John, 'Lords Break From Precedent: An Australian View' (1967) 14 *ICLQ* 808. The House of Lords had considered itself bound by its own decision since the judgment in *London Street Tramways Co Ltd v London County Council* [1898] AC 375.

the view that this had been caused by developments in Australia (in particular, *Parker's* case): 'The common heritage of our law would have soon ceased to be common unless something was done. Now the House of Lords, sitting judicially, will be free to follow these decisions of the Australian court, one of high repute.'[92] Technically, the Privy Council did not have to follow the House of Lords – they were not in the same court hierarchy – but as they were staffed by predominantly the same judges it was very likely that a decision binding on them as members of the House of Lords would be applied in the Privy Council. But while some thought the 1966 Practice Statement might have been made to assist in maintaining the unity of the common law,[93] the very forces that encouraged the *Parker* 'rebellion' militated in favour of an increasing diversity rather than commonality.[94] The place of exemplary damages in the law of defamation, and tort law more generally, became caught up in the wider questions of uniformity and divergence in a post-Empire world.

VII. THE END OF THE AFFAIR

There were a number of unusual features about the appeal to the Privy Council. As ACP won in the High Court, the appeal was against the reasoning of the High Court rather than the result which gave rise to a nice question, ultimately resolved in ACP's favour, of whether the Privy Council had jurisdiction to hear the appeal.[95] On the substance, ACP's arguments had two distinct prongs: on whether *Rookes* or *Uren v Fairfax* was right as a matter of law and on whether the High Court had a right to diverge from the House of Lords. Understandably, ACP's Australian counsel focused almost exclusively on the former. The reasoning of the four members of the High Court who engaged with Lord Devlin's opinion was unpacked and criticised at great length as was the argument that Australian law preceding *Rookes* was as definitive as some of the High Court members had suggested.[96] But counsel was harder pressed to find a reason why divergence was not allowed and was forced to argue that, while some discretion did exist, it was not a matter of complete discretion.[97] The weakness of the argument is evident from the citation of *Skelton v Collins*, a post-*Parker* case in which the High Court refused to follow a House of Lords decision, as somehow supporting the old view that *Piro v Foster* restricted any discretion.

---

[92] E St John (ibid) 811, quoting the Legal Correspondent of *The Times*. *cf* R Cross, 'Recent Developments in the Practice of Precedent – The Triumph of Common Sense' (1969) 43 *Australian Law Journal* 3, 5.

[93] E St John (ibid) 815.

[94] 'Parker's Case' (n 67) 151.

[95] *Australian Consolidated Press Ltd v Uren* [1969] 1 AC 590, 628–34.

[96] ibid 598–610.

[97] ibid 611.

Three of the judges in *Skelton v Collins* did indeed cite *Piro v Foster*,[98] none of them to support a view that it operated as a formal limitation and in Owen J's case to point out how *Piro v Foster* had been effected by *Parker*. In effect, it seems counsel were arguing that any discretion only applied where the House of Lords decision was somehow flawed. As *Rookes* was not such a decision, the reasoning of the High Court should be rejected.

Uren's counsel, led by Evatt, proposed three substantive options to the Judicial Committee, the second and third relating to the narrow legal points of whether *Rookes* was correctly decided or whether it did not extend to libel.[99] The first was the most profound: the appeal should be dismissed because the High Court of Australia 'has now obtained sufficient maturity as to be able to determine the province of the law of defamation and libel for Australian conditions'.[100] While arguments also addressed whether previous affirmations in Australian cases on exemplary damages meant to mirror Salmond's initial view that these were awards for solatium or not, they were made in the shadow of the main diversity argument.

Faced with the prospect of holding that a recent decision of the House of Lords was wrong or that the freedom of the High Court to prefer its own decisions to those of the House of Lords was limited, the Privy Council decided that discretion was the better part of valour. It held that it was settled law in Australia before *Rookes* that exemplary damages could be awarded in a wider range of cases than allowed for in *Rookes*. Moreover, even if Salmond had been the source of the language used in some of the High Court cases, it was clear that awards in libel cases that went beyond hurt to a plaintiff's reputation or feelings had been sanctioned. The only question was whether the High Court was in error in preferring its own established jurisprudence to subsequent, contrary House of Lords authority. While noting the criticisms of *Rookes*, the Privy Council did not find it necessary to give an opinion on them although it is hard to avoid the inference that they were given at least some credence.[101] Perhaps with the 1966 Practice Statement in mind, it was noted that whatever the benefits of uniformity of law in the Commonwealth or wider English-speaking world, development could come 'from any one and not from one only of those parts'.[102] Moreover, the virtue of uniformity was not the same in all areas of law and in matters of domestic or internal significance 'the need for uniformity is not compelling'.[103] The decision on whether and how to allow a punitive element could be resolved

---

[98] (1966) 115 CLR 94, 104 (Kitto J), Windeyer J (134), Owen J (137–39). Taylor J agreed with Owen J on this point.

[99] *Australian Consolidated Press Ltd v Uren* [1969] 1 AC 590, 612–13.

[100] ibid 612.

[101] The criticisms are set out in some detail: see ibid 639–41, 643–44. See Renaud (n 65) 444–45.

[102] *Australian Consolidated Press Ltd v Uren* [1969] 1 AC 590, 641.

[103] ibid.

'not so much by asserting that reasoning can lead to only one conclusion but rather by coming to a decision as to what the policy of the law should be'.[104] This is what the High Court had done:

> The issue that faced the High Court in the present case was whether the law as it had been settled in Australia should be changed. Had the law developed by processes of faulty reasoning, or had it been founded upon misconceptions, it would have been necessary to change it. Such was not the case. In the result in a sphere of the law where its policy calls for decision, and where its policy in a particular country is fashioned so largely by judicial opinion, it became a question for the High Court to decide whether the decision in *Rookes v Barnard* compelled a change in what was a well-settled judicial approach in the law of libel in Australia. Their Lordships are not prepared to say that the High Court were wrong in being unconvinced that a changed approach in Australia was desirable.[105]

Academic opinion on the case largely concerned the method by which the Privy Council had rejected the appeal rather than the substance. JR Lehane, then a third year law student, noted the limited discussion on 'the policy of law' as to awards of punitive damages in civil cases. As neither *Rookes* nor *Uren* advocated abolishing punitive awards, the issue was where to draw the line and in light of his support for Windeyer J's view that fault was too deeply embedded to be removed from the damages question, he thought the approach of the High Court more sound. He also correctly noted that, irrespective of the rejection of the categories approach of Lord Devlin, the acceptance of a formal divide between aggravated and exemplary damages now existed as part of Australian law,[106] albeit the acceptance was tinged with more scepticism than evidenced in *Rookes*.[107] The commentator in the *Melbourne University Law Review* could see the arguments for abolition but thought this could only be done through legislation. If exemplary damages were to be retained, the High Court's approach in *Uren* was preferred to *Rookes* as the latter's restrictions 'would appear to create far more problems than they solve'.[108] More generally, the Privy Council decision engendered even greater confidence that the House of Lords would reconsider Lord Devlin's categories when it had the opportunity to return to the issue.[109] In a persuasive argument, the John Latham Professor of Law at Monash Law School, David Jackson, noted that, if the *Uren* problem was to be minimised, English courts would need increased consideration of non-domestic authority. This was 'hardly novel' for jurisdictions outside England and he suggested

---

[104] ibid 642.

[105] ibid 644.

[106] See also R Hayes, 'Newspaper Libel – The Deterrent and Vindicatory Effect of General Damages Awards' (1967) 5 *University of Queensland Law Journal* 370, 374.

[107] JR Lehane, 'Stare Decisis, Judicial Policy and Punitive Damages' (1968) 6 *Sydney Law Review* 111, 117–19.

[108] Renaud (n 65) 445.

[109] ibid; 'Current Legal Developments' (1968) 17 *ICLQ* 234, 235.

the non-English practice should be followed by English courts.[110] While these were general comments, it was the *Uren* decision that had prompted them and no doubt he thought *Rookes* would be a likely target for the new multi-jurisdictional judicial Commonwealth.

When the House of Lords did get the opportunity to reconsider *Rookes* in a libel case, however, there was no clamour for Lord Devlin's views to be overturned. *Broome v Cassell & Co Ltd*[111] was complicated by the remarkable decision of a Lord Denning MR-inspired Court of Appeal to hold that *Rookes* had been decided *per incuriam* by the House of Lords.[112] Apart from rejecting the Court of Appeal's capacity to make such a finding, and holding that in substance the argument was incorrect, a seven-judge bench gave quite different responses to *Rookes*. While Viscount Dilhorne and Lord Wilberforce had difficulty in accepting the restrictions imposed by the categories,[113] and hence supported the pre-*Rookes* law which *Uren* had upheld, the views of Lords Reid, Diplock, and to a lesser extent Lord Hailsham of St Marylebone LC that exemplary damages were anomalous[114] supported the status-quo of *Rookes* as a compromise position as did the reluctance to depart from a recent decision of the court. While some of their Lordships cited the judgments of Windeyer J and Taylor J in their speeches,[115] the unanimous decision of the High Court in *Uren* rejecting *Rookes* did not cause a change of heart among the majority of their Lordships. Lord Diplock saw the different policy judgement of the courts in Australia, New Zealand and some Canadian jurisdictions in rejecting the *Rookes* limitation as cogent grounds for reconsidering the decision but not for rejecting it if it was (as he thought) a step in the right direction.[116] And with no doubt unintended irony, Lord Hailsham thought that Commonwealth courts might actually modify some of their criticisms of *Rookes* in light of the *Broome v Cassell* decision![117]

Broome v Cassell crystallised the differing scope of exemplary damages in defamation, and tort law more generally, in English and Australian law. But to the extent the difference was founded on a disagreement over the categories in *Rookes*, it masked a more fundamental question. As Julius Stone pointed out shortly after the *Broome v Cassell* decision, the problem with the *Uren* decisions

---

[110] D Jackson, 'The Judicial Commonwealth' [1970] *CLJ* 257, 279.

[111] *Broome v Cassell & Co Ltd* [1972] AC 1027.

[112] For contemporary criticism, see Stone (n 54).

[113] *Broome v Cassell & Co Ltd* [1972] AC 1027, 1108–09 (Viscount Dilhorne), 1119–20 (Lord Wilberforce).

[114] ibid 1086 (Lord Reid), 1127–28 (Lord Diplock), 1077, 1080 (Lord Hailsham).

[115] See, for example, ibid 1072, 1082 (Lord Hailsham), 1108 (Viscount Dilhorne).

[116] ibid 1127. By the time of *Broome v Cassell*, there was authority in both New Zealand (*Fogg v McKnight* [1968] NZLR 330) and Canada (*McElroy v Cowper-Smith and Woodman* [1967] SCR 425) that *Rookes* did not represent the law in those jurisdictions albeit that there was contrary authority in Canada (*Kirisitis v Morrell* (1965) WWR 123; *Sharkey v Robertson* (1969) 3 DLR (2d) 745.

[117] *Broome & Cassell & Co Ltd* [1972] AC 1027, 1083.

in both the High Court and Privy Council was that they avoided making findings on the key issue:

> In short, the core question in both the Privy Council and the High Court *should have been* not just *whether* the cases showed a wide range of the power to award something or other called 'exemplary' damages but *in what sense* of these terms they did so – Sir John Salmond's or Lord Devlin's?[118]

The difficulty was, as this chapter has shown, an analysis of the authorities provided no clear answer. Rather, Stone's argument was that, given the fuzzy dividing line between aggravated and exemplary damages, it was possible to accommodate virtually all the components of an exemplary award within aggravated damages. The characteristics of a defendant's conduct that founded an exemplary award would be mirrored by the non-pecuniary harm caused to the plaintiff in virtually all cases. The attractiveness of this option, however, depended on a normative evaluation of whether a punitive element ought to be allowed in damages awards in civil cases. The answer given by Lord Devlin in *Rookes* and Lords Hailsham, Reid and Diplock in *Broome v Cassell* was that this ought not generally to be allowed. Conversely, only Taylor J and Windeyer J dealt with the point in *Uren* and they were not prepared to be so restrictive. In particular, Windeyer J's reluctance to see awards of damages as serving a unitary interest, reasoning mirrored in the speech of Lord Wilberforce in *Broome v Cassell*, inevitably led him both to regard an absolute division between aggravated and exemplary damages as illusory as well as allowing him to be more sanguine about the limiting effect of Lord Devlin's categories. In hindsight, disagreements over the categories obfuscated the real issue: as Stone argued, the need was to 'cut through confusions, by attending to the functions served by damages with various labels, *rather than arguments about these labels*'.[119] Caught in the precedential question, the strengths and weakness of Lord Devlin's categories became the surrogate for the merits of wider arguments about the role of fault and punishment in awards of damages. They also hid the fact that the Australian adoption of Salmond's 'contumelious disregard' criterion represented a tangible transplant of a Roman law concept into the common law. Unfortunately, the lack of a direct common law equivalent to *injuria* robbed the term of the contextual meaning it had in Roman law and in the new setting it did not really assist in clarifying the nature of an award of exemplary damages.

VIII. ALL'S WELL THAT ENDS WELL?

The prospect of different rules for exemplary damages applying for defamation cases in England in Australia was subject to almost immediate qualification.

---

[118] Stone (n 54) 317.
[119] ibid 323.

As the dividing line between aggravated and exemplary damages was porous, it was an heroic task for a jury to separate components of the award into: 1) compensation for proved loss; 2) compensation for hurt, worry, and distress caused both by the publication and conduct of the defendant up to and including the trial; and 3) an award of damages which, even taking into account the punitive effect of an award under 2), was necessary to express disapproval of the defendant's conduct. Concerns over 'double counting' in 2) and 3) and the limited appellate review of jury awards made any award of exemplary damages potentially problematic. By the time of Stone's 1972 article discussed above, the prospect of legislative reform in defamation law in the jurisdiction which gave birth to the *Uren* litigation was taking shape. In October 1968 the New South Wales Law Reform Commission issued a working paper on the law of defamation, one of the suggestions being the abolition of exemplary damages and allowing awards of aggravated damages on account of the conduct of the defendant only on a direction of the judge.[120] The justification was, contrary to the confident contrary assertion of Menzies J in *Uren v Fairfax*,[121] that high awards of exemplary damages infringed freedom of speech. While the latter proposal was abandoned when the final report was published in 1971, the proposal to abolish exemplary damages in New South Wales was retained for many of the reasons Lord Devlin had stated in *Rookes*[122] and was implemented in 1974.[123] Thirty years later, this was legislated throughout all Australian jurisdictions when the uniform defamation legislation was passed. While *Uren* continues to govern awards of exemplary damages in the law more generally in Australia, it has ceased to be authoritative on its own facts.[124]

Conversely, in England *Rookes* has remained the law governing awards of exemplary damages in defamation claims although a recent study suggests that punitive damages are in fact awarded very rarely in these cases.[125] Despite recommendations from the Law Commission in 1997 that the categories should be removed in favour of a wider power to award exemplary damages when a defendant 'deliberately and outrageously disregarded the plaintiffs rights',[126]

---

[120] 'Reforming Defamation Law' (1969) 43 *Australian Law Journal* 38, 39.

[121] (1966) 117 CLR 118, 147.

[122] New South Wales Law Reform Commission, *Defamation* (Report No 11, 1971) paras 42–56.

[123] Defamation Act 1974 (NSW), s 46.

[124] But note the recommendation that exemplary awards be available for breach of a statutory tort for invasions of privacy if one were introduced: Australian Law Reform Commission, *Serious Invasions of Privacy in the Digital Era*, ALRC Report No 123 (2014), 233, which might also encompass some conduct covered under defamation.

[125] J Goudkamp and E Katsampouka, 'An Empirical Study of Punitive Damages' (2018) 38 OJLS 90.

[126] The Law Commission, *Aggravated, Exemplary and Restitutionary Damages* (Law Com No 247, 1997), para 5.44. The Leveson Inquiry also recommended that exemplary damages should be available in 'media' torts, including libel and slander (Lord Justice Leveson, *An Inquiry into the Culture, Practices and Ethics of the Press Vol 4*, HC 779 (2012), para 5.12) and the Crime and Courts Act 2013, s 34 allows exemplary damages to be awarded beyond Lord Devlin's categories against publishers of news-related material for (among other actions) libel and slander.

the *Rookes* categories have survived, only recently bolstered by the presumption in favour of judge-only trials in defamation cases.[127] The uniformity between English and Australian law so confidently predicted by the supporters of *Uren* has not occurred but the divergence has been turned on its head: the English position is now the more liberal. Yet there is one sense in which *Rookes* did create uniformity: by articulating a clear distinction between aggravated and exemplary damages, in both jurisdictions a greater focus was placed on whether an award of aggravated damages might be sufficient to deal with any punitive element the defendant's conduct might deserve.[128]

More broadly, however, the Uren litigation must be understood in the context of the express throwing off of any imperial yoke. The Privy Council was undoubtedly correct in noting that there were plausibly different views that could be taken over the limits to be placed on awards of exemplary damages. To allow a mature Commonwealth supreme court to take a different view to the House of Lords fitted perfectly with the new post-war British Commonwealth which would be defined by its differences as much as its commonalities.

After the Privy Council appeal, Uren began a new trial against Frank Packer's ACP in respect of the same publications and was awarded AU $20,002 (Australia having decimalised its currency since the original trial), the $2 being awarded for the Skripov counts.[129] Further appeals followed to the New South Wales Court of Appeal[130] (also established since the original trial) and to the High Court and a third trial was in prospect before Packer settled in July 1969.[131] After the settlement with ACP – which included the publication of an apology in the *Sunday Telegraph* in the same place as the original publication – Uren cleared his name in Parliament when, under pressure from Liberal Prime Minister Gorton, Dudley Erwin grudgingly accepted Uren's denial of any improper dealings

---

[127] Defamation Act 2013, s 11, amending Senior Courts Act 1981, s 69(1). *cf* the position in Australia, where under the uniform defamation legislation five jurisdictions retained a prima facie right to jury trials subject to a contrary court order (remembering that exemplary damages were abolished under that legislation). See Defamation Act (NSW) ss 21 and 22 and the equivalent provisions in Queensland, Tasmania, Victoria and Western Australia. There are no equivalent provisions in the Australian Capital Territory, the Northern Territory and South Australia. See generally D Rolph, *Defamation Law* (Sydney, Thomson Reuters, 2016) [5.150].

[128] For a contemporary example see *Johnstone v Stewart* [1968] SASR 142 and more recently *NSW v Ibbett* [2006] HCA 57, (2006) 229 CLR 638. See also the uniform defamation legislation which mirrors earlier New South Wales legislation (Defamation Act 1974 (NSW), s 46(3)) precluding the state of mind of the defendant being relevant to the award unless it affects the harm suffered by the plaintiff: Defamation Act 2005 (NSW), s 36 and the cognate legislation in the other States and Territories.

[129] *SMH*, 29 November 1967, 12.

[130] *SMH*, 1 May 1969, 7.

[131] Uren (n 4), 142; Transcript of interview with Tom Uren by Robin Hughes, 17 January 1996: www.australianbiography.gov.au/subjects/uren/interview11.html. Apparently Alan Reid was used as a go-between for the opposing parties during the settlement negotiations and after it was finalised Uren and Reid – whom Uren nicknamed 'poison pen' – were on 'amicable enough terms': Fitzgerald and Scott (n 14) 152.

with Skripov.[132] The settlements with Fairfax and ACP did not end Uren's involvement with the law of defamation – he settled an action against Fairfax in September 1979 arising out of an editorial in the *Sydney Morning Herald* on the final stages of the Vietnam War[133] – but his legal fame attached solely to the earlier proceedings. It took him six and a half years but he had the last laugh: with the proceeds of the Fairfax settlement he built a holiday house on land he owned and called it the Fairfax Retreat. With the ACP proceeds he bought another holiday home and called it Packer's Lodge.[134]

[132] Uren (n 4) 146–48.
[133] *Canberra Times*, 11 September 1979, 10.
[134] Uren (n 4) 145.

8

Charleston v News Group Newspapers Ltd *(1995)*

URSULA CHEER

I. INTRODUCTION

IN 1992, A very successful English tabloid newspaper, the *News of the World*, subjected two Australian television soap actors to a traumatic ordeal by publishing a sensational story about a pornographic computer game. Anne Charleston and Ian Smith were actors in a popular television soap opera, *Neighbours*, set in the fictional backyard BBQ paradise, Ramsay Street, where they played a respectable middle-aged couple named Harold and Madge Bishop. The Bishops had become well-known and loved characters to millions of viewers throughout Australia and the rest of the world, including the United Kingdom where the series was distributed. The actors were shocked, therefore, when, on 15 March 1992, the newspaper published an article under a very prominent headline in capital letters across most of the page which asked the question: 'STREWTH! WHAT'S HAROLD UP TO WITH OUR MADGE?' Below the headline was a large photograph of an almost naked couple in which the female was bent across some furniture while the man was, as Lord Bridge of Harwich in the House of Lords delicately put it, 'apparently engaging in an act of intercourse or sodomy with her.' In the picture, the lower bodies of both participants were covered by an outline map of Australia with the words 'CENSORED DOWN UNDER.' To the right side of this was a smaller image of the same woman dressed in fetish clothing exposing her breasts. Under the images was a smaller but still striking headline: 'Porn Shocker for Neighbours stars'.

The couple depicted in the images appeared to be Anne Charleston and Ian Smith. However, the captions in small print under the images provided an explanation: 'SOAP STUDS: Harold and Madge's faces are added to porn actors' bodies in a scene from the game' and 'RAMSAY RAVE: "Madge" in kinky leather gear'. The text of the article itself revealed that the makers of the computer game had used and superimposed the faces of Charleston and

Smith without their consent. The 'famous faces' were 'unwitting stars of a sordid computer game ... the stars knew nothing about it'.[1] Inset small images were captioned using the word: 'VICTIMS' and the tone of self-righteous indignation in the article contrasted 'oddly with the prominence given to the main photograph'.[2] Charleston and Smith sued the publisher.

Charleston v News Group Newspapers Ltd (*Charleston*) is the short appeal decision of the House of Lords on the preliminary question whether the publications complained of were capable of bearing defamatory meanings alleged by the plaintiffs. The plaintiffs argued the photographs and headlines in their ordinary and natural meaning said they had posed for pornographic pictures and behaved in a reprehensible manner which would shock viewers of *Neighbours*. The defendants denied that the photographs and words, taken in proper context, were capable of bearing any defamatory meaning. Having lost in the courts below, the plaintiffs also lost in the House of Lords, where their final appeal was dismissed. *Charleston* became a leading case and is authority for the proposition in defamation law taught to law students worldwide in the United Kingdom, Australia, Canada and New Zealand, that the natural and ordinary meaning of words is to be determined by taking into account the context of the words used and the mode of publication. The meaning can include any inferential meanings, but can only be that which the words would convey to the mind of an ordinary, reasonable and fair-minded reader. Fundamentally, even if the words might in reality suggest different meanings to different groups of readers, the law presumes and the jury must seek, a single meaning conveyed to a notional, reasonable reader. Therefore, plaintiffs cannot choose isolated passages and sue on those if other words throw a different light on things. *Charleston* is leading authority, then, exemplifying a fiction called the 'single meaning' rule, which itself relies on the application of another fiction – the views of an ordinary, fair-minded person, who is taken to have read and responded to the whole of the publication, not just part of it.

This chapter will describe the legal reasoning used by the House of Lords in *Charleston* in dismissing the appeal, in order to establish the decision in a historical setting. It will then analyse the case in the light of comparative case law and commentary. The discussion will examine arguments made that the decision was necessary to prevent the law from being too complicated. On the other side, there are arguments which suggest the House of Lords in *Charleston* gave too much weight to freedom of expression and left deserving plaintiffs without a remedy, and this position will be scrutinised also. The inquiry will include an analysis of the nature of the 'single meaning' rule as a legal fiction and whether it is good and necessary, as well as the question whether the doctrine referred

---

[1] *Charleston v News Group Newspapers Ltd* [1995] UKHL 6, [1995] 2 AC 65 (*Charleston*) 69.
[2] This statement of facts is taken from ibid 68–69.

to as the bane and antidote doctrine is a sound control mechanism for a 'single meaning' rule. That other legal fiction embraced in the decision the ordinary, reasonable, fair-minded person, also deserves inspection. Finally, the contemporary function and effectiveness of the rule will be examined, including its interrelationship with intellectual property law, and the impact of the internet.

II. THE DECISION IN *CHARLESTON*

As noted above, *Charleston* is a short decision, in which the House of Lords appeared very certain that it would dismiss the appeal. Lord Bridge gave the main speech, supported by Lords Goff, Jauncey and Mustill. Lord Nicholls gave a short separate decision also dismissing the appeal. After setting out the facts and describing the allegedly defamatory article in detail, Lord Bridge referred to it as a 'kind of gutter journalism'.[3] It is striking that he also noted the plaintiffs were complaining about 'degrading faked photographs', a phenomenon that has enormous currency and impact in the era of the internet, over 20 years after *Charleston* arose from publication in a hard copy of a newspaper. However, although his Lordship thought there was a strong argument the plaintiffs were deserving plaintiffs, he went on to make very clear that it was not the place of the House to determine or maintain the quality of journalism or journalistic ethics, or to seek to develop a novel tort.[4] The question for the House was to determine the meaning of the words, and here Lord Bridge revealed that the plaintiffs conceded, for the purpose the proceedings, that the publication as a whole was not defamatory. Indeed, his Lordship agreed with the concession, thinking it obvious that no defamatory meaning would have been inferred by any reader going beyond the first paragraph of the article.[5] As is discussed below, that concession has not been immune from later criticism.

The argument before their Lordships was mainly confined to what effect the publication had had on the minds of so-called 'limited readers' – those who only read the headlines and looked at the photograph and no more. The plaintiffs suggested limited readers made up a significant portion of the millions reading the *News of the World*. Such a group would think the actors had willingly participated in the pornographic photographs in some way, and therefore the plaintiffs wanted damages for being lowered in the estimation of the limited reader group. Lord Bridge immediately raised the daunting obstacle the plaintiffs faced, of a 'long and unbroken line of authority' establishing that plaintiffs cannot sue selectively by severing a damaging part of a publication from the context around it that removes or changes the damage by casting a different light

---

[3] ibid 69.
[4] ibid.
[5] ibid.

on it,[6] because an ordinary, reasonable reader is taken to have read and reacted to the whole of the publication. If damaging words exist within the whole, they may be cancelled out by other words in the publication – put another way, for every bane there may be an antidote.[7] This proposition was taken by Lord Bridge as so well-accepted as to be almost conventional lawyerly jargon,[8] and he went on to state that the bane and antidote doctrine requires a jury to take on an often difficult task of determining whether an antidote is effective or not. To do so, the jury may consider the mode of publication and what prominence is given its various parts. Issues may also arise as to what is part of the single publication for this purpose.

But no such issues arose in *Charleston* because of the concession made by the plaintiff that read as a whole, the article was not defamatory[9] – in other words, the context of the article provided an antidote for the bane of the headlines and main image. So instead, the plaintiffs had to argue that modern tabloid journalism such as that embodied by the *News of the World* presented a novel scenario for the courts. Counsel for the plaintiffs submitted that because sensational headlines and images (the *raison d'être* of the tabloid media) intentionally invite and create a significant limited reader group within the wider target audience, liability should follow based on any defamatory meanings taken from the publication by that limited group.[10] Lord Bridge was of the view that this argument was defeated by two well-established principles of libel law. The first is that the natural and ordinary meaning of words (legal innuendo aside), is determined by reference to the meaning an ordinary, reasonable, fair-minded reader (a notional reader) would take from them. The second is that when using the notional reader test, a jury should look for a single meaning conveying one sense in which *all* readers would understand the words.[11]

It is clear this approach is resolutely objective. Lord Bridge cited and approved dicta by Diplock LJ (as his Lordship then was) in *Slim v Daily Telegraph Ltd* (*Slim*)[12] which makes clear that it does not matter what meaning the publisher intended the words to have or how they were understood by those who read them. The question for the jury is the 'one and only meaning that readers as reasonable men [*sic*] should have collectively understood the words to bear',[13] and this approach would be defeated if either side could call witnesses to try to establish subjective meanings, or a plaintiff could do this without

---

[6] ibid 70, referring to *Duncan & Neill on Defamation*, 2nd edn (London, Butterworths, 1983) 13, [4.11]).

[7] ibid citing *Chalmers v Payne* (1835) 2 CM & R 156, 159; *Chalmers v Payne* (1835) 150 ER 67.

[8] *Charleston*, 70.

[9] ibid 71.

[10] ibid.

[11] ibid.

[12] ibid. Lord Bridge cites Diplock LJ in *Slim*, 171, for the latter proposition.

[13] ibid 72.

putting forward evidence at all. So the adjudicator at trial, usually the jury, is to seek the one and only meaning that a reasonable person would have collectively understood and damages are determined accordingly if that meaning is defamatory.

Having stated this position as the law, Lord Bridge went on to outline how a jury might determine whether a prominent, apparently defamatory headline, has been neutralised by text in an accompanying article. Acknowledging the exercise is a finely balanced one, his Lordship noted a number of indicia that are to be used and should be examined – these are the nature of the libel in the headline, the language of the potentially neutralising text, and the manner in which the whole of the material is presented.[14] Lord Bridge completed his speech with two points, powerfully made. He rejected the severance proposition put forward for the plaintiffs as unacceptable in the light of the principles discussed above. He also found that while limited readers would have existed in fact in the *Charleston* case and would have taken away a defamatory impression of the plaintiffs because they only read the sensational headlines and looked at the faked photographs but went no further, such readers could not be described as ordinary, reasonable, fair-minded readers. Accordingly, he dismissed the appeal.[15]

Lord Nicholls' separate speech endorsed that of Lord Bridge but further nuanced the interpretation of the law. His Lordship attempted to be realistic about the contradictions and weaknesses in the legal position. He began by discussing the reality of the nature of mass media as it was then represented by hard copy newspapers. It is obvious some time has passed since *Charleston* because the first statement made is that 'Newspapers get thicker and thicker'. Now, of course, the opposite is true.[16] However, the point made by his Lordship was that in 1992, the relevant edition of the *News of the World* was large – 64 pages long, making it a reality that readers would quickly scan headlines and turn the pages – 'Everybody reads selectively'.[17] Lord Nicholls acknowledged that common sense would appear to support the idea that newspapers should have no right to complain of a law, which, when they chose to produce a defamatory headline, then held them liable despite the use of neutralising contextual material. However, pragmatically, his Lordship then acknowledged that the law did not take a common sense approach, but instead adopted the

---

[14] ibid 72–73.

[15] ibid 73.

[16] ibid [7]. Worldwide, the advent of the internet has impacted negatively on the production and delivery of mainstream media, including hard-copy newspapers. As the market model has become less profitable, newspapers are becoming smaller and smaller or disappearing completely as publishing businesses fold: See M Hirst, W Hope and P Thompson, 'Australia and New Zealand' in *Global Media Giants*, B J Birkinbine, R Gomez and J Wasko (eds) (New York, Routledge, 2017) 353; N Newman with R Fletcher, A Kalogeropoulos, D A L Levy and R Kleis Nielsen, *Reuters Institute Digital News Report 2018*.

[17] ibid 73.

'single meaning' standard judged by the ordinary reader. Even more directly, he then admitted 'this is a crude yardstick'[18] because in some cases a deserving plaintiff will be without a remedy, but in others, a newspaper may have to pay damages even though many readers did not take a defamatory meaning from the words. Such is the playing field. The test is objective and the context must be taken into account. However, Lord Nicholls then emphasised that context may or may not cure a defamatory extract – each case will be different, depending on what the context is. In doing so, his Lordship recognised an element of relativity within the bane and antidote doctrine in the sense that the presence of an antidote will not automatically cure. He then went on to make a final point about headlines by asserting that context will always include layout of the article. The speech is not entirely clear but Lord Nicholls appeared to imply that the essential nature of a headline is that it demands more attention and should be given more weight. This means there can be no automatic objective expectation that later material tucked away below or on a continuation page would be read by the ordinary reader, thus providing a curative effect. To summarise, in his speech, although Lord Nicholls accepted the law as stated by Lord Bridge, he also acknowledged the rough justice aspect of the 'single meaning' standard confirmed in the case, and attached important caveats to how much weight is to be attributed to context where headlines contain the damaging words. Thus, he delivered the famous dicta: 'Those who print defamatory headlines are playing with fire'.[19] Having attempted to establish some sort of borderline, Lord Nicholls then found that *Charleston* was on the other side, because the ordinary reader would have read further than the headline and photo and when they put the newspaper down that day, would not have thought less of the well-known plaintiffs. In this, Lord Nicholls' and Lord Bridge's application of the ordinary, reasonable, fair-minded reader test to the facts of the case was the same.

In *Charleston*, then, the House of Lords looked backwards to well-established law to reject a claim that the existence of tabloid mass media had created a novel gap in the law which required filling by the courts. The House was not prepared to create or recognise a new rule allowing plaintiffs to bring defamation claims based on natural and ordinary meanings that only arise if the words are severed from their context, even if in fact, a significant portion of the audience to whom the words were published would have arrived at a meaning in this very manner and thus thought less of the plaintiff. The Law Lords endorsed an approach based on an assumption that the finder of meaning, usually a jury, would always be able to establish a single meaning for the words. The single meaning is reached using an objective test – it is the meaning an ordinary, reasonable, fair-minded person would agree on, after considering the

---

[18] ibid.
[19] ibid 74.

words in their whole published context. If the whole contains some words which appear defamatory, the defamatory effect (or bane) may be neutralised by other contextual words which operate as an antidote. The presence of an apparent antidote does not automatically cure, and the analysis is carried out by considering the nature of the libel, the language of the potentially neutralising text, and the manner in which the whole of the material is presented. Layout is also a relevant factor. Therefore, if the damaging words appear in a headline, the curative effect of other words may be harder to establish. The case acknowledges the challenging character of tabloid media which is highly incentivised to publish sensational material, and the strong potential for such material to damage a reputation. Nonetheless the House of Lords was not prepared to change law to make it easier for plaintiffs to sue such publishers. A 'single meaning' rule with the workings and indicia referred to prevails, even though described in the judgment as a 'crude yardstick'.

Charleston is an established leading case on the determination of the natural and ordinary meaning of words in defamation worldwide. In the United Kingdom, it has been cited in reported cases at least 50 times, substantively in 16 decisions.[20] In Australia, it has been considered in depth in at least eight cases[21] and cited in at least 12 others. In New Zealand, it has been discussed in detail in four cases[22] and cited in 12 other decisions. It has been applied by the Supreme Court of Canada and cited in other courts in that jurisdiction.[23] At least 55 articles worldwide have discussed it to a greater or lesser degree as well as 30 legal books and encyclopaedias. The decision will now be scrutinised comparatively, based on its treatment in the courts and by legal commentators worldwide. Critics have advanced a variety of concerns, including that *Charleston* was a borderline decision based on an incorrect concession made by the plaintiffs; that it was wrong about how an ordinary, reasonable, fair-minded reader would behave in relation to meanings; that the bane and antidote doctrine is not effective; that the case is not really a defamation case at all but rather evidences gaps in the law; and that a multiple meaning rule could work effectively and more fairly in some cases. These issues will be addressed in turn.

---

[20] See eg, *Mark v Associated Newspapers Ltd* [2002] EMLR 38, [2002] EMLR 839, [2002] EWCA Civ 772; *Curistan v Times Newspapers Ltd* [2008] EWCA Civ 432, [2009] QB 231, [2009] 2 WLR 149, *Ajinomoto Sweeteners Europe SAS v Asda Stores Ltd* [2010] EWCA Civ 609, [2011] QB 497; and *Monroe v Hopkins* [2017] EWHC 433 (QB), [2017] WLR(D) 188.

[21] See eg, *Chakravarti v Advertiser Newspapers Ltd* [1998] HCA 37, (1998) 193 CLR 519; *Kenny v Australian Broadcasting Corporation* [2014] NSWSC 190; and *Hockey v Fairfax Media Publications Pty Ltd* [2015] FCA 652, (2015) 237 FCR 33.

[22] See eg: *Thode v Coastline FM Ltd* unreported, HC(NZ) Tauranga, 1 October 1997, CP 31/95, and *McGee v Independent Newspapers Ltd* [2006] NZAR 24.

[23] See Hilary Young, 'But Names Won't *Necessarily* Hurt Me: Considering the Effect of Disparaging Statements on Reputation' (2011) 37 *Quebec Law Journal* 1.

III. THE SEARCH FOR A SINGLE MEANING

A. Policy and Balancing

At the heart of *Charleston* is an ancient[24] assumption that a single meaning can be found and indeed must be found for the law to work properly. Lord Bridge quotes with approval Diplock LJ in *Slim* where he explains why this is so:[25]

> [T]he notion that the same words should bear different meanings to different men and that more than one meaning should be 'right' conflicts with the whole training of a lawyer. Words are the tools of his trade. He uses them to define legal rights and duties. They do not achieve that purpose unless there can be attributed to them a single meaning as the 'right' meaning.

Juries, Diplock LJ goes on to say, must make unanimous findings on all issues before them, and the level of damages awarded in defamation depend on the meanings attributed to the words – the more serious the defamatory meaning, the higher the damages that will follow. Therefore the accepted justifications for the rule are that part of the bundle of legal rights and duties that make up defamation law would be too difficult to define, and juries would not be able to perform their functions, if a single meaning rule is not applied.[26] Juries do not give reasons for their decisions and typically employ an impressionistic approach to whether words are defamatory. Inevitably, trials would be more drawn out, difficult and expensive if plaintiffs could put forward different witnesses to establish meanings understood by a specific group, thereby inviting argument by the defendant on reliability and connected issues.[27] The law applies the 'single meaning' rule even though it is recognised that those engaging with publications will in fact take different meanings from both the whole or part, either by not reading properly, by just understanding differently, by having different levels of general knowledge or reading or seeing the words in different circumstances.[28]

Lord Nicholls' reference in *Charleston* itself to the rule as a 'crude yardstick' is an open acknowledgment of its imperfections. The rule has also been strongly criticised as 'anomalous, frequently otiose and, where not otiose, unjust'[29] and

---

[24] It has been suggested the 'single meaning' rule pre-dated 1792 (or at least 1840): Diplock LJ in *Slim*, 173–74.

[25] *Charleston*, [5], citing Diplock LJ in *Slim*, 171.

[26] Under Fox's Libel Act of 1792, the jury became the decider of meaning in civil (and criminal) cases. However, the judge must still decide the limits to the meanings the words are capable of having, and the jury's verdict must relate to the finding they have made as to the actual meaning: Sedley LJ in *Ajinomoto Sweeteners Europe SAS v Asda Stores Ltd* [2010] EWCA Civ 609, [2011] QB 497 (*Ajinomoto Sweeteners v Asda*), [2].

[27] Tom Gibbons, 'Defamation Reconsidered' (1996) *OJLS* 587.

[28] *Ajinomoto Sweetners Europe SAS v Asda Stores Ltd* [2009] EWHC 1717, [2010] QB 204, [30].

[29] Sedley LJ (Sir Scott Baker LJ agreeing) in *Ajinomoto Sweeteners v Asda*, [31]. The same judge referred to the rule as 'an immovable object … beyond redemption by the courts: [27], approving

'a pragmatic practice [which] became elevated into a rule of law and has remained in place without any enduring rationale'.[30] However, the rule is championed by its supporters as providing an appropriate and workable means of balancing the right to freedom of information against the right to protect reputation, and providing the certainty required by the public and the media and other publishers to order lives and businesses.[31] Nonetheless, those policy reasons have failed to convince some commentators and members of the judiciary that the rule should persist. The reasons for this are examined below.

B. The Ordinary, Reasonable Fair-minded Reader

Ordinary, reasonable readers have been described as having ordinary intelligence, experience and education, and being

> neither perverse nor morbid nor suspicious of mind, nor avid for scandal. They do not live in ivory towers and can and do read between the lines in the light of their general knowledge and experience. They do not engage in over-elaborate analysis in search for hidden meanings, nor do they adopt a strained or forced interpretation. They are not lawyers and their capacity for implication may be greater than that of lawyers.[32]

What matters in establishing meaning for the purpose of a defamation claim is the meaning which the ordinary reasonable person would as a matter of impression carry away in his or her head after reading the publication.[33]

In *Charleston*, Lord Bridge held that the ordinary, reasonable, fair-minded reader would have taken the trouble to find out what the article was all about, as well as looking at the headline and the images. Lord Nicholls thought so too, because neutralising captions accompanied the pictures, and in particular the caption to the smaller photographs contained the word 'victims' and the ordinary reader 'could not have failed' to see the captions. Additionally, the second sentence at the top of the article confirmed the actors knew nothing about the computer game.[34] There is ambiguity but Lord Nicholls appears to imply that

---

Diplock LJ in *Slim*, 179. See also Alastair Mullis and Andrew Scott, 'The swing of the pendulum: reputation, expression and the recentering of English libel law' (2012) 63 *Northern Ireland Law Quarterly* 27.

[30] Sedley LJ (Sir Scott Baker LJ agreeing) in *Ajinomoto Sweeteners v Asda*, [32].

[31] Eric Barendt, 'Review Article: Alan Durant, *Meaning in the Media*' (2011) 3 *Journal of Media Law* 143; Penelope Gorman, 'Strewth! Madge and Harold have no remedy in libel law' (1995) 139 *Solicitors Law Journal* 440. See also Tugendhat J in *Ajinomoto Sweeteners Europe SAS v Asda Stores Ltd* [2009] EWHC 1717, [2010] QB 204, [45], where he described the rule as a 'control mechanism'.

[32] *Hockey v Fairfax Media Publications Pty Ltd* [2015] FCA 652, (2015) 237 FCR 33, [64] (based on Lord Reid in *Lewis v The Daily Telegraph* [1964] AC 234, 257–58). See also *New Zealand Magazines v Hadlee*, unreported, CA(NZ), 24 October 1996, CA 74/96.

[33] *New Zealand Magazines v Hadlee*, unreported, CA(NZ), 24 October 1996, CA 74/96.

[34] *Charleston*, [6] and [8].

the ease of actually seeing the information meant ordinary readers would simply not take the headlines and pictures at face value – they would see all and no defamatory meaning could arise.

Charleston attracted criticism almost immediately for its vision of how mass media is consumed.[35] The most notorious rejection of the approach came a few years after the decision, from Justice Kirby in the High Court of Australia in *Chakravarti v Advertiser Newspapers Ltd*, where, discussing the principles used to determine the existence of defamatory words, he stated:[36]

> Respectfully, I cannot agree with their Lordships' opinion. In my view it ignores the realities of the way in which ordinary people receive, and are intended to receive, communications of this kind. It ignores changes in media technology and presentation. It removes remedies from people whose reputation may be greatly damaged by casual or superficial perception of such publications. And it overlooks the purpose of defamation law which is to provide redress when reputations are damaged in fact, not to reserve remedies to those cases only where detailed and thorough analysis of the matter complained of has been undertaken.
>
> …
>
> To the extent that dicta in *Charleston* or other cases suggest that the courts should attribute to the recipients of matter published in the mass media a close and careful attention to the entirety of the item published, I would not follow that opinion.

Kirby J's strong criticism has been approached with caution in Australia. *Charleston* is still applied, but it has been suggested that recipients of published information are not taken to give close and careful attention to mass media publications.[37] In *Hockey v Fairfax Media Publications Pty Ltd*, for example, where the relevant publications were headlined full newspaper articles, and posters and online tweets made up of few but striking words, it was emphasised that ordinary readers do not read in isolation but take the context into account, including the surrounding circumstances.[38] They are taken to have read the whole of an article, not just headlines, but importantly, the more sensational an article, the less degree of analytical care is expected, in contrast to serious publications which trigger an assumption of caution and close critique.[39]

---

[35] See eg, 'Court ruling on headlines' (1995) 16 *JML & P* 74; Sir Michael Davies, 'Neighbours in the House of Lords' (1995) 69 *Australian Law Journal* 590; Meredith Blake, 'The Gutter Truth' (1996/1997) 7 *Kings College Law Journal* 99.

[36] [1998] HCA 37, (1998) 193 CLR 519, [134].

[37] Andrew T Kenyon, 'Pleading defamatory meaning, fair report defences and damages: *Chakravarti* in the High Court' (1997) 7 *Torts Law Journal* 1; Andrew T Kenyon, *Defamation: Comparative Law and Practice* (London, UCL Press, 2006) 45. See also *Korolak v Bauer Media Pty Ltd* [2016] NSWDC 98, [22].

[38] *Hockey v Fairfax Media Publications Pty Ltd* [2015] FCA 652, (2015) 237 FCR 33, [65].

[39] ibid [65]–[67]. See also *New Zealand Magazines v Hadlee*, unreported, CA(NZ), 24 October 1996, CA 74/96, where a headline outweighed an antidote in the accompanying article. In *McGee v Independent Newspapers Ltd* [2006] NZAR 24, both the bane and a potential antidote arose as a story broke on television over a number of days. Nonetheless, the defamatory statements were put to the jury.

Considering a publication as a whole does not mean every part is assumed to get equal consideration. Therefore headlines and captions, which publishers insert conspicuously and deliberately to attract attention, can legitimately be given more weight by the recipient.[40] This approach could be described as a legitimate extension of that taken by Lord Nicholls in *Charleston*.

C. How do Ordinary, Reasonable, Fair-minded People Think?

Very little commentary has been devoted to testing the fiction of the ordinary, reasonable, fair-minded person referred to in *Charleston*, perhaps because this hypothetical audience has been the backbone of defamation law and is a close cousin to the 'person on the Clapham omnibus' who resides in the heart of tort law generally. However, Australian academic Roy Baker has carried out an extensive empirical research project using communications studies methodology which involved surveying over 3,000 randomly selected people, supplemented by focus groups, to attempt to determine who the hypothetical audience represents and what views they hold.[41] Each person taking part in the survey had the content of an anonymised but real potentially damaging media report read to them and had to respond as to whether they thought less of the subject of the report or not. Participants were also asked whether they thought ordinary, reasonable Australians would think the same. Baker found that in the case of all news stories used, the proportion of participants who personally thought less of the subject because of the news report was much smaller than the proportion who thought an ordinary, reasonable person would think the same. Baker identified this effect, where media is seen to have a greater impact on others, not ourselves, as the 'third person' effect,[42] and contrasted this result with his survey of legal practitioners and judges, the majority of whom would have found the articles to be potentially defamatory. Baker concluded that when a judge or jury is asked to decide whether a publication is defamatory, they do set aside their own views, as indeed they are meant to. However, when, as asked to, they identify and express the views of ordinary, reasonable people, they in fact express views of people who are gullible, prejudiced or both. He concluded that this outcome favours plaintiffs unfairly, excessively chills freedom of expression and misleads as to the prevalence of prevailing social attitudes.[43]

---

[40] ibid [70] citing *John Fairfax Publications Pty Ltd v Rivkin* [2003] HCA 50, (2003) 201 ALR 77, [26]. Mr Hockey's claim was successful in relation to the posters and Twitter publications only, where lack of any other context meant there could be no antidote to the bane.

[41] Roy Baker, 'Defamation and the Moral Community' (2008) 13 *Deakin Law Review* 1.

[42] First identified by W Phillips Davison in 'The Third-Person Effect in Communication' (1983) 47 *Public Opinion Quarterly* 1.

[43] Baker, 'Defamation' (2008) 34c35.

Baker's early work implied that if juries were allowed or encouraged, through the adoption of a subjective rather than an objective test, to express their personal views about whether a plaintiff has been defamed, they would in fact represent not only the ordinary person but also the reasonable person more truthfully and accurately. The jury would not only stand in the shoes of the ordinary and reasonable person, it would actually be that person. The legal fiction would thereby lose its fictitious character and become a more reliable test. Such an approach is based on a more optimistic view of how juries function, similar to that which prevails in contempt law. Baker went on to carry out further detailed empirical work on the third-person effect, and concluded the approach should abandon reference to the 'ordinary, reasonable person' test altogether. This later work reaffirmed his view that the third-person effect represents a collective misapprehension of public opinion which does disturb the balance in defamation law, resulting in an advantage for plaintiffs.[44] Baker ultimately rejected the idea of asking judges and juries to substitute their subjective views and favoured instead an approach that is as empirical as possible within the existing system. Therefore, he proposed that courts should use relevant empirical indicators which cast light on the real impact a publication has had on its audience. This would include witness evidence or other evidence indicating the plaintiff has lost status or become a social outcast. This would be a significant change as extrinsic evidence is usually not admissible except where innuendo meanings are pleaded. Baker concluded optimistically, and rather vaguely, that defamation law in practice must discover the reasonableness of the general community which is more tolerant and accepting than we think, rather than seek the views of the fictitious ordinary, reasonable person.[45] The suggested change would appear to require the jury to give up an instinctive approach to finding a single meaning and require jurors to instead become something akin to social scientists.

Charleston supporters might acknowledge the suggested approach could make the single meaning rule less of a fiction. However, they would also probably remain unconvinced that change of this kind is necessary. The rule has been openly acknowledged as a fiction from the outset, but justified by the policy reasons of the need for certainty and an efficient method of resolving cases. It remains unclear whether Baker's solution would create more certainty overall. It might, however, reduce plaintiff advantage, as the plaintiff's case would become more complex and would require collation and advocacy using social scientific material to present to the jury, with new rules as to what evidence might be admissible.

---

[44] Roy Baker, *Defamation Law and Social Attitudes: Ordinary Unreasonable People* (Cheltenham, Edward Elgar, 2011) 316.
[45] ibid 317–18.

D. Insufficient Flesh on the Bones for Judge-Alone Trials?

The House of Lords in *Charleston* did not go into detail as to how agreement about the assumed single meaning is to be reached. This could be seen as a weakness in the rule in jurisdictions where civil juries are not used for defamation cases, and instead, judges have to grapple with the problem and give reasons. Such a case is *Cornes v The Ten Group Pty Ltd*,[46] where, to overcome this problem, Blue J in the Supreme Court of South Australia suggested that where the choice is between more than one possible meaning, the *predominant* meaning should be chosen by the trier of fact. The judge suggested this approach avoided any need to adopt a fiction that words have a single meaning in the real world. This still left the issue of truly equivocal words, where Blue J noted the single meaning rule did not provide an answer at all. In such a case, the judge suggested that it assists to return to the policy and principles behind the rule and these say that the law must choose. Applying this, Blue J held that where a defendant makes a statement that is equally capable of being defamatory and not defamatory, the defendant is a still a wrongdoer because if the non-defamatory meaning is removed, the defamatory one remains. The plaintiff must have suffered injury and the defendant has made a defamatory statement and must compensate for it. Blue J therefore found that a statement made on a comedy television programme which appeared to suggest the respondent was an adulterer who had slept with a footballer while married could, and would be equally understood by ordinary reasonable viewers in a literal sense and (and thus defamatory) and also in jest (not defamatory). This meant the statement was defamatory.[47]

Although this may foreshadow difficulties which could arise if more jurisdictions abandon juries in civil trials, in fact, it does not appear that this sort of judicial side-stepping is common, and such difficulties may be rare. In *Cornes*, neither Kourakis CJ nor Gray J found it necessary to take such an approach, and were able to find the same meaning arose in the full context of the whole programme.

Further, where juries are involved, an English court has noted recently that:

> It is surprising – it might even be thought gratifying – that neither of the very experienced leading counsel appearing in the present appeal could recollect a case in which a judge had had difficulty in directing a jury in accordance with the single meaning rule, or in which a jury had evinced difficulty in applying it.[48]

---

[46] [2012] SASCFC 99, (2012) 114 SASR 46.

[47] See ibid [196]–[197].

[48] Sedley LJ in *Ajinomoto Sweeteners v Asda* [4]. Nonetheless, in that case, where the question was whether the rule should apply to malicious falsehood as well as to defamation, the Court refused to import it into the former tort because it would have unjust results when applied to statements made in advertising and similar contexts. The balance has therefore been left more in favour of plaintiffs in malicious falsehood.

E. Bane and Antidote

A number of commentators have questioned how the bane and antidote doctrine worked in *Charleston* and how it works generally.[49] The plaintiffs accepted throughout that the article as a whole contained words that could neutralise the bane of the headline and the prominent photograph. However, the appeal was about the preliminary threshold issue whether the article was capable of bearing a defamatory meaning, which is a question of law for the judge. Where, as in *Charleston*, an article contains a defamatory imputation that will perhaps be seen by a jury as cured by a reading of the whole context, it is very difficult to overcome the threshold test and avoid a finding that the words are at least capable of being defamatory.[50] Therefore the speeches in *Charleston* do not contain any detailed reasoning as to why and how any neutralising effect could be achieved. Lord Bridge notes only that the question is a nicely balanced one for the jury which depends on the nature of the libel in the headline, the language of the text relied on to neutralise and the manner in which the whole is set out and presented. However, he does not then apply this to the facts before him because he refuses to accept only a prominent headline and photograph can be sued on alone. This is then followed by an assertion to the effect that a reader who does not take the trouble to discover what the article was about could hardly be described as ordinary, reasonable and fair-minded.[51] Lord Nicholls also makes a declaration that the ordinary reader would not have failed to read the captions accompanying the pictures, and would see at once the headlines and pictures could not be taken at face value.[52] However, the only statement he makes which indicates why this is so is that the 'reader's eye needed to travel no further than the "victims" caption to the smaller photographs and to the second sentence at the top of the article'.[53] Yet their Lordships acknowledge the photograph and headline were large and prominent, and in contrast, the captions and the text in the article themselves were small. The prominent material was also highly salacious and sexualised, which would naturally attract and retain the attention of a reader. Arguably, it is entirely possible an ordinary, reasonable person would miss the detail in the smaller text of the captions and article in those circumstances. Perhaps a fair-minded person would not. Only Lord Bridge refers to a fair-minded person and he does not discuss what sort of person this may be, which is unhelpful.

---

[49] See eg, Peter Prescott, 'Libel and Pornography' (1995) 58 *MLR* 752; Davies, 'Neighbours' (1995) 590.

[50] See Samuels JA in *Morosi v Broadcasting Station 2GB* [1980] 2 NSWLR 418, 419–20.

[51] *Charleston*, [6].

[52] Whether this means, as argued by Satouris, that the ridiculous nature of the photograph and the accompanying warning were palpable, is not clear: Paul Satouris, 'The Role of Media Satire in Australia and its Relation to Defamation Law' (2002) 21 *Communications Law Bulletin* 1.

[53] *Charleston*, 74.

This lack of detail has produced disagreement among commentators about when something in the context will cure. McManus criticises the judgment as providing little guidance as to how an antidote will remove a sting.[54] Burrows regards the outcome of the application of the doctrine in the case as borderline, and has commented that Justice Kirby's judgment in *Chakravarti* is a warning that defendants may not always be so lucky as they were in *Charleston*, where the text diluted the defamatory meaning in the headline and some of the captions.[55] Other commentators suggest it is clear that a bane will only be neutralised by an antidote in extreme cases.[56] This uncertainty about application of bane and antidote could once again be seen as a weakness since it is inconsistent with the need for certainty policy argument' used to justify the single meaning rule. Rolph argues that taking context into account actually strengthens defamation law by helping provide broad protection against the making of false statements.[57] However, certainty is undermined when doubt persists as to how context is to be taken into account, and applying the doctrine is unavoidably a fact dependent exercise in each case.

F. Not a Defamation Case at all?

Bainbridge and Pearce point out that although the publication in *Charleston* was held not to be defamatory, nonetheless it undoubtedly caused the plaintiffs substantial distress, for which they were left without a remedy.[58] Other commentary has suggested the plaintiffs failed because the case was not a defamation claim at all, but rather an attempt to enforce a publicity right, a form of intellectual property (and possibly privacy) which is not generally recognised in most common law jurisdictions except the United States.[59] The argument goes

[54] Francis McManus, 'Back to basics in the law of defamation' (1995) 16 *Journal of Media Law & Practice* 160.

[55] John Burrows, 'Media Law' [1996] *New Zealand Law Review* 342. See also Jason Harkess, 'A Linguistic Inspection of the Law of Defamation' (1998) 8 *Auckland University Law Review* 653; Paul March, 'The end of the libel lottery' 9 *Entertainment Law Review* 222; John Burrows, 'Media Law' [2000] *New Zealand Law Review* 193, 198.

[56] See eg, Roger D McConchie and David A Potts, *Canadian Libel and Slander Actions* (Toronto, Irwin Law, 2004) 298; Michael Gillooly, *The Law of Defamation in Australia and New Zealand* (Sydney, Federation Press, 2006) 39.

[57] David Rolph, 'Irreconcilable Differences? Interlocutory Injunctions for Defamation and Privacy' (2012) 17 *Media & Arts Law Review* 170, 198.

[58] David Bainbridge and Graham Pearce, 'Tilting at Windmills – Has the New Data Protection Law Failed to Make a Significant Contribution to Rights of Privacy' (2000) *Journal of Information, Law and Technology* 2 [3.1.1].

[59] See Stephen Todd, Ursula Cheer, Cynthia Hawes and Bill Atkin, *The Law of Torts in New Zealand*, 7th edn (Wellington, Thomson Reuters, 2016) 787; S Che Ekaratne, 'Head-Swapped Photographs & Copyright: A New Zealand Perspective' (2017) 23 *Canterbury Law Review* 39, 42–43; J Thomas McCarthy *The Rights of Publicity and Privacy* (Toronto, Thomson Reuters, 2016) [10.37].

that when the actors complained about the faked image and the headline, they were really trying to protect an exclusive right to exploit their own image or personality.[60] However, without more, Lord Bridge refused to consider the possibility of a novel tort in *Charleston*, and the 'single meaning' rule prevented the claim from being successful in defamation. Had a publicity right existed, the misuse of the publicity would have been determinative, rather than the meaning of the publication as fixed by a test involving the application of a fiction inside a fiction. The limits of defamation law, as represented by *Charleston*, mean it is ineffective in preventing or remedying unauthorised and unwanted exploitation of personality. Thus it has been said that 'The mere exploitation of another's popularity is not defamatory'.[61] Although Robinson suggests courts might be becoming more open to the possibility of protecting such rights when using existing forms of action, she notes this still requires skilful advocacy,[62] and *Charleston* still represents a barrier to change in defamation law.[63] It may be that ongoing development in intellectual property law and in the burgeoning laws of privacy in common law jurisdictions will effectively plug any 'gap' in the law represented by *Charleston*, and this area of criticism of the case will fall away.

G. Future Application of the Single Meaning Rule

It is apparent *Charleston* and its crude yardstick sit uncomfortably within the common law, criticised by some, defended by others on policy grounds, barely tolerated by yet others by virtue of its longevity and a reluctance to change such a well-embedded part of defamation law. However, its relevance has been challenged in commentary in recent years which has raised a further issue whether the 'single meaning' rule together with the bane and antidote doctrine can be applied to new media delivery platforms, in particular those associated with new technology.

The issue is not as new as it appears. In a 1997 New Zealand case, *Thode v Coastline FM Ltd*,[64] the plaintiff argued that the bane and antidote doctrine should be applied differently to broadcast as opposed to print media. The alleged defamation arose from a light-hearted hoax birthday telephone call

---

[60] Guy Veysey, 'It's just not cricket' (2002) *NLJ* 1391; Jonathan Morgan, 'Privacy, Confidence and Horizontal Effect: "Hello" Trouble' (2003) 62 *CLJ* 444.

[61] Jan Klink, '50 Years of Publicity Rights in the United States and the Never Ending Hassle with Intellectual Property and Personality Rights in Europe' (2003) 4 *Intellectual Property Quarterly* 363, 376. See also Catherine Seville, 'Peter Pan's Rights: 'To Die Will Be An Awfully Big Adventure'' (2003) *Journal of Copyright Society USA* 1, 11–12.

[62] Felicity Robinson, 'How image conscious is English law?' (2004) *Entertainment Law Review* 151, 153.

[63] Franz Hoffman, 'The right to publicity in German and English law' (2010) 3 *Intellectual Property Quarterly* 325, 333.

[64] *Thode v Coastline FM Ltd*, unreported, HC(NZ), Tauranga, 1/10/1997, CP31/95.

made by a radio station in which the later part of the candid call made it clear it was a joke. The plaintiff argued that a radio listener may leave or enter a room, or stop concentrating and not hear all of the broadcast, and does not have the opportunity to review the material that exists for print media. Potter J rejected this argument, in part because the Defamation Act 1992 (NZ) abandoned any legal distinction associated with the spoken word (slander) and the written word (libel), merging these under the label of defamation.[65] However, the judge also reached this finding because she thought there would 'need to be powerful persuasion to draw a distinction between the treatment of the written and spoken word in the absence of authority'[66] *Charleston* was the authority relied on by the defendant and the judge concluded it was clear authority.[67]

Kirwan has similarly argued that *Charleston* might apply differently in respect of items presented on television, where there is much less time to reflect and absorb information.[68] In *McGee v Independent Newspapers Ltd*[69] which arose from publication of a story which broke over two days on television and on websites, the Court overcame any problems by holding that what was sauce for the goose was sauce for the gander[70] – this meant the bane and the antidote could arise over the period and be based on two broadcasts. On one day there were two broadcasts and two website publications, the latter of which contained an antidote. The judge considered all of these and found although the antidote required serious consideration, the alleged defamatory meanings would still be put to the jury.[71] Throughout the judgment, the judge appeared to have no difficulty applying *Charleston* to different media nor to a story breaking over time.

Harris et al note that *Charleston* is a modern example of publications which lack authenticity and integrity, and these have always existed. However, the authors also accept that recent developments in computer technology have elevated fakery to a new level.[72] Does this mean *Charleston* has become irrelevant, a dead letter? Gary Chan Kok Yew raises relevant complexities associated with hyperlinking in the light of the Supreme Court of Canada decision in *Crookes v Newton (Crookes)*, where it was held that hyperlinking to internet websites within a publication did not itself constitute publication of the material on the website linked to.[73] Yew suggests that *Crookes*, combined with

---

[65] Defamation Act 1992 (NZ), s 2.
[66] *Thode v Coastline FM Ltd*, unreported, HC(NZ), Tauranga, 1/10/1997, CP31/95, 14–16.
[67] cf *Gordon v Amalgamated Television Services* [1980] 2 NSWLR 410, 412.
[68] Brendan Kirwan 'Defamation, Isolation and the Ordinary Reader: *McGarth v Independent Newspapers*' (2004) 9 *Bar Review* 463.
[69] *McGee v Independent Newspapers Ltd* [2006] NZAR 24.
[70] ibid [50]–[51].
[71] ibid [53]–[58].
[72] Candida Harris, Judith Rowbotham and Kim Stevenson, 'Truth, law and hate in the virtual marketplace of ideas: perspectives on the regulation of Internet content' (2009) 18 *Information & Communications Technology Law* 155, 173–75.
[73] Gary Chan Kok Yew 'Defamation via hyperlinks – more than meets the eye' (2012) 128 *LQR* 346.

Charleston, would exempt hyperlinked material from consideration as context and thereby exclude any antidote contained in the linked publication. Whether the Canadian position will be adopted in other common law jurisdictions has yet to be determined.[74] It is clear, however, that the status of hyperlinking in defamation law will impact on how *Charleston* is to be applied in relation to context.

Roopani also examines these issues and suggests that *Charleston* can and should be retained and applied to new media.[75] She notes that it is possible for hyperlinks themselves and their surrounding context to appear defamatory if the linked content itself is not taken into account,[76] and that courts seem reluctant to develop a principled approach to the issue of what would count as context in such cases, preferring to take a fact-based approach.[77] After examining cases involving hyperlinking and online searches, Roopani poses the question whether 'courts will move towards an alternate approach to determining the scope of a publication which recognises that the ordinary, reasonable recipient of material on the internet may not necessarily read the whole publication for the purposes of ascertaining its meaning'.[78] She concludes no special new rules are necessary or desirable, but that courts may need to take into account the novel features of the internet when considering scope and content for meaning, such as whether the material is delivered by audio, text or video, and the different platforms used to deliver the internet content, such as mobile phones.[79]

Roopani accepts the validity of the *Charleston* approach and finds it adaptive to modern technology. Her view is essentially that there is no need to throw out the baby with the bathwater and she appears to be convinced by the policy reasons which have been put forward for the rule. However, as detailed above, there are powerful critical arguments which have exposed weaknesses in the rule and in the policy reasons put forward to support it. Lord Bridge in *Charleston* agreed with Diplock LJ in *Slim* when he rejected the possibility of words bearing multiple meanings and plaintiffs being able to sue on those multiple meanings. Some have argued that the 'single meaning' rule should be replaced by a multiple meanings rule. This possibility is the final issue to be scrutinised in this chapter.

---

[74] For example, New Zealand does not yet have binding authority. However, the High Court has shown some inclination to take a more nuanced approach to hyperlinking, based on intention and intervention by the linker: *Karam v Fairfax New Zealand Ltd* [2012] NZHC 887. See also *Visscher v Maritime Union of Australia (No 6)* [2014] NSWSC 350.

[75] Dinika Roopani 'The scope and content of a "publication" on the internet for the purposes of defamation law' (2015) 20 *Media & Arts Law Review* 33.

[76] ibid 38, citing Matthew Collins, *The Law of Defamation and the Internet*, 3rd edn (Oxford, Oxford University Press, 2010) 28, n 48.

[77] Roopani, 'Scope and content' (2015) 40.

[78] ibid 41.

[79] ibid 44–45.

H. Alternative Approaches

Barendt and others have argued that changing to a multiple meaning rule risks altering the current acceptable balance which exists in the law by increasing potential liability for a multiplicity of meanings. Writers and publishers are entitled to the degree of certainty as to whether or not what they publish will be considered defamatory by an ordinary, reasonable person.[80] However, the detailed examination of the rule contained in this chapter has shown that this vaunted certainty is arguably a chimera, based as it is on the views of a fictional person established to satisfy a test which has a fictional goal. This suggests that proposals to adopt a 'multiple meaning' rule are not outlandish and should be taken seriously.

Perhaps the strongest expression of why a multiple meaning rule is desirable and workable is the judgment in *Ajinomoto Sweeteners v Asda*,[81] where the English Court of Appeal refused to apply the 'single meaning' rule to the tort of malicious falsehood. Although the Court acknowledged that the reasons for the rejection of the rule for malicious falsehood included differences between the torts, nonetheless it also outlined general reasons for doing so. These included that the rule produces unfair and unjust results, has no enduring rationale,[82] and is based on fictitious premises.[83] In particular, Sedley LJ did not accept that adopting a 'multiple meaning' rule would make trials more unwieldy or too complex. The judge took care to state that this was not just because malicious falsehood claims, unlike defamation claims, are not usually tried by a jury – indeed, he noted that juries are quite capable of dealing with thorny directions. He concluded powerfully that altering the rule would make 'the trial of the issues fairer and more realistic' and that 'trial of plural meanings permits the damaging effect of the words to be put in perspective and both malice and (if it comes to it) damage to be more realistically gauged'.[84] Rimer LJ added: 'If the single meaning rule did not exist, I doubt if any modern court would invent it, either for defamation or any other tort'.[85]

The Scottish Law Commission, in its recent examination of the tort of defamation, was convinced by the reasoning of the Court of Appeal in *Ajinomoto* to recommend a 'multiple meaning' rule. It has said:[86]

> We are also of the view that the 'single meaning rule' that is applicable in actions of defamation should not apply in relation to proceedings ... We are in agreement with

---

[80] Tony Martino 'In conversation with Professor Eric Barendt: hatred, ridicule, contempt and plain bigotry' (2007) 18 *Entertainment Law Review* 48.

[81] [2010] *EMLR* 23, [2011] *QB* 497.

[82] ibid [32]–[33].

[83] ibid [43].

[84] ibid [34].

[85] ibid [43].

[86] Scottish Law Commission, *Report on Defamation* (Scot Law Com 248, 2017) [9.35]. The Scottish government is consulting further on the report, see letter dated 6 June 2018: www.scotlawcom.gov. uk/files/2415/2870/8097/Response_from_the_Scottish_Government_to_Report_on_Defamation_No_248_.pdf.

the view expressed in the Ajinomoto Sweeteners case that examination by the court of multiple meanings allows the damaging effect of the words to be put into perspective and malice and damage to be gauged more realistically.

This recommendation was made in the context of a report which recommends significant changes to the law, including a removal of a presumption of jury trial, to be replaced with a discretion in the court to determine the form the inquiry should take.[87]

Other alternatives have been suggested. In 2012, Mullis and Scott argued that the rule was unjust in the context of a discussion of a draft Defamation Bill published by the Northern Ireland Ministry of Justice that proposed the effective end for the role of the jury in determining meaning.[88] These commentators proposed that a claimant's inferred meaning should be at the heart of any subsequent consideration of the issue, but that inferred meaning should be subject to a test of reasonableness. More recently, Scott has recommended that Northern Ireland legislate to introduce a bipartite scheme recommended by the Northern Ireland Law Commission before it went out existence in March 2015.[89] Such a scheme would involve abolishing the single meaning rule but only in conjunction with the enactment of a jurisdictional bar to claims in defamation based on meanings that had been corrected or retracted by the publisher promptly and prominently. Scott has defended this proposal robustly by arguing that it will ensure only singular and contested meanings reach court after other unintended meanings have been weeded out. The proposal is, however, linked to a further recommendation that, like the United Kingdom, Northern Ireland should also legislate for a presumption against civil juries in defamation cases.

It is clear, then, that the suggestion of a 'multiple meaning' rule is now being taken seriously. Both a bipartite scheme, and a simple 'multiple meaning' proposal would alter the balance of the current law and therefore require careful consideration in the context of examining the desirability of other changes to defamation law, such as removing civil juries. Major change of this nature is best achieved by way of a government inquiry which allows extensive consultation to inform recommendations for statutory change.[90]

---

[87] ibid [8.19]. England and Wales has already removed this presumption: *Defamation Act 2013*, s 11, but has not abandoned the single meaning rule.

[88] Alastair Mullis and Andrew Scott, 'The swing of the pendulum: reputation, expression and the recentering of English libel law' (2012) 63 *Northern Ireland Law Quarterly* 5, at 14. See also 'Ceci n'est pas une pipe: the autopoietic inanity of the single meaning rule in libel law' in Kenyon (ed) *Comparative Defamation and Privacy Law* (Cambridge, Cambridge University Press, 2016) 40.

[89] Andrews Scott (2016) *Reform of defamation law in Northern Ireland*. Department of Finance, Belfast, UK, http://eprints.lse.ac.uk/67385/, [3.2]–[3.28], [3.32], [3.60]–[3.66], referring to Northern Ireland Law Commission, *Defamation Law in Northern Ireland*, NILC, 19(2014) and the submissions received during a consultation period that closed on 20 February 2015.

[90] The Law Commission of Ontario is investigating the law of defamation in the internet age, and may consider the issue of single meaning when considering how the context of publication on the internet is to be taken into account. See Law Commission of Ontario, *Defamation Law in the Internet Age*, Consultation Paper, November 2017, www.lco-cdo.org/wp-content/uploads/2017/12/

IV. CONCLUSION

This chapter has examined the leading House of Lords decision, *Charleston v News Group Newspapers.* We have seen that the case is a modern expression of an old rule that in defamation, when determining the natural and ordinary meaning of allegedly damaging words, the finder of fact must settle on a single meaning that would be taken from the words by an ordinary, reasonable and fair-minded person, and this determination is reached by looking at the whole context of the publication. This 'single meaning' rule has been recognised as a fiction and it has been openly acknowledged by courts that in fact multiple meanings may be taken by multiple audiences, some of which will be damaging to some plaintiffs. However, those plaintiffs are left without a remedy because it is said policy requires certainty for defendants to be able to order their lives and businesses and defamation trials should not be too long or complex. The 'single meaning' rule, labelled a crude yardstick from the outset, exploits a test involving not only the views of a notional person, but also a difficult and comparatively undeveloped canon called the bane and antidote doctrine, which may or may not reduce potential liability for defendants.

An analysis of judicial and academic commentary about *Charleston* reveals that its application of the 'single meaning' rule and the notional person test lacked a clear rationale and was ambiguous at best. Doubts persist as to how mass media is consumed and how this affects the meanings taken from publications by ordinary audiences. There is some empirical evidence that juries, forced to objectively express what they see as the views of the notional person, do not apply this test in a way that is fair to defendants or accurate. There is little guidance as to how a single meaning may be arrived at, although additionally, there is little evidence that this has caused great difficulty for juries or judges attempting to direct them. This suggests, however, that the process is instinctive and not well understood. There is lack of agreement as to when an antidote will neutralise a bane, in particular, whether it can only do so in extreme cases and whether more weight is to be given to contextual material such as headlines. Additionally, some commentators have suggested *Charleston* is not a defamation case at all, but rather a claim to protect a right of personality or publicity. Those commentators suggest that if such rights are recognised in the UK, Canada, Australia or New Zealand in future, plaintiffs such as those in *Charleston* would have no need to use defamation law and would not be left

---

Defamation-Consultation-Paper-Eng.pdf, 45, Question 7. Would legislative reform of the test for defamatory meaning be appropriate or should this area of defamation law continue to evolve incrementally through case law? If a new test were adopted, what elements should be part of this test? 7. Would legislative reform of the test for defamatory meaning be appropriate or should this area of defamation law continue to evolve incrementally through case law? If a new test were adopted, what elements should be part of this test?

without a remedy. Finally, it is apparent that while *Charleston* appears adaptive to new media, this occurs without achieving any greater certainty of principle.

This analysis has shown that lack of certainty at every stage of its application, in the end, is the reason why the principle/rule/crude yardstick enshrined in *Charleston* has not achieved its policy-based purpose. Applying the 'single meaning' rule and its composite parts is and has always been, a fact-based exercise arrayed in an elaborate costume of principle and doctrine. But the emperor has no clothes and the attainment of certainty is a pretence. Thus, it appears likely that calls from commentators and law reform bodies for a 'multiple meanings' approach to be adopted (perhaps in conjunction with a jurisdictional bar for corrected or retracted publications and elimination or reduction of the role of juries in defamation cases) will increase in the future. Such calls should be given serious attention.

9

Reynolds v Times
Newspapers Ltd *(1999)*

HILARY YOUNG

R EYNOLDS V TIMES *Newspapers* brought reasonableness into the law of
defamation, making the strict liability tort less of an outlier in modern
tort law. In so doing, it also tilted the balance between reputation and
speech in England, affected the way journalists do their work, and influenced
the law throughout the common law world. This is the story of *Reynolds* and
its famous 'privilege'.

In some ways, *Reynolds* is a simple case[1] about whether a newspaper defamed
a politician when it implied the politician was a liar and failed to publish his
explanation of events. At issue was whether an honest but mistaken news article about a politician was protected by the defence of qualified privilege. In
holding that the existing law of qualified privilege[2] *could* afford a defence for
media who report on matters of public interest, although not on the facts of
the case, *Reynolds* seems rather uninteresting. But its important innovation was
its holding that media have a duty to communicate on matters of public interest, and the public a reciprocal interest in receiving the information, so long as
the defendant behaved responsibly in publishing. It set out criteria to consider
in assessing responsibleness. In so doing, *Reynolds* introduced a negligence-
based defence into the largely strict-liability tort of defamation.[3] The House

---

[1] *Reynolds v Times Newspapers Ltd* [1999] UKHL 45, [2001] 2 AC 127 (*Reynolds*): 'On this
level [that it was about the plaintiff's honesty re events over a one week period] the action could be
portrayed as relatively simple'.

[2] 'My conclusion is that the established common law approach to misstatements of fact remains
essentially sound' (*Reynolds v Times Newspapers Ltd* [1998] EWCA 1172, [2001] 2 AC 127, 143
(*Reynolds* CA)). '[T]he House of Lords had not given the impression of doing anything particularly
new, and their opinions can be regarded as merely fleshing out a doctrine which was well known to
the common law' (Neville Cox, 'Public Interest Reporting and Defamation Law: Recent Irish Developments' (2007–2008) 2 *Quarterly Review of Tort Law* 20, 25).

[3] As discussed below, Australia had previously incorporated reasonableness into its statutory
qualified privilege defence, but *Reynolds* was the first to do so at common law, and its innovation
was broader and more influential.

of Lords decision was fairly narrow (applying the existing law of qualified privilege, applying to journalism, setting strict criteria of responsibleness), and some judges were initially hostile even to that narrow extension of the doctrine. Nevertheless, subsequent cases and legislation in England and abroad have expanded the scope of *Reynolds* privilege. *Reynolds'* negligence-based defence, or something like it, can now be found in defamation law throughout the common law world.

I. FACTS

The facts of *Reynolds* are so well-known that at least four journal articles have referred to the facts as well-known.[4] In the fall of 1994, Albert Reynolds was the Taoiseach (Prime Minister) of Ireland. A high-level judicial position opened up and Reynolds wanted to appoint his Attorney-General, Harry Whelehan. Reynolds' coalition partner, Labour Party leader Dick Spring, was unenthusiastic but initially agreed not to oppose the appointment on certain conditions. In October, before the appointment was finalised, a news story broke about Whelehan's apparent inaction on an extradition matter. A Catholic priest accused of child sexual abuse was wanted in Northern Ireland ('the Smyth case'). Whelehan's office of the Attorney-General had ignored the file for seven months.

On November 11, Whelehan provided Reynolds with a report, dated November 9, explaining the delay in extraditing Smyth. Among the reasons given was that a provision of the Republic's Extradition Act 1965 had never previously been applied and so the Attorney-General had to give extra attention to its interpretation.

That same day, the coalition cabinet discussed the judicial vacancy. Because of the revelations about the Smyth extradition, Mr Spring and his Labour MPs opposed Whelehan's appointment. They left the meeting so that their opposition would effectively be recorded in the minutes. Whelehan's appointment was approved.

On Monday, 14 November it emerged that the relevant provision of the Extradition Act 1965 had, in fact, previously been considered – by Whelehan himself ('the Duggan case'). Later that day, this information was brought to Reynolds' attention but it appears that its significance was not initially made clear.

---

[4] Ian Cram, 'Political Expression, Qualified Privilege and Investigative Journalism – an Analysis of Developments in English Defamation Law Post-*Reynolds v Times Newspapers*' (2005) 11 *Canterbury Law Review* 143, 146; Cox, 'Recent Irish Developments' (2007–2008) 24; Ailbhe O'Neill, 'Reporting Allegations: Reynolds Privilege Revisited in the UK Supreme Court Short Articles and Comments' (2012) 47 *Irish Jurist New Series* 185, 185; Neville Cox, 'The Future of the Reynolds Defence in Irish Defamation Law Following the Defamation Act 2009' (2014) 51 *Irish Jurist* 28, 36.

The next day, Reynolds spoke in the Dàil (Parliament) about the extradition matter, saying he was giving a 'full account'[5] and that there had been a failure in the Attorney-General's office. No mention was made of the Duggan extradition case. The impression given was that the Smyth case was the first to be considered under the relevant section of the *Extradition Act 1965*. The new Attorney-General had provided advice to the Prime Minister stating that 'it would be absolutely incorrect to inform the Dàil that this was the first time that the section [of the *Extradition Act 1965*] was considered. It was considered – though not in a profound manner in the Duggan case'. However, this advice was only delivered to Reynolds' office after he had left to give his speech in the Dàil. He did not see it until after giving his 15 November speech. When he did see it, he 'hit the roof'[6] and resolved to address the Dàil again to correct the record.

Before he could do so, however, his coalition collapsed. On Wednesday, 15 November, Spring met with the new Attorney-General and asked him when the file, containing information about the Duggan case, was found. The Attorney-General correctly replied that it had been found that Monday. But Spring incorrectly inferred from this that Reynolds had known about the case when he spoke to the Dàil (and perhaps also at the time of the earlier cabinet meeting) and that he had deliberately misled the Dàil. Spring announced that he would no longer continue the coalition. Reynolds tried to salvage things by making another speech in the Dàil, much more critical of Whelehan, but the damage had been done. Reynolds resigned as Taoiseach on November 17. Whelehan also resigned as President of the High Court.

On 20 November, the British mainland edition of *The Sunday Times* contained an article titled 'Goodbye gombeen man: Why a fib too far proved fatal for the political career of Ireland's peacemaker and Mr Fixit'. It included statements such as 'Reynolds had known all along that Whelehan's excuse did not hold water, yet in the dail on Tuesday he had backed his promotion to the High Court'. Importantly, the analogous story in *The Sunday Times'* Irish edition was more factual, balanced and unobjectionable.[7]

Reynolds sued Times Newspapers Ltd (*The Times*) in relation to the British mainland edition. In addition to its use of the word 'fib' in the headline, Reynolds objected to much of the text. He claimed the article implied that he had deliberately mislead the Dàil on 15 November, that he had mislead his cabinet colleagues, and had lied to them about when he had acquired relevant information.

The Times defended on several grounds: meaning; common law; and statutory qualified privilege, fair comment and justification, though the statutory qualified privilege and fair comment defences were eventually abandoned.

---

[5] *Reynolds* CA (n 1) 137.
[6] ibid.
[7] *Reynolds* CA (n 1) 219.

II. JUDICIAL HISTORY

A. Trial

In a jury trial, Reynolds won a Pyrrhic victory: he succeeded in establishing liability but the jury awarded him nothing in compensation. (The trial judge substituted an award of 1p.) The jury concluded that the allegations in *The Times* were not true, so justification failed, but that the newspaper did not act with malice. It remained for the judge to deal with costs and with qualified privilege.[8]

The qualified privilege issue was not a new one, but *The Times* suggested a new approach to it. It was long understood that common law qualified privilege applies where there is a duty to communicate the information to an audience and that audience has a reciprocal interest in receiving that information.[9] Courts had generally held that qualified privilege could not be made out in relation to publications to the world at large because there was rarely a duty to publish so broadly. Further, the media were held to have no special duty to publish.[10] The effect of the law was therefore especially harsh on the media, who publish to the world at large as a matter of course.[11] As a result, the law had a chilling effect on the media.[12] Because they generally had no duty to publish, the only defence usually available to the media was justification (truth). But even if journalists worked honestly and diligently, they could be liable in defamation if they made a mistake or were otherwise unable to establish the truth of a factual allegation years later in court. This in turn meant that important matters were not being reported, to the detriment of the public. Many thought the law was unfair.

Unsurprisingly, the trial judge applied the general rule that the media have no duty to publish to the world at large and held that there was no qualified privilege.

---

[8] *Reynolds* CA (n 1) 143.

[9] *Adam v Ward* [1917] AC 309, 334 (Lord Atkinson).

[10] 'Media publishers, generally speaking, were not seen as having a duty to publish nor the public an interest in receiving widespread publications, even in circumstances where such a publication concerned a legitimate matter of public interest.' See *Braddock v Bevins* [1948] 1 KB 580 (CA); *Blackshaw v Lord* [1984] QB 1 (CA); Jason Bosland, 'Republication of Defamation under the Doctrine of Reportage – The Evolution of Common Law Qualified Privilege in England and Wales' (2011) 31 *Oxford Journal of Legal Studies* 89, 90, fn 4.

[11] 'The English law of defamation had long been regarded as unduly harsh, especially in respect of defendants having published... to the world at large – in practice mass medias' (Eric Descheemaeker, 'A Man Must Take Care Not to Defame His Neighbour: The Origins and Significance of the Defence of Responsible Publication' (2015) 34 *University of Queensland Law Journal* 239, 251.) Also ibid Descheemaeker cites Paul Mitchell, *The Making of the Modern Law of Defamation* (Oxford, Hart Publishing 2005) 145, which at fn 117 notes that the rule can be explained in part by the courts' antagonism toward newspapers in the late 1800s.

[12] Writing before *Reynolds*, Barendt *et al* state: "We believe that our investigation of the impact of defamation law on various media has demonstrated clearly that the chilling effect in this area genuinely does exist and significantly restricts what the public is able to read and hear" (Eric Barendt et al, *Libel and the Media – The Chilling Effect* (Oxford, Clarendon Press, 1997) 191).

B. Court of Appeal

Both the plaintiff and defendant appealed – Reynolds on the basis of instructions to the jury, *The Times* on the qualified privilege issue. Reynolds succeeded in his appeal. A new trial was ordered. However, the Court of Appeal had to determine whether qualified privilege would be available in the new trial.

Lord Lester, representing *The Times*, argued for qualified privilege to be extended to political communications to the world at large. He was effectively arguing for a modified Australian approach. In *Lange v Australian Broadcasting Corporation,* Australia's High Court had recognised a narrow common law qualified privilege to speak to the world at large about 'government and political matters that affect the people of Australia'.[13] Unlike *Reynolds* privilege, however, this was not a policy-driven change to the common law; rather, the privilege was considered necessary to give effect to Australia's implied constitutional freedom of political communication. *Lange* privilege is defeated if defendants cannot prove their conduct was reasonable.[14] (Although Australia's reasonableness approach appears broad and flexible, in reality it has not often benefitted defendants).[15] What Lord Lester was arguing for differed from the law in Australia, however, in that the privilege would only be defeated by showing a lack of an honest belief in truth.

In arguing *The Times'* position, Lord Lester relied heavily on a New Zealand Court of Appeal decision, also brought by former New Zealand Prime Minister David Lange: *Lange v Atkinson.*[16] In that case, the court upheld a qualified privilege defence in relation to a media report about a politician. It held that publishing to the world at large was no bar to the application of qualified privilege, that the public has an interest in statements about government and politics, and that the breadth of that interest justified widespread publication on such matters. (The Court of Appeal decision in *Lange* NZ was later set aside by the Privy Council, but was good law at the time of the *Reynolds* appeal to the Court of Appeal.[17])

In its judgment, the Court of Appeal in *Reynolds* laid the foundation for what became known as *Reynolds* privilege. It reviewed the law of qualified privilege and noted that although it is impossible to clearly demarcate occasions of privilege, the defence promotes the 'common convenience and welfare of society'.[18] The court discussed several cases in which qualified privilege had been

---

[13] *Lange v Australian Broadcasting Corporation* (1997) 189 CLR 520. The privilege has been narrowly interpreted. For example, it does not apply to matters concerning the judiciary (*Herald & Weekly Times Ltd v Popovic* (2003) 9 VR 1, [2003] VSCA 161). Note that *Lange* qualified privilege exists alongside statutory qualified privilege (see eg Defamation Act 2005 (Vic), s 30).

[14] *Lange* ibid [572].

[15] See eg David Rolph, *Defamation Law* (Sydney, Thomson Reuters, 2016) 238, fn 196.

[16] *Lange v Atkinson* [1998] 3 NZLR 424 (CA) (*Lange* NZ).

[17] *Lange v Atkinson* [2000] 1 NZLR 257 (PC).

[18] *Reynolds* CA (n 1) citing *Stuart v Bell* [1891] 2 QB 341, 162.

found to apply where defendants had published to the world at large.[19] They involved matters of public importance. Based on this and other cases discussing the proper balance between reputation and free speech, the court concluded that the common law of qualified privilege had a three-part test: First, there must be a 'legal, moral or social duty' to publish (duty test). Second, the recipients must have an interest in receiving the communication (interest test). Third, the circumstances of publication must suggest that it is in the public interest to protect the communication (circumstantial test).

In order to flesh out when a privilege is warranted for the common convenience and welfare of society, the court reviewed statutes and cases, including from other common law jurisdictions and the European Court of Human Rights. These suggested tilting the balance toward greater protection of the press when reporting on political matters or matters of public importance: 'the common convenience and welfare of a modern plural democracy such as ours are best served by an ample flow of information to the public concerning, and by vigorous public discussion of, matters of public interest to the community'.[20]

Thus, on the duty branch of the test for qualified privilege, the court stated that the media have a duty to inform the public on matters of public interest, which is a category broader than political communications. This marked a significant shift from the previous case law in which the media were rarely said to have a duty to publish to the world at large. 'In modern conditions what we have called the duty test should, in our view, be rather more readily held to be satisfied.'[21] The same was true of the interest branch of the test. The public often has an interest in being informed of matters of interest to the community. Article 10 of the European Convention on Human Rights enshrines a right to receive information, which also weighs in favour of making the interest branch more easily satisfied.

More is needed, though, than a reciprocal duty and interest, in the sense described above. Otherwise it was thought that the press would have too much leeway to print defamatory statements on matters of public interest, to the detriment of those who operate in the public sphere. It would effectively protect all journalistic communications on matters of public interest, no matter how irresponsible, so long as there was no malice (ie improper purpose) in publishing. Instead, the third branch of the test, the circumstantial test, was intended to achieve the right balance between reputation and speech. It asks whether the circumstances of publication are such that it is in the public interest to protect the speech with qualified privilege. The court specifically mentioned the nature, status and source of the information as relevant factors

---

[19] *Cox v Feeney* (1863) 4 F & F 13, 176 ER 445; *Allbutt v The General Council of Medical Education and Registration* (1889) 23 QBD 400; *Perera v Peiris* [1949] AC 1; *Webb v Times Publishing Company Limited* [1960] 2 QB 535.
[20] *Reynolds* CA (n 2) 176.
[21] ibid.

and suggested that the circumstantial test was essentially like Australia's reasonableness test.[22]

As applied to the facts, the publication at issue was on a matter of public interest, such that there was a duty to publish and the public had an interest in receiving it. But the circumstantial test was not made out because *The Times* used an unreliable source, did not bring the publication to Reynolds' attention and, in particular, it failed to include Reynolds' version of events. The court therefore held there was no qualified privilege, upholding the trial judge's decision.

To summarise, the Court of Appeal applied the existing common law of qualified privilege insofar as the existence of a privilege depends on whether, on the facts of the case, a qualified privilege would promote the common convenience and welfare of society. In the case of media publications to the world at large, however, this was to be determined by a three-part test rather than the usual duty-interest test. The first two branches, duty and interest, will generally be made out when the matter is one of public interest, as the media have a duty to publish on matters of public interest and the public has an interest in receiving those publications. The test will then hinge on the third branch – whether the publisher acted reasonably in publishing (the circumstantial test).

The court's innovation was to borrow from Australia's approach without limiting the privilege to speech on political matters.[23] Although as we shall see, the House of Lords modified this test in *Reynolds*, and again in *Jameel*, and although England and Wales have replaced the defence with a statutory one, and although other jurisdictions have their own versions of *Reynolds* privilege, and although it is often not even a form of qualified privilege anymore, the fundamental features of public interest and reasonableness, set out in the Court of Appeal's judgment, persist.

C. House of Lords

On further appeal to the House of Lords, the only issue was qualified privilege.

Lord Nicholls, writing for the majority, canvassed other jurisdictions' approach to the issue and noted that the problem was a difficult one. On the one hand, freedom of expression is profoundly important, and the press plays a crucial role in disseminating important information. On the other, the media have the potential to do substantial harm if they get their facts wrong. 'No answer is perfect. Every solution has its own advantages and disadvantages'.[24]

---

[22] 'We question whether in practice this is a test very different from the test of reasonableness upheld in Australia': ibid [177].

[23] As noted above, common law *Lange* privilege is limited to speech about government. Statutory qualified privilege in Australia is much broader in theory, but in practice it has been applied narrowly. See fns 14–16.

[24] *Reynolds* (n 1) 201.

Ultimately, the existing common law approach was considered sound, so there was no reason to create a special category of privilege for political speech. That said, it was important to provide greater protection for free speech. Within the context of the duty/interest analysis, public interest should therefore be understood broadly. In addition, the court was willing to accept a certain amount of uncertainty in the law in exchange for flexibility. The burden was not thought to be too great on defendants. 'The common law does not seek to set a higher standard than that of responsible journalism, a standard the media themselves espouse'.[25]

And so *Reynolds* privilege was adopted by England's highest court.

The House of Lords modified the Court of Appeal's approach, rejecting the circumstantial test as a separate test. Instead, the nature, status and source of the material and circumstances of publication were held to be relevant to the question of whether there was a duty to publish. The House of Lords therefore restored the two-part duty and interest test for common law qualified privilege, while clarifying that a duty only existed where journalism was responsibly published.

To assess whether publication was responsible, Lord Nicholls set out an 'illustrative' and 'not exhaustive' list of factors to consider.

(1) The seriousness of the allegation. The more serious the charge, the more the public is misinformed and the individual harmed, if the allegation is not true.
(2) The nature of the information, and the extent to which the subject matter is a matter of public concern.
(3) The source of the information. Some informants have no direct knowledge of the events. Some have their own axes to grind, or are being paid for their stories.
(4) The steps taken to verify the information.
(5) The status of the information. The allegation may have already been the subject of an investigation which commands respect.
(6) The urgency of the matter. News is often a perishable commodity.
(7) Whether comment was sought from the plaintiff. He may have information others do not possess or have not disclosed. An approach to the plaintiff will not always be necessary.
(8) Whether the article contained the gist of the plaintiff's side of the story.
(9) The tone of the article. A newspaper can raise queries or call for an investigation. It need not adopt allegations as statements of fact.
(10) The circumstances of the publication, including the timing.

This list has been hugely influential, for better and for worse, and marks one of the most important contributions of the House of Lords decision in *Reynolds*.

---

[25] ibid [202].

As we shall see, the initial effect of this list was to make it difficult for defendants to establish they published responsibly. Although Lord Nicholls stated that these factors are merely illustrative, the ten criteria effectively became the test of responsible journalism, applied as a rigid checklist. Later, parts of the list were incorporated into common law and legislation in England and elsewhere.

Applying the new test to the facts, the House of Lords agreed with the lower courts that qualified privilege did not apply. *The Times* did not report on Reynolds' explanation to the Dáil about what happened. The allegations were serious. The publication was essentially unfair. The communication was on a matter of public interest but because it was not communicated responsibly, there was no duty to publish it.

III. THE AFTERMATH IN ENGLAND AND WALES

Commentators recognised the importance of *Reynolds* from the beginning. For journalists publishing on matters of public interest, it was no longer necessary to prove what you said was true so long as you were diligent in your reporting. There was now a negligence-based defence. *Reynolds* and its new qualified privilege were referred to as a 'landmark case',[26] '[g]round-breaking',[27] 'a seismic shift',[28] 'revolutionary'[29] and 'a massive change',[30] as 'momentous',[31] 'the most significant [development] that the English law of defamation has undergone since the Second World War',[32] as 'perhaps the most important libel judgment to date',[33] and as 'marking a historic shift in the law of libel'.[34]

That said, many tempered their optimism with caution; much would depend on how the defence was applied.[35] Its flexibility meant it was unpredictable.

---

[26] Eric Barendt, 'Balancing Freedom of Expression and the Right to Reputation: Reflections on Reynolds and Reportage' (2012) 63 *Northern Ireland Legal Quarterly* 59, 59.

[27] Katherine Rimell, 'A New Public Interest Defence for the Media? The House of Lords Decision in *Reynolds v Times Newspapers Ltd*' (2000) 1 *Entertainment Law Review* 36, 36.

[28] Amber Melville-Brown, 'The Impact of *Reynolds v Times Newspapers*' (2000–2001) 18 *Communications Lawyer* 25, 28.

[29] An English practitioner (1S) as cited in Andrew Kenyon, '*Lange* and *Reynolds* Qualified Privilege: Australian and English Defamation Law and Practice' (2004) 28 *Melbourne University Law Review* 406, 423.

[30] Another English practitioner (8B) cited in ibid.

[31] Eoghan Padraig McSwiney, 'Reportage Is a Fancy Word: An Appraisal of the Development of the Doctrine of the Reportage Defence and the Implications of the Draft Defamation Bill 2011' (2012) 2 *Queen Mary Law Journal* 43, 45.

[32] Descheemaeker, 'A Man Must Take Care Not to Defame His Neighbour' (2015) 239.

[33] Siobhain Butterworth, head of legal affairs at *The Guardian* and *The Observer*, quoted in Melville-Brown, 'Impact' (2000–2001) 29.

[34] Marin Roger Scordato, 'The International Legal Environment for Serous Political Reporting Has Fundamentally Changed: Understanding the Revolutionary New Era of English Defamation Law' (2007–2008) 40 *Connecticut Law Review* 165, 175.

[35] Melville-Brown (n 28), 28; Andrew Kenyon and Tim Marjoribanks, 'The Future of Responsible Journalism: Defamation Law, Public Debate and News Production' (2008) 2 *Journalism Practice* 372, 380.

It was a 'sniff test'.[36] A member of *The Times'* legal team stated 'it is difficult to see just how radical a change it will be… as the guidelines are very general and will have to be applied in each individual case'.[37]

That caution turned out to be justified. 'If anything, the sentiment that *Reynolds* would usher in a more protective era for investigative journalism has proved unfounded.'[38] 'Any hopes that the decision in *Reynolds* would greatly expand the freedom of the media to publish untrue defamatory allegations of real interest to the public were soon dashed by the approach of the courts in the following five or six years.'[39]

Initially, judges seemed to apply *Reynolds* in a way that reflected its spirit. Referring to cases like *Loutchansky*[40] and *Al Fagih*,[41] Ian Cram refers to this a Phase One of the post-*Reynolds* jurisprudence.[42] But in Phase Two, courts tended to apply *Reynolds* privilege restrictively. The High Court decisions in *Jameel v The Wall Street Journal*[43] and *Galloway v Telegraph Group*[44] reflect this trend, although there were certainly others.[45] These cases were both decided by Justice Eady.

Jameel involved a story in the *Wall Street Journal Europe*. It alleged that the claimant Jameel Group's bank accounts were being monitored by the Saudi Arabian central bank, at the request of the US government, in relation to possible funding of terrorism. The *Wall Street Journal* had interviewed several sources and had tried to get the plaintiff to comment.[46]

Before turning to the ten *Reynolds* factors, Eady J noted that 'some' think the defence introduced more uncertainty into the law, and that this had more of a chilling effect than the prior law of defamation.[47] He admonished readers to remember that *Reynolds* was 'less a breakthrough than a reminder of the

---

[36] An English practitioner (5QC) cited in Kenyon, '*Lange* and *Reynolds* Qualified Privilege' (2004) 423.

[37] James Price, cited in Melville-Brown (n 28) 28.

[38] Cram 'Political Expression' (2005) 146.

[39] Barendt, 'Balancing Freedom of Expression' (2012) 61.

[40] *Loutchansky v Times Newspapers* [2001] EWCA Civ 1805, [2002] QB 783.

[41] *Al Fagih v HH Saudi Research & Marketing (UK) Ltd* [2001] EWCA Civ 1634, [2002] EMLR 215.

[42] *Loutchansky* (n 40), took a broad approach to public interest and *Al Fagih* ibid found that using unreliable sources did not necessarily defeat the defence; Cram (n 4) 152–53.

[43] *Abdul Latif Jameel Company Ltd v The Wall Street Journal Europe Sprl* [2004] EWHC 37 (QB), [2004] EMLR 11 (*Jameel* HC) (note that this is the decision on the qualified privilege decision only).

[44] *Galloway MP v Telegraph Group Ltd* [2004] EWHC 2786 (QB), [2005] EMLR 7.

[45] '[I]n the more than six years since it had been handed down, libel defendants had rarely succeeded when relying on [*Reynolds*]' (Stuart Karle, 'Jameel on Appeal: Reynolds Revisited' (2006–2007) 24 *Communications Lawyer* 8, 8). Other examples include *James Gilbert v MGN* [2000] EMLR 680 (QB) and *Armstrong v Times Newspapers* [2004] EWHC 2928 (QB). Deirdre Kelly states that until *Jameel*, only three cases succeeded in establishing the *Reynolds* defence, but she does not state which cases (Deirdre Kelly, 'Bearing False Witness against Your Neighbour: The Evolution, Perils and Possibilities of the Development of Qualified Privilege in Defamation Law' (2007) 7 *University College Dublin Law Review* 106, 110).

[46] *Jameel v Wall Street Journal Europe SPRL* [2005] EWCA Civ 74, [2005] QB 904, [35] (*Jameel* HL).

[47] *Jameel* HC (n 43) [17]–[18] (Eady J).

width of the basic common law principles, although it was much more encouraging of their invocation than previous English decisions'.[48] It certainly did not, in his view, replace the duty analysis with a negligence standard.[49] Eady J rejected *Gatley's* interpretation of 'duty', in the *Reynolds* context, whereby a duty to publish effectively flows from the defendant having published responsibly. Instead, he adopted the plain meaning of 'duty', namely 'obligation'.[50] Eady J therefore framed the duty question as one of whether 'the public *needed* to have that information straight away, true or not'[51] (emphasis in the original). He believed the defence should be applied restrictively:

> Because it can on occasion afford such protection to allegations of the gravest and most damaging kind, and which may though false remain uncorrected when the defence is upheld, it is tolerably plain that it can only be sustained after the closest and most rigorous scrutiny.[52]

In applying the factors, Eady J began by interpreting the public interest question narrowly. It was not a question of whether terrorism or funding terrorism were matters of public interest. The question was rather whether it was in the public interest for the *Wall Street Journal* to identify the Jameel Group, on the specific date of publication, as being on a list of those whose financial transactions should be monitored.[53] Unsurprisingly he held that this was not in the public interest.[54] There was also held to be no urgency – at least in that the publisher could have waited another day to get Jameel's side of the story. Although several sources were consulted, Eady J held that they were not reliable, based on the jury's findings that the sources did not confirm the allegations made in the article.[55] Qualified privilege was held not to apply.

In *Galloway, The Daily Telegraph* had published a series of articles about a well-known parliamentarian, accusing him of being paid hundreds of thousands of pounds by Saddam Hussein's regime, and of taking a cut of funds for the Oil for Food programme. The allegations were based on documents found in the Iraqi Foreign Ministry after the fall of Baghdad, and those documents were published in full in *The Daily Telegraph*. Justice Eady rejected the qualified privilege defence for several reasons. Addressing each of the *Reynolds* criteria in turn, Eady J considered that the source was not reliable, because it was 'the tyrannical and corrupt government machine of Saddam Hussein'.[56] He noted that no attempt had been made at verification, and was unswayed by the *Telegraph's* argument that verification of the report was beyond their means.[57]

---

[48] ibid [27] (Eady J).
[49] ibid [23] (Eady J).
[50] ibid [28], [30] (Eady J).
[51] ibid [31] (Eady J).
[52] ibid [32] (Eady J).
[53] ibid [40] (Eady J).
[54] ibid [53] (Eady J).
[55] ibid [66] (Eady J).
[56] ibid [153], [161] (Eady J).
[57] ibid [161] (Eady J).

Eady J also rejected the *Telegraph*'s claim that the matter was urgent, in that it had to protect its scoop. He viewed the urgency matter from the perspective of the audience, saying the story would be of interest any time.[58] He faulted the *Telegraph* for not putting the allegations to Mr Galloway before publishing[59] and for its tone.[60] Reportage was rejected because the *Telegraph* adopted and embellished the allegations contained in the original Iraqi documents.[61]

Although *Galloway* is closer to the line than *Jameel*, Eady J's approach in both these cases (and the approaches of the Court of Appeal, which upheld the trial decisions)[62] has been called an application of the 'closest and most rigorous scrutiny',[63] as 'media-hostile',[64] and as 'hostile to the spirit of *Reynolds*'.[65] *Reynolds* privilege was turning out to be ineffectual.

But then, the House of Lords was called on to revisit *Reynolds* in an appeal of *Jameel*. That case 'breathe[d] life into *Reynolds*, restating, and possibly liberalising the *Reynolds* approach'.[66] Ian Cram, who referred to two phases of post-*Reynolds* jurisprudence,[67] was writing in 2005. But a third phase began in 2006 with the House of Lords decision in *Jameel*.

The outcome of the case was evident from paragraph 2 of the decision, in which Lord Bingham of Cornhill referred to the *Wall Street Journal Europe* as 'a respected, influential and unsensational newspaper'.

There were two issues on appeal: the application of *Reynolds* privilege and whether for-profit corporations had to prove special damages in order to succeed in defamation. On the second issue, a majority held that the existing law should be retained (there is no need for corporations to prove special damages).[68]

On the *Reynolds* privilege issue, the Lords were unanimous in overturning the Court of Appeal's rejection of the defence.[69] They agreed that lower courts'

---

[58] ibid [163]–[164] (Eady J).

[59] ibid [166] (Eady J).

[60] ibid [168] (Eady J).

[61] ibid [159].

[62] *Jameel* HL (n 46).

[63] Cram (n 4), 152, citing *Jameel* HC (n 43).

[64] ibid [155].

[65] *Jameel* HL (n 46) 56 (Lord Hoffmann).

[66] Kelly 'Bearing False Witness against Your Neighbour' (2007) 119.

[67] Cram (n 4) 152–53.

[68] Lord Hoffmann and Lady Hale, however, would have changed the law. Lord Hoffmann justified his position thus: 'In the case of an individual, his reputation is a part of his personality, the "immortal part" of himself and it is right that he should be entitled to vindicate his reputation and receive compensation for a slur upon it without proof of financial loss. But a commercial company has no soul and its reputation is no more than a commercial asset, something attached to its trading name which brings in customers. I see no reason why the rule which requires proof of damage to commercial assets in other torts, such as malicious falsehood, should not also apply to defamation': *Jameel* HL (n 46) [91]. Note that Defamation Act 2013, s 1(2) requires trading corporations to prove serious financial loss, thereby legislating the views of Lord Hoffmann and Lady Hale but going further and requiring the loss be serious.

[69] All but one held that qualified privilege applied on the facts. Lord Bingham would have sent the case back for the qualified privilege issue to be dealt with at trial.

approach was too narrow, and contrary to the spirit of *Reynolds*. Eady J had applied the duty/interest test strictly, holding that only if it were in the public interest for a particular statement to be published, in that way and at that time, would it be privileged. In fact, only if it could be said that it would have been wrong of the defendant *not* to publish would publication be responsible.[70] The Court of Appeal's approach was only somewhat less narrow. Lord Bingham stated:

> The Court of Appeal upheld the judge's denial of *Reynolds* privilege on a single ground… that the newspaper had failed to delay publication of the respondents' names without waiting long enough for the respondents to comment. This seems to me, with respect, to be a very narrow ground on which to deny the privilege, and the ruling subverts the liberalising intention of the *Reynolds* decision. The subject matter was of great public interest, in the strictest sense. The article was written by an experienced specialist reporter and approved by senior staff on the newspaper and *The Wall Street Journal* who themselves sought to verify its contents. The article was unsensational in tone and (apparently) factual in content. The respondents' response was sought, although at a late stage, and the newspaper's inability to obtain a comment recorded. It is very unlikely that a comment, if obtained, would have been revealing, since even if the respondents' accounts were being monitored it was unlikely that they would know.[71]

The Lords also made clear that the text as a whole should be examined, not simply the words complained of.[72]

The Lords criticised Eady J for his overly narrow application of Lord Nicholls' ten *Reynolds* criteria. They should be viewed as 'pointers', not 'a series of hurdles to be negotiated',[73] and 'They are not tests which the publication has to pass'.[74] Lord Bingham thought Eady J had 'subvert[ed] the liberalising intention of the *Reynolds* decision'.[75] Lord Hoffmann thought that by treating the *Reynolds* criteria as 'ten hurdles', Eady J had demonstrated hostility to the spirit of *Reynolds*.[76] Instead, there should be deference to editorial judgment.[77]

While the Lords agreed that the approach to *Reynolds* needed to be liberalised, they disagreed on whether *Reynolds* privilege is a form of qualified privilege or a standalone defence. Two were content to view it as a form of privilege.[78]

---

[70] *Jameel* HC (n 43) [32] (Eady J).
[71] *Jameel* HL (n 46) [35] (Lord Bingham).
[72] ibid [48] (Lord Hoffmann).
[73] ibid [33] (Lord Bingham).
[74] ibid [56] (Lord Hoffmann).
[75] ibid [35] (Lord Bingham).
[76] ibid [49] (Lord Hoffmann).
[77] ibid [51].
[78] Lords Bingham (ibid [30]–[32]) and Hope (ibid [105]) viewed it as a form of qualified privilege. It is somewhat unclear where Lord Scott stood on the matter.

Lady Hale and Lord Hoffmann, on the other hand, viewed the defence as now distinct from qualified privilege. Lord Hoffmann stated:

> Although Lord Nicholls uses the word 'privilege', it is clearly not being used in the old sense... I therefore agree with the opinion of the Court of Appeal in *Loutchansky v Times Newspapers Ltd (Nos 2–5)* [2002] QB 783, 806 that '*Reynolds* privilege' is 'a different jurisprudential creature from the traditional form of privilege from which it sprang.' It might more appropriately be called the *Reynolds* public interest defence.[79]

Repeating the language from *Loutchansky*, Lady Hale thought:

> It should by now be entirely clear that the *Reynolds* defence is a 'different jurisprudential creature' from the law of privilege, although it is a natural development of that law... In truth, it is a defence of publication in the public interest.[80]

Lady Hale and Lord Hoffmann were convinced by the fact that *Reynolds* protects speech based on its content and the behaviour of journalists, not the occasion of publication.[81] In addition, it made little sense to think of malice defeating the defence when there would rarely if ever be responsible publication where publication was motivated by malice.[82] Finally, there was concern that qualified privilege's duty/interest analysis tended to be applied narrowly.[83]

But the Lords agreed that the privilege applied on the facts.[84] The publication was on a matter of 'great', 'undoubted' and 'considerable' public interest. 'It might be thought that this was the sort of neutral, investigative journalism which *Reynolds* privilege exists to protect'.[85] According to Lady Hale, 'If ever there was a story which met the test, it must be this one'.[86] Lord Hope found that *Jameel* 'has all the hallmarks of responsible journalism'.[87]

Jameel revived *Reynolds*, which was at risk of becoming obsolete. Why spend a great deal of money trying to prove the defence if the chances were that you'd be unsuccessful? *Jameel* affirmed the speech-friendly nature of *Reynolds*. It also laid the groundwork for future extensions of the defence in England and abroad. For example, Lord Hoffmann stated that the defence applies to everyone – not just journalists.[88] The statutory equivalent of *Reynolds* privilege in

---

[79] ibid [46] (Lord Hoffmann).
[80] ibid [146] (Lady Hale).
[81] ibid [46] (Lord Hoffmann).
[82] ibid.
[83] ibid [146] (Lady Hale).
[84] Although Lord Bingham would have sent the matter back to be retried, and therefore would not have held that the test was made out, it was he who said 'It might be thought that this was the sort of neutral, investigative journalism which *Reynolds* privilege exists to protect', suggesting a certain amount of agreement with his colleagues on this point, even if it was for a jury to decide (ibid [35]).
[85] ibid.
[86] ibid [148] (Lady Hale).
[87] ibid [111].
[88] ibid [34] (Lord Hoffmann): 'Lord Nicholls was speaking in the context of a publication in a newspaper but the defence is of course available to anyone who publishes material of public interest in any medium.'

England certainly applies to everyone,[89] and the Canadian Supreme Court took up Lord Hoffmann's words in creating a defence that apparently applies to all.[90] That said, *Jameel* didn't solve all the problems that plagued Phase Two; the *Flood* case demonstrated that even after *Jameel*, some courts would continue to apply the defence narrowly.[91] Yet *Jameel* is known for 'breathing new life' into *Reynolds*.[92]

Notwithstanding this 'new life', *Reynolds* has not been unproblematic or uncontroversial. Thus far I've focused on the scope of *Reynolds*, on what it means to communicate responsibly, and have implied that its changes to the law have been positive. However, the doctrine has been criticised for reasons other than its narrow application in Phase Two. Some think it is inappropriate to have a fault standard in defamation law, such that a false statement can remain uncorrected. It is said to devalue truth. 'Clients do not really care whether the journalists were ethical or not; they care that a falsehood has been stated about them'.[93] This means that some plaintiffs' reputations will not be vindicated, despite the fact that the truth of the statement hasn't been proven. Of course, the same could be said of most victims of negligence; they don't care whether the people who injured them were careless – just that they be compensated. And yet tort law tends to require fault.

Another criticism relates to the effect of the case on the practice of journalism. Media companies, many with access to staff lawyers, work to '*Reynolds*-proof' their cases. They insist that the subject of a story be asked for comment, for

---

[89] Defamation Act 2013, s 4 abolishes *Reynolds* privilege and replaces it with a 'publication on a matter of public interest' defence.

[90] *Grant v Torstar Corp*, 2009 SCC 61, [2009] 3 SCR 640 (*Grant*). That said, many Canadian courts have been interpreting this case as though the defence only applied to journalists and bloggers. See Hilary Young, '"Anyone… in Any Medium"?: The Scope of Canada's Responsible Communication Defence' in Andrew Kenyon (ed), *Comparative Defamation and Privacy Law* (Cambridge, Cambridge University Press, 2016) 17.

[91] In *Flood v Times Newspapers Ltd* [2010] EWCA Civ 804, [2010] EMLR 26, *The Times* ran a story about a named police officer who had been accused of taking bribes by an anonymous informant. The story indicated that the allegation had been made and that police were investigating. That was true, but the plaintiff pleaded that the article was defamatory in suggesting that he *was* taking bribes. When the police investigation found nothing, the online version of the original story was not removed or amended. While the trial judge found that the print publication was protected by *Reynolds* privilege, the Court of Appeal overturned. (The Supreme Court reversed *Flood v Times Newspapers* [2012] UKSC 11, [2012] 2 AC 273 (*Flood*).) The Court of Appeal's decision made some wonder whether *Jameel* had changed anything. 'Those who thought the legal landscape was altered radically by Reynolds and Jameel appear to have been quite deluded': Afua Hirsch, 'Times libel ruling shows Reynolds privilege is of little practical use' *The Guardian*, 21 July 2010, www.theguardian.com/law/2010/jul/21/times-libel-ruling-reynolds-defence. '[T]he decision of the court of appeal in [*Flood*], back in 2010, left some of us wondering whether the ingredients necessary to succeed in a defence of Reynolds privilege – also known as the responsible journalism defence and the Reynolds public interest defence – could ever be found in the real world': Siobhain Butterworth, 'Flood versus the Times: Reynolds privilege defence is back' *The Guardian*, 21 March 2012, www.theguardian.com/law/2012/mar/21/flood-times-reynolds-privilege-defence.

[92] Kate Beattie, 'New Life for the *Reynolds* "Public Interest Defence"? *Jameel v Wall Street Journal Europe*' (2007) 1 *European Human Rights Law Review* 81.

[93] An English interviewee (21QC) cited in Kenyon (n 29) 425.

example, even if that would otherwise not have been done, to improve their chances of succeeding in a *Reynolds* defence, should it come to that.[94] The implication is that there is something inappropriate or cynical about this, or that it unfairly benefits larger media organisations that can afford regular legal advice.[95] Alternatively, it forces journalists to write in a way that they prefer not to.[96] Others, however, suggest that this has been positive in helping ensure stories are fair before they are published.[97]

Less debatable is the problem of cost. Media attorney Mark Stephens says it costs £100,000 to £200,000 to mount a *Reynolds* defence.[98] On the claimant's side, Andrew Kenyon cites an English barrister as saying that *Reynolds* is 'very expensive to defeat'.[99] This is because *Reynolds* added complexity to the law, which inevitably increases costs.[100] The cost and complexity issue presumably persists under s 4 of the Defamation Act 2013. (More on this below.) Some say this high cost encourages reasonable settlements[101] but it must also have an effect on access to justice.

Related to the cost and complexity issue is the problematic role of the jury under *Reynolds*. Juries make relevant findings of fact but judges decide whether the defence is made out. One criticism of *Reynolds* was that because juries had to answer complex questions of fact under *Reynolds,* the 'jury's role [became] far more difficult, if not "almost impossible"'.[102] At trial in *Loutchansky v Times Newspapers*, Gray J referred to the jury's task as setting an 'examination paper'.[103] The Ministry of Justice also noted the jury problem: 'difficulties had been experienced in juries considering issues relating to the *Reynolds* guidelines because of the range and complexity of the issues requiring determination as questions of fact'.[104] Although the issue has been rendered largely moot in England by s 11 of the Defamation Act 2013, which abolished the right to jury trials for defamation, it remains an issue in other

---

[94] Russell Weaver et al, 'Defamation Law and Free Speech: *Reynolds v Times Newspapers* and the English Media' (2004) 37 *Vanderbilt Journal of Transnational Law* 1255, 1305–06.

[95] Jacob Rowbottom, 'Defamation Act 2013: The public interest defence and digital communications', *Inforrm's Blog*, 30 January 2014, www.inforrm.org/2014/01/30/defamation-act-2013-the-public-interest-defence-and-digital-communications-jacob-rowbottom. According to Kenyon's study, the role of lawyers in the English editorial process increased, rather than diminished, after *Reynolds* (Kenyon (n 29) 1097).

[96] Weaver et al, 'Defamation Law and Free Speech' (2004) 1304.

[97] 'The *Guardian's* editors conclude that the change demanded by *Reynolds* is "not a bad thing journalistically" because English media culture is highly aggressive' (ibid 1302).

[98] Stephen Bates, 'Libel Capital No More – Reforming British Defamation Law' (2011–2012) 34 *Hastings Communications and Entertainment Law Journal* 233, 250.

[99] Kenyon (n 29) 425.

[100] Cram (n 4) 152.

[101] Kenyon (n 29) 425.

[102] ibid [427] citing English barrister 12B.

[103] *Loutchansky v Times Newspapers Ltd* [2001] EMLR 898, 912.

[104] Ministry of Justice, 'Report of the Libel Working Group' (2010) http://webarchive.nationalarchives.gov.uk/20110322191207/http:/www.justice.gov.uk/publications/docs/libel-working-group-report.pdf, 39.

jurisdictions. In Canada, for example, where jury trials are still common in defamation actions, the Supreme Court cited problems with the jury's role under *Reynolds* in deciding to make responsible communication a question for the trier of fact alone.[105]

Although reportage is not discussed in *Reynolds* itself, there have also been debates about at least two relevant aspects of the doctrine. According to the repetition rule, repeating a libel is as actionable as authoring it.[106] But reportage creates an exception where the public importance of the publication lies in the fact that a statement was made rather than in its truth and there is no endorsement of the facts as true.[107] The first reportage issue was whether reportage is doctrinally a subset of *Reynolds* privilege. Bosland argued it is not, while others disagreed.[108] The other issue was whether, in trying to fit reportage within *Reynolds* privilege, the courts had diluted *Reynolds* to the point of making it 'vague and unspecific'.[109] These issues were effectively resolved when the Defamation Act 2013 made reportage a subset of the statutory publication on a matter of public interest defence.[110]

Other debates about *Reynolds* also became academic with the enactment of the Defamation Act 2013, which abolished *Reynolds* privilege in England and Wales. With it went the need to parse Lord Nicholls' ten factors (although they are still often relevant to the statutory analysis), the need to question whether it is a form of qualified privilege or a standalone defence, and the need to ask whether it applies to everyone or just journalists. However, the statute contained a defence of publication on a matter of public interest that raised a new set of questions.

The text is as follows:

4 Publication on matter of public interest

(1)   It is a defence to an action for defamation for the defendant to show that—

(a)   the statement complained of was, or formed part of, a statement on a matter of public interest; and

---

[105] In holding that whether communication was responsible is a question for the jury, the majority in *Grant* (n 90), 134 stated: 'The *Reynolds* model, where "primary facts" are determined by the jury but the decision on responsible journalism is made by the judge, entails a complex back and forth between judge and jury and may lead to interlocutory rulings, and in due course appeals from those interlocutory decisions. Moreover, confining the jury's role to preliminary fact-finding would entail seeking jury responses to numerous detailed questions, which may in turn "thwart many of the benefits sought through the doctrinal changes": Kenyon, at p. 433; see also Lord Phillips, M.R., in *Jameel v. Wall Street Journal Europe SPRL*, [2005] EWCA Civ 74, [2005] 4 All E.R. 356, at para. 70, lamenting the division of roles that has taken shape in English courts under *Reynolds*.'
[106] *Cookson v Harewood* [1932] 2 KB 478, 485 (Lord Greer) approved by Lord Devlin in *Lewis v Daily Telegraph* [1964] AC 234, 283–84.
[107] *Roberts v Gable* [2008] WLR 129 (CA) para 61 (Lord Ward).
[108] Bosland, 'Republication of Defamation under the Doctrine of Reportage' (2011) 91–92; McSwiney, 'Reportage Is a Fancy Word' (31) 52–53; Barendt (n 26) 73.
[109] Descheemaeker (n 11) 249 citing in particular *Flood*.
[110] Defamation Act 2013, s 4(3).

(b)   the defendant reasonably believed that publishing the statement complained of was in the public interest.

(2)   Subject to subsections (3) and (4), in determining whether the defendant has shown the matters mentioned in subsection (1), the court must have regard to all the circumstances of the case.

(3)   If the statement complained of was, or formed part of, an accurate and impartial account of a dispute to which the claimant was a party, the court must in determining whether it was reasonable for the defendant to believe that publishing the statement was in the public interest disregard any omission of the defendant to take steps to verify the truth of the imputation conveyed by it.

(4)   In determining whether it was reasonable for the defendant to believe that publishing the statement complained of was in the public interest, the court must make such allowance for editorial judgement as it considers appropriate.

(5)   For the avoidance of doubt, the defence under this section may be relied upon irrespective of whether the statement complained of is a statement of fact or a statement of opinion.

(6)   The common law defence known as the Reynolds defence is abolished.

On its face, the provision is significantly different than the common law defence it replaces. The word 'responsible' does not even appear.[111] 'Public interest' is used in two different ways. It would seem that the question of objective reasonableness has been subsumed by a question of whether the publisher subjectively thought it was reasonable to publish. How much difference this will make is still being determined.[112]

IV. THE AFTERMATH OUTSIDE ENGLAND

While *Reynolds* privilege was undergoing its transformation in England from case to case, and was then codified as s 4 of the Defamation Act 2013, it was also influencing laws in other jurisdictions. The Supreme Court of Canada created a defence of responsible communication on matters of public interest.[113] Ireland has a statutory *Reynolds* defence in s 26 of the Defamation Act 1990 (Ireland).

---

[111] As noted in Descheemaeker (n 11) 248.

[112] 'There is room to debate how far a shift in focus from the "responsibility of journalism/communication" to the "reasonableness of belief that publication is in the public interest" would entail any substantive change.' (Andrew Scott and Alastair Mullis, 'A new style public interest defence in libel law ensures that rights and interests of claimants, defendants and the wider public are properly protected' http://blogs.lse.ac.uk/politicsandpolicy/a-new-style-public-interest-defence-in-libel-law). Also, 'The better view is therefore that, as far as the historical "*Reynolds*" segment of the defence of [responsible] publication on a matter of public interest is concerned, nothing of substance has changed in English law with the Defamation Act 2013 (UK)' (Descheemaeker (n 11) 250). According to *Gatley,* it is too early to tell: 'It remains an open question whether the move from the common law privilege to the statutory defence will entail any substantive change': Alastair Mullis and Richard Parkes, *Gatley on Libel and Slander*, 12th edn (London, Sweet & Maxwell, 2013) (*Gatley*) [15.4].

[113] *Grant* (n 90).

New Zealand's Court of Appeal recently recognised a public interest responsible communication defence, overturning its earlier rejection of such a defence.[114] The common law in Northern Ireland,[115] South Africa,[116] Malaysia,[117] India,[118] Brunei,[119] the Commonwealth Caribbean,[120] and Hong Kong[121] has been influenced by *Reynolds* to varying degrees. Australia has largely resisted broadening its approach, grounded in political speech.

V. THE FUTURE OF *REYNOLDS*

Nineteen years after it was decided, the influence of *Reynolds* in England and abroad remains significant and it seems indisputable that *Reynolds* will continue to affect defamation law in a number of jurisdictions for years to come. More difficult is to assess *how* its influence will be felt. Will responsible communication defences truly be applied to all kinds of communications instead of privileging journalism? Will the role of the negligence fault standard expand in defamation until, perhaps, the tort is subsumed within negligence law?[122] Time will tell.

In the meantime, if properly applied, *Reynolds* and its progeny should help defamation law to adapt to major changes in values and technology. Defamation law has been criticised for being hopelessly out of date, for being grounded in an era of duelling and the printing press, and therefore for not appropriately protecting freedom of expression in the twenty-first century. The world in which

---

[114] *Durie v Gardiner* [2018] NZCA 278. On the issue of overturning the previous *Lange* approach, see paras 55–57.

[115] *O'Rante v Trimble* [2010] NIQB 135.

[116] *National Media Ltd & Ors v Bogoshi* (579/96) 1998 ZASCA 94, 1998 (2) SA 1196 (SCA). Note that this case predates the House of Lords decision in *Reynolds* but it relied on the Court of Appeal's approach.

[117] *Dato'Seri Anwar Bin Ibrahim v Dato'Seri Dr Mahathir Bin Mohamad* [1999] 4 MLJ 58 (HC); *Halim bin Arsyat v Sistem Televisyen Malaysia Bhd* [2001] 6 MLJ 353 (HC). See also Andrew Kenyon and Hean Leng, 'Reynolds Privilege, Common Law Defamation and Malaysia' (2010) *Singapore Journal of Legal Studies* 256.

[118] *Rajagopal v State of Tamil Nadu* (1994) (6) SCC 632 is often cited for India's reliance on *Reynolds* but that case arguably adopted the 'actual malice' rule from *New York Times v Sullivan* 376 US 254 (1964) instead. But in *National Stock Exchange of India v Moneywise Media Ltd* (2015) TaxPub (CL) 0570 (Bom-HC), (2016) 125 CC 0201, (2015) 132 SCL 0312, the Bombay High Court clarified that Indian law is closer to *Reynolds* than to *Sullivan*, 22.

[119] *Rifli bin Asli v New Straits Times Press (Malaysia) Berhad, Rifli bin Asli v Ahmad Khawari Isa and Berita Harian Sdn Bhd* [2001] Brunei Law Reports 251 (HC); *Rifli bin Asi v New Straits Times Press (Malaysia) Berhad, Rifli bin Asli v Ahmad Khawari Isa and Berita Harian Sdn Bhd* [2002] Brunei Law Reports 300 (CA).

[120] *Bonnick v Morris* [2002] UKPC 31, [2003] 1 AC 300.

[121] *Abdul Razzak Yaqoob v Asia Times Online* [2008] 4 HKLRD 911 (HC).

[122] See eg Descheemaeker (n 11) 241, who notes that *Reynolds* is a step toward convergence with negligence and later states that this represents an appropriate middle ground between protecting reputation and protecting speech: ibid 263. *The Law of Defamation in Canada*, vol 4 (Toronto, Carswell, 1999) 27–58, fn 155 states: 'the preferable course is to bring defamation into line with the larger tort doctrine of negligence'.

substantive and procedural defamation law evolved has changed in important ways. For example, publication to the world at large is no longer primarily the purview of and educated and trained group of professionals with codes of conduct. As a result, such publications no longer necessarily have the credibility they once did. It may also be harder for individuals to put allegations behind them, thanks to the internet and search engines.

Yet although *Reynolds* was a traditional journalism case involving old-fashioned print media, the flexibility of its reasonableness-based defence allows defamation to adapt to changing technologies and changing values. Properly understood (and that is certainly a caveat), *Reynolds* can be a defence of responsible tweeting,[123] of responsible blogging, of responsible Facebooking, of responsible investigative journalism, of responsible restaurant reviewing, of responsible pamphleteering, of responsible satire,[124] of responsible letter-writing, speech-making and of every other kind of expression on matters of public interest.

Reynolds' flexibility is not only helpful in dealing with a changing world, but arguably also in combatting a tendency to find liability where there is little or no reputational harm. This is perhaps surprising, given that *Reynolds* is seen as subsuming truth and vindication to the principle of fault-based liability.[125] Reputational harm need not be proven in defamation, but given the law's aims, its limitations on speech would be indefensible if it too often imposed liability in the absence of reputational harm. Yet there is reason to think this happens regularly. Reasons for this include a literal approach to meaning and the third-person effect.

Although meaning should be assessed contextually, some of defamation's rules are incompatible with a contextual approach, such as the rule that an allegation of criminality is inherently defamatory.[126] Sometimes it is not rules but their application that is insufficiently contextual. In *Barrick Gold v Lopehandia,* the court treated as defamatory rambling, extreme and, in my view, not credible accusations against a mining company.[127] There are many other

---

[123] Paul Bernal, 'A Defence of Responsible Tweeting' (2014) 19 *Communications Law* 12.

[124] Although the defence used to only apply to statements of fact, and satire is usually interpreted as comment, the Defamation Act 2013, s 4 is not limited to fact. The defence may, therefore, apply to satire.

[125] Recall the barrister who said 'Clients do not really care whether the journalists were ethical or not; they care that a falsehood has been stated about them' (n 93).

[126] It is slander per se to allege the commission of a crime. See *Gatley* (n 112) [4.6]. However, if you state that a notorious murderer is a murderer, you do not defame him since no one thinks less of him as a result.

[127] *Barrick Gold Corp v Lopehandia*, 71 OR (3d) 416, 239 DLR (4th) 577 (ON CA) involved a disgruntled businessman who made over-the-top allegations against a multinational mining company. They seem not to have been taken seriously. (For example, the allegations were not picked up by the mainstream media, which they surely would have been had there been any truth to them.) Yet the trial court and Court of Appeal found for the plaintiff. See Hilary Young, 'But Names Won't *Necessarily* Hurt Me' (2011) 37 *Queen's LJ* 1 for other examples.

examples of defendants being 'convicted more by the dictionary than by the law'.[128]

Consider also the third-person effect, in which people overestimate the negative effect of disparaging speech on people's reputations. In other words, people are likely to treat as defamatory speech that does not, in fact, cause reputational harm, or to assume the harm is greater than it actually is.[129] '[H]arm to reputation is consistently overestimated, to the unjust advantage of the plaintiff' in a defamation action.[130]

Given how bad defamation law can be at ensuring liability is only imposed when there is reputational harm, and at assessing the extent of that harm, it may be a step forward for courts to take a step back and simply ask: 'was it reasonable to say what was said, in all the circumstances?'

Of course, there is always a risk that courts will apply too much hindsight or will assess reasonableness with the 'closest and most rigorous scrutiny'. I think that risk is somewhat mitigated by the history of *Reynolds, Jameel* and all that led to the Defamation Act 2013. It has been made clear time and time again that the defence is a contextual and speech-promoting one. Yet the flip side of flexibility is a lack of predictability.

Albert Reynolds died in 2014. His legacy is wide-ranging, from helping end the troubles in Northern Ireland to negotiating Ireland's role in the EU, to raising seven children. Yet outside Ireland, and to lawyers, he is best known as the plaintiff in *Reynolds v Times Newspapers*. Regardless of the future of his eponymous defence, the *Reynolds* case has earned its place in legal history by increasing the role of fault in defamation law, by providing more protection to journalism in particular, and by influencing the law throughout the common law world.

---

[128] Young, ibid [18].
[129] Roy Baker, 'Defamation and the Moral Community' (2008) 13 *Deakin Law Review* 1.
[130] ibid [3].

10

Dow Jones & Company
v Gutnick *(2002)*

KYLIE PAPPALARDO[1] AND NICOLAS SUZOR[2]

I. INTRODUCTION

THERE ARE FEW Australian cases that have had the global attention of *Dow Jones & Company v Gutnick*. Coming in the early days of online governance, it marked the first time that a country had 'allowed jurisdiction over extraterritorial parties based solely on content downloaded from the Internet'.[3] Originating proceedings were filed in 2000[4] and the case reached the High Court of Australia in 2002,[5] not long after John Perry Barlow had declared that cyberspace was independent of the sovereignty of nations[6] and Johnson and Post had argued that the internet should be considered a separate jurisdiction beyond the regulation of individual countries.[7] In *Dow Jones v Gutnick,* the High Court stated unequivocally that local courts could – and would – assert jurisdiction over online interactions that affected persons in their territory. With this decision, the High Court of Australia handed down what was to become a landmark case in internet jurisdiction and defamation law.

[1] Queensland University of Technology (QUT) School of Law, k.pappalardo@qut.edu.au. Many thanks to Tess Van Geelen for excellent research assistance.
[2] Queensland University of Technology (QUT) School of Law, n.suzor@qut.edu.au. Suzor is the recipient of an Australian Research Council DECRA Fellowship (project number DE160101542). This research is supported by infrastructure provided through the Australian Research Council – funded *Tracking Infrastructure for Social Media Analysis* (TrISMA – LIEF LE140100148).
[3] N Garnett, 'Dow Jones & Co. v. Gutnick: Will Australia's Long Jurisdictional Reach Chill Internet Speech World-Wide?' (2004) 13 *Pacific Rim Law and Policy Journal* 61, 61–62.
[4] *Gutnick v Dow Jones & Co Inc* [2001] VSC 305 [3].
[5] *Dow Jones & Company Inc v Gutnick* [2002] HCA 56, (2002) 210 CLR 575.
[6] J Barlow, 'A Declaration of the Independence of Cyberspace' (*Electronic Frontier Foundation*, 8 February 1996) www.eff.org/cyberspace-independence (accessed 25 January 2018).
[7] D Johnson and D Post, 'Law and Borders – The Rise of the Law in Cyberspace' (1996) 48 *Stanford Law Review* 1367.

Concerns about the *Dow Jones v Gutnick* judgment reverberated around the world. The Australian High Court had claimed jurisdiction over a defamation dispute because the defamatory content had been downloaded and read in Australia, even though the defendant's business was based almost entirely in the United States. Commentators worried that this reasoning, if adopted by other nations, would mean that internet content might be subject to the laws and regulations of every country in which it could be downloaded – creating almost boundless liability for publishers.[8] This 'spectre of global liability' seemed likely to cause risk-avoiding behaviour and chill speech, radically undermining the freedom and neutrality on which the internet was based. In short, many commentators feared that the Australian decision might inadvertently break the internet.

In the years that followed the *Dow Jones v Gutnick* judgment, the dire predictions of commentators did not eventuate. Online publishers learnt, by and large, to manage the risk of liability for publishing potentially defamatory content. Larger publishers and online hosts often have access to legal counsel to help them evaluate legal claims, and the number of claims for defamation has not proved overwhelming. Smaller hosts who do this evaluation without legal support do tend to be more risk averse than their larger counterparts – their internal policies may be more restrictive than what the law actually requires – and this may be a concern for the free expression interests of their users. But publishers and hosts with no assets and little interest in Australia can often simply ignore the law, relatively secure in the knowledge that Australian defamation law and the judgments of Australian courts are unlikely to be enforced by a court in their own jurisdiction. Large publishers with the technological capacity have also been able to implement geoblocking systems that constrain the impacts of Australian law to only block content for Australian users. Thus, as a practical matter, internet publishers have worked around the jurisdictional conundrum created by the Australian High Court in *Dow Jones v Gutnick*.

But *Dow Jones v Gutnick* is about more than jurisdiction. Fundamentally, it is about the enduring tension between social and technological change and the development of the law. The High Court grappled with understanding what was different about the internet and how big of a change it actually posed to existing modes of regulation. The appellants in *Dow Jones v Gutnick* had asked the Court to radically reconsider and adapt existing defamation law to the internet age. The High Court declined to do this, preferring an approach that applied, as best as possible, existing law to a foundationally new setting like the internet.

---

[8] See generally, Garnett, 'Dow Jones' (2004); S Bone, 'Private Harms in the Cyber-World: The Conundrum of Choice of Law for Defamation Posed by *Gutnick v Dow Jones & Co*' (2005) 62 *Washington and Lee Law Review* 279; M Richardson and R Garnett, 'Perils of Publishing on the Internet' (2004) 13 *Griffith Law Review* 74, 90.

In *Dow Jones v Gutnick*, the High Court expressed scepticism about arguments that the internet presents a special case requiring major changes to the common law. As one of the first major decisions to consider how existing law would apply to a global communications network that many thought would be unregulatable, its echoes have been substantial. The High Court set the scene for later cases, in defamation law and beyond, that have continued to reject arguments that the internet requires fundamentally different rules. Importantly, while the Court in *Gutnick* warned that the application of pre-existing principles to internet publication would likely cause some problems, it did not think that these problems were serious enough to warrant change to the common law. The Court considered the possibility of adapting the defences to defamation, but unlike the way that the common law had earlier developed the defence of innocent dissemination for newspaper vendors and libraries, the Court ultimately thought that any such change would today have to come from the legislature.[9] Fifteen years later, while some of the problems that were predicted in 2002 are now more visible, no legislative change has emerged.

In the Web 1.0 era, when *Dow Jones v Gutnick* was decided, online publication largely mimicked the publishing structures in place in the offline world – publication was performed by firms with a high degree of control over their employee and contractor writers. The ramifications of *Dow Jones v Gutnick* are different in the web 2.0 world, however, where many publishers are intermediaries with little capacity to properly assess claims that user-generated content is defamatory. Problems of scale are significant, but not insurmountable, and are not the main reason why the implications of *Dow Jones v Gutnick* are different now. Differences now lie in information gaps and asymmetries – intermediary publishers do not have the same ability to determine whether a writer held an honest opinion or had made best efforts to establish truth as employer publishers did. In most cases, they cannot truly know whether a post is defamatory or not, without a full judicial determination.

These differences suggest that the questions raised in *Dow Jones v Gutnick* about new defences are now ripe to revisit. In 2003, Brian Fitzgerald argued that 'the [*Gutnick*] decision highlights the need to better understand how cyberspace has opened us to a new life that is only partially rooted in territorial existence'.[10] In 2017, we argue that the internet has opened us to a new life that is only partially rooted in the notions of legal responsibility and systems of oversight and control that permeated the *Dow Jones v Gutnick* decision. The internet is much different 15 years on, and publishing structures have changed significantly. It is worth asking whether our understandings of defamation liability and defences should be different too.

---

[9] *Dow Jones* (n 5) [51] (Gleeson CJ, McHugh, Gummow and Hayne JJ).
[10] B Fitzgerald, '*Dow Jones & Co. Inc. v. Gutnick* – Negotiating American Legal Hegemony in the Transnational World of Cyberspace' (2003) 27 *Melbourne University Law Review* 590, 611.

II. *DOW JONES & COMPANY v GUTNICK*: AN OVERVIEW

In December 2002, the High Court of Australia handed down its decision in *Dow Jones & Company Inc v Gutnick*. It was a decision that was to prove controversial the world over. The appellant, Dow Jones, was the publisher of the *Wall Street Journal* and *Barron's* magazine, and operated a subscription news site at WSJ.com. The appellant's main editorial offices were in New York City and its servers for WSJ.com were in New Jersey. Dow Jones was sued by the respondent, Mr Joseph Gutnick, who alleged that he was defamed in an article published in *Barron's Online* (on WSJ.com) and *Barron's* print magazine in October 2000. Gutnick sued in the Supreme Court of Victoria. Gutnick lived in Victoria, Australia, and conducted most of his business there; he undertook to only bring an action in Victoria.

The originating process to commence the action was served on Dow Jones outside of Australia. Dow Jones entered a conditional appearance and applied for an order permanently staying further proceedings or setting aside the originating process,[11] on the basis that Victoria was a clearly inappropriate forum for determination of the action.[12] Dow Jones argued that publication of the relevant article, for the purposes of defamation, occurred when the article was uploaded to its servers in New Jersey and that New Jersey was therefore the appropriate jurisdiction for the legal action.[13]

Justice Hedigan of the Victorian Supreme Court dismissed Dow Jones's application, holding that publication of the defamatory matter had occurred in Victoria when downloaded by Dow Jones subscribers there, and that Victoria was not a clearly inappropriate forum for trial. Dow Jones sought leave to appeal to the Victorian Court of Appeal, but leave was denied by that Court, which held that the decision at first instance was plainly correct. Dow Jones was then granted special leave to appeal to the High Court of Australia.

The High Court had three issues to determine: (1) whether the Court had jurisdiction to decide the action; (2) if jurisdiction existed, which law applied to the dispute; and (3) having regard to the resolution of the first two issues, whether the proceedings should be stayed or set aside on the basis that the Australian jurisdiction selected by the respondent was an inconvenient forum.[14]

---

[11] Under rr 7.01(1)(i)–(j) of the Supreme Court (General Civil Procedure) Rules 1996 (Vic). See *Dow Jones* (n 5) [3].

[12] *Dow Jones* (n 5) [5].

[13] In making this argument, the appellants relied, in part, on the 'single publication' rule under US law, which states that where a defamatory imputation is published in multiple copies of a newspaper or book, for example, there is no need to plead each copy of the publication separately. The appellants applied this reasoning to the internet, arguing that publication online occurs only once – where the content is uploaded – and not each time the content is accessed by a reader. The single publication rule additionally states that the relevant jurisdiction will be the location where the 'single publication' being litigated was published. See *Dow Jones* (n 5) [18]–[37].

[14] *Dow Jones* (n 5) [69].

The principle accepted by the Court and the parties was that 'in trying an action for tort in which the parties or the events have some connection with a jurisdiction outside Australia, the choice of law rule to be applied is that matters of substance are governed by the law of the place of commission of the tort'.[15] The question was where the tort of defamation had been commissioned. More specifically, given that the tort of defamation requires the *publication* of defamatory matter – where had the publication of the material in question occurred?

In their joint judgment, Gleeson CJ and McHugh, Gummow and Hayne JJ held that publication is a bilateral act, not a unilateral act on the part of the publisher alone. To be published, defamatory material must be both made available by the publisher and comprehended by the reader, listener or observer.[16] They stated, 'It is only when the material is in comprehensible form that the damage to reputation is done and it is damage to reputation which is the principal focus of defamation, not any quality of the defendant's conduct'.[17] Where material is on the internet, their Honours held that the material is not available in a comprehensible form – and thus not 'published' for the purposes of defamation law – until it is downloaded on to the computer of a person who is browsing the web.[18] Given that persons had downloaded the relevant *Barron's* article in Victoria, and that Gutnick had a reputation there, the Justices held that the tort had been committed in Victoria and that Victoria was not a clearly inappropriate forum for trial.[19] The other High Court justices, Gaudron, Kirby and Callinan JJ, broadly agreed with the joint judgment findings in separate judgments.[20] The High Court unanimously dismissed Dow Jones's appeal.

III. THE SPECTRE OF GLOBAL LIABILITY

The jurisdictional implications of the High Court's decision in *Dow Jones v Gutnick* were thought, at first, to be potentially dramatic, even catastrophic. If defamatory content was 'published' everywhere it was downloaded, then internet publishers would need to be cognisant of the defamation laws in every jurisdiction in the world in which there was internet connectivity. As the appellants argued, 'a publisher [would be] forced to consider every article it publishes on the World Wide Web against the defamation laws of every country

---

[15] ibid [9].
[16] ibid [42] (Gleeson CJ, McHugh, Gummow and Hayne JJ).
[17] ibid [44] (Gleeson CJ, McHugh, Gummow and Hayne JJ).
[18] ibid.
[19] The Court therefore rejected the single publication rule. *Dow Jones* (n 5) [48] (Gleeson CJ, McHugh, Gummow and Hayne JJ).
[20] *Dow Jones* (n 5) [65] (Gaudron J), [151]–[153] (Kirby J), [202] (Callinan J).

from Afghanistan to Zimbabwe'.[21] This could have a chilling effect on online speech – to avoid liability, publishers might tailor their posts to conform to the laws of the most speech-restrictive jurisdictions.[22]

The High Court justices acknowledged these concerns in their judgments, but were dismissive of them. The plurality judgment described the risk as 'unreal',[23] and Kirby J warned that the 'spectre of 'global' liability should not be exaggerated'.[24] Callinan J stated that 'The fact that publication might occur everywhere does not mean that it occurs nowhere. Multiple publication in different jurisdictions is certainly no novelty in a federation such as Australia'.[25] The judges noted that, as a matter of practicality, a plaintiff will only be able to recover substantial damages in a jurisdiction where they have a reputation – usually the place in which they live – and so a person is unlikely to sue in a jurisdiction where a judgment in their favour 'would be of no real value to them'.[26] Frivolous suits brought in jurisdictions where the plaintiff did not have a reputation would presumably be thrown out under the *forum non conveniens* test.[27] The costs and practical difficulties of bringing an action against a foreign publisher would also likely serve as a deterrent to most potential plaintiffs.[28] Finally, Kirby J noted that publishers might simply ignore proceedings brought in jurisdictions where they have no assets or interests, particularly where the application of foreign laws might be considered offensive to their own legal customs, and save their contest for a court in their own jurisdiction if and when an attempt is made there to enforce the foreign judgment.[29]

In fact, the High Court was largely unsympathetic to any claims that online dissemination created different, special or more difficult compliance circumstances for publishers.[30] Their Honours found that publishers would be readily able to identify the person potentially defamed in an article, as well as the place where that person ordinarily resides and has a reputation.[31] It would therefore not impose an excessive burden on the publisher to require them to be aware of the defamation laws in that place.[32] '[T]hose who make information accessible

---

[21] ibid [54].

[22] Garnett (n 3) 68.

[23] *Dow Jones* (n 5) [54] (Gleeson CJ, McHugh, Gummow and Hayne JJ).

[24] ibid [165] (Kirby J).

[25] ibid [186] (Callinan J).

[26] ibid [53] (Gleeson CJ, McHugh, Gummow and Hayne JJ), see also [151] (Kirby J), [184] (Callinan J).

[27] *Voth v Manildra Flour Mills Pty Ltd* [1990] HCA 55, (1990) 171 CLR 538.

[28] *Dow Jones* (n 5) [165] (Kirby J).

[29] ibid.

[30] The lower court was also unimpressed. See further, D Rolph, 'The Message, Not the Medium: Defamation: Publication and the Internet in *Dow Jones & Co Inc v Gutnick*' (2002) 24 *Sydney Law Review* 263, 269–70.

[31] *Dow Jones* (n 5) [54] (Gleeson CJ, McHugh, Gummow and Hayne JJ) [134], [151] (Kirby J), [199] (Callinan J).

[32] ibid.

by a particular method do so knowing the reach that their information may have,' the plurality wrote.[33]

The High Court's decision in *Dow Jones v Gutnick* elicited widespread concern from scholars and commentators worldwide. Concerns were expressed that the decision was 'contrary to traditional notions of sovereignty and jurisdiction',[34] and that it would result in uncertainty about which legal standards would apply to online speech.[35] Writers opined that defendants like Dow Jones would face 'liability without end',[36] particularly where the plaintiffs might be international figures with international reputations.[37] Online publishers, naturally, were worried that they would face difficulty and expense defending suits all over the world.[38]

A. A Web 1.0 Decision

For the internet of 2002, the *Gutnick* decision seems somewhat inevitable, even if not ideal. It reflects a refusal by Australian courts to allow US law to dominate, and it recognises that internet publishers who seek to operate in a given jurisdiction have a responsibility to abide by the rules of that jurisdiction.[39] Publishers who wanted to deal only with the laws of their home jurisdiction could protect themselves from liability in Australia by keeping their business and assets elsewhere.[40] Certainly, internet companies have made this type of decision in the time since *Gutnick*; almost a decade later, Google notoriously decided that it was no longer willing to abide by Chinese law as the cost of doing business in China and closed its operations in 2010.[41] This was a major decision for a major internet company; but smaller companies with little presence in foreign jurisdictions generally have much less to worry about, particularly since foreign defamation judgments are almost impossible to enforce in US courts.

For a publisher who has assets or business in Australia, complying with Australian law is costly, but is not an overwhelmingly difficult task. We conducted a series of semi-structured interviews in order to better understand the internal

---

[33] ibid [39] (Gleeson CJ, McHugh, Gummow and Hayne JJ).

[34] Garnett (n 3) 62; see also R Garnett, '*Dow Jones & Company Inc v. Gutnick:* An Adequate Response to Transnational Internet Defamation?' (2003) 4 *Melbourne Journal of International Law* 196, 201.

[35] Garnett (n 3) 75; Bone, 'Private Harms' (2005) 309; Richardson and Garnett, 'Perils of Publishing' (2004) 90.

[36] Bone (n 8) 307.

[37] ibid 308–9; see also Richardson and Garnett (n 8) 77 (discussing international reputation).

[38] Garnett (n 3) 62; R Winfield, 'Globalization Comes to Media Law' (2006) 1 *Journal of International Media and Entertainment Law* 109, 110–11.

[39] *Dow Jones* (n 5) [186]–[187] (Callinan J), [151] (Kirby J).

[40] ibid [53] (Gleeson CJ, McHugh, Gummow and Hayne JJ), [151] (Kirby J).

[41] See R MacKinnon, 'China's "Networked Authoritarianism"' (2011) 22 *Journal of Democracy* 32.

decision-making processes of internet hosts. We collected 19 interviews with representatives from content creators, moderators, and hosts, as well as legal counsel and third parties involved in various disputes over content.

When Australian hosts receive defamation claims, they typically spend a substantial amount of time evaluating the merits of the allegations. Larger hosts may have in-house counsel to deal with complaints, and smaller hosts may get external legal advice for the more complex or serious claims. Most claims, however, seem to come from unrepresented individuals, and they do not always set out a firm legal basis for the allegations. The experiences of our interviewees suggest that individual claimants and small businesses may seek to use defamation law to try and get personal information or negative reviews removed in a way that is often out of the scope of a legally actionable claim in defamation.

Most of the time, operators of small Australian hosts need to investigate claims they receive without the assistance of legal counsel, and they try to develop lay expertise to enable them to assess the validity of claims and their exposure to risk. In many cases, this can lead small operators to be quite risk-averse; they develop policies about permissible content on their sites that are substantially more restrictive than would be strictly required under Australian law. For example, we spoke to the operator of a website that allowed users to post reviews and comments about their experiences with other businesses. In order to avoid complaints by third parties, they engage a team of community moderators who edit or remove posts that contain broad opinions. They try to limit discussion to predominantly factual explanations of a particular user's experiences, even though honest opinion is protected under Australian defamation law and even though corporations with ten or more employees have no cause of action under defamation.[42] In cases where the threat exceeds a threshold of risk that the host is comfortable with, we saw that they will often make a decision to remove all the content related to the complainant rather than retain a solicitor to contest it – including, in some cases, developing a policy that no discussions about that company would be permissible on their site in the future.

Larger Australian operators who receive a greater number of defamation complaints have more sophisticated processes to evaluate their legitimacy. We spoke to the operator of a business that specialises in moderating user-generated comments on major news websites. All comments on the news sites he

---

[42] Under the uniform defamation legislation in Australia, corporations of more than ten persons (or with fewer than ten but related to a larger company) are not eligible to sue for defamation. The exclusion does not apply to not-for-profits. See Civil Law (Wrongs) Act 2002 (ACT), s 121; Defamation Act 2006 (NT), s 8; Defamation Act 2005 (NSW), s 9; Defamation Act 2005 (QLD), s 9; Defamation Act 2005 (SA), s 9; Defamation Act 2005 (TAS), s 9; Defamation Act 2005 (VIC), s 9; Defamation Act 2005 (WA), s 9. Corporations may have a claim in injurious falsehood, but we did not find that the recipients of takedown requests had much experience with senders making a clear allegation under this head of liability.

is responsible for go through an approval process before they are published, and his team of moderators each receives specific training in defamation law from the in-house counsel of the news organisation. He explains that potential defamation liability is treated very seriously; moderators are not allowed to approve comments until they have undergone training in defamation 'because that is absolutely so crucial that we make sure we don't allow defamatory comments to be published'. When a potentially defamatory comment is identified, the moderators try to correlate the potentially defamatory imputation with reputably reported news. They check, for example, whether a commenter's claim that a politician is corrupt is sufficiently substantiated by independent news reports. In one instance, our interviewee explained how an administrative agency's determination that a politician had engaged in corrupt behaviour would not be sufficient to approve a comment – they were only willing to approve the comment once they could find confirmation that a court had found the politician guilty. Again, the approach taken here is often very risk-averse: 'if there is any doubt, we do reject the comments to avoid the possibility of defamation'. In the great majority of cases, the moderators make these decisions themselves, without escalating to legal counsel.

What we see in Australia is that defamation law has a strong effect on internet hosts. They take claims seriously, and often develop preventative measures to identify and remove any potentially defamatory material before it is published. This is a relatively costly exercise but, it must be noted, not one that our interviewees complained about. One of our participants, an editor for an independent news publication, routinely deals with defamation concerns, and noted that there was an emerging industry norm that apparently defamatory comments posted by users should be removed within 24 hours. This, he reflected, was a reasonable expectation – but apparently only one that his publication could afford to abide by because they had the generous support of pro bono counsel that he estimated he consulted two to four times a week.

For internet publishers outside of Australia, the complexity of dealing with complaints under Australian law is greater, but again not necessarily prohibitive. Many sites based in the US apparently choose to simply ignore Australian defamation complaints. These organisations benefit from a great deal of comparative certainty under US law, where the tests for liability under libel law are substantially different from those under Australian defamation law.[43] US courts are also unlikely to enforce foreign defamation judgments.[44] The publishers that

---

[43] For a successful action of libel, US law requires the plaintiff to discharge the burden of proof that the publication was false. In the case of public figures, the plaintiff must also show that the publication was motivated by actual malice (the publisher knew or was reckless that the statement was false); see *The New York Times Company v L B Sullivan* 376 US 254 (1964), 270, 279–80. See further A Kenyon, 'What Conversation? Free Speech and Defamation Law' (2010) 73 *Modern Law Review* 697, 713.

[44] See J Maltby, 'Juggling Comity and Self-Government: The Enforcement of Foreign Libel Judgments in U.S. Courts Notes' (1994) 94 *Columbia Law Review* 1978; D Rendleman, 'Collecting a Libel Tourist's Defamation Judgment' (2010) 67 *Washington and Lee Law Review* 467.

do need to worry about Australian law are the larger publishers with business interests and assets within Australia. These are the organisations who cannot afford to ignore a court order in Australia, either because of the financial cost or the risk to their ongoing reputation (or 'social licence to operate'[45] within Australia). For these publishers, the High Court's admonition that they, just like Australian firms, need to factor in the costs of a duty not to defame Australians into the costs of doing business in Australia is hard to fault.[46] The major caveat, of course, is that the long-term implications of *Gutnick* and the ongoing challenges of defamation law are not faced by the same types of publishers as the *Wall Street Journal* – for the current targets of defamation law, the intermediaries who have little direct control over user-generated content or direct knowledge about the allegedly defamatory claims, Australian law may pose a much greater challenge.

B. The Web 2.0 Era and the Ongoing Implications of *Dow Jones & Company v Gutnick*

The internet has changed radically since the *Gutnick* decision. Shortly after the case had wound its way through the Australian appellate system, the dot com bubble burst. Only two years later, in late 2004, Tim O'Reilly and John Battelle had given a name – Web 2.0 – to the fundamental change on the internet that emerged from the crash.[47] Web 2.0 represented a greater decentralisation in internet publishing. Previously, anyone with access could theoretically make a website and have a global presence, but the barriers to access were still high, both in terms of technical skill and cost. The rise of Web 2.0 was a rise of the 'platforms' – services that made it easy for people to connect and communicate with others. This was the 'user-generated content' revolution, whose ascendance was signified by books like Clay Shirky's 'Here Comes Everybody'[48] and *Time* magazine's 2006 cover: 'You – Yes, You – Are TIME's Person of the Year'.[49]

In 2002, a majority of the High Court were of the view that existing differences between publishing on the internet and publishing through other media were not so significant that they warranted a departure from established rules

---

[45] J O'Brien, G Gilligan, A Roberts and R McCormick, 'Professional Standards and the Social Licence to Operate: A Panacea for Finance or an Exercise in Symbolism?' (2015) 9 *Law and Financial Markets Review* 283.

[46] *Dow Jones* (n 5) [186] (Callinan J).

[47] T O'Reilly and J Battelle, 'Opening Welcome' (Speech at the State of the Internet Industry Forum, San Francisco, California, 5 October 2004).

[48] C Shirky, *Here Comes Everybody: The Power of Organizing without Organizations* (New York, Penguin Press, 2008).

[49] L Grossman, 'You – Yes, You – Are TIME's Person of the Year' (*Time*, 25 December 2006) http://content.time.com/time/magazine/article/0,9171,1570810,00.html (accessed 19 October 2014).

of defamation.[50] The rise of Web 2.0 publishers and, several years later, social media platforms, throw into sharp relief the unique features of internet publishing that were not easily visible back in 2002. The High Court in *Gutnick* thought that an internet publisher's potential liability in defamation could be relatively easily mitigated by routine checks about the subjects of the content they published and the laws of their home jurisdiction.[51] All of this presupposes that the publisher knows – or should know – what content they are distributing, just as a newspaper publisher would be expected to know the contents of the material they print.

The implications of the *Gutnick* decision are very different in the context of user-generated content and social media. Defamation liability applies to all publishers, whether they created the content or merely helped in its distribution. The foundational principle of the modern internet, dominated by media platforms, is that those platforms do not know or control in advance what content their users post. The arguments about scale presented by the defendants and intervenors in *Gutnick* were relatively easy to dismiss, as Callinan J did: 'Publishers are not obliged to publish on the Internet,' His Honour said; 'If the potential reach is uncontrollable then the greater the need to exercise care in publication'.[52] This is not as simple in the social media age; the sheer scale of content posted every day by users means that it is impossible to imagine the internet we have today with any form of pre-publication review.

The problem of scale, on its own, is not insurmountable. Only a miniscule proportion of the content posted online will ever be the subject of a defamation complaint. Where a publisher is not the creator of a defamatory statement, defamation law does not require them to know about the content they help distribute. The defence of innocent dissemination in Australian law protects internet platforms who are 'subordinate distributors' from liability for content posted by their users – up until the point where the matter is drawn to their attention.[53] Clause 91 of Schedule 5 of the Broadcasting Services Act, introduced in 1999,[54] goes slightly further: it nullifies the effects of any State and Territory laws that would effectively subject internet hosts to liability where they do not have knowledge about the content, as well as any laws that effectively require internet hosts to proactively monitor what its users are uploading.

---

[50] *Dow Jones* (n 5) [39] (Gleeson CJ, McHugh, Gummow and Hayne JJ), [125] (Kirby J).

[51] ibid [151] (Kirby J).

[52] ibid [182] (Callinan J).

[53] *Emmens v Pottle* (1885) 16 QBD 354; *Thompson v Australian Capital Television Pty Ltd* [1996] HCA 38, (1996) 186 CLR 574, 585–90; Civil Law (Wrongs) Act 2002 (ACT), s 139C; Defamation Act 2006 (NT), s 29; Defamation Act 2005 (NSW), s 32; Defamation Act 2005 (QLD), s 32; Defamation Act 2005 (SA), s 30; Defamation Act 2005 (TAS), s 32; Defamation Act 2005 (VIC), s 32; Defamation Act 2005 (WA), s 32. For a detailed analysis of the application of innocent dissemination to internet publishers, see D Rolph, 'Publication, Innocent Dissemination and the Internet after Dow Jones & Co Inc v Gutnick' (2010) 33 *University of New South Wales Law Journal* 562.

[54] By the Broadcasting Services Amendment (Online Services) Act 1999 (Cth).

If scale were the only problem, post-publication review would be manageable – there is no reason to expect that a contemporary internet platform would have any major difficulty identifying the jurisdiction where a complainant has a legal claim after a complaint has been made.

While scale is important, it is not just the amount of content that distinguishes the modern internet from the early commercial internet of the turn of the century. The bigger problem is the much larger degree of difficulty that contemporary service providers face in evaluating the merits of a claim as compared to a publisher like Dow Jones. For platforms – the types of internet businesses that host content created by users – evaluating a defamation complaint requires more than identifying the most probable jurisdiction and understanding its laws. It is relatively easy for a social media platform like YouTube or Facebook to identify whether an uploaded video or a post contains a defamatory imputation according to the laws of Australia once an Australian complainant has drawn it to their attention. Identifying whether any defences may apply, however, is often much more difficult.

The *Gutnick* decision was centred on a model of mass media publication, where the content was directly created by an employee or contractor under the control of the publisher. Evaluating a defence like justification in this context can be difficult, but is usually not prohibitively so; mass media publishers have been doing this offline for many decades. When the content is posted by a third party, however, a platform has only incomplete information. Without a large degree of trust in the poster or access to a trustworthy record of the allegedly defamatory material, there is no easy way to be confident in its truthfulness. Similarly, a platform has no real ability to identify whether an opinion expressed is based on an honest belief, as required under the defence of honest opinion.[55]

This is a problem that matters most at the margins – predominantly for major platforms with interests in operating in Australia, and for user-generated speech that, while potentially defamatory on its face, might be covered by a defence. Nevertheless, it is a real problem for speech, since it is those defences that provide the safeguards for socially valuable critical speech. The major defences that protect valuable critical speech in defamation – justification and opinion – remain difficult to establish, and even more so for intermediary publishers.[56]

In recent years, digital media platforms have come under increasing pressure on freedom of expression grounds to resist attempts by third parties to pressure

---

[55] See Civil Law (Wrongs) Act 2002 (ACT), s 139B(4); Defamation Act 2006 (NT), s 28(4); Defamation Act 2005 (NSW), s 31(4); Defamation Act 2005 (QLD), s 31(4); Defamation Act 2005 (SA), s 29(4); Defamation Act 2005 (TAS), s 31(4); Defamation Act 2005 (VIC), s 31(4); Defamation Act 2005 (WA), s 31(4).

[56] See A Kenyon, 'Six Years of Australian Uniform Defamation Law: Damages, Opinion and Defence Meanings' (2012) 35 *University of New South Wales Law Journal* 31; A Kenyon, 'Perfecting Polly Peck: Defences of Truth and Opinion in Australian Defamation Law and Practice' (2007) 29 *Sydney Law Review* 651.

them to remove content.[57] The public debate around whether foreign internet companies should remove content is increasingly framed around freedom of speech as a fundamental human right. The United Nations *Guiding Principles on Business and Human Rights* set out the principle that businesses have a responsibility to respect human rights and to mitigate the effects of human rights violations with which they are involved.[58] This language of responsibility has been adopted by a range of civil society groups and academics in attempts to articulate standards through which to hold internet companies accountable for their decisions in removing or not removing internet content. Ranking Digital Rights evaluates major telecommunications providers and digital media platforms on their performance against freedom of expression values when they receive requests to remove content from law enforcement agencies, courts or private parties.[59] The Manila Principles, a joint statement of civil society groups and academics, sets out the strong proposition that: 'Content must not be required to be restricted without an order by a judicial authority'.[60] Important reports from UNESCO[61] and the UN Special Rapporteur for freedom of expression[62] have stressed the impact on speech rights of decisions by internet intermediaries to restrict content.

This increasing pressure means that major technology companies – particularly those based in the US – are faced with increasing criticism when they make decisions to remove content in response to pressure from third parties. Some companies have developed informal preferences or formal policies to resist requests to remove content unless required by law. This leads to difficulties when they are faced with a claim under Australian defamation law. Because liability

---

[57] See N Suzor, T Van Geelen and S West, 'Evaluating the Legitimacy of Platform Governance: A Review of Research and a Shared Research Agenda' (2018) 80 *International Communication Gazette* 385.

[58] J Ruggie, *Guiding Principles on Business and Human Rights: Implementing the United Nations 'Protect, Respect and Remedy' Framework* (HR/PUB/11/04, New York; Geneva, United Nations Office of the High Commissioner for Human Rights, 2011), www.ohchr.org/Documents/Publications/ GuidingPrinciplesBusinessHR_EN.pdf (accessed 7 November 2016); endorsed by United Nations Human Rights Council, *Human Rights and Transnational Corporations and Other Business Enterprises* (A/HRC/RES/17/4, 2011), https://documents-dds-ny.un.org/doc/RESOLUTION/GEN/ G11/144/71/PDF/G1114471.pdf?OpenElement (accessed 23 January 2018).

[59] See New America Foundation, '2017 Corporate Accountability Index' (*Ranking Digital Rights*, 2017), https://rankingdigitalrights.org/index2017 (accessed 8 January 2018).

[60] *Manila Principles on Intermediary Liability: Best Practices Guidelines for Limiting Intermediary Liability for Content to Promote Freedom of Expression and Innovation* (Manila, 2015), www.manilaprinciples.org (accessed 15 February 2017).

[61] R MacKinnon, E Hickock, A Bar and H Lim, *Fostering Freedom Online: The Role of Internet Intermediaries* (Paris, UNESCO, 2014), www.unesco.org/new/en/communication-and-information/ resources/publications-and-communication-materials/publications/full-list/fostering-freedom-online-the-role-of-internet-intermediaries.

[62] D Kaye, *Report of the Special Rapporteur on the Promotion and Protection of the Right to Freedom of Opinion and Expression* (A/HRC/32/38, Geneva, United Nations Human Rights Council, 2016), www.ohchr.org/EN/Issues/FreedomOpinion/Pages/Privatesectorinthedigitalage.aspx (accessed 16 February 2017).

starts after the internet company is put on notice about the defamatory content, a decision whether to accede to the request must be made relatively quickly. In order to make this decision, the foreign company needs not only some familiarity with Australian law, but also often familiarity with the context of the allegedly defamatory material. They also need to assess the risk that the plaintiff has the resources and willingness to bring a suit in Australia.

One of the core concerns for speech on the internet of today is that national laws may impose liability on internet hosts for the content they carry without guaranteeing effective standards of due process or protection for freedom of expression. Justice Kirby raised concerns about freedom of speech in *Gutnick*, but noted that the ICCPR also provides that 'No one shall be subjected to arbitrary or unlawful interference with his privacy, family, home or correspondence, nor to unlawful attacks on his honour and reputation'.[63] Defamation law has long attempted to balance concerns over restriction on speech with harm to reputation[64] – even if the precise balance that is struck differs between jurisdictions. But because the protections built into defamation law for speech are in the defences, they can only really be effective where a defendant has an incentive to contest a potential plaintiff's complaints. Platforms have some incentive to stand up for the speech rights of their users, but this is likely a weaker incentive than that of the mass media defendants around whom the defamation defences have been developed. If we consider that in addition to having somewhat weaker incentives to protect speech, platforms also have only incomplete information at best about whether a defence may be applicable, we would expect them to be much more likely to err on the side of caution and remove content than their mass media analogues.

The *Gutnick* case, as presented to the High Court, was not a perfect vehicle for in-depth reconsideration of how established defamation principles apply to the internet. As a question of jurisdiction, the Court was asked by the defendant to adopt a rule that would require Australian courts to decline jurisdiction in cases brought by a meritorious Australian plaintiff who had suffered harm to their reputation within Australia. This would have required a major change to the rules of defamation that were not readily justifiable on the grounds that the internet presented a form of distribution different from older media.[65] The High Court was reluctant – to put it mildly – to take such an exceptional approach to the internet. Kirby J was most sympathetic to the challenges posed by the internet, stating, 'the Appellant (and interveners) have established real defects in the current Australian law of defamation as it applies to publications

---

[63] *Dow Jones* (n 5) [116] (Kirby J); *International Covenant on Civil and Political Rights*, opened for signature 16 December 1966, 999 UNTS 171 (entered into force 23 March 1976) art 17.

[64] See generally F Schauer, 'Uncoupling Free Speech' (1992) 92 *Columbia Law Review* 1321; M Weiland, 'Expanding the Periphery and Threatening the Core: The Ascendant Libertarian Speech Tradition' (2017) 69 *Stanford Law Review* 1389; Kenyon, 'What Conversation?' (2010).

[65] Rolph, 'The Message, Not the Medium' (2002) 277.

on the Internet'.[66] Ultimately, though, it was almost impossible in 2002 to imagine what massive structural changes to the internet lay ahead over the next few years. Justice Kirby considered that significant change to the law exceeded judicial function, and that the issue was best left to the legislature.[67]

Australian legislative bodies had the opportunity to respond to the issues raised by *Dow Jones v Gutnick* in 2005, when negotiating and ultimately enacting uniform defamation legislation across Australian states and the Australian Capital Territory.[68] But although they harmonised a number of features of defamation law across Australian states and territories, including the question of how legal jurisdiction is determined between those states and territories, the legislature failed to look beyond its own borders to the broader regulatory disruption occasioned by the internet. The Standing Committee of Attorneys General (SCAG) Working Group of State and Territory Officers recommended, simply: 'There should be no legislative change arising from the High Court decision in *Dow Jones v Gutnick* at this time'.[69] 'This time' has proved to be a long time – over a decade later, there have been no further statutory amendments updating Australian defamation law for the internet age.

IV. 'AMERICAN LEGAL HEGEMONY' AND THE 'SPLINTERNET'

Of all the possible outcomes of the *Gutnick* case, none are wholly satisfactory, and all had their critics. If the Court had agreed with the defendants and the intervenors and adopted a rule that defamation should be governed by the laws of the speaker, it would have abdicated its responsibility to Australians and undercut the protections of democratically developed law in favour of an 'American legal hegemony'.[70] On the other hand, if Australian law applied, and other jurisdictions followed similar rules, commentators worried that we might end up producing 'a chilling effect on Internet speech worldwide by reducing the level of speech protection on the Internet to the lowest common denominator'.[71]

The long-term results of *Gutnick* are somewhat different to these early fears. The High Court's assertion of jurisdiction in *Gutnick* was extensive – given the very small number of subscribers in Victoria, the claim that a US publisher

---

[66] *Dow Jones* (n 5) [137] (Kirby J).

[67] *Dow Jones* (n 5) [136]–[138] (Kirby J).

[68] On 1 January 2006, new uniform defamation legislation came into force throughout the States of Australia and in the Australian Capital Territory. Each of the States has passed a Defamation Act. Each of the States' legislation is modelled on the proposed uniform defamation laws developed by the Standing Committee of Attorneys General. See generally, D Rolph, 'A Critique of the National, Uniform Defamation Laws' (2008) 16 *Torts Law Journal* 207.

[69] Standing Committee of Attorneys General (SCAG) Working Group of State and Territory Officers, *Proposal for Uniform Defamation Laws* (July 2004) recommendation 21.

[70] *Dow Jones* (n 5) [200] (Callinan J).

[71] Garnett (n 3) 61.

should necessarily take into account Australian law could reasonably be viewed as overreaching. In normative terms, it hardly seems desirable that a foreign publisher that has only tangential interests in a jurisdiction should be bound by that jurisdiction's laws, merely because its services can be accessed globally.[72] The long-term impact of *Gutnick*, however, has been mitigated by three key practical factors. First, content hosts with little connection to a jurisdiction can and do routinely exercise what Svantesson calls 'selective compliance'. We have already seen that many internet hosts, as Justice Kirby predicted,[73] have been able to ignore the law of Australia, since they have no assets or interest in the jurisdiction. *Gutnick* itself was settled, but the contemporaneous attempts of French courts to assert global jurisdiction over Yahoo! eventually ground to a halt in the face of a refusal by US courts to enforce the foreign judgment.[74] Since that time, the gap between a court asserting jurisdiction and a plaintiff actually being able to enforce an order somewhere that the defendant has assets has worked well to temper the more dire predictions of the effects of the *Gutnick* decision.[75] Second, we also have not seen in the intervening 15 years a great deal of forum shopping – the threat that courts will use the *forum non conveniens* test to refuse to deal with opportunistic plaintiffs seems to have been sufficient so far.[76] Third, we have seen the routine deployment of geoblocking technology in the regionalisation of internet content – a trend that the High Court did not think possible in 2002.

Back in 2002, geoblocking technology was only in its infancy. Justice Kirby noted how easy it was for internet users to disguise their location by using privacy enhancing technologies, which meant that 'the nature of Internet technology itself makes it virtually impossible, or prohibitively difficult, cumbersome and costly, to prevent the content of a given website from being accessed in specific legal jurisdictions when an Internet user in such jurisdictions seeks to do so'.[77] To an extent, this is still the case today: no system of geoblocking is perfect, and it is always possible for users to use virtual private networks or other tools to circumvent them.[78] Nevertheless, geoblocking is commonly deployed and is

---

[72] D Svantesson, *Solving the Internet Jurisdiction Puzzle* (Oxford, Oxford University Press, 2017) 97–98.

[73] *Dow Jones* (n 5) [165] (Kirby J).

[74] *La Ligue Contre le Racisme et l'Antisémitisme v La Société YAHOO! Inc*, Tribunal de Grande Instance de Paris, Court File No 00/05308, 22 May 2000 and 20 November 2000; *YAHOO! INC v La Ligue Contre le Racisme et l'Antisémitisme*, 169 F Supp 2d 1181 (N Dist Cal, 2001) rev'd 379 F 3d 1120 (9th Cir, 2004) and 433 F 3d 1199 (9th Cir en banc, 2006).

[75] Svantesson, *Solving the Internet Jurisdiction Puzzle* (2017) 99.

[76] ibid 172–73.

[77] *Dow Jones* (n 5) [86] (Kirby J).

[78] For example, users have demonstrated resilience in overcoming efforts to restrict content to a particular geographic region on other grounds, including copyright and offensive content: see P Dootson and N Suzor, 'The Game of Clones and the Australia Tax: Divergent Views about Copyright Business Models and the Willingness of Australian Consumers to Infringe' (2015) 38 *University of New South Wales Law Journal* 206, 225; D Bambauer, 'Filtering in Oz: Australia's Foray into Internet Censorship' (2009) 31 *University of Pennsylvania Journal of International Law* 493, 510.

routinely effective for a large proportion of the population. The importance of geoblocking technology for dealing with some of the worrying potential implications of *Gutnick* should not be underestimated. Geoblocking allows platforms that want to comply with the law of a given jurisdiction to do so without restricting content in other jurisdictions. This goes some way to protecting individuals' freedom of expression on the global stage, and to alleviating concerns expressed by international bodies such as UNESCO and the UN Special Rapporteur for freedom of expression.[79]

A. Geoblocking and the Scale of Online Defamation Complaints

In order to try to understand the scale of defamation complaints on social media today and the responses of major transnational platforms, we turned to a number of different sources. In general, there is almost no good information that explains when platforms make decisions to remove or geoblock content on defamation grounds. To examine this question in detail, we created a set of tools that monitor a sample of social media content and attempt to detect decisions to restrict access to individual posts. Our infrastructure generally monitors content as close as practicable to the time it is posted, and then attempts to test its availability again between two and four weeks later. Unfortunately, the error messages of most social media platforms are not very descriptive; it is often impossible to tell when a post has been removed on defamation grounds, as opposed to another head of legal liability or a decision made under the platform's rules of acceptable conduct. However, it is possible to get a sense of the scale of defamation requests by focusing on the platforms that do provide descriptive reasons when they remove content. YouTube is one such platform. YouTube hosts user-generated content – it is the largest host of video on the web, ranks as the second website globally by volume of internet traffic, with over a billion users watching over a billion hours of video per day.[80] When YouTube removes a video that has been uploaded by one of its users, it provides a relatively detailed explanation. When a video is geoblocked on defamation grounds, YouTube returns an error message: 'This content is not available on this country domain due to a defamation complaint'.[81] We developed a tool that tests the availability of videos from an Australian IP address in order to identify videos that were removed from YouTube pursuant to Australian law.

In a random sample of 37 million videos posted to YouTube in 2017, zero videos had been removed or blocked in Australia with a message that

---

[79] See nn 61–62.

[80] See Amazon, 'youtube.com Traffic Statistics' (Alexa, 2018), www.alexa.com/siteinfo/youtube.com; Google, 'Youtube for Press' (Youtube, 2018), www.youtube.com/yt/about/press.

[81] Note that this error also occurs on the main YouTube.com domain when accessing videos blocked in Australia, even though YouTube does not have a separate country domain in Australia.

indicates they were removed because of a defamation complaint. These videos were collected from the YouTube API within two minutes after they were first published and form as close to a random sample as we are able to construct without greater access to internal YouTube data. Each video was then tested again between two and four weeks after it was first posted (most videos were tested 14 days after they were posted). It is possible that there were videos that were removed more than two weeks after they were posted – it may take complainants longer than two weeks to engage a solicitor and write a complaint to YouTube. Because social media posts tend to receive most attention early, however, we assume that the most serious likelihood of harm from defamatory videos would be within the first few weeks, when the videos are presumably most visible to a large audience.

In addition to the random sample, we also tested a sample of 85 million YouTube videos linked to on Twitter in 2017. These videos were collected through the Twitter search and streaming APIs, selecting tweets that contain a link to a YouTube video. We then tested the availability of each of these videos on YouTube as close as possible to the collection time and between two and four weeks later. This is not a random sample; it is a set of videos that are shared on Twitter, and will therefore skew towards videos that are more popular. Of these 85 million videos, 11 were geoblocked with the defamation complaint error message for Australia.

As a fraction of videos posted to YouTube, the number of videos explicitly geoblocked as a result of a defamation claim in Australia is vanishingly small. It is important to note that the actual number of complaints may be significantly greater, however. In the random sample, approximately 307,000 videos were removed from YouTube with a generic message that indicated the video violated YouTube's Terms of Service; 5.3 million were removed by the user; two million were removed because the user's account had been terminated on unspecified grounds; and a further 11,000 were geoblocked without explanation (excluding approximately 66,000 videos that were geoblocked on copyright grounds). This is an extremely large set of videos (up to 20 per cent of our random sample) that were not available to a viewer on an Australian IP address without a clear explanation. It is possible that some of these videos were unavailable because of defamation complaints, but because YouTube's reporting is not detailed, it is impossible to estimate how many.

Some companies, including Google and Twitter, send copies of some of the incoming content removal requests they receive to the Lumen Database. Lumen, formerly known as the Chilling Effects Clearinghouse, is a collaboration between US law schools and the Electronic Frontier Foundation, and is hosted by the Berkman Klein Center for Internet & Society at Harvard University. Lumen attempts to bring some transparency to the ecology of cease and desist letters concerning internet content. It is most complete for copyright notices sent under the Digital Millennium Copyright Act (DMCA) – a range of internet intermediaries routinely provide a copy of DMCA takedown notices that they receive to Lumen. Because DMCA notices have particular validity requirements, they generally contain similar types of information in similar formats. Lumen's store of defamation notices, on the other hand, is patchy at best.

In December 2017, we collected a copy of all the notices sent to Lumen that were categorised as defamation complaints – 113,041 notices in total. The overwhelming majority of these notices (112,345 – 99 per cent) were addressed to Google (including YouTube). Of these, only ten were recorded as a claim under Australian jurisdiction – four to Google complaining of URLs in its web search index, and six to other websites and blogs. The complaints range from 2011 to 2017, although most (six) were in 2016. We checked this figure with Lumen and Google, and were advised that there was a problem with the data sent to Lumen, which was addressed for new notices received from January 2017. When we checked again in July 2018, there were 1,161 complaints to Google under Australian defamation law over the previous six months, requesting removal of 2,584 distinct URLs – an average of just over six requests and 15 distinct URLs per day. 1,089 of these were filed by a single 'reputation management' company, on behalf of both corporate and individual clients. Of all 2,584 URLs complained about, 1,155 were requests to remove reviews of businesses on Google Maps. Most of these are unlikely to present credible defamation claims – incorporated bodies are only eligible to sue for defamation if they have fewer than ten employees or are non-profit organisations. Some of these complaints allege defamation against an employee, but most are using defamation law as a mechanism to request the removal of negative or allegedly false reviews. The portion of complaints that do raise a credible allegation under defamation law are difficult to evaluate – many reviews are phrased as opinions, and will be protected as long as they are based on 'proper material', and any review that is truthful will not be defamatory. For a company like Google, there is no easy way to identify whether a review is truthful or an honest opinion. Google do not report how many reviews it removes from its Maps service for defamation, so there is no way to easily assess the impact of unclear defamatory liability on the flow of socially beneficial negative reviews. The remaining 1,429 URLs complained about to Google were an array of webpages on over 600 distinct domains. Many of these allege defamation in some form, although there are also complaints about private information, cyberbullying, fake reviews, as well as a handful of requests from people who posted content themselves but are unable to remove it from the site they posted to. Some of these can be immediately rejected – they do not present a colourable claim of defamation – but many of the allegations in these notices seem almost impossible to accurately verify without knowledge of the underlying facts that a search engine does not possess. Because Google faces strict liability if it chooses to reject an allegation, defamation law imposes a strong structural bias to censor speech in this area of uncertainty.

We also checked Twitter for tweets that had been geoblocked from Australian users. We used the TrISMA infrastructure,[82] which collects tweets by accounts identified as Australian. When Twitter geoblocks a tweet according to the law of a given country, it will return an error message that the tweet has been 'withheld' in that country. The TrISMA infrastructure does not capture tweets from accounts based outside of Australia, so we have no way of knowing whether there are a large number of international tweets that are the subject of an Australian defamation complaint. We also have no way of tracking whether Twitter receives a large number of complaints under Australian defamation law where it deletes, suspends the sender's account, or ignores the request without geoblocking it. But from the information that is visible for analysis, of the 141 million tweets that were captured by the TrISMA infrastructure from January to April 2017, only 23 were blocked in Australia. It is impossible to tell which, if any, of these were blocked on defamation grounds. Twitter has only reported a single Australian defamation complaint to Lumen, from an Australian Senator in 2016, for which it took some action to remove or geoblock the material complained of.

Quantitatively, there is limited evidence of an unmanageable load of defamation notices from Australians. Clearly, however, the notices passed on to Lumen are only a subset of the total requests to remove content made under Australian defamation law. Most publishers and internet intermediaries would be unlikely to provide a copy of any notice they receive to Lumen. Google's search engine is one of the primary global targets for takedown requests – it receives more than 80 million copyright takedown notices a month – but apparently only receives several thousand Australian defamation requests per year. Clearly many more intermediaries are dealing with complaints under Australian defamation law than are represented in our data. Unfortunately, however, without better data practices and transparency procedures, it is impossible to assess the extent of incoming defamation requests under Australian law.

Ultimately, the volume of defamation requests made under Australian law about online content over the last 15 years since *Dow Jones* is hard to estimate. Many of these complaints are dealt with informally, and never get so far as a plaintiff filing a suit. While major telecommunications companies and digital media platforms have started issuing transparency reports and filing copies of takedown notices with Lumen, almost none of these firms systematically provide details of defamation takedown requests. Almost all large hosts of internet content explicitly retain the power to remove content posted by users at the sole discretion of the host.[83] Even for the large internet intermediaries

---

[82] See A Bruns, J Burgess, J Banks and T Highfield, 'TrISMA: Tracking Infrastructure for Social Media Analysis' (Brisbane, Queensland University of Technology, 2016), http://trisma.org.

[83] N Suzor, 'Digital Constitutionalism: Using the Rule of Law to Evaluate the Legitimacy of Governance by Platforms' (GigaNet: Global Internet Governance Academic Network, Annual Symposium, September 2016).

that report on court orders they receive, when they make a decision to remove or block content according to their internal policies they do not report on these decisions in any way.[84]

Nevertheless, we have to assume that the absolute number of defamation complaints is lower than was feared at the time that *Gutnick* was handed down. One of the ways we can tell is actually by the absence of good data. Transparency reporting, as a practice of telecommunications and internet firms, emerged not just from a desire to protect freedom of expression and privacy, but also out of a resistance to increased regulation.[85] Google started reporting copyright takedown requests to Lumen back in 2002,[86] and started issuing transparency reports in 2010.[87] When the EU Court of Justice handed down its 'right to be forgotten' ruling and hundreds of thousands of Europeans sought to have search results that were inaccurate or outdated removed from Google's index, Google created a new transparency report focusing on these requests.[88] This is not unique to Google; most of the major platforms provide summary information about only two types of content removal: copyright takedowns and government censorship. Requests about defamation have never been a large enough volume to compare to copyright or right to be forgotten requests, and have never been taken quite as seriously as low-volume but high-impact government censorship.

Qualitatively, however, defamation takedowns are potentially more worrying. While the cost to publishers and platforms may be manageable, there are serious costs to freedom of speech and access to information. Internet intermediaries will find ways to manage their risks and limit their costs – presumably, they will often acquiesce to notices that are not clearly invalid, even if a defence to defamation could conceivably apply. Unlike under copyright law, there is no takedown procedure for defamation that allows the person whose speech is removed to file a counternotice and have the content reinstated. When we spoke to representatives of major platforms and the lawyers who advise them, we heard concerns about the difficulties they experienced in making decisions

---

[84] Suzor, Van Geelen and West, 'Evaluating the Legitimacy' (2017).

[85] See C Parsons, 'The (In)effectiveness of Voluntarily Produced Transparency Reports' (2017) *Business & Society* (online); J Kopfstein, 'Silicon Valley's Surveillance Cure-All: Transparency' *New Yorker*, 1 October 2013, www.newyorker.com/tech/elements/silicon-valleys-surveillance-cure-all-transparency (accessed 31 January 2018); K Bankston, R Schulman and L Woolery, 'Case Study #3: Transparency Reporting', *New America* (undated), www.newamerica.org/in-depth/getting-internet-companies-do-right-thing/case-study-3-transparency-reporting (accessed 31 January 2018).

[86] D Gallagher, 'New Economy; A copyright dispute with the Church of Scientology is forcing Google to do some creative linking' *New York Times*, 22 April 2002, www.nytimes.com/2002/04/22/business/new-economy-copyright-dispute-with-church-scientology-forcing-google-some.html?src=pm (accessed 31 January 2018).

[87] D Drummond, 'Tools to visualise access to information', *Google Public Policy Blog*, 21 September 2010, https://publicpolicy.googleblog.com/2010/09/tools-to-visualise-access-to.html (accessed 31 January 2018). See also Google, 'Google Transparency Report' (various dates), https://transparencyreport.google.com/about (accessed 31 January 2018).

[88] See Google, 'Google Transparency Report: Search removals under European privacy law' (undated), https://transparencyreport.google.com/eu-privacy/overview (accessed 31 January 2018).

about user-generated content where a defence to defamation may apply. Many of these companies appear genuinely concerned not to remove their users' posts unnecessarily. Ultimately, however, these transnational platforms make decisions based on their potential exposure to risk, and will often err on the side of caution and remove or geoblock content where there is a real possibility that they might be sued. Given the high volume of flawed and suspect notices in the Lumen dataset, it is reasonable to assume that a lot of lawful content, includes important information that is in the public interest, is likely to be removed by intermediaries adopting reasonable risk mitigation strategies.

B. From Geoblocking to Global Orders: Coming Full Circle

When the *Gutnick* decision was handed down, there seemed to be a real risk that national laws would be applied globally in a way that would work to stifle freedom of speech and access to information. Practically speaking, major internet publishers have found ways to constrain the effects of domestic laws – either by ignoring them, in the case of smaller publishers, or developing geoblocking solutions, in the case of the major transnational platforms who cannot avoid the laws of the countries in which they operate. By and large, this generally works reasonably well – at least in the sense that we have not seen many major controversies over different national standards for acceptable speech in the last 15 years. It allows national legislatures and courts to assert jurisdiction and set out standards of acceptable conduct without giving in to 'American legal hegemony' or subjecting the entire internet to their rule. Dan Svantesson notes that what he calls 'bark jurisdiction' (the assertion of jurisdiction with no real expectation of enforcement, as distinguished from 'bite jurisdiction') can be useful in enabling nations to assert the legitimacy of their local rules and guide behaviour within the jurisdiction.[89]

From this perspective, we should distinguish the legal ruling in *Gutnick* from its long-term practical effect. In legal terms, the Australian High Court set out a strong assertion that it would not cede sovereignty over internet publications to US law. The decision provides a basis to frame later debates over internet regulation in a way that continues to assert that Australian legal values matter, and that Australians who come to harm online deserve the protection of our law. At the same time, the practical effects have been more limited. Small- to medium-sized foreign publishers with little interest in Australia, most of whom are unlikely to inflict serious damage within Australia, have been mostly protected by the assurance that Australian defamation law is unlikely to be enforced by a competent court in their jurisdiction. Large publishers have developed geoblocking systems that constrain Australian law to mainly affect Australian users. There are still legitimate concerns that Australian law is not sufficiently

---

[89] Svantesson (n 72) 136–38.

protective of freedom of speech, but these concerns do not rise to the same level as worries in 2002 that Australian law was going to break the internet.

In recent years, however, there is some suggestion that the old questions raised by *Dow Jones v Gutnick* still haunt courts, policy-makers, and internet publishers around the world. In areas outside of defamation law, there appears to be a worrying and growing dissatisfaction with the practical detente that internet publishers came to after *Gutnick* and the French Yahoo! case.[90] In the wake of the Right To Be Forgotten case,[91] Google initially sought to delist results on its European search domains, and not Google.com. France's data protection regulator has now referred the matter to the European Court of Justice, arguing that Google should be required to remove offending results from all its country domains.[92] In Canada, the Supreme Court of British Columbia ruled in 2015 that Google should be enjoined from returning search results to particular websites selling counterfeit goods to any user, worldwide. In reasoning that echoes the Australian High Court's much earlier ruling in *Gutnick*, the Canadian Court dismissed concerns of jurisdictional overreach:

> Google raises the spectre of it being subjected to restrictive orders from courts in all parts of the world, each concerned with its own domestic law. I agree with the chambers judge that it is the world-wide nature of Google's business and not any defect in the law that gives rise to that possibility.[93]

Back in Australia, the expansive jurisdictional approach of the High Court in *Gutnick* also continues to echo through judgments. The New South Wales Supreme Court in a 2017 case expressed little hesitation in ordering Twitter Inc, a company incorporated in Delaware, to globally block future attempts of some of its users to leak an Australian firm's confidential information through the network.[94] None of these are defamation cases, but they show that the basic legal principles in *Gutnick* are still not settled. All three of these cases have been subject to extensive criticism about the potential for global overreach of national courts.[95] In both the earlier Yahoo! case and the more recent Canadian Equustek case, US courts have refused to enforce the order of the foreign court.[96]

---

[90] *La Ligue Contre le Racisme et l'Antisémitisme v La Société YAHOO! Inc*, County Court of Paris, Interim Court Order No RG 00/05308, 20 November 2000.

[91] *Google Spain SL v Agencia Española de Protección de Datos (AEPD) (Costeja)* (Case C-131/12) [2014] EUR-Lex 62012CJ0131.

[92] See A Hern, 'ECJ to Rule on Whether "Right to Be Forgotten" Can Stretch beyond EU', *The Guardian*, 20 July 2017, www.theguardian.com/technology/2017/jul/20/ecj-ruling-google-right-to-be-forgotten-beyond-eu-france-data-removed (accessed 30 January 2018).

[93] *Equustek Solutions Inc v Google Inc* [2015] BCCA 265, (2015) 75 BCLR (5th) 315 [56].

[94] *X v Twitter Inc* [2017] NSWSC 1300, (2017) 95 NSWLR 301.

[95] See, eg, S Kulk and F Borgesius, 'Privacy, Freedom of Expression, and the Right to Be Forgotten in Europe' (SSRN Scholarly Paper ID 2923722, Social Science Research Network, 2017), https://papers.ssrn.com/abstract=2923722, accessed 30 January 2018; M Douglas, 'The Exorbitant Injunction in X v Twitter' (2017) 36 *Communications Law Bulletin* 11; but *cf* G Frosio, 'Right to Be Forgotten: Much Ado About Nothing' (SSRN Scholarly Paper ID 2908993, Social Science Research Network, 2017), https://papers.ssrn.com/abstract=2908993 (accessed 30 January 2018).

[96] *Yahoo! Inc v La Ligue Contre Le Racisme et l'Antisémitisme*, 433 F 3d 1199 (9th Cir 2006); *Google LLC v Equustek Solutions Inc*, 2017 WL 5000834 (N D Cal, 2 November 2017).

V. CONCLUSION

The legacy of *Dow Jones v Gutnick* is an important one, and longer-lived than some might suppose. In response to the prospect of global liability that the *Dow Jones v Gutnick* decision threatened, online publishers were able to organise around governance systems and technological solutions that limited the impact of the regulation of potentially defamatory content so as not to stifle free expression. One important response was the use of geoblocking technology to restrict the reach of a jurisdiction's laws to only those internet users who resided in the relevant physical jurisdiction. But now a small collection of judicial decisions, very much in the vein of *Dow Jones v Gutnick,* seem set to threaten anew this delicate balance between regulation and speech.

Courts in Europe, Canada and Australia have seen fit to grant orders requiring online publishers like Google and Twitter to block content across geographical domains and well beyond national borders. As Svantesson has argued, we should be concerned about the scope and implications of worldwide blocking orders.[97] The echoes of *Dow Jones v Gutnick* can be heard in these decisions, even if faintly, when courts deny the massive structural changes that have occurred to the internet in the last decade and which the internet itself has wrought on models of publishing and flows of information. While US courts are still resisting the application of global blocking orders made against US companies by foreign courts, it is clear that there is still a real tension when courts are willing to exercise jurisdiction in very broad terms.

Since the rise of online platforms in the Web 2.0 era, the bounds of defamation liability have shifted. Secondary publishers that distribute content, but do not create or control it, cannot truly be confident of the defamatory nature of content, even after they have been notified of a potential claim and have therefore lost the defence of innocent dissemination. Their ability to properly evaluate the merits of a claim is highly suspect, because they cannot know what defences might be realistically open to the original speaker. They are not, for example, in the position to determine the truth of a statement made by an individual internet user.

Platforms are apt to manage the risk of liability by complying with demands to remove or block content. So far, large platforms have been able to constrain the full impact of these blocking decisions by restricting them to specific jurisdictions through the use of geoblocking technology. When courts chip away at these processes, however, by ordering platforms to implement broad and even global blocking, they also chip away at the (admittedly imperfect) protections that platforms have built into their governance systems to safeguard free expression.

---

[97] Svantesson (n 72) 186–89.

The real risk here is to freedom of speech for users. Most claims never make it to court. The costs of defending a defamation action are often prohibitive, especially compared to the much simpler option of removing or geoblocking content in response to a complaint. Without the due process guarantees recommended by the Manila Principles on Intermediary Liability,[98] platforms will continue to take measures to limit their risk by blocking or removing content. Because intermediary publishers have only a limited ability to evaluate claims of defamation and potential defences, and only limited incentives to do so, the threat of liability increases the risk that they will restrict legitimate expression to a greater degree than is socially optimal. This problem is exacerbated if courts around the world continue to order content to be removed not just in their own jurisdiction, but globally. While we have not yet seen evidence of a large volume of defamation takedowns in proportion to the massive volume of total social media posts, platforms certainly are receiving complaints that are difficult to assess, and a real threat to user speech does result.

The 'spectre of global liability' that was raised in *Dow Jones v Gutnick* and which has lay dormant for 15 years is now a real concern once again. It may be that this risk does not fully eventuate in the coming years, just as it failed to do so in the years following the *Gutnick* decision. Nevertheless, it is a call for caution and for care. Justice Kirby in *Dow Jones v Gutnick* acknowledged the internet's enormous impact on human affairs and its power as a communication technology.[99] These are features which should be protected; as Fitzgerald has argued, 'we must be innovative in building a legal framework in which [the internet's] distributed and ubiquitous nature can prosper'.[100] It may be that it is finally time to revisit the suggestion made by the plurality judgment in *Dow Jones v Gutnick* to develop new defences to defamation that are more appropriate to publishers in the internet age.

---

[98] *Manila Principles on Intermediary Liability: Best Practices Guidelines for Limiting Intermediary Liability for Content to Promote Freedom of Expression and Innovation* (Manila, 2015), www.manilaprinciples.org (accessed 15 February 2017).

[99] *Dow Jones* (n 5) [123] (Kirby J). See also Fitzgerald, '*Dow Jones*' (2003) 611.

[100] Fitzgerald (n 10) 611.

Index